A Texas Crossroads Bar & Grill

Trish Butte Varner

First Edition Design Publishing
Sarasota, Florida USA

A Texas Crossroads Bar & Grill Copyright
2012 Trish Butte Varner

ISBN 978-1506-909-79-0 AMZ PBK
ISBN 978-1622-872-33-6 EBK
ISBN 978-1622-875-49-8 PBK

LCCN 2014933994

Published and Distributed by
First Edition Design Publishing, Inc.
February 2014, 2020
www.firsteditiondesignpublishing.com

Dedicated to Steve Ritchie
USAF fighter Ace, Vietnam

In loving memory of my longtime friend,
Martin Caidin
1927 - 1997

and
my Dad.

With special thanks to:
My husband Bobby, for the steady supply of coffee shoved
under the door -and his unflagging encouragement

"RISE ABOVE" is what you do instead of giving in to despair.

CHAPTER ONE

As usual, I was behind in my bookwork and as usual, I didn't care.

My books weren't all that big a deal so I decided to let them slide, opting instead to wash ALL the glasses behind the bar. Not that they needed washing, but it's either do the books or the glasses, I don't vary. I'm in a well-worn rut I know, but that's the way I like it -no surprises. I had enough of them in Vietnam with land mines, booby traps, and wired children. Nowadays, I like it slow, predictable, and stress-free. I own a saloon that sits out on a crossroad in the middle of nowhere. It was built back in the 1800's and was probably called, "The Long Branch Saloon" or "Longhorn Saloon" –I don't know, but if you'll just bear with me, I'll get around to telling you how I came to find it.

Right off, you'd think a place like this would be on a Texas ghost town preservation list but it isn't. I suppose it's because it's located in a spot so damned hot and remote that nobody cares about coming here. Still -this is the kind of place that should be preserved. It's a piece of western heritage. At one time, the crossroads must've been a stagecoach stop because nothing's come by since, that's for sure.

The saloon is about a city block long and just as wide with a wooden door; (not swinging doors.) The bar is just like you see in westerns. It's made out of solid mahogany with a mirror behind it running the entire length of the wall. Straight ahead further on down, is one of the biggest stages you'll ever see in a domestic bar. It still has a painted canvas backdrop hanging from the rafters and if you squint just right, you can make out the faded trees and mountains on its surface.

To give you some idea of how enormous the place is, it was an opera house as well as a gaming establishment.

Three opera boxes overlook the stage from the north wall. They're big and roomy and were designed to hold at least eight people comfortably. The sides bow out like a potbellied pig; probably bent by someone who knew what he was doing like a ship builder. Each box is hand carved and built next to each other in a staggered design for the best viewing. They would cost a fortune to build today, but wood was plentiful a hundred years ago and the evidence shows throughout the saloon.

The real expense was in the "extras" like the chandeliers and red drapes inside each box. They would've had to be imported by ship from Europe to San Francisco -and then over land by stage. Getting them from there-to-here however, could take anywhere from ten months up to two years; depending on the outlaw-holding-up-stages situation.

One day I climbed up there to see what it was like. The chairs were covered in cobwebs, but still sitting exactly where they'd been left. Their legs had tilted some and the upholstery rotted, but they still had a royal air about them. A pair of dark red drapes was tied back on each side to give the opening a softer look. I'd forgotten how fragile things were in here and without thinking, I made the mistake of touching them and the material disintegrated in my fingers. I backed away from the drapes to test the floor with my foot. The dark wood seemed solid enough, but it had an uneasy springy feel to it and creaked when I walked across the boards. I was well aware that these boxes had long been unsafe, but it would take an act of God to make me tear them down. They were beautiful testaments to a bygone era that we'd never see again.

That was my first and last time in the opera boxes. Wanting to leave them undisturbed, I boarded them off and now all that occupies them is a few spiders, scorpions

...and maybe a ghost or two.

CHAPTER TWO

Back in its heyday, this saloon would've been the first stop for a cowboy after a long cattle drive. With six months back wages burning a hole in his pocket, he would want nothing more than to kick up his heels and drink himself into oblivion while pretty dance hall girls shilled for the house. He'd give no thought at all to gambling his earnings away on faro, poker and roulette. Naturally he'd be cheated out of every last cent he'd just spent a whole year in the saddle earning, but easy come, easy go. And before the night was over, I'm sure more than one cowboy wound up on this floor with his life's blood leaking out over some black-eyed Mexican beauty -or an ace hidden up the sleeve. Somebody said Buffalo Bill once came in and sat in on a game-and I'd like to THINK he did- but I doubt it. The West is full of unsubstantiated stories like that but I guess that's why people like me are drawn to it. It must've been a hell of a time to be a man back in those days.

The mirror behind the bar reflects the room like a milky cataract. Brownish age spots look like cancerous growths behind its thick glass. But the most interesting flaw in the mirror is a crackdown in the lower left corner. The crack originates from a hole made by a .45 bullet and zigzags upward across the center. I often gaze into that mirror from time to time, hoping to discover some faint image still inside, however, so far, the only thing from that era I've seen reflected in it, is the old baroque gilded cash register.

How I got here still isn't clear to me -and probably never will be. All I know for sure is that I was more dead than alive in both body and spirit. Just living through each day was a hard-won victory. But in time, things in me AND the bar, slowly began to come alive again.

...And I did it all without duct tape.

CHAPTER THREE

My name is Matthew Sean McIntyre. My friends call me Mac and I'm an ex-Vietnam vet.

My dad fought in the Korean War so when Vietnam came along, it was a natural choice for me to go. I'd heard stories all my life about the undying friendships he and his buddies formed in Korea as they slugged it out against the enemy. Most importantly, Dad told me about the homecoming parades and crowds of people lining the streets waving little American flags when they came back home. So naturally I went overseas thinking my country would be just as proud of me as it had been of my dad.

Only that's *not* how it went. For whatever reason, it was a war nobody liked; made all the worse by draft dodging assholes back here and "Hanoi" Jane's traitorous visit. What an idiotic thing for ANYone to do. Her cavorting with the enemy was thoroughly despicable and demoralizing to every soldier over there. But most especially to the P.O.W.'s that she could've helped -and *didn't*. I personally, will never forgive her for that.

My tour in 'Nam was almost over when we got word that Saigon was just hours away from falling. Every American soldier that could still stand on both feet was deployed and I hope to God I never see anything like that again. What a nightmare! When the Americans started to pull out the panic escalated into sheer Hell. People back here have NO idea what it's like to suffer like that. What got to me the worst was the children; tiny things no more than two- or three-years old wandering alone in the blinding smoke and bombs going off everywhere. It was pure chaos; a stampede of madness, screams, and explosions -and these babies were right in the middle of it. I personally scooped up as many as I could and put them on choppers, but it seemed like I didn't even make a dent. For every two or three I got on board, I'd turn around and see fifty more.

-and it's something that will *forever* plague me.

However, for as bad as Saigon was, I wasn't prepared at all for the reception I got here at home.

I stepped off the plane and was completely taken back by the sheer *force* of anger and hostility that greeted us at the airport. When the crowds broke through the police lines and rushed us, I freaked; it was Saigon all over again. As I tried to push my way past them, I was called a "baby killer," spit on, and had garbage thrown at my uniform. I couldn't believe it; what the hell had _happened_ to America? I'd never experienced such cruel mindless conduct; made all the worse by knowing that these were the very people I'd been over there fighting for. I'd just come through Hell in one piece, but this was too freaking much and it's a damned good thing I didn't have my weapon within easy reach.

It didn't get any better either. I became a pariah if the subject of my being in Vietnam came up and people turned away and gave me the cold shoulder. I felt more and more like a stranger in my own country and didn't take long before I stopped telling anyone I'd been there.

This just wasn't right and I would've given anything to have my dad around to talk to; not that I think he could've understood it any better than I did. So much had been taken away from me while I was away. But –I was discovering that life is like those tire spikes you can't back up over; there are no "do-overs" and once yesterday is gone –it's gone. My center crumbled and I climbed into a bottle to numb myself against all the hatred. Unfortunately, it was a mistake that put me on a path that was more Hell than Nirvana. However, I didn't see it that way and wouldn't have cared if I did. I stopped shaving, combing my hair –even bathing regularly. What was the point?

But it wasn't just the "warm" welcome I got when I returned home that started me on my long dark journey. I received three life shattering letters while still overseas. Two came from my family and one from my girl. Those three letters were enough to knock me off any sane path, but losing the Core of my being after coming home was the final nail in the coffin.

And I wish I could say it didn't leave me bitter and cynical; but it did.

The first letter came from my parents about four months after I got shipped out, telling me that my grandparents had been killed in a freak accident. They went to visit my great-aunt in Oklahoma; arriving on a rainy day that spawned a tornado on top of them that night. The house was totally destroyed and everyone killed. Nothing was left but splintered toothpicks, torn pictures, and rags that once were clothes hanging in a closet. I remember going through my whole tour without it really sinking in. I guess without being there for the funeral, it didn't have the same impact. Then eight months before I was to come home, my mom wrote to tell me that my dad had been coughing a lot over the last six months. She didn't want to tell me about it, but when he started to cough up blood, she forced him to go see the doctor. It was lung cancer and by then of course, it had spread too far. He died within weeks of his diagnosis and I got her letter two days after the funeral.

The shock of dad's death ended whatever childhood I had left. Up to that time, no matter how intense the fighting got, I made it through the darkest days with a single thought in mind -to get back and tell my dad all about it. My entire life had been built around us sharing this time together and now- just like that- he was gone. And if that wasn't hard enough, I had the extra weight of knowing mom had to handle this by herself. My parents had been married 45 years and I could already tell by her letters, that she was beginning to crack under the strain. Her handwriting wasn't the firm, steady script it'd always been; it was all over the place now –like a childish scrawl.

I worried about her constantly. She'd simply lost everyone she loved in too short a time and there was nobody for her to lean on. The Army granted me emergency leave but mom was adamant that I stay. I told her I was coming home anyway and started to pack, but she insisted I give her this time alone. She said it was easier if I wasn't around. That didn't make any sense to me but I was between a rock and a hard place. Finally, I gave up and stayed. But I didn't like it one bit.

I'd heard about one mate following another in death and sure enough, six weeks later, she was gone. The doctor said she died from a heart attack; but -it was a broken heart that took her.

I should've listened to my better instincts and gone home. My not being there with her was just one more thing in a long string of things, I never forgave myself for.

I had everything when I left home.

When I came back, it was *all* gone.

CHAPTER FOUR

I grew up on my grandfather's farm in rural in Lancaster County, Pennsylvania.

His two-hundred-acre farm was right in the heart of Amish country, and I loved it when I'd see their buggies coming down the shady country road running by our farm. I'd climb up and lean over the fence to get a closer look at the gleaming red spoke wheels. They'd wave to me and I'd wave back. The Amish are good people. They treat their animals well and you won't find a more beautiful well cared for horse anywhere.

Summers in Lancaster were wonderfully hot and green. I spent the July heat with my friends cooling off down at the old swimming hole. An Amish kid named Jake Darby and I loved to swing out over the cold water from a rope he tied to the branch of a tree. We especially got a kick out of splashing water on the girls who'd squeal and pretend to be mad (but got mad for real if we didn't.) Jake's family didn't believe in any kind of modern technology so there wasn't much he couldn't build from a few scrapes of wood, twine or rope. With his help, we built one of the coolest forts out under the shade of an old elm tree –and painted a sign that read: NO GIRLS ALLOWED! (A few months later, we both turned 14 and abandoned the sign.)

Winters in Lancaster County were cold and just as wonderful to play in as summer. The powdery hillsides made perfect places to slide down on the lid of a garbage can. We never wanted store bought toys (even if we could've afforded them) because Jake showed us so many great things we could make from odds and ends. And Christmas was the best time of all. I could always find my grandmother in the kitchen up to her elbows in white flour. I vividly remember the baking smells that greeted me when I'd come running in the kitchen after playing outside in the cold. The second I cleared the backdoor, I'd sniff the air and race off to see if there was a spoon or bowl I could lick.

I loved living on a farm. Farms taught us the stuff schools couldn't. Everyone had their job to do or you didn't eat. Hay had to be pitched and animals must be cared for every day –rain or shine. I learned about the Cycle of Life and Death, along with the importance of having chores to do - and doing them well. My grandparents taught me both character and where to find a sleeping giant called Courage deep inside me. My grandfather's wisdom was a mixture of sage humor and truth. I don't know where he got it, but we'd be sitting on the riverbank with our poles in the water, and out of the clear blue sky he'd say, "Son, always remember; ain't nobody's opinion of you important less it changes your opinion of yourself."

He had a lot of those sayings -and I'm especially fond of this one these days;

"Nobody can make a fool outta you boy, without a lotta help from you."

I didn't pay much attention to them at the time, but his words came back later on when I reached the Dark Ages (--which is what I call the time between thirty-five and Death.)

CHAPTER FIVE

The year I turned fifteen, my dad decided to try his luck in the big city of Chicago. Jobs were plentiful and people everywhere were striking out further and further from their rural roots. Chicago seemed to offer a better life and more money, so one day he just up and moved us away. It wasn't something I wanted to do, but after I got settled and enrolled in junior high, I have to admit I learned a lot from city life. I liked the cars, the music and oh yeah, the girls.

However, the thought of going back home someday never left my mind entirely. I missed the Amish way of life and seeing my grandparents. I made up my mind to go back after I graduated, but the Vietnam War came along and I enlisted instead. I was still in Basic Training when dad wrote to say he and mom were moving *back* to the farm. I was pissed until I read further on down to the part that said granddad was getting too old to run the place without some help and needed him to come back. And truth be told, I don't think dad minded going –I could tell by his letters that he was tired of the Windy City and longed for the farm just like I did.

However, instead of finding the farm the way he remembered it, dad discovered so many things needed repairing or out and out replacing that he was shocked. Apparently, granddad's health had been going downhill for a while. But it's hard for a man to admit he's getting old and he'd tried to handle things like always, until it just got too much for him to do alone. Dad wrote me that he might have to take a mortgage out on the farm to get it up and running again. I told him to go ahead; I'd pay it off just as soon as I got back. But when he wrote back, I nearly choked when I saw the interest rates. I immediately opened a savings account at a bank in Chicago and socked away every dollar I could. To make a long story short, I kept up with the payments just fine until the unexpected deaths of my family. When that happened, the bank didn't bother troubling themselves to send me any papers on the farm. Instead, they wasted no time calling in the loan, foreclosing and tearing everything down. They had the livestock and land sold to developers before my mom was even cold in her grave. And since I wasn't there to fight it, the rip-off was a slam-dunk for them. I asked once why they hadn't notified me. They just blinked and smiled a syrupy grin.

"We *did* Mr. McIntyre, but the papers must've gotten lost in the mail; so when we didn't hear back from you, we had no other choice but to go ahead and foreclose."

Yeah...right.

So. That was it. Losing the place hit me hard. I took it for granted that it'd always be there. Without knowing what else to do, I went back to Chicago -which brings me to the aforementioned letter from my girl. Her name was Jenny. We met in high school and fell in love at first sight. Like all young lovers, we became inseparable -just the three of us; my best friend Paulie, Jen and me. Paulie and I were joined at the hip so to speak and we pretty much went everywhere together. He had a girl but they weren't serious like Jen and me. We'd double date to the drive-in or just hung around together. It seemed as natural having my best friend involved in the circle as it did Jenny; so when I said I was going to go to Vietnam, my good friend Paulie, assured me he'd take good care of her for me. (Looking back now, I can see that had disaster written all over it.)

I was still reeling from the news of my grandparents when Jenny sent me a "Dear John."

I don't know if she knew about what happened but doubt she would've given it any thought one way or the other if she had. (Funny how you never notice such glaring flaws as selfishness when you're in love. The emotion must *truly* render you blind.)

I'll never forget the day that letter arrived. I had just dragged my weary war-torn butt back to camp after a particularly hellish firefight and found the wrinkled envelope lying on my bunk.

The jungle was exploding all around me, but seeing that letter lying there on my blanket blotted out everything. I lived for those letters. Exhausted as I was, I tore open the envelope with renewed strength and savored her angel sweet handwriting like it was manna from heaven. But as my hungry eyes devoured her words like a hungry man devours a steak, my grin slowly dissolved into a deep frown. She'd written to say "how wonderful what we had had been, but it wasn't fair to ask her to wait" until I got back. She went on to say how she'd met somebody else and they were "crazy about each other." She closed with how "she just KNEW I would understand and be happy for her newfound love" -with *my* *best* friend. My *no-good*, draft dodging, hippie, pot smoking, back stabbing, best friend. I tore the letter into a million pieces then shot it at least fifty times with my rifle. I despised both of them from that moment on and the hatred that grew inside me consumed everything good.

I began killing the enemy with no feeling of remorse. I got three Purple Hearts; one for wiping out an entire nest of NVA while getting shot up and don't remember feeling a thing.

However, I <u>DO</u> remember hearing my grandfather's words of wisdom every time I thought of Jen and Paulie.

"No one can make a fool out you boy, without a lotta help from you."

CHAPTER SIX

After I got back to Chicago, I asked myself a thousand times why I came back. Nothing was the same. High school was over, my girl and best friend had betrayed me the minute my back was turned, and I didn't ever remember the city being this dirty and unfriendly. I wandered the Southside, drank in rundown bars and slept in my car. I did everything I could to resist the pull of going to Jenny's old neighborhood. I don't know *why* we need to do crazy things like that, but we do and I finally give in to it. I drove to her neighborhood late one afternoon and parked a few doors down from her house. It was autumn and leaves of red and gold fluttered around my car as I settled back in my seat to wait. I didn't mind sitting there; it was the first time of feeling almost clean. After a while, the sun sank behind the trees and the blazing colors took me back to Lancaster County. Then the sun set and it turned chilly.

People came home and pulled up in their driveways. I watched them get out of their cars and go inside their houses. One-by-one lights blinked on behind windows and gray smoke rose lazily up into the twilight sky lazily brick chimneys. The smell of wood smoke reminded me of my football playing days. What days those had been; the cheering crowds, the bands playing loudly, cheerleaders doing cartwheels. I felt my heart soften. It wasn't *that* long ago that Jen and I had loved each other. Maybe she and dickhead hadn't worked out. I sat up. Was it too crazy to think that maybe I could talk to her and put things back the way they used to be?

I looked down at myself. I was a filthy mess. I'd need to come back after I cleaned up. But as I sat there in my car, I saw Jenny's front door open and she came out of her house with Paulie. They looked very much together and she looked very much pregnant. He helped her into his car and they drove right past me without ever even looking over. The second they turned the corner, I angrily started the car vowing NEVER do that to myself again. I drove straight to the nearest bar and *that* was my <u>last day</u> of sobriety for the next three years.

CHAPTER SEVEN

It took every bit of those next three years to drown the Hope that sprang up that night in Chicago. The normalcy of the neighborhood had fooled me into thinking I could go back to the way things were and loneliness had sucker punched me into believing again.

So I stopped believing. I wandered from bar to bar. I never ate and I slept in my car until something happened to it. (One day it was there; the next it was gone.) It either got stolen or I forgot where I left it –probably the latter. Whatever happened, I was a rudderless ship –and I didn't care.

Then one day, I woke up to find myself lying on the floor of this rundown spider infested building, (–which pretty much describes the condition I was in.) I blinked my eyes open without sitting up; thinking I was in some old warehouse in Chicago. But when my eyesight cleared, I saw odd wooden rafters overhead; not the vacuous space of a warehouse. I slowly raised myself up on my elbows and winched. My head felt like a brain tumor ready to explode. I eased down again and fell back into blessed blackness.

I don't know how long I was out but when I came to, I wondered where the hell I was all over again. Wherever I was, it was dark, gloomy, and looked like nothing living had been in here in *quite* a while. It was still daylight outside and amber sunlight filtered through multiple cracks in the walls. I could see sand, dust, and cobwebs covering everything in a thick blanket. This place had just gone to sleep one night and never woke up again.

As my eyes focused more and more in the dim light, the surroundings took on a very familiar look. Seeing the overturned tables, chairs and other debris, it dawned on me that I was in a bar! I turned my head to the right and sure enough, there was a long bar confirming it. I rubbed my grizzled chin and busted out laughing. Life was a REAL riot. Here I was; a drunk in a bar.

Then I passed out again –and this time, I stayed out.

For days, I swam in and out of the weirdest dreams. My booze soaked brain saw ghostly cowboys in fights and heard unearthly laughter. I saw these characters quite a lot before the hallucinations slowed down long enough for me to come around again. When I opened my eyes, I had no idea how long I'd been unconscious. (Time and me had parted ways long before I got here anyway.) My clothes were filthy from constant sweating and drying out again. I was dehydrated as hell and my bellybutton was kissing my backbone. No argument about it; I was a mess and by all rights, I should have been dead.

They say God looks out for drunks and fools. He sends angels when we're in trouble –and I was in *deep* trouble. But angels don't all come in white robes with long golden hair and Victoria Secret wings. Oh no, I couldn't be that lucky. The one He sent me came in the form of an old geezer. He must've been 190 years old with white chin whiskers and worn out overalls. A little burro loaded down with pick axes, shovels and other supplies followed close behind. I got the impression that he used this place on his way out to the desert and was *really* annoyed to find me here. He didn't say much, but after seeing my condition, I guess he realized I wouldn't be going anywhere anytime soon.

I didn't expect to see him again after his first visit, but he came by every morning before sun up with coffee strong enough to scare away even the worse D.T.'s. He was a cranky old coot, but I looked forward to seeing him and always knew when he was coming. I could hear his pots and pans clanking a mile away as he and his little burro made their way towards me. (Funny how you think you're so strong and don't "*need*" anybody; then one day you wake up half dead and find yourself looking forward to some old hermit and his little donkey coming by.)

We never talked (which I didn't feel much like anyway,) but one day I did ask him about my whereabouts and he answered in the sparsest words possible. He said, "You're in Texas, boy. Down by th' Mexican border" (-and that was our one and ONLY conversation.) I asked him which part of the Mexican border but he never said another word. I took it to mean that I wouldn't know even if he did tell me and didn't push the subject. It really wouldn't have surprised me to discover that I was on the moon, but finding out I was in the great state of Texas DID astonish me -*and* that I'd gotten here with no recollection of it. THAT fact alone was a bit scary, but finding out I'd somehow made it all this way and lived defied explanation.

In the week that followed, I sweated out most of the poisons in my system. I had enough water to get through in between visits but as I got stronger, he came by less and less. Days at a time would pass with no sight of him and just when I'd given up on ever seeing him again, he'd show up with more coffee, hardtack and water.

Then one day he came in before sun up as usual. He poured a cup of water out of his canteen and handed it to me. While I drank it, he took out a dozen or so sourdough biscuits and wrapped them up in a piece of cloth. He laid the bundle down along with a full canteen of thick soupy broth and four canteens of fresh water. Before I had a chance to say a word, he'd closed the door behind him and was gone. With a sick feeling in the pit of my stomach, I stared at the door until the morning sunlight come through the cracks. I sighed and reached into the cloth bundle to pull out one of those brick hard biscuits. I chewed on it without chipping a tooth then closed my eyes and went to sleep. Sleep was more than healing; it was a blessing in passing time. And maybe when I woke up, I'd find that I had just dreamed about an old prospector.

Five days went by without hearing the pots and pans and I knew the old man wasn't coming back. I was on my own again -and I didn't like it. Three years ago, I had shut life down and I didn't know how to kick start it. Living was going to be a lot harder than I thought. And I wasn't at all happy about trying it again 'way out here.

CHAPTER EIGHT

With food and water just about gone, I was going to have to get back on my feet. This presented a challenge. My muscles were like Jell-O. I had to get my body working again. The first couple of days were like trying to climb Mt. Everest. Nothing worked. My legs couldn't stand and if they did, they couldn't hold me. But I didn't give up. After two days, I was able to stand if I held on to something. I took my first step and I fell flat on my ass with my head spinning like it had been hit by a two by four. I hadn't eaten anything decent in years so getting back on my feet was going to be a long and difficult task. My body was starved from the lack of nutrition as well as the alcohol.

It took almost a week but I finally could walk without falling or holding on to something. The following day, after finishing off both the rock hard biscuits *and* the water, I decided to venture outside. I said a silent prayer, asking God to take care of the next phase of survival then I put all worries out of my mind and got to my feet. I pulled the door open and had all the air sucked out as a blast of white-hot heat hit me in the face. I held on to the door jamb with both hands to keep my emaciated body from hitting the ground. I never felt such heat. It was exactly high noon and the blinding white-hot sun burned straight down on this Godforsaken place.

I closed the door with my heart pumping in my chest and shakily crossed the warped planks of the veranda. The saloon took up this whole portion of the street and was covered by a tin roof that provided some protection from the elements. But shade or no shade it was still a furnace out here. Everything was burning white. Rivers of sweat ran down my face, neck and back. What the hell had I gotten myself into?

I stood out there with my lungs on fire and scanned the landscape. This was a ghost town if ever there was one. Except for the saloon, the only other buildings were a row of abandoned stores on the other side. The whole street was a set out of a Wild West movie. Horse troughs baked in the sun next to hitching posts distorted by waves of heat coming off the burning hot sand road. As if to make the picture completely authentic, a tumbleweed blew aimlessly down the middle of road in the hot wind. I noticed something odd about the buildings and went back to looking at them. All the stores had glass fronts but not one window was broken. My eyes scanned each building carefully. Everyone had been deserted for over a century -so why weren't any of the windows busted out? It wasn't natural. I mean, it's just human nature to throw a rock through the window of a deserted building.

The question begged to be answered and it irritated me that I couldn't find one. Surely some form of human life had passed this way in the last 100 years. I was too hot and tired to think about it now and had decided to go back inside when I saw a door open across the street. I thought I'd imagined it and looked again. The building had once been a hardware store because remnants of red letters on the glass front read: LEGRAND'S HARDWARE. While I stood there with my mouth open, a man walked out and went inside the building next door. When he closed the door behind him, the building looked as deserted as the rest of them.

What the *hell*? That HAD to be a mirage. If I'd been in better condition, I would've run across the street and pounded on that door. Instead, I waited to see if he came back out. Ten minutes went by with no sign of him and I laughed to myself. I was convinced now more than ever that I was losing what was left of my mind and needed to get out of this heat as soon as possible. But just as I turned around to go back inside, the door of the building across the street opened and the same man came out again.

That did it! I grabbed a post and yelled, "HEY –YOU THERE!!!"

The sound of my voice startled him as much as seeing him startled me. He stopped dead in his tracks and turned to look at me. I was getting really dizzy and having a great deal of trouble breathing. The moisture kept evaporating in my lungs as white spots fluttered before my eyes. I knew my knees were about to give out and clung to the post with both arms like a drowning man. The man crossed the dusty road and stepped up on the veranda. He squinted at me like I was a ghost. "Who're *YOU*?" he asked in a stunned tone of voice.

The damned spots were getting worse and I couldn't make out his face.

I panted, "My name is..." just as my knees gave way and my hands slid away from the post.

CHAPTER NINE

I woke up with a throbbing headache and a stranger kneeling over me holding a cold cloth on my head. I recognized him as the guy I'd seen earlier. "W-Where am I?" I muttered.

"Are you okay? Man, you had me worried."

I gently pushed his hand away. "I'm okay...what happened?"

The stranger got up. "You called to me as I was coming out of th' bank," he said.

I tried to comprehend what he was saying, but nothing computed. He must've picked up on it because he said, "Don't you remember callin' me when you were outside?"

"I don't even remember being out-" then it hit me. "Did you say *bank*?"

He nodded. "First Cattlemen's –right across the street."

"What are you talkin' about?" I demanded. "There ain't nuthin' out here but some old buildings and tumbleweed."

"Yeah I guess it DOES look that way," he grinned. "Don't get me wrong; this IS a real ghost town, but -no ghost."

I put my hand up to my forehead to see if I was running a high fever. I wasn't.

"I know what you just said makes sense on some level, but I'm damned if I can find it."

"Take it easy; I'll explain it all in good time. Meanwhile, you look terrible. When's th' last time you had bath or shaved?"

"When's th' last time th' Cubs won the World Series?"

"That long, huh."

I pushed myself up to a sitting position.

"What's your name?" he asked. "Where do you come from –an' how'd you get *here*?"

His questions weren't offensive and I didn't take any.

"My name is Mac McIntyre. I'm from Pennsylvania originally –Chicago lately, and I have NO idea how I got here -or even where "here" is."

"My name is Legrand Johnson an' I own th' hardware store across th' street."

I looked at him. "You mean you're a for real Legrand an' that's a for real store?"

"Real as rain on both."

"This can't be happening," I frowned.

He picked up a canteen and shook it. "You're all out," he said. "I squeezed out 'bout all I could to wet this cloth for your head." He poured the remaining few drops of water out on the cloth and handed it back to me. "Put this back on your head and lay down again."

I did as he asked.

"From th' looks of you I'd say you haven't eaten much lately?"

I shook my head. "I haven't had real food in years," I said. "Been on a liquid diet..."

"Well then, seems to me that th' first thing we need to do is get some hot food in you."

"Great," I said. "An' just where're you going to find it out here –you gotta lunch box?"

"Don't need one -there's a diner three doors down from my store."

I sat bolt upright. "You mean to tell me a diner has been right across the street this *whole* time –and I've been eating sawdust?" I was furious. "I thought there was NObody out here but me!"

"Well, nobody knew YOU were here either," he shrugged. "Which brings us back to how <u>did</u> you get here?"

I sighed. There was no getting around it; I was going to have to give some kind of explanation –no matter how bizarre it was. I didn't want to, but I began to explain as much of the fragmented story as I could remember. I touched on losing my family and glossed over the foggy haze I'd been in since Vietnam. I completely left out the part with Jenny and ended my tale of woe with waking up here. "Oh yeah," I added. "I guess I owe my survival to an old prospector...until he quit coming." I picked up the canteen. "He left me these th' last time he was here and some rock hard hardtack."

Legrand nodded when I mentioned him. "That would be Rocky. He's been a fixture 'round these parts ever since I was a boy. God only knows how old he is. Doesn't talk much though–"

"No kidding? Maybe you just don't know how to get him to open up," I said sarcastically. "He was a regular chatterbox with me –except for failing to mention anything about you being here or a diner across the street."

"That was Chicago humor –right?"

"Sorry," I said. "I get cranky without my teddy bear."

"Got'cha. I'll see if my daughter's got one she ain't usin'," he smiled. "Anyway, ol Rocky probably wasn't too happy findin' you here. He thinks of this place as his own personal Holiday Inn. But he's a good hearted old soul."

"I sort'a got that impression."

"Well, that's quite a tale," Legrand said. "But it don't really tell me a whole lot. You could be some psycho serial killer on the run from th' law, for all I know."

"Right, and just why would I pick *this* place? As far as I knew there wasn't a living soul out here."

"And that would matter because...?" he asked.

"No victims," I answered flatly.

"Ya gotta point," he nodded.

CHAPTER TEN

"Look, I'm no killer or psycho and I don't blame you one bit for being leery of any guy that shows up here lookin' like I do –especially if they didn't have a better story on how they got here. But it's th' truth and I'd appreciate any help right now on tryin' to solve this mystery. I mean, you gotta look at it from my side too. You tell me this IS a ghost town –but it ain't. What's going on?"

Legrand gave it some thought. "Okay –you're right. Not many strangers ever show up here, so naturally, we're suspicious. But," he grinned, "if you turn out to be an asshole, I'm gonna have to kill ya. There's a bounty on assholes out here in Texas."

I relaxed. "Fair enough," I said.

Legrand reached into his pocket and pulled out a cigar, then he picked up a chair and propped it back up on its legs. He sat down and crossed his legs. Once he got the cigar going, he took it out of his mouth and asked, "You mind?"

I didn't, but I said, "Would it matter?"

"No," he said, (exhaling enough smoke to need a paramedic.) "Okay, here's th' story. Back in the 1800's there was nothing out here but sand, coyotes, and cactus. Then the stage lines needed a way station for changing horses and decided this was a good place to put one in. About six months after they did, the town sprang up around it. Later on a hotel was built for people who wanted a good night's rest before continuing on their journey west."

"Was the saloon here then?" I interrupted.

"Th' saloon was one'a th' first things built," he grinned.

I looked at the stage and opera boxes. "What about those?" I asked. "I can't see a bunch'a cowboys really giving a shit about opera."

No, th' only things in here were th' bar and gaming tables. But it wasn't long before the town started attracting people who wanted to stay and raise families. They added the stage strictly because these folks wanted to encourage something more than just wild drinkin' and gambling."

"Is the hotel still here?"

"Sadly it was destroyed by lightning sometime after the turn of the century."

"Couldn't it be saved?

He shook his head. "The one thing they forgot to build was a fire house," he grinned. "An' it didn't rain long enough to wet th' wood. Everything's so dry out here that it went up like a match."

That angered me that it was gone. "Damn, that's a shame. If it looked anything like this place, it must've really been something.' You have any idea what it looked like?"

"I've only seen old photos of it, but it was like you see in th' movies; two stories with rooms upstairs overlookin' th' lobby an' registration desk."

"Isn't there anything left of the hotel?"

Legrand stared at me. "You sound like a man who has a lot of appreciation for these things."

"You don't see places like this anymore," I frowned. "This town is a true piece of Western heritage. In fact, I'd like to see *this* place saved." I was talking off the top of my head but the words came spilling out all over the floor. "Too bad I don't know how to buy it."

I glanced up. "Believe it or not, I do have some money."

Legrand's ears perked up. "If you're serious about stayin' around here, we might be able to work somethin' out. Nothin's impossible," he said with a twinkle. I didn't know what he meant by that, but was too exhausted to find out. I'd been through enough surprises for one day.

"So what happened to the town?"

"Well, rumors of gold being found began to spread. Before you knew it, miners flocked out here by the hundreds. It became a real Dodge City. Th' place was so jammed with people comin' an' goin' that th' stage lines added more stages to carry 'em all." Gesturing around the room with his cigar, Legrand added, "This saloon was packed every night." My eyes lit up in total fascination. I could hear the honky-tonk music, loud laughter and see the chandeliers sparkling brightly. "Anybody famous ever come in –like Wyatt Earp?" He laughed. "Wyatt was a gambler and lawman, in that order, so I'm not sure that he would'a come through here, but I'm sure somebody infamous did at one time or another. Gold fever attracts men from every corner of the country -and that just naturally brings outlaws-like saloons bring cardsharks."

I nodded, completely caught up in the moment. "Where did they strike gold out here?" I asked.

"They didn't," he said. "There never was no gold. I imagine a cowboy who had jest a tad more redeye than he could handle prob'ly made it up trying to impress some little ol' saloon gal. But it doesn't take much to start something like that and th' rumor spread like wildfire. The town exploded with gold fever an' was bustin' its seams for a year or two -until no gold was found. Then overnight, this place became a ghost town. Pretty soon,

17

the stages quit comin'. Nothin's come by since then an' th' town just withered up an' died."

I looked around at the dusty rafters and cobweb-covered chandeliers. I scanned the enormous stage with its tattered backdrop and overturned bar stools lying all over the floor. Everything was covered in layer upon layer of dust and cobwebs. It was as if someone had fired a starter pistol and everyone left at the same time...and never looked back. "You mean they just up and *left* everything?"

"As sudden as they came, they were gone. Pulled up stakes and headed for California."

I took the cloth off my head. "So nobody stayed," I sighed disappointedly.

"Not quite," he said. "Several families put down roots outside town and had no intention of leaving. My great granddaddy was one of them. He loved th' wide open spaces and wasn't about to leave. Land was twenty five cents an acre, so he after he bought a thousand acres, he bought a few head'a cattle and started a ranch." Legrand uncrossed his legs and sat up in his chair. "You don't know it," he said, "but you're surrounded by some of th' biggest, oldest, wealthiest, cattle ranches in Texas."

"*WHAAAT?*" I cried. I put the wet cloth on my head again. "This is too mucking futch," I muttered.

"And everybody out here likes this town just th' way it is, so we keep it that way. It doesn't invite trouble."

"So, you run a hardware store and there's a bank across th' street. What else is here in town?"

"Just th' diner," he said. "We only have what we need. My grandfather opened th' hardware store when th' ranches needed barbed wire, fence posts and mending tools on almost a daily basis. Otherwise it was a two day drive by wagon to get supplies."

"Oh yeah," he smiled, "and I still have th' ranch. I've added twenty five hundred more acres though an' about twice that many heads of cattle."

"How do you run both?"

"My foreman runs it."

"And th' bank?"

"The bank has only been here for the last ten years. Ranchers have daily transactions that concern big money. They can't be hobbled by travelin' back 'n forth to a bank that's miles away or risk hold-ups, so Cattlemen's Bank was started across th' street by one'a th' biggest ranching families in th' state."

"And *they* built the bank in that rundown cracker barrel across th' street??" I cried incredulously.

Legrand raised a knowing eyebrow. "You gotta be kiddin," I snickered. "Why a five year old could bust into that rundown place with a tricycle. I don't think *looking* deserted is gonna protect you." He tilted his head and stared thoughtfully up at the ceiling while puffing on his cigar. After a minute, he snubbed it out on the floor and leaned towards me. "*Ree-ally*...would you care to make a bet on that?"

I stopped laughing.

"That bank is fortified with eight inches of the toughest steel made. The wood outside was carefully removed then put back on. There are locks and time locks in there that 007 couldn't get through with a blowtorch. And if he did get one open, he'd just run into three more. It would take the most skilled thief at least *two days* to get through one lock. And *anyone* stupid enough to even try is inviting more booby traps than they can imagine."

I gulped. "That last one was aimed at me, wasn't it." He sat back and crossed both his arms and legs. "Only if you need th' warning," he smiled.

"Okay...first off, let me reassure you that I don't have any designs on robbing your bank," I said. "Hell, I had a hard enough time unlocking my car when I *had* one." Legrand stared at me without blinking. "I don't know anything about you," he said. "But sometimes a man's gotta go with his gut instincts. I've taken a big chance tellin' you all this and only time will tell if I'm right or wrong. And if I AM wrong, ONE of us is gonna be sorry. Care to guess which one it'll be?"

I sighed. "No..."

"Now, how 'bout that bath we talked about earlier?"

CHAPTER ELEVEN

I was more than ready for a shower.

However, without any plumbing and running water, I didn't see how that was possible. Legrand offered to take me to his place. He said his wife was one of the best cooks in the county; I could have supper, shower and spend the night. It was mighty tempting, but I looked down at myself and said, "Thanks, but no thanks. I'm just not ready to look the rest of the world in the face yet." Then I smiled jokingly. "But how 'bout those old horse troughs out in front of th' bank–they got any water in them?" His eyebrows shot up when I said that. "You just reminded me of something," he said, checking his watch. "It's just going on 3:30..." He jumped up and went out the back door without waiting for a response. I wondered what he was up too and waited patiently for him to return. He came back in wiping his hands with a rag. "Just as I thought," he said. "There's an old well out back covered over with planks. I'll get my guys over here an' I think with a lot of elbow grease, we can get it working again."

"What?" I said. You think you can get water in here?"

He nodded.

"You're sure it'll work."

"It'll work," he answered.

I had serious doubts but decided to humor this deluded Texan anyway. "Okay," I said, "let's say you <u>do</u> get it pumping again -what makes you think the water's drinkable?"

He finished wiping his hands off and put the rag in his hip pocket. "You ever wonder what th' name of this town was?" he asked.

"Yeah –often." It's called Rio Escondido."

"Hidden River," I said. "How in hell did a town 'way out in the desert get that name?"

"There are caverns big as cathedrals underground. A river a quarter mile wide with sandy beaches on both sides flows all the way into Mexico. The river is fed by a spring that starts somewhere up from here and is filtered through layers of sand. It's th' purest, clearest water you've ever seen –like glass."

"Caverns –*here*?? How -isn't th' ground too sandy?"

"A bedrock of limestone lies deep underneath all this sand and formed th' caverns thousands of years ago –prob'ly when th' world was a lot greener than it is now."

"I noticed you didn't say it was formed millions of years ago. Don't tell me I've run into an intelligent man who knows better than to believe in Darwin."

"Never did cotton to that idiot theory," he frowned. "Even if I was an atheist -which I'm not, there are too many holes in it. For one thing, I've never known of a species to "evolve" from an entirely different species –no matter how similar they are outwardly."

"Well, I suppose you could argue that a mule comes from a horse and a donkey..."

"True, but mules are still in the same species –and are born sterile."

I laughed and Legrand asked me what was so funny. "I just had a funny image pop into my mind. For all the twisted bullshit that's been invented to try to make Darwin's theory work," I said, "I've never seen a man impregnate an ape –or vice versa."

"An' you never will unless something very hinky is done to manipulate it. For one thing, the body temperatures are different. Sperm can't live in the different climate under natural conditions."

"People wouldn't be so fast to accept Darwin's "theory" if they fully understood that the man was the biggest racist since Hitler."

Legrand sighed. "Yeah, it was Darwin's theory that Hitler based his Master Race on."

"And look how well that worked out."

Legrand's face darkened. "Maybe it didn't work out that time, but Man hasn't quit trying to achieve what Hitler set in motion -and science has come a loooong way since then."

"Now *there's* a nasty thought," I frowned. "So –you ever go down and see that river and caverns?

"Not me! I'm strictly an above ground guy. But Rocky has."

"Is there any place he hasn't been out here?"

"Not that *I* know of."

CHAPTER TWELVE

Legrand, along with three of his guys from the hardware store spent the rest of the day working on the old well. I wasn't able to offer much help in my emaciated condition so I stayed out of their way. About an hour before sundown, they came back inside looking filthy and dripping with sweat. "We got it workin' -sort of," Legrand said. "But it's a bitch!" He wiped off his forehead with the back of his arm. "I'm gonna have to come back tomorrow when we can see. Th' pump is suckin' up too much air 'cause I can't see how far down th' water level is. It has to have dropped some since it was last used, but I need sunlight to see where it is." He looked at me apologetically, "Sorry, Mac, looks like you gotta fight them cooties for one more night."

"Ah well," I sighed. "It'll give me a chance to say goodbye. We've been together so long I gave 'em names."

He looked at his watch. "Okay, guys -its 6:30; go on home -but be back here by 8 in th' morning' so we can finish this thing up."

They nodded and said good night. After they left, he turned back to me. "I'm going over to th' diner an' get you some supper then I'm goin' home and take a long hot shower; I am *filthy*."

My stomach jumped at the mention of food and my mouth watered noticeably. I was tired, thirsty and very hungry. Thirty minutes later, Legrand was back with my food. I expected a sandwich, but he came in with two white cardboard boxes; one in each hand. He handed me one and I couldn't wait to open it. Inside was a feast of homecooked fried chicken, mashed potatoes (with real milk gravy) green baby limas and cornbread soooooooooo soft it melted in my mouth. "Ooh lord, Legrand," I mumbled with my mouth full. "This is the best food I've ever tasted except for my grandmother's." After saying that, I shut up and concentrated on eating. When I finished sopping up the last drop of gravy with the last crumb of cornbread, I was still hungry enough to eat a horse and was delighted when he said, "Here's one more box."

"There's *more?*" I asked, trying not to grab it from him. I opened the box and saw two of the biggest, thickest, slices of homemade apple pie ever. "*Holy* cow!" I whispered. "There's half a pie in here..."

"One'a them is mine," he said, "Got us both some pie an' coffee," he said, handing me a Styrofoam cup the size of Texas. "Pie ain't no good without coffee -hope black is okay..."

I took the coffee suddenly feeling like a bum. "Legrand," I began, "I don't know what to say. You've done so much for me that I-" my voice cracked and I cleared my throat. "I don't have any money...well, I *DO* but it's all been goin' in a bank back in Chicago..."

"Dammit Mac, if you *ever* mention money to me again when I do somethin' for you," he interrupted with fire in his eyes, "I swear I'll take you apart. So just shut up an' eat."

I looked at him sheepishly. "Does this mean we're engaged?"

"No," he growled, "but it *does* mean we're friends and that ain't somethin' I say lightly."

"Friends -an' just when did that happen?"

"Somewhere between you likin' this town and hatin' Darwin."

CHAPTER THIRTEEN

Legrand got the well working the next day and that night I finally got a bath (–well, two really.) I was so dirty that I poured out the first bathwater and refilled the tub. The second time, I got down to skin. Legrand was pretty ingenious about getting water in from the well. He ran a silver accordion dryer hose from the well to the tub, which was an oblong galvanized horse trough.

Of course the water was cold but Legrand was right; it was pure and clean.

We grew to be good friends over the next few weeks. He burned my old clothes and brought me new ones. We ate meals at the diner and with his help I began to come alive again.

One day over breakfast he said, "You given anymore thought to settlin' down here?"

I set my coffee down and nodded. "I have," I said.

"...And to buyin' that ol' saloon?"

"I'd sure like to talk about it," I said. "You got any idea how I could go about it?"

"I might," he nodded.

"Shit," I grinned. "There ain't nothin' around here that you don't know about."

After paying for breakfast, Legrand asked me to follow him over to his store. He took me into his office and pointed to a chair. "Sit down," he said, while he went around his desk and pulled out one of the top drawers. He took out an old metal box and set it on top of his desk.

"If you're serious about buyin' the saloon," he said, "then make me an offer."

His comment caught me completely off guard and I was speechless for almost a minute. When I found my voice again, I wasn't entirely convinced he wasn't pulling my leg.

"Are you serious?" I asked.

He nodded. "Serious as a heartattack."

"How can *I* buy it?"

"Easy," he answered. "I own it."

I closed my eyes and waited for the blood to come back into my head. "*You* own it. And all this time you never said a word..."

"I had to get to know you, Mac; had to see if you were serious about wantin' to stick around. Like I said before; we don't take to strangers much out here, so we don't volunteer information easily."

"Well, how much would you- you know -want for it?" I asked hesitantly.

"If I tell you the price, you promise to pay it?"

(Oh God -what was I getting myself into?) "If I can," I said. He took a paper out of the metal box. It looked like a legal document. "I had this drawn up at th' bank yesterday. It's all legal and binding; all it needs is your signature if you agree to the terms."

He handed it to me. I couldn't believe the terms and re-read them before looking at him. "Wait a minute, Legrand -what is this –a joke?" I looked at the selling price again and said, "You're kidding, aren't you."

"Why," he asked, "somethin' wrong?" He took the paper back and looked it over.

"Looks okay to me," he said.

I got up. "You're selling me the saloon and all its property for *A DOLLAR??*"

"Too much?" he asked. "I mean, if you ain't got it, I can wait."

CHAPTER FOURTEEN

I signed the paper, had my bank back in Chicago wire all my assets out here, and paid Legrand his dollar. As soon as the saloon was mine, I rolled up my sleeves and got to work. It was my intention to bring her back to life and open up again for business. I uncovered a century's worth of cobwebs from chandeliers and dusted decades of dust out of darkened corners. I nailed rafters back in place and rubbed layers of dirt off the mahogany bar. It took the better part of a week to sweep out a century's worth of sand, but to my delight, each layer uncovered a historic treasure. I found an old garter, one withered boot, a Morgan silver dollar and more bullet holes than I could count.

After I got the place a little more in order, Legrand and I installed plumbing, a septic tank, hot water heater and stainless bar sinks behind the bar. I put up glass shelves in front of the old mirror and last but not least, Legrand got an electrician he knew over in Brownsville to wire the joint. Everything I did to update the place would've been almost impossible without his help. Materials and their availability were a third of the cost because of him.

I couldn't go on sleeping on the floor, so once the bar was in shape I turned my attention to me. In the back, there was a large storeroom with a window. It was about twenty feet by thirty and plenty big enough for me to use. We remodeled it by putting in a bathroom. Legrand's wife gave me an area rug, a twin bed and a quilt she made to throw over it. (A coat of paint would've cheered things up, but I wasn't complaining.)

With my living quarters finished, I was just about ready to open now, but I still had a few more things to do; like buy booze. I went over to Legrand's and called the phone company from his place to come install a pay phone at the end of the bar, then looked up a supplier in the yellow pages and ordered beer, bourbon and tequila. It was a shoestring business, but it was all I needed. The phone company was installing the pay phone two days later, when a delivery truck pulled up. A nice-looking Afro-American man got out, wearing shorts and a short-sleeved shirt like the UPS guys wear. He came inside and introduced himself as Michael (*–not* Mike) and we shook hands. Although I tried hard not to, I grimaced and he let go with an apology.

Michael looked to be around 27 or 28 and could've played defensive tackle for Green Bay any day of the week, and seeing him hoist my beer kegs one at a time up on his shoulder, I figured right then that if the guy wanted to be called Michael *I* was going to call him Michael. Watching him unload the kegs, I realized he was so damned strong from lifting all this stuff, and never meant to shake my hand so bone crushingly hard. The two of us unpacked the liquor checking for any breakage; then lined the bottles up on the counter. I signed the order slip and when I handed it back to him, he said, "Ya know, this place needs one more thing –I'll be right back!" He went out to his truck and came back with a couple of neon beer signs to hang behind the bar.

"Wow, these are great -what do I owe you?" He smiled and said they were compliments of the supplier. I thanked him and walked him out to his truck. He got in, started it up and waved as he drove off. He turned north at the crossroad and I went to get the ladder and my tool box. Getting out a hammer and a couple of nails, I climbed the ladder and hung the signs on each side of the mirror. Then I plugged them in and BINGO -Michael was right –the signs were *just* what the place needed. I stood back and admired all the work I'd done since coming here. The bar was starting to look like a real saloon. I had running water, sinks, restrooms, liquor, and now -neon beer signs. What more could I ask for? Hmmm, what indeed? I rubbed my chin thoughtfully. The neon was a definite improvement, but something was still missing. The place was lacking a very important feature, but I couldn't put my finger on what. Then it came to me. Music! *That's* what was missing. I had to get a jukebox in here before I could open.

I grabbed the yellow pages again and called my liquor supplier up in Brownsville. He put me in touch with a place that sold or rented jukeboxes to bars. I called them and it arrived within ten days. They installed it for me near a support pole in the middle of the dance floor. The next day I opened up for business. There was no confetti or balloons -just an OPEN sign hung out on the door. I was now the proud owner/operator of a real western saloon.

Not surprisingly, I didn't have any customers outside of Legrand and his guys, but it didn't take long for word to get around. Business picked up and by the second week, I had all the paying customers I needed.

...But I've made <u>sure</u> Legrand never pays for anything.

I was forever in his debt, whether he wanted it or not.

CHAPTER FIFTEEN

That was five years ago.

In that time, the saloon has never stopped doing a steady business. Nights are usually unremarkable, but one night that changed. It was just a regular Thursday night. Everybody was sitting at the bar discussing their day. Ninety nine per cent of my customers are cowboys, so they like a beer or two after a long hard week of roping cattle, mending fences and - whatever else they do. The jukebox was playing Randy Travis when the unmistakable sound of air brakes outside overrode the music. I knew it was a bus and looked up to see what kind; thinking it was a Greyhound. However, it wasn't a commercial bus; it was a private customized one that carries VIP's and entertainers. The doors hissed open and several guys got out. They walked up to the bar and introduced themselves. It was plain to see they were musicians –and sure enough, they were in a band called "Texas Chainsaw." I'd never heard of them, but that's no revelation. I introduced myself and asked what could I do for them? They explained that they were on their way to Houston to do a concert. They didn't have to be there until late the next afternoon, so they wanted to know if they could bring in their instruments and play for us to kill some time. "We could use the practice," one of them laughed.

I was dumbfounded, but everybody at the bar hooted and hollered, so I said, "Sure, make yourselves at home." I have no equipment but these bands are self-contained so they brought in everything they needed and played until closing (which is any time before sun-up.)

Over the years, I've had countless hundreds of entertainers stop by- (even guys that I DO know who they are.) One night Waylon, Willie and Jerry Jeff Walker walked in; another night, it was David Allen Coe. They put on a show and drank until I thought they'd fall down.

But, the night I'll *never* forget is the one when the Eagles walked in. I don't usually get goosebumps but that night, I was covered with them. The Eagles probably have the finest harmony of anyone I've ever heard. Each of the members is a World Class musician in his own right –but together they're an extraordinary spiritual experience. I remembered how music did something and it gave me an idea. The jukebox was probably enough but I'd long thought about adding live music, so when three high school kids came in one day and asked if I'd hire them to play on the weekends, I said yes.

They aren't all that good, but they're loud -and IF a female ever comes in, they get the boys up on their feet. (Another noticeable thing out here is cowboys can't dance worth a damn.) Maybe it's just that they don't care; I don't know -but whatever it is, they're the happiest-go-lucky bunch I've ever seen. It's still the 50's for them and they couldn't care less if the world goes by without them.

Every place in the Universe has its own rhythm, but this town is different in that not much ever changes here. Hard work ends at sundown and Sundays are for family and worship. God's seasons are appreciated and mark definite times to do what should be done –just like in Amish country. Folks don't care if you're rich or poor; just so long as you're honest and trustworthy. Nobody cares to be complicated or make life that way for anyone else. The Golden Rule is alive and well and a man's word is more ironclad than anything written on paper.

Yep, I guess you could say my life was perfect. That is, until one day when she came in and *nothing* was ever the same again.

CHAPTER SIXTEEN

It was just another sizzling hot Texas day. The July sun was beating down on everything until you could fry an egg on the wooden sidewalks. I was behind the bar drying glasses and humming along with Johnny Rodriquez's, "Thumbin' My Way to Mexico," when the door suddenly swung open -and *stayed* open. The noonday sunlight bounced off the mirror like a laser, blinding the hell out of me. I put my arm up and yelled, "WILL YOU SHUT THAT DOOR BEFORE I GO BLIND!" The door closed, but it took a moment for the white explosions in my eyes to disappear. When they did, I stared at the young woman standing just inside the door. "Oh," I stammered, "I-I'm sorry ma'am...I thought you were one'a the cowboys." She didn't say a word- just stood there holding a raggedy little suitcase in one hand and clutching the neck of her sweatshirt with the other. I spoke to her again while wondering how she could stand being covered up like that in this sweltering heat. She stared off in space like she didn't see or hear anything and I wasn't sure she knew I was there. Finally she blinked and took a few unsteady steps towards me. As soon as she was close enough, I could see she'd been on the road a long time. She was covered in dust from head to foot. Sweat rolled down her face, leaving shiny wet tracks along her sunken cheeks. Even worse, I recognized a hangover when I saw one, and hers had been running one into another for a loong time. I thought it best not to speak to her again as she continued to make her way over to the bar. I didn't want to say anything that might break her concentration, so I slowly eased my towel off my shoulder to watch. Every few steps, she put her hand out to steady herself on some invisible handrail. If she didn't have the suitcase as a counterbalance, I think she would've tilted clean over.

...And don't you know that when she *finally* made it, she had trouble getting on the stool.

CHAPTER SEVENTEEN

I crossed my arms and leaned my butt against the cooler to wait for her to sit down. She set her suitcase on the floor so she could hold on to the stool with both hands. She griped each side of the stool in order to lift her leg up and slide across, but her hands were shaking so bad that she kept knocking the damned thing over. I lost count how many times she did this, but every time it crashed to the floor she bent down without looking at me and picked it up; only to knock it over again. It was pathetic. I never knew getting on a barstool could be so challenging and couldn't help thinking Ringling Brothers should see this.

After countless failed attempts, she finally made it by holding on to the bar with both hands and inching her fanny across the seat. I didn't know whether to applaud or ignore her. When she seemed pretty sure she wasn't going to fall off, she looked at me like she just noticed I was there. She gave me a tired smile and I sighed, "Can I get you something?"

"Yes," she said softly, "a glass of water, please."

"WATER??" I frowned, shaking my head like I didn't hear right. "Did you say...*water?*"

She nodded and raised a trembling hand to smooth dark hair piled haphazardly on top of her head. It was a useless gesture; (nothing short of a team of high priced hairdressers out of Hollywood could help that mop.)

I cursed silently as I got down my biggest glass. I filled it to the brim with ice, poured water over the crushed cubes and set it on a clean napkin in front of her. She muttered a weak thanks, but I'd already turned my back.

If I hadn't been so hell-bent on being indifferent, I would've known she was embarrassed --and broke. She probably was dying for a beer –and it wouldn't have killed me to give her one. But unfortunately, I was strictly a bartender these days; not a baby-sitter for life's emotional cripples. I'd told myself over and over that it was best not to care. After all, nobody gave a damn when I was puking my guts out in some filthy alley. Yeah, these days, I was a real bastard when it came to the Milk of Human Kindness.

But no matter how hard I tried to play the role of a hard ass, I kept glancing up in the mirror and to my utter aggravation, found myself watching her. She leaned both elbows on the bar, trying to get her hands around the glass and bring it to her lips. However, she was shaking so bad that more water sloshed all over the bar than made it into her mouth. I rolled my eyes and shook my head. To hell with it! Fascinated as I was, I was NOT going to be drawn into her little web of female helplessness. I grabbed a bar towel and roughly wiped up the spilled water while making a point of ignoring her. I threw the towel under the sink and turned my back on her again.

A minute later I looked up to see what she was doing. She was backing off the stool by holding on to the edge of the bar with the same death grip as when she got on. I thought her fingers were going to leave eight little grooves in the wood. She looked up and catching my eye in the mirror, asked, "It says bar and grill outside --do you serve food?" She spoke so softly I almost didn't hear her. I shook my head. "We don't have a grill." (...like she could afford to buy anything.)

She weaved a bit but persisted. "Then why does it say Bar and Grill?"

Sweat was pouring down her face. I took note of how deathly pale she looked and resented my interest. "Because," I answered with patient sarcasm. "Bar and microwave just sounds, oh, I don't know --less romantic." My acid retort went right over her head.

"Oh!" she said with a hopeful raise of her eyebrow. "Then, you DO have a microwave?"

"Yes," I answered, pointing tiredly to the one in the corner covered in spider webs. "But it doesn't work. It quit a week after I bought it at a garage sale, so all you can do in here is drink!" I grabbed another towel and rubbed the bar to punctuate my indifference to her problems.

Whatever small trace of hope I'd seen a moment ago, disappeared from her face as she said softly, "oh...I see." Her shoulders sagged as she bent down to pick up her suitcase again. "Well then, I guess I've taken up enough of your time..."

I stood there with a bored look and thought, "You bet your sweet ass you have," but didn't say anything. She held on to the bar until my silence made it clear that I had no interest in starting a conversation with her, then she let out a tired sigh and thanked me for the water. I watched as she turned to leave, but after taking three steps towards the door, she just crumbled to the floor. I was sure she was faking and got really pissed. I said, "Oh, that's cute, but do you mind getting up? This ain't a motel."

When she didn't get up, I *really* got angry. I threw my towel down again and ran around the end of the bar. I stood over her with both hands on my hips, convinced that she was just playing opossum. "Look, I'm not kiddin'...get up."

She didn't move.

Tightening my lips, I frowned and dropped down on one knee. I was pissed and slapped her on the cheek with the back of my fingers. "Miss-wake up..." I said harshly. "Hey, can you hear me?"

She just lie there; out cold. I sat back on my heels. She wasn't faking, damn it; I was sure of that. I reached down and felt her forehead. She was burning up and her breathing was practically nonexistent. Crap! I needed this like a hole in the head. I picked her up in my arms and was shocked at how light she was. Beneath her baggy clothes, she was just skin and bones. (No wonder she asked if I had any food.) I hurried to the storeroom trying to remember the old saying, "starve a fever; feed a cold." No, no, that was wrong! Food makes phlegm while fevers burn up everything in your body trying to kill infection. It was "*starve* a cold; *feed* a fever." Right! That was it! She needed food.

As I carried her across the dance floor, her hair came down and almost reached the floor as it swung back and forth. I was surprised to see how long and dark it was. (I liked long dark hair...) I laid her down on the bed. She didn't move. I picked up the quilt and was just covering her up when I heard the front door open and cowboy boots walk across the floor. It was odd that anyone should be in this early, so I tucked the quilt in all around her and hurried out.

I saw it was Harold Davidson. Everybody calls him, "Harley" and he was one of the few I would call "a close friend." I tried to sound casual as I called out, "Hey, Harley, how's it hangin'?"

He was just pulling out a bar stool and turned around to see where I was.

"Hey, Mac," he smiled. "It's hangin' just fine...an' you?"

"Oh...same as always," I answered absently, slowing my pace and finally stopping halfway to the bar. My mind was on the girl. I couldn't help but worry about her dying; which I didn't care about as much as her doing it here.

Harley took off his Stetson and laid it on the bar next to him. He ran his hand through his hair before taking out a handkerchief and wiping it across his forehead and down the back of his neck.

"It's hotter'n a brandin' iron out there, today," he said stuffing his handkerchief back into his hip pocket. He turned to look at me. "You gonna stand there all day or what?"

"Huh? Oh, yeah...comin' Harley." I took another quick glance back towards the storeroom then continued on behind the bar.

"Kind'a early for you to be in here ain't it -you get fired or somethin'?"

He took a deep breath. "Nope, we jest finished all'a that fencin' up in th' north pasture, so Ah told th' guys to take off early after they get everything bedded down for th' night."

"Pretty hot to be fencin' ain't it?"

"Yeah, but it had'ta be done, so..." he shrugged.

Harley was a tall lanky man of ageless description with piercing black eyes over high cheeks bones. His complexion was the color and texture of tanned leather. At six, six and around one seventy, he was pure cowboy from the top of his black Stetson hat to his straight leg jeans and handmade Mexican boots. (Harley was what my mother would've called, "a tall drink of water.") He was also foreman on the third largest ranch out here and remembered when cowboys rode horses instead of A.T.V.'s -which he hated. I made small talk while trying to figure out what to do with my new roommate. "So, how long you been at it up there?"

"Over a week now," he said. "Took us longer than usual."

"How come?"

"It's more mountainous than the south pasture is. It's so steep and rocky that we had a hard time gettin' the equipment up there. Them stupid good-for-nothin' all-terrain vehicles couldn't cut it." He paused and gave me a half smile. "But th' good news is we took horses."

"An' how'd it feel to be back in th' saddle?"

"Only place for any decent, self respectin' cowboy to be," he snorted. "My horse don't understand them new-fangled things AT all!" I put a napkin down in front of him. "So, what'll it be --th' usual?"

"Yep, no need to change now." I got down a shot glass and filled it with Jack Daniels then drew a Millers into an icy mug from the cooler. I set them in front of him and wiped my hands on a towel. I stood back and waited for Harley to pick up his beer, but he didn't move. Instead, he just cocked an eyebrow and scratched the back of his neck. "Somethin' botherin' you, Mac?" he squinted at me. I took another quick glance at the storeroom. "Uh, no, I don't think so—why?"

"Because you know I don't drink Millers!"

"Huh?" I blinked.

"Millers..." he repeated. "I don't drink it." I looked at him, then down at his beer. Finally it registered. "Oh, jeese, I'm sorry, Harley." I said, taking the beer back. After replacing it with a Michelob, he said, "You sure act like a man who's got something on his mind. I never seen you so jumpy."

"Yeah," I sighed, "guess I am actin' a bit weird."

"Well, spit it out."

I took a deep breath and thought about it for a second, then exhaled. "You know much about th' D.T.'s?" I asked. He sat up and narrowed his eyes suspiciously. "The *what*?"

"Th' D.T.'s," I repeated.

"You mean them things you get from drinkin' too much?"

I nodded.

31

"What th' hell kind'a question is THAT?" he demanded, pushing his beer away.

"No, no," I said, pushing it back. "I don't mean you, I mean in general."

"I don't guess I know anything about 'em...why?"

"Because," I began, "the damnedest thing happened about ten minutes before you came in. This girl came in and..." I stopped in mid-sentence and scratched my head, trying to find some way to explain. "Yeah...go on," Harley said. "Well, she didn't look right -like she'd been on th' road for a long time or somethin'. Anyway, she asked for a glass of water -which I gave her, but after she drank it, she stood up an' just passed out dead on th' floor."

"Yeah, that's why I don't drink water," he grumbled. "Stuff'll kill ya."

I sighed and rolled my eyes. "Will you just *listen* for a minute?" I frowned.

"Sorry, go on..."

"I'd just carried her back to th' storeroom and laid her on the bed when I heard you come in."

A frown crossed his face. "Who is she?" he asked.

I shrugged one shoulder. "Don't know. Never saw her before in my life, but she's burning up an' it don't take a rocket scientist to see she's been on th' bottle for a long time."

He tossed down his Jack Daniels, then stood up and put on his hat. "Well, let's go see how she is," he said.

We saw she was still passed out.

"Is she..." and he made a tipping motion with his hand like he was drinking, "now?"

"Nah," I whispered. "I'm positive she ain't."

"How do YOU know?" he snorted. "You some kind'a authority?"

"Actually I am," I grumbled. "So, what'd'ya think -should I send for Doc Wright?"

Harley stared at her then nodded. "It might not be a bad idea."

Doc Wright was a veterinarian, but he was the only doctor around.

"Do you know where he is?"

"Yeah," he nodded. "He's over at th' Johnson ranch. I saw him on my way in."

"Well, could you go get him? I can't leave her or th' bar."

"I'll go," he said simply.

I hurriedly walked him out to the door. "Listen," I said, "get on back soon as you can, okay? I don't want her dyin' on me."

"I will," he nodded. I watched him pull away while anxiously chewing on my lip, then went back inside to pace back and forth. I rubbed my chin, wondering what to do. I was a nervous wreck. Damn it, I didn't need this aggravation. I decided to fill a towel with ice. As I got the ice out of the cooler, I wondered if a sip of booze might help, but since I didn't know what was wrong with her, decided against it. I took the ice back to her, but the second I put the towel across her forehead, she arched her back suddenly and started to roll back and forth like a gut shot buffalo. She tried to push my hand away but I held the towel down firmly on her forehead. She didn't wake up during the scuffle, but her face had an angry look on it and I didn't know if she was having a bad dream or a grand mal seizure.

"Don't TOUCH me!" she screamed, clawing my hand with both of hers. She dug her nails into in to my flesh, but I bit my lip and held on. Then she wrapped her fingers around my wrist with all the strength of a vice grip and smacked my hand away so hard, it knocked the towel to the floor. Ice skidded across the floor in every direction. I picked up what I could, but when I went to put it back on her head, she flailed the air and growled, "I MEAN IT!! Get AWAY." (...And *again* with the towel and ice all over the floor.) I started to pick it up again when I saw that she was going to roll off the bed. Forgetting the ice, I quickly grabbed her shoulders and held her down. She kept struggling against me.

"Get your filthy hands off me, you bastard!" she hissed. "You can't make me come back! If you do, I *WILL* run away *again*!" The little minx clawed the air like a wildcat and I held my head back to keep my face from being scratched to pieces. I held her down but it wasn't easy. She kicked wildly and was stronger than her skinny frame would have you believe. I wondered how much longer I could hold her, when she suddenly relaxed and all the fight went out of her. She lay there with her head turned to one side and her eyes still closed. She was limp as an overcooked noodle.

I slowly took my hands away from her shoulders and staring down at her, wondered *what* was the hell was wrong with her. Had something -or *somebody* hurt her like this? The way she fought me sure looked like somebody had treated her real bad. If I was right, then *no* wonder she drank. The back of my hand was bleeding and looked like it'd been through a shredder. I wrapped the cold wet towel around it and touched her forehead again. She was even hotter than before. I was alarmed to see rivers of sweat running down both sides of her face flatting wisps of her hair against her head. Her breathing came out fast and shallow and her face was getting redder by the second. I quickly picked up a piece of ice from the floor and held it to her lips. The ice melted so quickly against her burning skin, that I wouldn't have been surprised if it evaporated into steam. I bent down closer. She was now in a deeper sleep than I liked and her breathing was becoming more and more ragged. I was starting to come unraveled when I heard the door open. I jumped up and ran out. It was Harley.

"Thank God you're back!" I cried. "What the hell took you so long?"

"Got back soon as I could," he stated matter-of-factly, taking off his Stetson. "Took me a while to find him." Doc came in close on his heels. "What's wrong, Mac?" he asked breathlessly. "Harley pulled me away from a sick calf over at Legrand's, but wouldn't tell me what the trouble is."

"Didn't 'zactly know how to," Harley shrugged.

"Yeah...it IS kind'a hard to explain," I said. "Maybe you'd better just come with me and see for yourself."

We hurried into the storeroom, but as soon as Doc saw her, he said, "You're kidding me, aren't you."

Harley and I shook our heads in unison. Doc adjusted his glasses and frowned. "I don't know, Mac, this is a bit out of my line."

"I know, but you gotta help her. She's really been actin' crazy...saying all kind of things that don't make sense! ...And she's got a bad fever."

"Yes, I can see that," Doc said sitting down on the edge of the bed. "Her face looks like she's on fire." He opened his black bag and as he pulled out his stethoscope, he grumbled, "Don't you ever dust in here?" (Since dusting is a big waste of time out here, it was a rhetorical question.) He put the stethoscope in both ears and pulled out his pocket watch. Taking her wrist gently between his thumb and first two fingers, he timed her pulse. Without saying anything, he pulled out a pin light and lifting her eyelids one at a time, shined the light on her glazed pupils. "Hmmmm," he muttered. "Dialated. Not good."

When he finished his exam, he took a deep breath and sat up. "Exactly what kind of things has she been doing?" he asked. I quickly told him everything, including my theory about the D.T.'s and grand mal seizure. Doc listened carefully. "Grand mal seizure, eh?" he smiled.

He took his stethoscope and checked her heart and lungs. Again he shook his head. "I don't know what it is, Mac, but I'm thinking it's a case of exhaustion, lack of food, and emotional stress. At least, that's all I'm hoping it is," he sighed, "Because there's no doubt she's very ill."

He lifted her arm gently and checked her pulse again. "She's in bad shape," he said. "She hardly has any pulse at all and just see how thin she is."

I already knew how thin she was.

He took out a thermometer, eased it under her tongue and held her mouth closed by gently cupping her chin in his hand. Several minutes later, he took it out and held it up to the light.

"A hundred and three and a half," he frowned. "If it goes any higher we have to get her to a hospital –which is exactly where she should be now." He shook the thermometer down and put it back into his bag. (Although it was a disposable, supplies were hard to come by out here, so everything got used over and over until it fell apart.)

"So, why's she got a fever?" I asked.

"Infection most likely –or maybe just rundown from some kind'a bacteria her immune system can't fight it off due to her not eating."

"Is she --contagious?"

"I don't know -it depends on what's infecting her." Doc rubbed his chin thoughtfully. "But it's my guess that she hasn't been taking care of herself—and she definitely shows signs of alcohol emaciation. However," he added, "we need to do something to break this fever right now." He looked at her and shook his head. "People don't generally let themselves go to hell like this without reason. I'd say she was running away from something."

"Or somebody," I frowned. Harley stopped fiddling with his Stetson and looked at me. Without looking at him, I asked, "So, what now?"

Doc scratched the back of his head and sighed. "I'm going to give her a wide spectrum antibiotic and hope it works."

He reached into his black bag again and felt around for a second then brought out the biggest syringe I ever saw. It was almost as big around as my fist and had a needle that must've been fourteen inches long.

"Good lord!" I gawked. "Y-You're not going to use *that* on her, are you - isn't that for horses?"

Ignoring my stupidity, Doc untwisted the needle and replaced it with a smaller one. Holding the syringe up to the light, he filled it part way with some kind of liquid. The giant syringe and its disproportionate smaller needle looked like something out of a bad horror movie. When he finished filling the syringe, he flicked the glass side with his finger then pressed the plunger until a thin spray of the clear liquid shot across the room. Holding the syringe up in his hand like a water pistol Doc said, "About all I can do now is hope she isn't allergic." He turned around and was just about to inject her, when Harley spoke up. "Hold on a sec, Doc," he said. "Isn't that stuff for horses?"

With a long patient sigh, Doc straightened back up and acknowledged that it was. "Yes, but it's the same exact medicine used for people; just different dosage." Seeing the skeptical look on both our faces, Doc held up the bottle. "See? Made by the same pharmaceutical company as the stuff you take." We leaned forward and squinted at the label. Yep. It was the very same stuff. (Man, these drug companies really had the best of both worlds.) I shrugged. What choice did we have? Doc was it. "Okay," I sighed, "do whatever you can for her."

Harley and I looked away while Doc rolled her over and injected her in the hip.

"About all we can do now," he said, "is wait."

When he was finished, I turned back around. "So...what if she is –you know, allergic?"

"Then we're in big trouble," was all he said.

Everybody fell silent as we held our breath and waited to see if she was going to accept the medicine or not. Fifteen of the longest minutes went by before Doc let out a deep sigh of relief. "Okay," he said, checking her heart again. "She seems to be all right. Now I'll give her a mild sedative to put her into deep sleep and hopefully provide the rest her body needs." This time he injected her in the vein. "That's all I can do," he said, "the rest is up to her and God." He turned to me. "Listen, Mac. It's imperative that you stay close by and don't leave her alone tonight. She's in very bad shape and treating her has been like playing Russian Roulette for me."

"Meaning...?" I shrugged.

He took the stethoscope from around his neck, folded it in quarters and stuffed it back into his bag. "Meaning, I've tried to under medicate her, but I still had to guess at the dosages. And not only that, but she very well could have something else wrong with her other than an infection."

I frowned. "Like...?"

"Like, she could have appendicitis or hepatitis! She could even be diabetic. Without a lab around to do any kind of blood workup, I have NO way of knowing. An X-ray would help, along with an E.K.G. and an E.E.G. to tell me what shape her head and heart is in. She could have had a recent head injury or even an old one -that's resulted in epilepsy. A MILLION things could be wrong with her! Hell man! I don't even know what's causing her fever!"

My lips tightened and a deep frown creased my forehead. Shit! It just didn't stop. The list of things that could be wrong with her was endless. I nervously ran my fingers through my thinning hair and seriously contemplated pulling out what little I had left. Doc wasn't helping any either as he continued to paint a very black picture. "If this fever doesn't break tonight, Mac, she's GOT to get to a hospital immediately. She SHOULD be on a saline I.V. She's badly dehydrated and her white blood count must be sky high!"

"This sucks," I muttered under my breath.

"And I don't even want to THINK about her having diabetes; *especially* if she really IS abusing alcohol."

"Well," I whined, "can't you tell by lookin' at her?"

"Read my lips: NO, Mac, I can't! I'm a VET, for God's sake."

I paced back and forth rubbing the back of my neck. This whole thing was starting to sound like a bad routine of "Good News, Bad News." WHY did she have to stop in here of ALL places? God, I thought I was finally far enough away from the world that I'd NEVER have to deal with women again -and here one was- on my doorstep! "This is just GREAT," I moaned. "How th' hell am I going to run a bar an' keep an' eye on her, huh -will somebody please TELL me?" I stopped pacing and looked at Harley. "Hey don't look at me, man," he said, backing away. "I gotta ranch to run. 'Sides, I don't know nothin' about women -sick OR well."

Doc snapped his bag ·shut and stood up. "I hate to bring it up, Mac, but there IS one more thing."

My shoulders sagged. "Oh *goody*," I sighed, looking at him like he'd just run over my dog.

"If she makes it through the night without any further complications, her chances will go up tremendously for a full recovery. But <u>only</u> if that fever comes down and nothing else is wrong with her." He started for the door, then stopped and looked back at me. "Oh yes...and get some food in her."

I hung my head and stared at the floor. I knew when I was beaten. I said I'd keep an eye on her <u>and</u> sleep on the floor by her bed after closing.

"Good man," Doc nodded, taking one last glance at her. She was sleeping peacefully and her breathing had returned to deep and natural. That pleased Doc and we went out.

As we headed for the bar, Doc said, "Give her two aspirin in about four hours and call me right away if she takes any change for the worse."

I nodded and went behind the bar while they sat down. Harley laid his Stetson on top next to him and looked over at Doc. "How 'bout a taste, Doc? Mac's buyin'."

"In that case," Doc said, "I'll have a bourbon 'n branch, if it's no trouble, Mac."

"Who says I'm buyin'?" I huffed.

They both glared at me.

"Okay, okay -I'm buyin'," I sighed.

I went to get their drinks and when I got back, they were talking about the heat.

"About this girl," I interrupted as I sat their drinks on fresh napkins in front of them. "I hate being responsible, Doc. I mean, what if she...you know...dies, or somethin'."

Doc took off his glasses and pinched the bridge of his nose before pulling out a handkerchief and wiping both lenses. Putting them back on, he looked at me and said cheerfully, "Well, you could always throw her back out in the street. It's not like anyone would notice 'way out here."

I gave him a dirty look. "Thanks!" I glared. "That's a real helpful bit of advice."

Ignoring my sarcasm, Doc raised his glass to Harley. "Cheers."

Harley nodded. "Back at ya," he said.

I could see I wasn't going to get any help from either of them, so I left them to their drinks and wandered off to think. How the hell did I get in this mess? What was I going to do with some...girl? Hell, I didn't even LIKE females anymore. (Don't get me wrong -it's just that I'm a confirmed bachelor these days.)

Doc noticed I wasn't joining in and called me over. "Look, Mac, you have every right to be worried, but this is something that life dumps on our doorstep every once in a while. For whatever reason God put her here, He must think you're the right person to handle it—and it wouldn't hurt to ask for His help tonight."

"Yeah," I said sarcastically. "I'll be SURE to thank Him for this."

But Doc was right and I liked living in a place where you still heard folks speak of God with knowing familiarity. I was a real ass for thinking only of myself when this girl needed my help. I looked at him sheepishly. "Sorry Doc. I didn't mean to be so self-centered."

He stood up and reached across the bar to pat my shoulder. "I know you didn't, Mac -and don't hesitate to call if you need me. I've got to be getting home now; thanks for the drink."

He tucked his bag under his arm as Harley got up. "Ah'm gonna mosey on too," he said, putting on his Stetson. "Ah got an early day tomorrow." They walked out together and Harley held the door open for Doc before waving to me and going out too.

I leaned back against the cooler and rubbed my fingers across the day old stubble on my chin. Today was what –Wednesday? That meant my chances of a quiet night were good. It was already going on eight o'clock and nobody had come in yet. (Of course that didn't mean anything.) An hour passed with no customers, then another went by and I decided to close up. I took a swipe at the counter and left the few dirty glasses there were in the sink. After locking the door, I turned off the lights and went back to sleep on the stupid floor in the storeroom. Whatever spark of humanity Doc had ignited in me earlier, was now doused.

I left the lights off inside the storeroom and quietly eased in, not wanting to wake her. I pulled my shirttail out of my jeans and sat down in the straight back chair across from the bed to take off my boots. Moonlight filtered through the little window over the bed, casting an angelic light across her face. I stood up and took my shirt off. Throwing it over the door, I started to unbuckle my belt when I heard her stir and froze, waiting to see if she was going to wake up. When she didn't move anymore, I finished taking off my belt and hung it over the door next to my shirt, then walked over to touch her forehead. It was still warm but nothing like it was when she came in. Maybe Doc's visit had done more good than any of us had dared hope. I smiled to myself; if she was on her way to recovery, she'd be leaving; which made *me* feel a whole lot better.

I pulled the quilt up over her. She had her head turned slightly to the left with her hand resting next to it, palm up. I pulled the chair closer and straddled it. I wasn't sleepy so I sat there and studied her face closely for the first time. The longer I looked her, the more I had the feeling that I'd seen her before. She had a famous movie star familiarity but I couldn't put my finger on it. I tried to think where I could've run into her, but drew a blank. I rested my chin on my forearms and tried to think who she reminded me of. It wasn't Jenny; Jen had brownish blonde hair and hers was a rich dark brown. Maybe she wasn't anybody; maybe she was just one of those people that just looked like somebody. Besides, she was 'way too young for me to know her...or- was she? I noticed a line or two around her eyes along with an overall maturity in her face. I sat up and rubbed by chin. She really wasn't half bad looking. Get a little meat back on her bones and she might even be decent.

I got up from the chair and took off my jeans. I balled them up and tossed them on the floor to use as a pillow. Grabbing my old Indian blanket robe off the back of the door, I got down on the floor and pulled it over me as I rolled over on my side. Nine hours later, I woke up stiff and sore, wondering how the hell I'd ended up down here. I'd completely forgotten all about the girl until I saw her and it all came back like a bad dream. I groaned. This is NOT how I wanted to spend my day.

I got up, threw the robe on over my skivvies and went in to splash cold water on my face. Looking in the mirror, I said to hell with shaving and dried off. When I came out of the bathroom, she was curled up in the quilt like a kitten. I sighed and tiptoed out. The sun was just peeking through the cracks around the front door and I looked at my watch. It was only 8:30; way too early to be up. I sighed, knowing it was going to be a looooong day.

CHAPTER EIGHTEEN

I went behind the bar and got out the coffee. I put it on then went outside for a newspaper.

We don't have a newspaper per se out here, but a "Houston Times" truck periodically comes by and leaves a few of their extras on my front porch. Of course, the news is so old by the time we get it, that the paper is free. I picked one up and read the headlines. Seeing that no one had dropped the atom bomb on us yet, I figured it was going to be a good day.

It was quiet on the veranda and I was in no hurry to go back inside, so I propped my shoulder against a post and enjoyed the coolness that still lingered in the air. With no cloud cover during the day, the temperatures were drastic; nights were freezing while days would melt the paint off a barn. I closed my eyes and took a deep breath. The faint smell of coffee told me that it was ready, so I took the paper and went back inside.

I got out a mug, filled it and sat down at the bar to read what was going on in the world. I used to enjoy reading the newspaper, but lately it was printing stuff I knew wasn't fair OR honest. I'd noticed a strong bend towards the Left; which really burned me because I didn't need these draft dodging assholes telling me what to think. And political mudslinging had worsened, reaching an all-time low.

We hadn't had a war since Vietnam and although there were rumblings the Middle East, surely we'd do better in the next century –which was just around the corner. I sipped my coffee and read several more pages of pure propaganda before throwing the paper in the trash. All this political nonsense was stirring up my Irish "everything-is-a conspiracy" and "paranoia-is-perfect-awareness" thinking. Clearly if I was to keep an unbiased ability to know the Truth, I was going to have to avoid reading newspapers.

I drank what was left of my coffee then decided to go see if I could wake Sleeping Beauty. Since she'd slept through the night, I hoped maybe she'd be better today. I filled a glass with some tomato juice out of the cooler and carried it back to the storeroom. Setting the glass down next to the bed, I gently shook her shoulder.

"Hey, time to wake up," I said. But she didn't move. In fact, she just stayed there in the same position she'd been in all night. I felt myself getting pissed and roughly pushed her shoulder again. "HEY -PRINCESS! WAKE UP."

Nothing.

"Listen," I said louder, "You HAVE to wake up!" Again nothing. I swore under my breath and seriously considered throwing a bucket of cold water on her. It hadn't occurred to me yet that she might be...you know...so I stood there like an idiot, staring down at her. I finally snapped out of it and leaned over to work my left arm under her neck and shoulders. When I had a good grip, I lifted her about a foot off the pillow and tried to pour some tomato juice in her mouth. Her head rolled slowly to one side and the juice flowed back out of her mouth like blood.

"Well!" I thought. "THIS is definitely not good!"

As I stared at her lifeless body, a cold panic started to work its way into every part of my formerly warm body. And speaking of warm, she now felt unnaturally cold. All my anger immediately evaporated and I was really scared. I chanted over and over, "Oh God, please, please, *please*, don't let her be dead!" I sat the tomato juice down again and gently laid her back on the pillow. Taking her chin between my thumb and forefinger, I lightly shook her. "Miss, can you hear me?" I said, trying to control the waver in my voice. "P-Please say you can—*please*?" Again nothing -not even the flutter of an eyelash. Looking at her chalky white face, I whispered, "Oh man! This is NOT good -NOT good AT all."

It was time to call Doc.

I sprinted out to the bar and fished a quarter out of the cash drawer. I ran to the pay phone, yanked the receiver off the hook and dropped the coin on the floor three times before finally getting it in the slot. My hands were shaking so bad, I could barely dial the number. When I finally got through, I listened to Doc's phone ring over eight times and was about to hang up when he answered.

"Doc! Oh thank *God* you're still there! THIS IS MAC," I screamed, as all my endeavors to stay calm went out the window.

"Hello, Mac," he answered. "How's our patient doing this morning -is everything all right?"

I swallowed again before answering. "Th-That's what I'm callin' you about, Doc. She seems to have grown real fond of that dreamless sleep you put her in last night." Realizing how that statement could be misinterpreted, I hastened to add, "I mean, she's okay -I think, but oh *hell*, I can't tell."

"I'm not surprised," Doc said evenly. "It's probably the first good sleep she's had in a long time, and you're right, it probably was dreamless."

I squeezed my eyes shut and pressed shaking fingers against bloodless lips. "No, Doc, you d-don't understand. I tried to wake her, but she's...oh, I-I don't *know*..."

"She's what, Mac?"

"VERY asleep," I blurted out. (I just couldn't bring myself to say the "D" word.)

"Hmmm," Doc mused. "Did you happen to touch her?"

"Well...yeah..."

"Okay, so how did she feel -was she cold or clammy?"

Feeling faint, I closed my eyes again and rubbed my forehead. "Oh God...I-I don't know...I'm not sure."

"Well, how did it go last night?"

"Like -in what way?" I asked, trying to get some grasp of reality.

"I mean, did she sleep through the night; or is she stiff this morning and in the same position as you last saw her in?"

Stiff?? *That* did it. My eyes flew open and an icy hand squeezed my heart. I tried to breathe while hysteria had a field day throughout my body.

41

Suddenly I couldn't get my breath. "Oh lord," I whispered, closing my eyes once more and leaning my forehead against the wall. My hands and arms were shaking so bad now that I could hardly hold the receiver up to my ear.

"Mac?"

Straightening back up, I said, "Uh, yeah, I-I'm still here. I d-don't know," I admitted, "but I don't think she's...you know...stiff." I closed my eyes again and tried not to faint.

"I think you're overly alarmed, Mac," Doc said. "If she had expired during the night, believe me, you'd know it by looking at her this morning. Death has a definite look."

"Please d-don't say that," I said. "There's no way I can handle it if-if she's..."

"Listen, Mac, I was just heading over to the Lazy Y, but I'll stop by and check on her first if you'd like, okay? Have some coffee waiting."

I croaked out a "thanks," and hung up. It took a lot of effort, but I made it back to the coffee pot and shakily poured myself another cup. As I tried to bring it to my lips, I decided a liberal shot of bourbon was exactly what it needed. I poured out most of the coffee, replacing it with bourbon and when the front door opened ten minutes later, I was much, much, calmer.

"Is that coffee I smell?" Doc called. I slammed my mug down. "Boy-am I glad to see you!" I slurred with a glassy-eyed grin. I handed him his coffee and asked if he'd like it with or without something in it. Taking the mug from me, he raised an eyebrow and said, "Without, thanks -but I'd say you had it with."

"Had to," I nodded vigorously. "It was either that or stand here and shake to death."

"Come on," he smiled. "Let's go look in on her."

Taking his coffee with him, we headed for the storeroom. If he was the least bit worried, he didn't show it and some of my optimism began to return. I jogged alongside him, chatting like a manic magpie. When we got to the door, I opened it and we went inside. Suddenly I felt uneasy. I didn't know if she was dead or alive, but made myself glance at her. She still looked dead to me, but Doc didn't think so.

"Oh my," he smiled brightly, "she looks much better today, Mac. See? Some of her color is back."

I squinted at her. "If you say so," I muttered.

He got out his stethoscope and listened to her heart for a moment then smiled again. "Ah, yes, she's doing much better today. Her heart is much stronger."

I was never so glad to hear anything in my whole life.

Doc checked her temperature. "One hundred, even," he said. "That is VERY GOOD! I'm going to give her a B-12 injection then I think it's time we got her to sit up and take some nourishment."

Remembering the tomato juice, I picked it up from the floor and said, "I was tryin' to get some of this in her, but I couldn't wake her. That's when I called you."

He looked at it and frowned suspiciously. Reading his mind, I let out a long sigh. "It's just plain ol' tomato juice," I huffed.

"It'd better be," he said. "Tomato juice is good...but NO alcohol!"

"Here," I said, giving him the glass. "Taste it for yourself."

"I believe you," he said, "but I had to say it anyway." He took the tomato juice and gently shook her to see if he could get her to wake up. Her head rolled to the other side and she let out a little moan.

"SEE?" I yelled excitedly. "That's JUST what she did when I tried to wake her -only, she didn't moan."

Doc shook his head and handed the tomato juice back to me. "She's just plain exhausted," he said. "I'll give her the vitamin injection then try to wake her." He gave her the shot in her upper arm as I stood back and waited to see if there'd be any response. She didn't even flinch when the needle went in. After a minute, Doc shook her again -this time hard. She groaned softly and pushed his hand away. It took a couple more good shakes before she finally realized we weren't going to let her slide back to the arms of Morpheous. She frowned and rolling over on her back, her eyes fluttered open. She didn't say a word -just stared at the ceiling like a zombie. Finally she mumbled, "Where am I?" Her eyes came into focus and she saw us for the first time. She frantically jerked the quilt up to her chin and screamed, "WHO the HELL are YOU two?"

"Now what?" I frowned as Doc sat down on the edge of the bed.

"Good morning," he said. "I'm Doctor Wright, and this is your host, Mac McIntyre."

Her forehead wrinkled in anger and she looked around the room. "Am I dead? Is this Hell? Because if it is, I knew it would be bad, but not THIS bad."

I rolled my eyes.

"No, my dear," Doc said sternly. "You're not dead, but you came mighty close."

"Did I?" she asked dully. "Well, then I blew it, 'cause I was sure tryin' to make it all th' way."

"Don't sound so disappointed," Doc said coolly. "You're still not out of the woods."

She sighed. "So? Where am I -in some kind of ...strange hospital?"

"No, no, nothing like that," Doc assured her. "You're in the storeroom of a bar."

She stared at Doc for a long moment then her eyes narrowed down and she said tonelessly, "A...bar?"

Doc and I both nodded.

"What-the-hell-am-I-doing-in-the-storeroom-of-a-BAR!" she asked in measured words.

Before we could explain, she suddenly sat up and started to crawl backwards in bed. When she backed herself into the corner, she drew her knees up and clutched the quilt to her chin like it was going to protect her from whatever evil her mind thought we were up to. I never saw anything like it; her whole demeanor changed in the blink of an eye. Her face hardened into granite and fire shot out of her eyes as she pointed her finger at us. "You're in on it, aren't you!" she accused through clinched teeth. "HE sent you, didn't he? Well, forget it! I AIN'T GOIN' BACK and HE can't MAKE me! I'd rather DIE first!"

She was so far back in the corner, I thought it'd take a tow truck to pull her out.

I wanted to reach over and yank her out by the hair, but Doc didn't try to touch her. Instead he just said, "I honestly have no idea what you're talking about."

Her eyes narrowed. "Yeah, I just BET you don't!" she yelled. "This is a-a mental ward, isn't it!" Her voice softened and she cocked one eyebrow. "Yeah...it figures he'd have me put away." Then she was back to yelling again. "Well, I AIN'T crazy! Not YET anyway, but it's a WONDER!"

Doc grew concerned and tried to get her to calm down. I also wondered what the hell she was talking about and started to feel real uncomfortable. I didn't like all this talk about mental wards and being crazy. I was still walking my own tightrope.

"Stop for just a moment and think back," Doc said quietly. "Do you remember yesterday, at all?"

Her eyebrows knitted together. She swallowed hard and shook her head.

"Well, you came in yesterday afternoon and asked for a glass of water, which Mac here, gave to you. After you drank it, you started to leave, but passed out on the floor instead."

Doc is a no nonsense type of guy and I think she could tell he wasn't lying to her. Just the same, she stayed in the corner with the quilt clutched in both fists. Finally she said, "I don't know how he did it, but he had you put somethin' in th' water to make me pass out, didn't he? He's gonna try an' take me back, ain't he!" Her eyes looked at us like a doe caught in somebody's headlights.

I wondered who the hell "HE" was. Whoever he was, he'd done a number on her, that was clear.

I still had the tomato juice in my hand. Doc took it from me and said softly, "No one put anything in your water. We haven't the faintest idea who you are or what you're talking about." He held the tomato juice out to her. "Here, why don't you drink this and try to relax." She dropped her eyes to the tomato juice, then back at him and squeezed her lips together tightly. The look in her eyes said she'd like to kill both of us.

Mule headed female.

"No need to act like such a child," he said evenly. "No one is going to make you go anywhere you don't want to." I left the room for a moment and brought back a small table. I pushed it next to the bed and Doc set the glass down. "And you don't have to drink this if you don't want to."

He got up from the bed and took off his stethoscope. "Well Mac, if there's nothing else, I'll be going." He tucked his stethoscope in his bag and snapped it closed. A second passed before she warily reached out and took the juice from the table and held it without drinking. Doc looked at her. "Well," he said. "I'm glad to see you're beginning to act reasonable."

She took a sip, frowned and looked at us.

Doc took a vile out of his coat pocket. "And I'd very much like it if you'd take these with that juice," he said, shaking out two tiny tablets

"I don't take anything unless I know what it is," she said suspiciously. "Could be rat poison."

"A very wise thing to do," Doc acknowledged. "But it's just a weak dose of Valium to help you relax. However, you don't have to take them if you don't want to."

The way she looked at them, I would've bet a whole week's pay that she wouldn't take the pills, but damned if she didn't toss them in her mouth and wash them down with the whole glass of tomato juice.

"I hope that WAS poison!" she spat.

Doc never wavered. "No you don't," he said calmly. "Now give me your arm. I want to check your pulse." She gave a bored sigh and extended her arm straight out in an exaggerated childishly fashion. Doc checked her vital signs and said, "You're doing fine. Just stay in bed until you're feeling better -and be sure to eat!"

"Right," she shot back. "And just *what* do you suggest I eat? I haven't had a bite in four days; and PLEASE spare me the joke about biting me."

I spoke up then. "Not to worry. I'll feed you."

She crossed her arms over her chest and cocked that one eyebrow. Looking at me for the first time, she huffed, "Not to worry? Boy...you're sure not from around here, are you."

I looked at Doc. "She must be gettin' better, Doc -she's getting testy."

45

"I'll just leave you two to work this out," he said. "I've got patients waiting for me over at the Lazy Y."

"Wait JUST a minute," she said. "The Lazy Y? That doesn't sound like a hospital to me; that sounds like a ranch." Doc stopped in the doorway. He turned to look at her. "It is," he answered. "I'm a vet."

"A VET!" she screamed. "You called a VET to take care of me -ARE YOU *CRAZY*!"

She jumped up and picked up the empty tomato glass. "Uh oh," I said, as she drew her arm back.

We quickly left and were halfway across the dance floor, when Doc and I heard the sound of a glass smashing against the wall. We looked at each other, but kept walking. When we reached the front door, I said, "Thanks for coming Doc. I was so damned worried that she was...you know. But you never let it get to you." His shoulders slumped a bit and he suddenly looked very tired. He said, "You have no idea how worried I was when you called this morning, Mac."

I was shocked. "You -you...were?" I blinked.

"I'm a vet, Mac. If anything had happened to her, it would've meant my license and probable incarceration. I could've spent the rest of my days in jail."

The enormity of his statement bounced around my head and my mouth fell open. "No," I whispered. "How could you be blamed for helping someone in trouble?"

"The law is VERY specific, Mac," he said. Then he smiled. "But, you're right; somebody had to help her and that someone just happened to be me."

That was Doc -always worried about the other guy; never himself. I took a long hard look at him and it was like I was really seeing him for the first time. He wasn't anything like those jive ass yuppie doctors you go to today with their profit sharing margin conglomerates and "bottom lines." You know -the new breed of Harvard grad George Clooney wanna-bees with their ponytails and sloppy white coats thrown over an L.L. Bean plaid shirt. Young know-it-alls who can't be bothered to explain things to you; who wear their stethoscopes slung around their necks like a love charm. ...And if you're over forty -forget it. If you have insurance or medicare and come in with a sinus headache; they'll rush to schedule you for a cat scan.

No, Doc was more like one of them doctors you see on old westerns. The kind you trusted. His shoulders were perpetually bent from all his years of stooping over taking care of animals. His Albert Einstein white hair was thick and unruly, and he was nearsighted as hell without his ever-present wire rimmed bifocals perched on his nose over a neat mustache. His jacket smelled of pipe tobacco and no matter how hot it got, he never went anywhere without a vest and tie over a clean white shirt. As far as I was concerned, he was on the endangered species list.

"I'm mighty proud to know you, Doc," I said sincerely.

He handed me his coffee mug and patted my shoulder in that fatherly way that never failed to reassure.

"But," I added hotly, "she is a *NUT* an' if she tries to sue you for helping her, I'll kill her!"

He laughed. "Thanks for the coffee, Mac, and don't get so worked up. I'm sure she's a lovely girl."

"Yeah," I said. "A real peach!"

"If it'll ease your mind any," Doc smiled, "I'm pretty sure the worst is over. However," he held up his finger, "call me right away if there's any change -no matter how minor you may think it is. You understand?"

I nodded.

"Here are the rest of those tranquilizers. It's important not to give her too many, but in her agitated state, it's also important that she stay as calm as possible." He pulled out another vile from his inside breast pocket. "This is the antibiotic I gave her in capsule form. The directions are on the bottle."

"What kind is it?" I asked...like I'd know.

"It's five hundred milligrams of Tetracycline. That's a massive dose to take orally, but it should kill just about any infection she has. Stay on her about taking them because it does more harm to start them and not stay on them. Give her one tomorrow and make sure she has food in her stomach first. Oh, and keep her out of the sun. This medicine makes the patient's eyes and skin very photosensitive to sunlight -and don't give her any kind of dairy product other than yogurt because cheese and milk products cancels out the medicine."

"Did you say to "keep her outta th' sun? What is wrong with you –does this look like Club Med?"

"Good bye, Mac," he said and went out the door.

So far, my morning was off to a rotten start; the good news was that she didn't die on me, but the bad news was that she might sue Doc for saving her life -and the bitch probably would too. Suddenly the phone rang scaring the life out of me. I ran over and ripped the receiver off the hook.

"HELLO!" I yelled angrily and heard Harley's laugh in my ear.

"Rough night, Pardoner?"

"Yeah," I exhaled tiredly. "An' it ain't gonna get any easier either. Doc just left, an' he says she's gotta stay here 'til she's better."

"And how long does he say she's gotta stay?"

"I have NO idea," I sighed, "but I'd guess in th' neighborhood of about twenty more pounds."

"I got some special grain here for that," Harley said. "Want me to bring some along when I come by later this afternoon?"

"ANYTHING that'll get this show on th' road," I answered.

We hung up and I wondered where to start first. I decided the best place to start was with the fridge behind the bar and went to see if I had any kind of food in there for her to eat. I saw three eggs along with a half-eaten block of moldy cheese. I could boil her one of the eggs in hopes that it was still edible. I went back to ask her if she felt like eating and was surprised to find her propped up reading a magazine that she'd found on the floor. The pages were all tattered and torn, but she turned each one like this was a perfectly normal way to read a magazine.

I cleared my throat. "Will you eat some hard boiled eggs, if I fix 'em?" She ignored me and continued to flip the torn pages. I repeated the question and waited for a response. Finally, she turned and looked at me. "YOU'RE going to cook?" she blinked all innocent like.

My quills bristled. "Yes," I answered. "What's wrong -you gotta problem with that?"

"Gee, and just what would YOU cook—some secret recipe your mom handed down?"

Now my blood began to boil. Not only was she ruining my day and messing up my life, but she needed a good ass whupping –which I was just itching to give her. But I held my tongue and took a deep breath before answering. "No," I sniped back. "I stumbled on the recipe of boiling water ALL by myself!"

"What if I want 'em soft boiled?" She narrowed her eyes. "Or is HARD boiled all you know?"

My back stiffened at the veiled sarcasm. "HARD boiled is all I know."

Tossing the magazine back on the floor, she said, "I'd rather have a double brandy. Remy Martin preferably."

"Tough," I said. "It's tomato juice or eggs. That's th' menu."

She said, "Well, it sucks."

I shrugged indifferently. "Fine, let me know if you change your mind." I turned around to leave.

"HEY!" she yelled. "No need to bite my head off. Come on back here an' talk with me for a while. I'm lonely."

I kept right on walking.

"Please?" she added softly.

I stopped and said, "I don't know; I'm pretty busy. TOO damned busy to babysit, THAT'S for sure!"

"I'll be good," she said. "I promise." I took my time strolling back to the storeroom. When I got back inside, I took the chair and flipped it around. "I'll only stay if you tell me who you are," I said, straddling it.

"Don't push it," she scowled.

I slid the chair back and started to get up.

"God, you're sensitive," she said. "Okay, okay, my name is Samantha, but I'd prefer you just call me Sam."

"Okay, Sam, an' you can call me, Mac. Now that we know each other, where are you from?"

Boom! Her guard went back up. "Why do you want to know that?" she asked coldly.

"Well, at th' rate you're tryin' to kill yourself, I need a name to call -like a next of kin -or maybe a...husband?"

I was hoping there *WAS* somebody who'd come down here and take her off my hands; I'd call them in a New York minute! But she just sniffed and looked away without answering. I was going to have to use better bait.

"Or a boyfriend, maybe?" I pressed.

"Stop it!" she demanded. "I'm not tellin' you jack an' that's <u>that</u>! There ain't nobody -so just forget it!"

"Nobody, huh?"

She twisted her head around to glare at me. "Are you dense? I said, NOBODY!"

The emphasis of her words cut through me like a knife. I'd struck out and was irritated as hell about it, but I'd also hit a raw nerve. "Okay, suit yourself. It's a big prairie out there. Just tell me where to put th' marker."

"Put it up your-" She didn't finish. Instead she took a deep breath and let it out in a long sigh. She leaned her head back on the pillows, looking drained. "I'm sorry. I've just...always been healthy as a horse and I guess I kind'a...took it for granted." She closed her eyes for a moment and when she opened them again, I noticed they were cornflower blue. Her lashes were thick, long and dark. She smiled a little and looked at me with those blue eyes. (Damn, but they were the *prettiest* shade of blue....) "I guess I'm a pretty rotten patient, huh," she said in a voice soft and civil. Between those mesmerizing eyes and her soft voice, I felt something stir deep inside and I smiled back, thinking maybe she was okay after all and I should ease up a bit. I had my mouth open to say something nice when she suddenly shifted on her pillow. Her incredibly rotten mood was back. "Can I ask you somethin'?"

"Sure," answered.

"Jjust why th' hell are you going out of your way to take care of me?" she blasted. "You SURE don't strike me as th' Mother Terasa type."

That did it! She was back on my list again. "Yeah, well, not all of us look like what we really are," I said.

"What's *THAT* supposed to mean?" she demanded.

"Like you - you don't look like royalty, but you sure act like it! You always been this demanding and ungrateful?"

"I really hadn't ever given it any thought," she sniffed arrogantly. "But, probably."

"You a born an' raised Texan?" I asked. The sudden shift in conversation made her suspicious. "What's it to YOU, if I am?"

"Because," I informed her, "you should know better'n to look a gift horse in th' mouth."

(Secretly, I'd always wondered what the hell that meant and made a mental note to ask Harley about it one day.)

"Yeah, I guess I should," she said with a shrug. "But I ain't goin' BACK with him!" she threatened. "If he comes here for me, I'll fight TOOTH AND NAIL -an' if *you* gotta problem with that, then just deal with it!"

"Oh, I gotta problem with it all right!" I fumed. "I gotta BIG problem with it. I didn't ask for you to bring your sorry-ass in here and faint on my dance floor, you know!" My blood pressure was skyrocketing through the roof. "So, the SOONER you get to feelin' better, th' sooner you can get OUTTA here!" I was about to explode. "Which'll suit me JUST FINE!"

Her eyes flashed fire. "Well, excuuuuse me all to hell, Mister! I didn't MEAN to cause you NO TROUBLE!"

We squared off like two rabid pit bulls about to sink our fangs into each other when I noticed her hair. It was twisted up in a knot on top of her head with hair sticking out all over like a pincushion. She looked so damned comical that I had to look away to keep from bursting out laughing. She noticed the diversion and asked coolly, "Is something WRONG?"

She had this really irate pissed off look on her face punctuated by the pincushion hair-do.

I thought I'd die laughing and bit my lip until I tasted blood. My throat burned from the laughter gurgling up inside me. I looked down at my feet and squeezed my lips together as tight as they'd go, but I still made little giggling sounds like, "haa-ahem uh ahmmmm ha ha mmmm."

I coughed and put my hand over my mouth to stifle my giggling. Tears were burning my eyes. When I finally got some control back, I cleared my throat and tried to say I was wondering if she might feel like a shower. I still couldn't bring myself to look at her. She cooled down a little and said it might help get her over the "woozies." Then I made the mistake of glancing at her again and almost exploded. I clamped my hand over my mouth and hurried towards the door.

"The bathroom is uh- over here," I pointed with my back to her. "Clean towels are hanging up by the sink."

Staring after me, she sat up in bed. "Are you all right?" she frowned.

I nodded furiously making sure to keep my back to her as I hurried out the door.

Without turning around, I heard her mumble a confused "thanks" as she got out of bed and went into the bathroom. I was halfway across the dance floor when I heard an ear-piercing scream and nodded knowing she'd just looked in the mirror.

CHAPTER NINETEEN

I started to wash last night's glasses, forgetting there wasn't any pressure with her in the shower. I turned off the water just as the front door slowly opened and Juan came in with his ever-present boombox under his arm.

"Juan, muchacho! Que pasa!" I smiled.

He stood in the door and waved. "Buenos dias, Senor Mac. Como esta usted?"

"Muy bein, muy bein." I answered. "Well, c'mon," I motioned. "Get your caboose on in here, boy." He came inside, reverently closing the door behind him.

It was broiling outside and sweat was running down both sides of his face. I got a glass down and poured a Coke over lots of ice. He came over to me and put his boombox down on the floor. Climbing up on a stool, he took off his Dallas Cowboys baseball cap and set it down next to him on the bar. "Mucho gracias," he beamed, wrapping both hands around the glass.

"Pretty hot outside, yes?" I asked.

He nodded vigorously and took a long sip before answering. "Si! Muy caliente!"

"And I don't guess its gonna cool off anytime soon," I mused.

He shook his head. "No, I think so." I laughed at his English and gave him a nuggie on top of his head. "Well, I gotta get these glasses washed; let me know when you're ready for seconds on th' coke."

He nodded again and went back to sipping his soda.

Juan was a good kid and I liked him a lot. He was about five six, a hundred pounds, and had glossy straight black hair that looked like his mama turned a bowl over to cut. The beat-up Dallas Cowboys baseball cap was a treasured fixture and he'd rather die than part with it. ...And he brightened up the place every time he came in.

I was drying the few glasses I'd left in the sink and setting them back on the shelves when he asked, "Do you have any work for me today?"

"Yeah, as a matter of fact, I do." I said, turning back to him. I put my towel down and picked up his empty glass. His face broke out in a grin. "I am so glad."

I poured him another Coke and set it down in front of him. "But finish this first. Don't want you dying from thirst in this heat."

"Okey-dokey," he grinned.

I puttered around behind the bar while he drank his soda. When he finished he said, "Do you want me now to begin the working?"

"Well, not this very minute," I laughed, taking his empty glass.

"Okay, Senor Mac! Whatever you tell me."

"It's "whatever you say," I corrected, getting a quarter out of the drawer. "Here, go play us something on th' jukebox."

"But I have thee rad-e-o," he said.

"Later, right now I want to hear some George Jones."

He took the quarter and went over to the jukebox.

I smiled as I watched him, remembering the day about a year ago, when he came in to ask me if I'd let him sweep up the place. At first, my distrustful nature told me he was most likely an illegal little punk who was over here staking out the joint, but something about him made me decided to give him a try anyway. I soon learned that he was not only a hard worker, but one of a very few who didn't indulge in illegal activities; actually preferring to do honest work no matter how little it paid. (And it sure didn't pay much these days -especially here.)

As it turned out, Juan DID come over illegally every week to work for me, but in the evening he always went back across the border where he lived in a little shack with his parents, four brothers and five sisters. Although they lived in squalor, he was always clean and his parents had been very sure to teach him to have respect for adults in general, family in specific, and not to fall for the Devil's easy money. In their own way, they had taught him the true meaning of life: Live by The Golden Rule, honor your parents, and be content with what you have.

His values were firmly in place and he never took anything without asking first; not even a glass of water. Over time I came to look on him as a little brother, and have had a lot of fun with him mangling English and me doing the same to Spanish.

"Como esta su linda madre, Juan?" I asked.

He gave me quizzical look and wrinkled his forehead trying to decipher what I was asking. When my question in all wrong Spanish content finally registered, he laughed and shook his head. "Oh, mi mother es bueno. Mi whole familia es muy bueno," he smiled. "Gracias."

"And how's your English coming along?"

He smiled proudly. "Oh, I learn THREE new words, Senor Mac!"

"And they are...?"

"They are, "chair"...casa, I mean "house"...and "Toyota.""

"Well, two outta three ain't bad."

"Como, Senior Mac?"

"Nothing," I shrugged. "I guess Toyota is probably as American as apple pie these days. Listen, I've kind'a got my hands full with some unexpected problems today."

"Si?"

"Si. Do you mind taking this can of spray polish and rubbing a light coat down the sides of the bar? I'll pay extra dinero."

"Oh, no, Senor Mac," he protested. "I do eet for no extra. You always muy, I mean, very kind to me. But what es these?" he asked taking the can.

"It's polish."

He frowned and I tried to explain, but was getting nowhere. Finally I took a towel and sprayed some wax on the lower part of the bar to demonstrate. I rubbed the polish with the rag and his face lit up. He took the towel from me. "I do now," he grinned. I gave him the polish and he sat down on the floor, taking a bent wire coat hanger out of his back pocket. He reached over and slid his boombox towards him then stuck the mangled hanger in where the aerial should've been. The radio was an outdated model that I hadn't seen in years. It was bulky and looked like it had been thrown from a speeding car. Knowing Juan, I was positive he'd found the radio in some trash pile and worked on it until he got it to play again. (NObody would steal such a thing.) He secured the wire hanger in the empty aerial slot and turned it on. Mariachi marimbas, trumpets and guitars spilled out into the quiet room.

I smiled and patted him on the shoulder. "It ain't George Jones," I grinned, "but its good. I'll be in the back if you need me."

"Okay," he nodded.

When I reached the storeroom, I yelled, "Hey -are you decent?" but got no answer. The door was closed so I knocked. "Hello? Sam?" Still no answer. I called, "Hellllloooo," again and opened the door an inch. I peeped in until I saw her. She was lying across the bed with the quilt wrapped around her. Wanting to make sure she was okay, I eased the door open and quietly tiptoed into the room. She was sound asleep, but I noticed she'd taken a shower and washed her hair. She smelled like delicate flowers on a misty morning and for a moment, I lost myself in the wonderful aroma. Her hair looked so...soft...like you could lose yourself in it.

Without thinking, I reached out to touch it, but caught myself just as my fingers were about to wind themselves around her long dark locks. I quickly yanked my hand back and cursed. *DAMN IT!!!* I didn't like this feeling looking at her gave me. There was NO room for <u>anyone</u> in my life and as *SOON* as she was well she got her walking papers -no IFS ands or BUTS! Besides, she already had someone else in the picture and that suited me JUST fine. If she wanted to run away from the screwed up problem, let her learn the hard way, like I did. I had my life just the way I liked it thank you very much; and it did NOT included some danged woman with an attitude!

I started to leave when I saw her ratty little suitcase lying open on the floor with its meager contents strewn everywhere. I surmised she'd taken out whatever clean clothes she had to put on after her shower. Seeing her pathetic few things lying there like that suddenly made me feel sorry for her. It was the first time I'd felt anything akin to compassion in a very long time. She moaned softly, rolling over and kicking off the quilt. All she had on was a pair of white cotton bikini panties with a short white T-shirt. It was all I could do not to gasp as I stared mesmerized at the sight of her. Even in her anorexic condition, her figure was stunning. Her bust was more than ample and her legs were long and slender. Her waist was so small I could get both hands around it with fingers left over. Every part of her was perfectly proportioned.

She was beautiful.

As I stared at her, a jolt of hot electricity ran through my lower body. I raised my eyebrows in stark surprise at the feeling. Since I hadn't felt anything like this in decades, I was positive these feelings were long dead. She let out a soft moan and pulled her legs up in the fetal position. Ignoring the butterflies in my stomach, I went over to pull the quilt over her. But as I picked up the corner, I hesitated for a second. Her eyelashes were so long and dark against her cheeks, and this time, before I realized what I was doing, I reached down and lightly touched her face.

Her skin was so soft and sensual that I instantly felt the heat in my loins. My eyes slowly drifted down her body, lingering over every inch. She was stunning -no doubt about it. I wanted to run my hand over her breast and down her ribs to feel the hard flatness of her smooth tan stomach. It was like I was in junior high all over again. I couldn't control myself and almost touched her when I suddenly snapped out of it and jerked my hand away for the second time. I angrily pulled the quilt up over her then yanked the faded curtains tighter over the window. Without looking at her again, I turned away and headed back to the bar.

On my way out, I kicked a sheet of paper on the floor next to her suitcase. It must've fallen out when she got her clothes. I knelt down to pick it up. I'm not a snoop but it was half unfolded and when I saw words scrawled in pencil, I tried not to read them, but couldn't stop myself. The paper contained some kind of poem with each line ending in a downward slant -a sure sign of sadness or depression. I started to put it back then changed my mind. I thought this might give me a clue as to what was going on with her-or so I rationalized. I unfolded the rest of the wrinkled torn paper. The penciled words were smudged, but still readable. I started to read them as my curiosity canceled out whatever morals I might've had.

The words read:
"So...once again your heart has been broken...
By words that have been spoken,
Of a love that was ever so true...
And once again, you've been made a fool of by lies
Believed in by an ever lovin' you.
And now all your joy,
Like a broken toy that can never be the same again...
Has taken on a second hand glow like a broken bow
...And a picture in a broken frame.
Knowing full well,
That Love IS hell,
And you'll never be the same again.

For it's not only your heart
That's fallen apart,
But other's too...who are close to you.
And whether stranger or friend,
There IS an end
For all who believe,
In a love hard to find with a broken mind,
Left alone with your heart on your sleeve.
So...farewell Joan of Arc
...And all others who embark
On a journey that ends with Morpheous...
For the Pure of Heart
End up worse off than they start
And if only one can agree with me...
Then I feel deeply for the both of us."

The words made me weak in the knees. I'd studied Greek and Roman mythology during my senior year of high school, so I knew who Morpheous was. She was the favorite goddess of all junkies; the Goddess of Sleep (-and where we got the name "morphine.") In the case of this poem however, the mention of Morpheous could mean sleep or death; since some consider sleep a form of death. After all, death would be the one place a wounded soul could withdraw to in hopes of finding some peace. I know, because I'd often considered it myself and reading this had reopened my own wounds; something I didn't want reopened.

I read the last line again.

"...And if only one can agree with me...then I feel deeply for the both of us."

"Both...of us..." I whispered.

I looked at her again –this time with a much deeper admiration than physical. I carefully folded the paper again and put it back where I found it. Then I quietly left, feeling like I'd just invaded the most private of all territories; her heart. Her words were still haunting me when I reached the bar and I swallowed hard, trying to wash the bitter taste from my mouth.

"I am about feeneshed with thee rag, Senor Mac," Juan said. "I weel do thee sweeping next?"

I was so lost in my thoughts that Juan's voice startled me. I'd forgotten all about him.

"Huh? Ooh...Juan. Right"

"Ees something wrong, Senor Mac?" he asked.

"Uh, no, no," I sputtered, wiping away beads of sweat from my forehead.

"Do you weesh I sweep in the back?" he asked, referring to the storeroom.

When I didn't answer, he tugged on my shirt. "Senor Mac...?"

"I'm sorry, Juan—what did you say?"

He repeated the question and I grabbed the broom from him. "NO!" I cried.

Juan jumped back like I scared him.

"Oh jeese, I'm sorry, Juan. Look, don't bother with the storeroom today. I have a sick amigo that's sleeping in there."

He relaxed and smiled. "An hombre who have too much Tequila?" he nodded knowingly.

"No...actually this is a senorita," I said without thinking.

He winked. "Ohhhh, a SENORITA!" he smiled.

I shook my head vigorously. "No, no, not THAT way," I laughed. "This is some girl that came in yesterday and ended up in a dead faint on my floor."

Juan frowned, "Como?" Then fear suddenly replaced his smile and he took a step back.

"La senorita esta muerto?" he asked, quickly making the sign of the cross.

"No, Juan. She's not dead, she's just sick."

"B-But you say she...daid. Eef she es..."

"I meant she fell on the floor," I interrupted. "You know, fainted -uh, desmayo? Is that the correct word?" Juan looked more confused than ever and shook his head slowly back and forth. I could see he was not getting the picture. Crap, I saw the only way to get my point across was to demonstrate by closing my eyes and falling down in a swoon. I felt like a damned fool lying there on the floor, but Juan found it highly comical. "OH! SI! Hoy comprende."

I got up from the floor and told him I was so glad. As I dusted my sleeves off, he asked seriously, "But there ees something else bothering you, Senor Mac?"

"Yeah," I said, brushing the knees of my pants. "She needs to eat, but I don't know how to cook all that good."

"I can have mi madre feex you some'a her sopa," Juan offered. "With real pollo."

I scratched the stubble on my chin. "Mexican chicken soup? I didn't know such a thing existed."

"Oh, si!" he assured me.

It wasn't a bad idea. Juan's mother HAD to be a better cook than I was, to say nothing of knowing what to do for an ailing girl better than me. "All right, Juan. Ask your mother to make my friend some of her soup. And tell her to make SURE it's good'n spicy!"

Juan looked at me as if to say, "There is another way?"

"Si, Senor, of course."

I went behind the bar and hit the register "NO SALE" key. Taking sixty bucks out of the ancient cash register, I handed it to him. "This is for the work you did today and for your mama's trouble."

He was dumbfounded. "These es TOO much dinero," he exclaimed.

"Take it," I ordered. "Just make sure to come back tomorrow with the soup, okay?"

Juan stuffed the money into his pocket and pulled on his Dallas Cowboys baseball cap. Picking up his radio, he tucked it under his arm and walked briskly towards the door. He turned and waved "Adios" before going out.

"Hasta manana, Juan," I called after him. "MANANA," I repeated.

"Si, si, manana, Senor Mac," he called out from the other side of the door.

"Via con Dios, Juan," I yelled, but he was already gone.

CHAPTER TWENTY

Sam slept for the rest of the day, and I didn't try to wake her. I felt like sleep was more important than eating right now. Besides, she wasn't missing anything by waiting another day for Juan's mother's soup. I wasn't lying when I said I knew how to boil water; I just failed to admit that it was the ONLY thing I knew how to cook.

A few of the guys came in for beers around six and we shot the breeze until I got a spurt of busy from about eight to nine thirty. By eleven thirty the place was empty so once again, I got to lock up early and sleep on the floor next to Sam's bed. I was beginning to feel like a Golden Retriever. The night passed uneventfully and the next morning, I was up at nine forty-five. By then, I was sitting at the bar drinking coffee and reading the same paper (after digging it out of the trash.) I'd just got a second cup when Juan arrived with a large rather new looking thermos tucked firmly under his arm. "Juan!" I said as he handed it to me, "you're a good man!"

"Mi madre says to say she is...how you say? Uh, HONORED," he beamed.

"And tell your mother I said she's a saint!"

Juan beamed at the compliment. "I buy the botella termos yesterday weeth the dinero you give to me. Is good, si?" I unscrewed the cap and drooled all over myself as the aroma drifted up my nose. "Oh, yes," I sighed. "Is pure heaven."

"She say she make more if you weesh," Juan said.

"Tell her I wish an' will take ANYTHING she wants to send." I handed him another twenty, which he refused until I told him, "For your mama."

"Si, gracias," he said, taking it and again stuffing it into his pocket. "Mi madre say to thank you muy, muy, mucho." He didn't say anything else, but I felt a kind of anxiety radiating from him as he scratched his neck and shifted from one foot to the other.

"What's the matter, Juan?"

He readjusted his baseball cap nervously. "I am sorry, Senior Mac, but I cannot stay. I must go back and help with the chores. There ees mucho work for to do. I am so sorry. Please do not be disturbed with me."

I smiled at his wrong phrasing for "angry" and pulled the brim of his baseball hat down over his eyes. "Oh, I'm disturbed all right—just not with you. Anyway, Yo comprende...now get outta here." His face broke out in a wide grin and he pushed his cap back up. "Gracias, Senor Mac. Hasta luego," he waved.

"Hasta luego," I waved back.

As soon as the door closed, I grabbed a clean mug. I wanted to get this soup into Sam while it was still good and hot. I poured the thick broth into the mug and hurried in to wake her. To my surprise, she was sitting up staring blankly at the wall.

"Well, hello, sleepyhead," I said, sitting down next to her on the bed.

She yawned and shook her head. "Huh?"

"Still a little groggy, eh? Well, just WAIT 'til you taste this! This'll get you movin' in th' right direction."

"Uge," she said, turning her head. "If that's food, get it away from me."

"I don't think so," I said, waving it under her nose. "I went through too much trouble to get it." The aroma was all she needed. She turned her head back to me again. Her eyes brightened and she asked eagerly, "What IS that wonderful smell?"

"It's honest-to-God REAL Mexican homemade chicken soup -and there are kings that would kill for just a thimbleful. Had it smuggled in overnight. Here," I said, spooning some into her mouth, "taste it." Her eyes teared up and she fanned the air with both hands. "WOW!" she inhaled. "Good God, I haven't tasted anything this good since I was a child. Gimme!" she said, grabbing for the mug. I offered her the spoon, but she only wanted the mug...which I watched her upend and drain.

I don't care what the food industry says. There is nothing like good, old fashioned, homemade food. Sam took the mug away from her mouth, leaving a thin mustache over her upper lip. "God! I LOVE this soup! It's so thick and spicy! Is there more?"

"Well...yeah," I said, cradling the thermos protectively to my chest. She held her cup out to me with both hands. "But a-are you sure you want...more?" I asked, sadly. (I'd hoped to get a bowl of it for myself.) She nodded again with a big smile and I reluctantly poured the rest of that wonderful smelling soup into her mug -filling it to the brim. Sam finished the soup. Drained it dry. There wasn't a drop left. I shook the thermos. Oh well, I pouted; it was more important that she ate.

She had the most disgusting look of contentment on her face as she laid her head back on the pillow. Turning to me she said, "You had that smuggled in, huh, an' I was right—you CAN'T cook."

"We only discussed boiling water," I frowned, still disappointed over not getting any soup.

"Hmm," she mused. "I've heard of drug smuggling, but never soup smuggling. Is it at all lucrative?"

"This is my first attempt and so far -no."

"Where did you smuggle it in from?"

"There's this kid named Juan that crosses th' border to come do little odd jobs for me, like sweep up an' make a few honest dollars to help his family out. He's a good boy."

"Did HE make it?" she asked.

"No, dummy, but he stopped by yesterday an' I asked him to ask his mama about makin' somethin' that might help you get back on your feet. He suggested some of her soup...and, well, you know—or rather ate—th' rest."

"And I can't remember when I last tasted anything that great!"

"So I noticed," I said, frowning at the empty thermos I was holding.

"So –how're you feeling?" I asked, (without saying, "you little piggy.")

Sam patted her stomach and sighed. "WONDERFULLY full and a little zoned, but not enough to go back to sleep."

"Probably still feeling the effects of the tranquillizers from yesterday. That stuff stores up in your liver –which reminds me…" I got up, reached into my pocket and pulled out the vile of Valium. "Doc left you these, but don't take them unless you really need to." She nodded and set them on the little table next to her bed. "I'll need them tonight. All this lying around makes it difficult to just fall asleep."

"He left these antibiotics too." I handed them to her. "The instructions are on the bottle, but you should take one now since you've got food in your stomach." She shook out a pill while I went into the bathroom and got her a glass of water. She popped the antibiotic in her mouth and swallowed the capsule without any resistance. (I was astounded there was any room left in her stomach.) "You're SURE that wasn't some godforsaken horse pill your vet left for me?" she asked. I assured her it wasn't.

"Man, I can't believe I've gotta VET for a doctor." She handed me the empty glass, readjusted the quilt and leaned back on the pillows "So. Where am I and how did I get here?"

I pulled the chair up and sat down. I told her she was in the middle of nowhere and I had no idea how she got here. "It all happened just the way Doc said -you walked in around noon, asked for some water and just keeled over as you started to leave." She looked like she was trying to go over it in her mind. After a long silence she said, "I don't remember comin' in here. I wish I could, but th' truth is, I don't."

"Well, don't strain yourself over it," I said, remembering my own experience. "It happens."

I started to get up, but she grabbed my hand. "Wait a minute, Mac," she said. "I didn't happen to..*say*... anything while I was running a fever, did I?"

"Like …what?" I hedged.

She stared at me with eyes cold as steele. "Like –anything personal."

I looked down to avoid her eyes. I didn't want to tell her that I'd read the poem I found on the floor. "Uh -no," I answered. "You didn't say much of anything."

She narrowed her eyes at me. "You...SURE?" she pressed.

I looked up and met her eyes. "Does it matter?"

"Yes, actually -it does," she answered nervously.

I thought about it for a moment. "You were pretty out of it," I said. "You came in, asked for a glass of water, then after drinking it you turned to leave and passed out on the floor. I thought you were faking until I touched your head. You were burning up. I carried you back here when a friend of mine came in and we thought it best if we called Doc to come look at you.

60

True, he's a vet, but he's the only doctor around this side of Brownsville or Houston and he's probably a better doctor for animals *or* humans than any one of them up there." I stopped to catch my breath before going on. "Anyway, sometime after Doc got here, you started saying stuff like, "Get away from me," and that you weren't going to go back...but you never said go back where."

She looked worried. "Was that all?" she asked with a frown and I nodded.

She took a deep breath and let it out before asking if she'd mentioned anyone by name.

I told her she didn't and she seemed satisfied. I decided to push it and asked, "Is there anything you'd like to talk about?"

She shook her head. "No. Nothing." Her protective wall was up again and I knew now that she was definitely running away from somebody. But it was *far* from being over.

"Look," I said gently. "I've been around th' block. I know what it is to be hurt so bad by someone you love that you crawl into a bottle just to stop th' pain an' loneliness..."

"Stop right there," she demanded, and glaring at me, she said, "I'm *sure* you do, but it's not up for discussion, okay. We don't need to trade stories..."

She spoke to me with all the cutting warmth of a drill sergeant and I didn't like the dressing down. I stood up again. "Fine," I said hotly. "I thought I could help, but I see you've got it all figured out and under control!" I started to leave but she grabbed my wrist and her face softened. "I apologize. It's been a million years since I could talk to or trust, anyone."

"Yeah, well believe it or not, I DO *know* the feeling," I said angrily. I was hot and pissed, but eternally glad that she had refreshed my resolve to NEVER bring another woman into my life.

She suddenly yawned. "Oh, excuse me. I didn't realize I was so tired. I think I'll take a little nap now. I'm feeling pretty sleepy after that soup." She slid down in bed, pulling the quilt up over her. She smiled at me like nothing had just happened and I found it unnerving the way she could switch moods in the blink of an eye. "'It's so quiet here," she mumbled, rolling over on her side. "I could just stay here forever." Her voice trailed off and I stood in the doorway with her words still ringing in my ears. I felt my back stiffen. I didn't *want* anybody staying here forever -and certainly not HER!

CHAPTER TWENTY-ONE

Sam slept off and on for the next three days. Between the food Juan brought and the pills giving her some much needed rest I saw color coming back in her cheeks. On the fifth day, she stopped taking the tranquillizers and felt like sitting up. She asked if I'd come in to sit and talk with her. It was early afternoon and business was slow, so I didn't mind sitting down for a while. I figured maybe if I spent a little time with her, she'd finally open up to me. We'd been getting along fairly civilly, so I opened the conversation with, "So, what would you like to talk about today?" Her curt answer made the ground rules clear. "Anything but me...."

"Fair enough," I nodded. Not wanting to set her off, I decided to talk about the first thing that popped into my mind. "Hey- how 'bout movies - what's your favorite?

She wrinkled her forehead thoughtfully. "I've got several. It's hard to nail down just one, but I guess "Harold and Maude" would be right up there with whatever's Number One."

I looked at her quizzically. "Sorry, but I don't think I've ever heard of that one."

She giggled and it sounded like music. "I'm not surprised. It's a B movie that's become a cult classic."

"What's it about?"

"I don't know if I can explain it. You really have to see it to appreciate it, but it's about a lonely boy whose family has all the money in the world. He has no brothers or sisters and lives with his mother in this mausoleum of a mansion. I guess his father is dead because it's just him and his mother – who's very "Old Rich" conventional and always trying to hook him up with a "nice" girl. He, of course, is a very uptight, closed off young man who has no desire or interest in what his mother wants, and is always committing suicide in front of her. She ignores his-"

"*Wait* a minute," I interrupted. "How do you commit suicide more than once –if you're successful, that is?"

"That's why you have to see the movie." She looked at me and laughed. "If you think you're confused now, wait until I tell you that he DOES finally fall in love, but it's with an 80 year old free spirit who lives in an old derailed Pullman train car."

"*What*??" I frowned.

"Oh yes," she nodded. "They meet at a funeral. See –they both like going to funerals. It doesn't matter who's it is -and ten times out of ten they don't even know the person being buried."

"Don't tell me anymore," I said. "It just gets more and more bizarre."

"That's an understatement," she grinned. "It's a romantic dark comedy, but I love it and could see it over and over again."

"Why -are you warped or something?"

"Because it proves REAL love doesn't care what you look like; it's what's inside your heart that counts. In fact, my favorite part in the movie is when they go to a carnival and he makes her one of those old metal discs that prints out whatever you want. Later on that evening, they're sitting by a lake watching fireworks and he pulls it out to give her. It says, "Harold loves Maude." After she tells him how much she loves and treasures it, she flings it into the lake. He asks her why she did that –and she tells him because now she'll *always* know where it is."

"Oh brother! Don't tell me they get married and live happily ever after."

"Noooo. But Harold DOES want to marry her. He adores her and plans to propose on her upcoming 80th birthday. They're celebrating it in her train car with a candlelit dinner and champagne. She's adorable dressed in a silk flowered kimono with flowers in her hair. Everything is perfect."

"They open the champagne and as they toast each other, he asks her to marry him. She's thrilled by his proposal, but explains that she can't marry him because it's always been her destiny to leave this plane after turning 80 and she's already taken the poison. He freaks out and rushes her to the hospital, where she dies as happily as she lived."

She smiled at me. "See? A beautiful love story."

I was speechless -this wasn't at all what I had in mind when I asked her what movie she liked.

I had hoped her answer would be, "Gone with The Wind," or something equally romantic that might give me some insight to her mysterious past. Boy –did *that* idea backfire. I was at a complete loss now as to what to do next. I scratched my head and said, "Well. I sure didn't expect you to say a movie like that was a favorite."

She leaned back against the pillow. "I love the Rocky Horror Picture Show," too. Tim Currey looks better in a bustier and black stockings than Marilyn Monroe."

I'd never heard of that one either. "Well, don't tell me about it," I said. "I'm having enough trouble with that last one."

She looked at me with a mischievous twinkle in those blue eyes. "Y'a know, I just thought of something; maybe we're like Harold and Maude. You're pretty uptight. Maybe I'm Maude an' you're..."

"I'M uptight? Hah! I'm as laid back as they come. Just because I don't go around committing suicide..."

"You might try it sometime," she said. "It's very...freeing."

I cocked my eyebrow and glanced at her sideways.

I wondered what the hell that meant, but wasn't going to ask.

CHAPTER TWENTY-TWO

So far my talking to her had only confirmed she was still unstable and that she did still have someone in her life. Outside of that, I had no clearer picture of her than I did a few days ago when she walked through my front door. I decided to give it up for now.

"I've gotta get back to th' bar and get things ready for later on," I said, getting up. "You want anything?"

"Yeah," she said. "Give me one of those Valiums and some water if you don't mind."

I picked up the vile from her night table and took off the cap. "You really want one?" I asked. "You've been doing pretty well without them"

"Well, I want one now -in fact, make that two..."

I stopped shaking the pills out in my hand. "Two?? I don't know...two seems excessive..."

"Look, Nurse Jane, two five milligram Valium won't kill me,"

I looked at the two pills in my hand. "You seem to know an awful lot about these things," I said. "How'd you know these were five milligrams?"

"By th' color," she answered. "I knew what they were th' day th' doctor—I mean, th' *VET*, handed me one. I've eaten enough Valium in my lifetime to know what milligram they are just by lookin' at them." I stared at her, remembering her statement about suicide being so "freeing."

"An' don't look so worried; if I ain't dead by now, I'm not going to die on you."

I raised my eyebrows. "And *THAT* would mean...?"

By the look on her face, I could tell something unpleasant had triggered her memory. Her face turned dark and hard. "It means that only th' GOOD die young apparently an' th' REST of us have to stick around and SUFFER."

"Apparently," I sighed, handing her the pills.

She took them and I returned to the bar. I tried to get my mind on other things, but couldn't help wondering who the guy was behind all this. Things were not black or white in life. On the one hand you had the way you *thought* things were and on the other, you had the way things *looked* like they were. The way they *really* were, was somewhere in between. In the short time I'd been around Sam, I knew she wasn't an ordinary girl. She was an enigma –and I thought it might be time I examined my own feelings about her. I knew I was attracted to her physically, but it was much more

than that. I also wanted to protect her from- what? I frowned in disgust.
This shit had to stop. Just then the door opened and Legrand walked in.

"Hi, Mac."

"Hey, Legrand."

He sat down at the bar and ordered a Coors.

"Where's the rest of th' troops," I asked.

"There's a rodeo up in Brownsville this weekend, so I let 'em off early."

"Then I guess it'll be pretty quiet 'round here for th' next few days."

I drew his Coors and set down it in front of him. "What's new?" he asked.
"Th' girl doin' any better?"

I nodded. "Yeah, seems to be getting' some color back now that she's
eating regular and resting."

"What're ya gonna do with her when she's back on her feet?"

That was a good question. "I didn't take her to raise," I shrugged, "so I
guess she'll be on her way."

He laughed. "Yeah –right."

"What does *that* mean?" I frowned.

He sat up and let out a deep sigh. "She's a pretty darn good lookin' piece
of horse flesh," he smiled. "Or hadn't you noticed."

"She ain't a piece of anything –much less horse flesh," I said sternly.

"Oh, ho, ho," he laughed. "You've noticed, all right."

Legrand finished his beer and I asked if he wanted another. "No thanks,
I gotta be skeedaddalin' but you take good care'a that li'l ol' gal." He got up
to leave when he remembered something and came back to the bar.
"Listen," he said, "a guy came in th' store yesterday. He said he was down
here doin' some surveyin' for a highway they're gonna run north of here to
some place just outside El Paso."

"They're not thinkin' of coming this way are they?" I asked.

"No, no…it has nothing to do with us," he answered.

"Then why is he here?"

"He's just stayin' somewhere near here while he does th' work; listen,
Mac, forget about all that! Th' point is that he didn't have no place to stay
while working on th' project, so the D.O.T. bought him a nice new trailer
and set it up with a septic tank an' everything. Its pretty good size, too. I
think he said it was around 80 by 20. It has two bedrooms but only one
bath. Anyway, now that he's done doin' his job, they don't need th' trailer
anymore and will most likely scrap it. He wondered if I knew anybody that
might want to buy it and I thought of you. Its brand new –only six months
old."

Wow. I hadn't given any thought to ever having a home out here, but
this was a damned good idea.

"Yeah, I'm interested," I said. "How much does he want for it?"

Legrand laughed. "You know government agencies," he grinned. "He said they'll take ten cents on th' dollar."

"DAMN!" I cried. "You bet I'm interested! Find out how much that is and I'll see if I've got enough saved over at th' bank."

"Okay, but if you ain't got enough, I can float you an interest-free loan." I smiled. "No, if I have to borrow any, I'll pay interest. You've done enough for me."

He shrugged. "I'll get back to you on this," he said and left.

Except for Harley and Doc, the rodeo kept the place empty for the next couple of days. Doc came by to check on Sam's progress and Harley wasn't interested in the rodeos they put on today calling the ones who participated in them, "Coca Cola Cowboys."

Doc was happy to see Sam was on the mend. He said when she finished the antibiotics, she could start getting out of bed for an hour or so if she felt like it –but to still stay clear of direct sunlight. He was especially pleased about the good food she was being provided for by Juan's mother. He didn't stay for a drink, but Harley stayed with me until around nine, then put on his Stetson and waved good night. After he left, I was all alone for the first time on a Friday night since opening up. (Even my band had taken off to go to the rodeo.) Bored with nothing to do, I thought about going back to see if Sam wanted to play cards or something -then remembered she'd taken the Valium. I got down a glass instead and poured myself a double shot of bourbon. I tossed it back in one swallow and refilled the glass, then sat down with my drink to think about the trailer Legrand found. It would be great to have a home again. I smiled at the idea and tossed down my drink. Having exhausted all there was to do, I got up from the bar and decided to hit the hay early.

After I washed the glass and closed up for the night, I headed back to wash my face and brush my teeth. Sam was sound asleep. I decided to give her some privacy by not sleeping in the storeroom. I quietly closed the door and got undressed. I balled up my jeans for a pillow then got down on the floor, hoping my nights down here were numbered. I pulled my old flannel robe up over my shoulders and fell asleep with visions of a good solid queen size bed floating around my head.

The next day, Juan showed up early with food for Sam. He brought soup, fried chicken, and flan, a delicious custard-like dessert. Sam wolfed it down with her usual truck driver gusto then said she wanted to get up. She had taken most of the antibiotic, so I told her Doc said she could do whatever she felt like as long as she stayed out of the sun. With a radiant smile, she got up, dressed, and met me at the bar. "Is it always this dead?" she asked, looking around.

"Well, it IS a ghost town," I smiled.

66

"What's th' deal?"

"Rodeo up in Brownsville," I said.

"Oooohh, that's right."

"You know about it?"

She nodded. "Uh huh, we have a lot of annual rodeos here in Texas. But the BEST one is th' one th' prisoners put on up in Huntsville at th' prison. It's a no-holds-barred rodeo. The prisoners are lifers and got nothin' to lose, so they go for the wildest, meanest, craziest, bulls they can get. You should go sometime."

"Th' chances of me going anywhere are slim to none," I said, picking up a glass and filling it with ice. I poured a Coke over the crushed cubes and set it down in front of her. "I have no desire to leave this place and go back to what's laughingly called "civilization."

" I can understand that," she sighed.

She looked like a teenager with her hair brushed to a high gloss and tied back in a ponytail held by a blue ribbon. She didn't have on any make-up but her skin glowed and her cheeks were apple rosy. If I'd been younger, I would've asked her to the prom.

"So," I said, leaning on my elbows across the bar. "You're from where did you say –Conroe?"

She frowned and said, "No, I'm from Da-"

She caught herself and stopped.

I frowned. "What was that," I said.

She looked down and stammered. "Uh...that's right...Conroe." I knew she was lying but didn't know why and it angered me to see that this was yet another piece of the puzzle that didn't fit. "Look," I said hotly. "I'm getting' tired of you thinkin' I'm an idiot. Can you *possibly* tell the truth about ANYTHING?" She started to get up and I grabbed her by the wrist. "Oooh no, you don't. You stay right *here* and come clean." She yanked her arm away but sat back down. I waited. Finally she let out a sigh and said, "Okay, I'm from Dallas. I said Conroe because I was afraid if you knew where I was really from you'd send me back to-"

"To *who*?" I pressed. She shook her head and looked away. "It's complicated and just better if you leave it alone."

"Look," I said. "I don't know who -or what's hurt you, but running away doesn't help. It always catches up to you; so if you wanna talk about it, maybe I can protect you –or help in some other way..."

She didn't.

CHAPTER TWENTY-THREE

Neither of us said another word and the silence was deafening. She took a few sips of her soda then got up. "I'm going out an' look around –okay?"

"Be my guest," I said, indifferently. "But don't get lost out here. Doc'll kill me…"

I watched her leave and wondered if I'd pushed too hard and she might not come back. When she was out of sight, I threw my towel down across the bar. "Damn it," I swore. I felt like a man in limbo and didn't know why. What was it to me if she wanted to leave? Wasn't I anxious to get rid of her? (Yesterday that question had an answer; today I wasn't so sure.) It was only eleven in the morning, but I poured myself a stiff drink.

Around two, Sam still hadn't come back and I was about to go looking for her when the door opened and she came in holding a bunch of Black-Eyed Susans. "Look what I found at the end of the sidewalk," she grinned. I let a sigh of relief, surprised as hell at how *glad* I was to see her. "Well, let's put them in some water," I smiled, filling a large glass and handing it to her.

"I'm going to set these next to my bed," she beamed proudly, "then I'm going to take a shower." She waved and took the flowers back to her room without another word about our earlier argument. For whatever reason, it was good to see her come back smiling. I didn't know why her happiness was important to me now, but it was and my life seemed to be taking on new purpose.

When I heard her singing in the shower, I sat down at the bar and got out my bankbook to see how much money I had. I'd always made deposits without ever looking at the bottom line, so I was surprised to see there was almost 50 thousand in my savings. Most of it came from the small amount the bank <u>had</u> to give me from the sale of my grandfather's farm, but between what the bar made and my military check, I'd contributed almost 20 thousand since being here. I closed the book, slapped it against my palm and tucked it in my back pocket.

Maybe I wouldn't have to borrow any money from Legrand after all.

CHAPTER TWENTY-FOUR

The first of the week, everybody was back from the rodeo and business picked up again.

On Tuesday, my house band came in and waved to me as they trooped up to the stage.

"Hey, Mac dude."

"Hey band dudes," I waved back. "What're you guys doin' here?"

"We got a new mike and wanna set it up –that okay?"

"Sure," I nodded. "You guys comin' in this weekend?"

"Yep, we'll be here."

"Okay, then," I smiled.

Although it was only the first part of the week, by nine, I was as busy as the proverbial one-legged man at an ass kicking contest when Doug Metcalf came in looking for Noreen. Doug's a curly blond biker who's a die-hard Lorenzo Lamas fan. I'm positive his man hood is wrapped up entirely in his Harley Hog and tattoos and he's living proof that blonde jokes ain't exclusive to females.

He came over and slapped the top of the bar. "Hi, Mac! You seen Noreen?"

I cringed at the mention of her name and shook my head. "Not yet," I said.

He unzipped his leather jacket and frowned. "Damn that woman," he mumbled. "She's a sho'nuf heartbreaker."

"Yeah well...only if you're dizzy enough to fall for her."

"I guess," he mumbled again. "But she's so...so..." and because his vocabulary was so woefully lacking, he was at a loss for words in describing his passion for her.

"Wild?" I offered.

He straightened up and his whole face brightened. "YEAH, that's IT!" he cried. "She is WILD!"

I cocked an eyebrow. "You gotta give up diet sodas, Doug. Trust me, Aspartame kills off more productive brain cells than booze --no matter how much the industry denies it."

He gave me a vacant look. "Huh?"

"Never mind," I sighed. "You're a lost cause, my friend."

He ordered a beer, which I got for him and he wasted no time drinking. "My, you're thirsty. Want another one?" He reached into his jeans and pulled out the liner of each pocket, smiling sheepishly. I rolled my eyes and let out another long sigh. "It's on me," I said.

"Gee, thanks, Mac," he smiled. "You're an okay dude, you know that?"

"Well golly, Doug. That just makes me all tingly."

I got him another beer, which he drank a lot slower this time and I knew he was killing time waiting around for Noreen. Each time the door opened, he'd jerk his head in that direction to see who came in. This went on for over half an hour. When she didn't show, he stood up and asked me to tell her he'd been in looking for her.

"Well," I said with a sarcastic edge. "I know she'll be absolutely bummed over missing you."

Zipping up his jacket, he beamed. "You think?"

"Oh, yeah," I assured him, shaking my head no.

He laughed and shoved away from the bar. "Thanks for th' beer, Mac," he waved. "See ya."

The theme from "The Twilight Zone" ran through my head as I watched him leave.

I picked up Doug's glass and looked out at the dance floor. Everyone was in a dancin' mood and it was packed. I didn't know where they found them, but from time to time the cowboys come in with an actual female date. While I washed and dried Doug's glass, I smiled at the Sea of Stetsons two stepping to the jukebox and low lights. Every girl being driven backwards by her cowboy dance partner was short with Big Hair and looked like Brenda Lee –(except for one who looked like Sally Field.)

The night was going by fast, which suited me just fine. When I'm busy, it keeps my mind occupied and before I knew it, it was time to give last call. By the time I finished getting everyone out, counting the receipts and locking up, it was coming up on three a.m. I dragged my way back to the storeroom and once again, sat my tired body down on the floor just outside Sam's door. After pulling off my boots, I lay down and yanked the flannel robe over my skivvies. I was so tired, I didn't even remember closing my eyes.

It felt like only five minutes had gone by when someone started shaking the tar out of me. Without opening my eyes, I rolled over and grumbled, "Stop it," and pulled the old Indian robe over my head, but they just shook my shoulder harder.

"Mac! Wake up!" an unfamiliar voice kept saying. "It's one o'clock! GET UP!"

"Leave me alone," I mumbled. "I just got to sleep..."

"No Mac. It is one o'clock -IN THE AFTERNOON!"

My eyes sprang open and I sat straight up. "ONE O'CLOCK?" I'd slept so sound that I didn't even know morning had come -and gone.

"Cheese'n crackers, why didn't you get me up earlier?"

Sam was standing over me, staring at me. "I've been trying to wake you for fifteen minutes," she said.

I dropped my face in my hands. "I was so tired," I mumbled through my fingers. "The last thing I remember is locking up." I was seriously thinking about grabbing another fifteen minutes when Juan come flying through the front door. "Senor Mac! Senor Mac!" he yelled. "Come queek!"

I winced as the front door loudly banged into -and bounced off of- the wall. (I could just see the cavernous ding left by the doorknob.) God –I was in the middle of a traffic jam already today.

"Senor Mac...jou must geet up NOW! " Juan was beyond excited as he came over and started pulling on my arm. My legs weren't awake yet, so it took a minute before I finally managed to untangle them and stagger to my feet. "What *is* it, Juan?" I frowned.

"Come queek," he cried excitedly. "A car! It just heet a little dog! I think it is still alive, but it is muy caliente outside and he weel die in the hot!" We both took off for the door. "Why didn't you just bring him in to me?" I asked as we ran out.

"I did not know eef eet would break heem," Juan answered logically and I nodded, understanding what he meant, perfectly.

When we reached the dog, it was lying unconscious by the side of the road. It was a little brown mutt with long wiry hair; probably one of the thousands that ran wild out here. The heat was unbearable and I knew nothing could last long out here -especially injured. I knelt down to see how he -or she –was and didn't like the small trickle of blood I saw by its mouth -*or* the pool underneath its little head. I was sure it was dead, but Juan was so insistent that I decided to give it a shot. "Let's go," I said gathering the animal up in my arms. Its small head lolled to the side and its fur was matted with blood. I adjusted the crook of my arm to brace his head and neck. "C'mon, we gotta call Doc Wright right away!" I yelled, not wanting to tell Juan that I thought the little dog was gone. He nodded and we hurried back to the bar as fast as possible.

I was well aware that if the dog was alive it could have bitten me, but it was a chance I'd just have to take. The dog would only bite out of pain or fear -or both.

As soon as we got inside, I laid the dog on top of the bar. That was when I noticed he was still breathing. I grabbed a towel and covered him up in case of shock then called Doc. He was out of course, but his answering service in Houston said they'd page him and have him call right away. After the longest eight minutes of Juan's life went by, the phone rang. I grabbed it on the first ring and told Doc what had happened. He said to give the dog some water, but only a drop or two from the tip of my finger in case of internal injuries. Then he said to keep the animal warm. I told him I'd already done that part. He said he was on his way and I went back to wait with Juan.

Juan hadn't left the little dog's side since I brought it in. He talked to it in low soothing tones, while gently stroking its small body. The dog lay limp and lifeless and his breathing had gotten a lot more shallow since we'd come in. I didn't like the looks of it and silently shook my head. More blood had pooled under its head. It didn't look like he was going to make it and it hurt.

Juan looked up at me with tears brimming in his eyes and whispered, "I pray for thee perro to bee okay." His face added more hurt on top of what I already felt.

I patted his shoulder and tried to think of the right thing to say. "You did a good thing, Juan," I said brightly. "If he lives, it will be because of you." He nodded, but when he didn't say anything, I knew he was crying. Finally after what seemed like an eternity, Doc rushed through the door. He came up to the bar and sat his medical bag down next to the dog.

"This is the second patient I've come here to see," he said tersely. "You going out of the bar business?"

"No," I said grimly. "Just th' luck of th' draw."

"Well, thank God, this time it's a patient I'm familiar with."

The dog opened his eyes at the sound of our voices and I felt a spark of hope. Doc gently poked around and to the little guy's credit, it never once tried to bite him.

"I'm not positive, but I don't think anything is broken," he said, peering into its ear. "I think she was just badly grazed. Her ear is bleeding...but it's on the outside."

"Please tell me you didn't just say "she," I moaned.

"Well, I did," Doc answered, without looking up. "Looks like she lost a few teeth, too, but I can't tell if there's any internal damage without doing an X-ray. I want to check her head -and eardrum, which might've been ruptured."

"Then do it," I said, looking at Juan. "I can't have this on my conscience."

"Let's get her into my car," Doc said. I nodded and wrapped the poor little thing up in an old Army blanket.

As I laid her carefully in the back seat of Doc's old '58 Buick, I couldn't help thinking how I'd like to KILL the son-of-a-bitch who hit her and hadn't stopped. Man OR woman, pricks like <u>that</u> deserve to die hurt, broken, and ALL ALONE in the unforgiving heat of the sun!! Cruelty and self-centered concern made my blood boil.

Doc checked on the dog to make sure she was quiet and comfortable. She just laid there with trusting eyes and tried to lick his hand. He smiled and closed the back door. He got in the front and turned the key and the big engine roared to life. I couldn't help thinking it was a good thing the dog didn't get hit by his car—it was a tank! (...And to think, it still ran on regular.)

"I'll call you later when I know something," he yelled out his window, and with that, left us in a cloud of dust. We watched them disappear into the heat and I put my arm around Juan's shoulder. "She'll be fine, Juan...I just know it."

I stood there with my arm around him and silently prayed my words would go straight from my mouth to God's ear. However, she most likely had internal injuries and I felt like such a *liar*.

To make matters even worse, Juan wiped his eyes and smiled up at me when he said, "You are a good man, Senor Mac."

I swallowed the lump in my throat and reminded him, "Oh, I don't know...you're the one who came'n got me." Then I muttered, "But what I want to know is, who's going to keep her if she makes it?" He looked up at me again and his face brightened. "I know what to do, Senor Mac!" he smiled. "Let us geeve her a house with thee amigo who ees seek -they can get well together!"

My first thought was, "Oh, no, not another mouth to feed," but when I gave it some thought, I got to thinking how that wasn't such a bad idea. Sam's healing might go faster if she had something to take her mind off her own worries. I rubbed my chin thoughtfully. "Damn, you just may have an excellent idea there, Juan."

"May I come for to visit?" he asked.

I ruffled his hair. "Of course you can."

His optimism was infectious and I got to believing the dog just might make it after all.

Later that evening, Doc called to tell us that other than losing three teeth and having a bruised forehead, the dog looked like she was going to be all right. "There's no internal injuries or any sign of a concussion that I can see from looking at the X-rays," he concluded.

"What about her ear?" I asked.

"Just a small cut," he answered. "Probably happened when her head hit the gravel or on a rock. That kind of wound bleeds profusely but isn't as bad as it looks. It only required three stitches."

"Was her eardrum ruptured?"

"No ruptured eardrum," he confirmed. "I'm going to give her a mild sedative and let her sleep through the night. If no complications occur, I'll drop her off when I leave to make my rounds in the morning. Just be sure she takes it easy for a day or two. Head injuries -no matter how minor, need to be watched."

"But...she *IS* gonna be okay...right?"

"Far as I can tell..."

I hung up feeling like I'd just won the lottery and turned around to Juan with a big smile.

"She just glanced off th' bumper an' is gonna be fine. Doc wants to keep her overnight to make sure she's okay, but he's gonna bring her back here tomorrow."

Juan's face beamed. "Muy bien! I weel bee here...at what ees thee hour?"

"Come by around noon," I said.

"I weel come weeth thee food for jour amigo," he nodded, happily.

"Well!" I said, slapping the bar. "THIS calls for a celebration. I'm going to have a Jack Daniel's. What do you want -Coke or Sprite?"

"A Coke, por favor," Juan smiled.

"Coke it is," I said, and we spent the next half hour toasting ourselves the dog and Doc. When he finished his drink, Juan stood up and announced, "Eet ees late and I must go now, Senor Mac, but I weel return manana. Muchas gracias for all you deed, Senor Mac. I weel not bee able to sleep without no bad worries tonight." I laughed, knowing what he meant, but didn't bother to correct him. "Hasta manana, mi amigo," I said.

He sprinted for the door and waved. "Hasta luego," he called. I swiveled back around to the bar on my stool. Damn! I hadn't felt this good since Dad and me birthed a calf a hundred years ago. I'd completely forgotten about that cold December morning when we brought a little calf into the world, and watched in total amazement as it immediately tried to stand up on four wobbly legs.

I could still hear the drizzle of the rain on the barn's tin roof outside and the smell of wet wood, mixed in with the fragrance of hay and manure. How brief those times are. It takes something like what happened today, to pull us back to those warm places in the heart. To my surprise, I discovered it's when a life hangs in the balance that you find out what you're really made of. There's no such thing as a life being unimportant. (I'd pulled many a lizard out of the rain barrel.)

My chest swelled up a bit with pride and I poured myself another shot of Jack. Maybe I was just a little bit like a cowboy after all. Hot tears rimmed my eyes as I raised my glass in a silent toast. "Here's to you, Dad."

CHAPTER TWENTY-FIVE

Doc called the next day to tell me my new puppy was still bruised and sore, but ready to come home. "And this time you're getting a bill!" he said.

"Puppy?" I groaned. "How old?"

"Hard to pinpoint, but between seven and nine months, so unfortunately, the teeth she lost yesterday were most likely permanent.

However, they were all on one side in the back, so she can still chew whatever cheap dogfood you buy her."

I frowned at that, but chose to ignore it. "When can she be spayed?"

"I'd wait about a month. Let her get over this first," he said. "I'm leaving here soon as we hang up and will be there in about fifteen minutes."

"Okay, and schedule her for a spaying A.S.A.P!"

Twenty minutes later, the door opened and Doc came in holding the puppy. Except for the shaved fur around her right ear and three new stitches, she looked much better than the last time I saw her. She was so damned cute. One ear stood up and the other one flopped over. I took her from Doc and patted her head. "Well hello, girl." She gently licked my cheek and wagged her tail. I was smitten.

Doc smiled. "She's a very good dog," he said. "She never once fought me while I did the examination. She'll make an excellent companion."

I agreed. "She's a smart little thing," I smiled. "She looks at us like she knows we tried to help her yesterday."

Doc nodded. "Animals –especially dogs-respond to kindness. Their love and devotion goes far beyond understanding. Nothing else gives back so much for so little." He stroked her head then said, "Well, I've got to be going now -you take good care of her."

"Before you leave Doc, what should I feed her?"

"I'd suggest keeping her on soft food until her gums heal up. Canned dog food with bread mixed in to prevent diarrhea would be perfect."

"Canned dog food and bread?" I had no idea where I could find that.

"Legrand carries a limited supply of milk, bread and dog food," Doc said. "Along with some other things like candy, band-aides and rubbing alcohol."

"I didn't know that. I thought he only carried hardware."

"He started getting the other things in when folks ran out and couldn't run to the corner store –look, I've gotta run."

"Okay, and thanks for everything," I said.

After Doc left for his morning rounds, I took the puppy in to meet Sam. She'd been there when Juan came running in and was on pins and needles waiting to hear the outcome. When we reached the storeroom, I opened her door and introduced her to Sam, who immediately brightened up and held out both arms. I put the puppy in them. She smothered her with kisses (and I felt just a twinge of envy.) "Oooooooh, you are just *adorable,*" she cooed, holding her up in both hands. "What are we gonna name you –huh?" She looked at me. "Any suggestions?"

"How 'bout callin' her "Allstate" 'cause she's in good hands?"

Sam frowned. "No," she giggled, 'but you did just give me a good idea," and she named her "Freeway," (because "Crossroads" didn't work.)

CHAPTER TWENTY-SIX

From the moment they saw each other, there was no question that Freeway was Sam's dog. They took to each other like tequila and salt, and Freeway never left her side. Within 48 hours of the little dog coming into her life, Sam's whole demeanor changed. She got out of bed every morning, hurried to get dressed, and off they'd go to spend the day outside exploring. It was magic the way that dog transformed not just Sam, but all of us. Juan came often to play with her. Sometimes he'd bring her a ball (or some other toy he found) after spending hours cleaning it up. Legrand ordered special cases of dog food and loved her as much as the rest of us.

As the days went by, I watched Sam's health improve by leaps and bounds. Pretty soon, she and Freeway started to take longer and longer walks in the late afternoon. She'd rush in just before dark with her eyes sparkling and have to tell me all about a sunset she'd just seen.

It was like Sam was seeing everything in life for the first time.

She'd say, "Isn't life wonderful, Mac."

And lately, I thought it was.

Wherever Sam went, Freeway was an appendage on her heels. And I've got to confess, Freeway was the cutest mutt I ever saw. She had a round little fuzzy body on short tiny legs. Her mug was that of a Scottie and she had the cutest way of turning her head inquisitively when you talked to her. Her brown fur was tipped with black and I bet she didn't weigh fifteen pounds soaking wet. Sam brushed her every night like she was a pedigreed Afghan.

One day when Juan came by, I watched the two of them faun over Freeway.

"That dog is going to be spoiled rotten," I scowled.

"Si," Juan laughed. "But what ees thee good to have thee life, eef there ees no-thing ever to love?" I was stunned; Juan had just summed up the real reason for living. A Master Poet Lauriat couldn't have done it more simply or eloquently. Sam kept brushing Freeway as looked at me and snorted. "You can try that "tough guy" routine all you want, Mac, but you don't fool me ONE little bit! You're a big softy an' you would've been the biggest blubberer at Freeway's funeral if she hadn't made it."

I raised my eyebrows. "You're absolutely right," I admitted

CHAPTER TWENTY-SEVEN

About five weeks after Sam was fully recovered, she became really, really, bored and started to clean *everything*. She scrubbed the storeroom, washed the sheets, the quilt, rug, my old Indian blanket robe, curtains -and the one towel I owned. When that was done, she started on the tables, dance floor, and bar. She was a woman possessed and it really started to get on my nerves.

In no time, she had the place sparkling and I had to make her stop.

"Keep this up, an' nobody will come in," I told her. "Besides, dust gives th' joint character, an' that spider over in th' corner, is one of my best friends." Sam stopped scrubbing a table long enough to look at me thoughtfully. "You know..." she said, pointing her sponge at me, "you need to just go ahead and hire me."

"WHAT?" I cried.

She came over and put her hands on both hips. "HIRE me," she repeated.

"But, I don't need any help," I argued. "Juan does th' sweeping an' I handle th' rest."

"Juan can *still* do th' sweeping. I can wait on tables so your cowboys don't have to come up to the bar."

I hadn't given any thought to having a waitress *or* the fact that she'd want to stay on here. "You're -you're serious about this, aren't you."

"I am!" she sniffed. "I've gotten to know everybody around here and they like me, so what would be th' problem?"

"Th' problem is, I can't pay anybody else to work here," I frowned. "Th' guys in th' band only make twenty five dollars for th' whole weekend."

"I don't care...I'm sure I'll make enough in tips."

I saw that she was dead set on this idea and found myself saying, "The pay sucks, but th' job does come with a roof over your head and all the popcorn you can eat."

"Throw in some'a that soup Juan's mama makes and a case of dog food for Freeway, and you got yourself a waitress," she grinned.

What could I say? "Okay," I shrugged. "Job starts tonight."

"Oh goody," she beamed. She untied her apron and hurried back to her room. Twenty minutes later, she came out looking like a little country Barbie doll. She had changed into a tight pair of faded dungarees with a pink-and-white checkered blouse. Her long hair was brushed back in a ponytail and a pink bow trailed down her back. "Ready," she smiled. "Where do I start?"

"Just take care of table orders tonight," I said. "We'll go from there."

She nodded and tied her apron on again. I watched her get a tray out from under the bar and found myself warming to the idea of having her

77

around. I was just thinking what a nice addition she'd be to the place, when Noreen's face flashed in front of my eyes.

Oh no!

I'd completely forgotten all about Noreen!

CHAPTER TWENTY-EIGHT

I'm not ashamed to admit when I'm afraid of something and Noreen was a *force* to be reckoned with. It was just a matter of time until she came in and saw Sam. I tried to think of some way to keep them from ever running into each other, but there would be absolutely no way of keeping them from meeting face to face. In fact, I wondered why Noreen hadn't been in already. She was usually around on weekends, but I hadn't seen her since about a week before Sam showed up; which only meant one thing; she was shacked up with some poor sap that had money. I sighed, wishing I'd taken out more life insurance -or better yet -maybe God could just strike me dead now.

I tried to put the impending doom out of my mind and concentrate on work. Although the night went by slow, it was steady. Sam did surprisingly well handling drink orders, but the acid test would be this weekend when it was packed. Just after closing, she brought her tray up to the bar and said, "This was too easy. There has to be more to it."

"It's only Wednesday," I said. "Wait'll this weekend."

"But isn't there more you could show me to do?"

I thought about it. "Tomorrow night you can come behind here and I'll show you how you can help out if we get really busy."

"Great -I'll look forward to it," she said, taking off her apron and laying it across the tray. She waved good night and said she was going to bed.

"You want a little somethin' before hitting th' hay?" I called. She shook her head and kept on walking. I got down a glass, poured myself a shot then went to bed –on the floor -wondering when Legrand was going to come back with some news on the trailer.

The next afternoon, I went over to his store to see him, but he wasn't there. No one knew where he'd gone, so I just left word that I'd been there. When I got back, Sam was waiting for me behind the bar. "Well, are you gonna show me what you want me to do, or what?"

"Holy cow," I frowned. "It's only four thirty –you *must* be bored!"

Grabbing my apron off the cooler, I tied it on and said, "Okay, this is simple. Glasses get washed as soon as you get 'em. Now, you may have noticed there are two sinks. You wash 'em in this sink an' rinse 'em in the second one, which has a special disinfectant in it. Then you let 'em air dry on this rubber mat here. See? It has an open honeycomb design so the mouth of th' glasses don't touch anything, but air can still get in underneath." I picked up a mat to demonstrate. She looked at the mat blankly, then me. I put the mat down and turned to show her the next step. "The glasses that don't get used get put up here on these glass shelves in front of the mirror; which as you can see I've also lined with honeycomb mats. Be sure to always place the glass mouth down. Any questions?"

With a look of disgust, Sam huffed, "You *gotta* be kiddin'."

I pulled on my earlobe and gave her my best choirboy look. "Why...whatever do you mean?"

"You're teaching me how to wash dishes -something EVERY woman knows how to do from CHILDHOOD?"

"Well," I stammered, "I didn't know if you knew about the...um, disinfectant."

My face heated up as she glared at me just like my mother used to do when she caught me with my hand in the cookie jar.

"You're a real Fruit of th' Loom, you know that?"

I rolled my eyes and said, "Need I remind you that I'm the boss and shouldn't have to take this abuse. Besides, I didn't say you had to be a rocket scientist to do this!"

"Well," she glared. "I think I can handle it -but if I DO run into trouble, I CERTAINLY know who to call."

I was seriously thinking of choking her when the door opened and Harley strolled in with Doc. Taking off his Stetson, Harley nodded at us and said, "Evenin' Mac...Sam." They sat down next to each other and Doc set his black bag on the bar next to Harley's Stetson.

Sam smiled brightly. "Hello Harley, hi, Doc." I glanced up at the old Hamm's Beer clock rotating on a rusted chain swaged over the mirror. It was like the hands weren't moving. "It's not even five o'clock yet; a bit early for you guys to be in here, ain't it?" I smiled. Doc nodded, while Harley ran his hand over his hair without taking his eyes off Sam. "Good to see you up an' about, Sam," he said.

"Thanks, Harley," she smiled. "Michelob and Jack back?"

"Yep."

My jaw fell as I watched her skillfully pull the Michelob tap and fill a shot glass with Jack Daniel's; placing it all nice and neat in front of Harley - right on a clean napkin. (Well!! I hadn't even gotten around to showing her THAT part.)

"Why...thank you, Sam," he smiled, then he looked at me with the barest trace of a smile and raised an eyebrow.

"And what can I get for you, Doc?" she smiled cheerfully. Sam was Doc's most ardent admirer since he saved Freeway's life.

"I think I'll just have some coffee," Doc smiled back. "And a little brandy, if you have any around."

He occasionally drank brandy; another reason Sam liked him; he had "taste," she said. She made a point of telling him in a loud voice, "It's just bar brandy. Not the GOOD stuff."

I frowned at her. "You think maybe you could yell that a little louder –I don't think the guys over at Legrand's quite heard you."

"Whatever you got, is fine," he said.

She served Doc and the two of them fell into conversation about Freeway's latest escapades, while Harley drank his beer in silence and gave me a funny little grin every now and then. I tried to ignore him but when he did catch my eye, I'd give him a dirty look. Thirty minutes later, Doc got up and said he had to be going. Sam hugged him goodbye then told me she was going to feed Freeway. After they were gone, Harley sat there looking at me like the cat that had swallowed the canary. Finally, he said, "Don't tell me. You got Sam workin' for you."

I leaned back and nodded then took a deep breath and looked at him helplessly.

"Are you crazy?" he laughed. "Do you have ANY idea how Noreen's gonna take this?"

His grin got bigger and bigger as he shook his head. "Boy-oh-boy, YOU are a dead man, my friend. I sure hope I'm here when she sees Sam for th' first time. If I'm not, I know I'll sure see th' skyrockets."

"Hey! I thought you were my amigo," I groaned.

"Where Noreen's concerned," he said, "it's every man for hisself."

That was true. Out here, women are scarce and Noreen was just about the only game in town. Even worse, she considered this bar her very own personal turf.

"Yeah well, I'm just surprised she hasn't been in here already," I sighed. "She must be holed up out of town with somebody."

"If she is," Harley said, "God help the poor sucker." That being said, we both fell silent and instinctively lowered our eyes to say a silent prayer for the poor bastard -whoever he was.

CHAPTER TWENTY-NINE

Standing over six feet in her stocking feet, Noreen was...hard to describe. Without apology, she slept with whomever she pleased. Noreen may not have known who discovered America, but she sure knew EVERYTHING about sex and how to profit from it. In that area, she was a human calculator with a cash register heart -but if anyone was a living example of somebody who had taken life's lemons and made lemonade, it was Noreen.

Born in a rundown shack just outside of town to parents who were living proof on the drawbacks of inbreeding, Noreen was a survivor. The shack had been left abandoned for years and the wind had pounded the building relentlessly until it leaned to one side in a gravity-defying slant. The walls were missing so many boards it was a mystery as to what kept the damned thing from falling over, and piles of sand filled every corner – even after they moved in. The floorboards were warped like the ribs of a Spanish galleon and the roof looked as if it had seen a meteorite or two. Without a shard of glass left in the busted out windows, the family had plenty of natural heating and air-conditioning at the wrong times of the year. But by the time they found the shack, they were just glad to have a place to call home. Her parents already had three teenage idiot boys, but her ma was pregnant again with Noreen, so she was born here, making her maybe the only true non-Indian native of this place.

Since good impressions weren't high on her father's list, it didn't take long before the front yard was littered with rusted-out cars and the shack "furnished" with whatever discarded furniture he and the boys found. The stuff they dragged in was so indescribably nasty that nobody in his or her right mind would've sat on anything without getting a tetanus shot first. Noreen's uncle also lived with them, making the men outnumber the women five to two -and all in all a retarded gorilla had a higher I.Q. than the combined male population of her household. Her mother however, was the total opposite. She was a sweet natured woman who didn't weigh ninety pounds soaking wet. Although Noreen never spoke about her family, I do remember her commenting once how she never remembered a time when her mother's red raw hands didn't smell of bleach.

Before her mother met her father, she managed to get all the way through the eleventh grade. She probably would've graduated too, if it hadn't been for him. So of course she was better educated than her father and he resented the hell out of it. He was a mean man who drank constantly. As a child, Noreen saw him beat her ma without provocation - and I can't say as I blame Noreen for turning out the way she did. She *had* to have felt powerlessness.

Like everyone else around here, I knew nothing about her past and, like everybody else, thought she was an insufferable air-headed nut –and I *probably* would've *gone on* thinking that if it wasn't for Doc. Long before I arrived or Doc moved here from New England, I'd heard about another doctor; a practicing G.P. with an office on the outskirts of town. He was a well-respected grandfatherly type who treated folks from both sides of the border (rich or poor) for pretty much little or nothing right up until he died about twenty years ago. He had no family, so nobody bothered to clear out the building after his death. All his medical records and files were just boxed up and forgotten -as so many things are out here.

CHAPTER THIRTY

Then one day about eight or nine months after I opened the bar, a gentleman came in. He was wearing a tweed jacket with suede patches on the elbows and a damned *vest*, white shirt and tie. Thinking he must be lost, I smiled and thought to myself, "Now what th' hell is this?"

After he introduced himself to me, he said he was a veterinarian from Boston and had just moved out here with his wife. He went on to say he planned to take over the old doctor's building on the outskirts and open a vet's office for the ranchers. I was both surprised and pleased.

"I know that old building," I said. "It hasn't had anybody in there in over twenty years."

"I know," he nodded.

"Well, good luck. No tellin' *what* you'll find in there." I invited him to sit down and have a drink, but he said he had to be going. "I just came by to meet you," he said, shaking my hand.

"I'm sure glad you did, Doctor Wright -an' next time bring your wife," I grinned.

"I'll do that," he nodded. "And just call me Doc –everybody else does."

A few days later, he came in with Anna. After they sat down at the bar, Doc introduced her to me. Her warm blue eyes twinkled and she flashed a smile that lit up the place. "It is so *nice* to meet you, Mac," she said in a sincere voice that reminded me of my grandmother.

"Same here, Anna...it's about time some folks with class showed up around here. Welcome!" Just then the door opened and Harley walked in. He came over and I introduced him to everybody. Harley took off his Stetson and laid it on the bar then pulled up a stool and sat down next to

Doc and Anna. After he got settled, I said, "Western hospitality dictates that all your drinks are on the house today, folks, so what'll it be?"

"Mine too?" Harley asked.

I frowned then rolled my eyes and sighed, "Yeah.... yours too."

We spent the next hour getting to know each other and by the time they left, I'd learned that both Doc and Anna came from a long line of New Englanders. He'd been born and raised just outside Boston to a very wealthy family of doctors, lawyers, and judges. His family was "old money" while Anna's family wasn't exactly impoverished. They became sweethearts in junior high school, married right after graduation and have been lifelong partners for over fifty years. Although they wanted children, they weren't able to, so they lavished all that love on each other.

Neither had ever been outside of New England, therefore it took a real Leap of faith for Doc to pull up stakes and move west now in his autumn years. But he was getting tired of the battling the bitter New England winters and wanted to retire from all the hustle and bustle of his rich clients and their pampered pets –yet, he didn't want to quit altogether. He knew he wanted to do something more worthwhile than giving a poodle rabies shots, he just didn't know what. He considered teaching at the university, but that still had him shoveling tons of snow every winter. Also there was their home. It was a lovely old three-story brick mansion that had been in his family for generations and Doc hated the thought of ever parting with it. However, Anna had arthritis in just about every part of her body and climbing stairs was all but impossible anymore. So after weighing the pros and cons, Doc felt it was time to think about moving some place warm and dry. Anna's comfort was far more important than the house.

"Well how in the hell did you ever find *this* place?" I wondered. "I mean, Boston is light years from here –both geographically *and* culturally."

Doc said that maybe it was just luck -or Fate -that made him stop by his favorite coffee shop one cold afternoon after he finished up with his last patient. The slate gray sky and blistering cold wind was just the kind of day that made Doc want to pack up and leave. He was in a foul mood and wanted nothing more than a hot cup of coffee before heading home. He'd just sat down in a booth by the front window, when a truck driver he knew walked by with his collar turned up against the wind. As soon as he saw Doc, he waved and came inside. He slid in across from Doc and they both ordered a sandwich and coffee. The man was a coast-to-coast driver who worked for a large well-known trucking outfit, so when Doc casually mentioned that he was thinking about retiring and moving some place dry and warm with *no* city traffic, the driver immediately said, "I know just the place you're looking for..."

To be polite, Doc asked about it, but mentally dismissed it as soon as he learned it was in the middle of nowhere down in the hottest part of Texas. His ears did perk up though when the driver went on to tell him about all the cattle ranches out here with no vet to take care of them. He said a vet had to either make an all-day drive from Houston or be flown in by one of the ranchers. At first, Doc didn't think much about it, but after the first snowstorm dumped over eleven inches on them, he recalled the conversation vividly and told Anna about it. However they still didn't seriously entertain the idea of moving to such a Godforsaken place until the next snowstorm dumped ten more inches on top of the former eleven. That was all it took and the next spring, they sold their house, packed up, and headed west.

CHAPTER THIRTY-ONE

Doc had done his homework and contacted a real estate agent in Brownsville before leaving Boston. The agent sent him several photos of houses in and around the area, but most were too small, too rundown or just flatly too far away from the proximity of the ranches. Anna honed in on one photo of a four-bedroom "fixer-upper" that was in the right location. It was the best of the lot, but Doc wasn't used to this kind of architecture and thought the outside was dreary and unimaginative with its square shaped adobe structure. However, there wasn't much of anything else available and the price was laughable. Still, Doc wouldn't commit to buying. Then he received another envelope one day, from the real estate agent. Wondering what he could be sending, Doc opened the envelope and was delighted to pull out a floor plan showing the inside of the house boasted of thirty five hundred square feet. The note enclosed said that while the house did need some minor cosmetic work, it *was* the largest within a hundred miles and in perfectly sound condition. He thought Doc should take another look keeping an open mind.

That evening, he and Anna went over the floor plan inch by inch. A third of the footage was devoted to the living room with its high ceilings, fireplace, wood floors, and wide spacious windows. The kitchen included plenty of counter and cabinet space with a dining room separating it from the living room. Anna fell so in love with the single-story dwelling that Doc gave in after seeing the potential of turning it into a lovely New England cottage with just a few additions -like a front porch, colonial windows and shutters -*after* he covered the entire pink stucco monstrosity with vinyl siding.

I knew the house and had even looked at it a few years back, but it was bigger than anything I'd ever need so I passed on it, much as I hated to. However, it was a great place and I was glad it was going to be lived in again.

The next few months were spent with Anna busily unpacking all their belongings, while Doc moved into the former doctor's building. Being from New England, Anna had the house looking like a home in no time. She hung white crisscrossed Priscilla's in the living room windows with dark green drapes on each side and set two overstuffed chairs in front of the fireplace. She covered the bare wooden floors with an artistic hand-woven area rug from their home in Boston. In the dining room, a flower arrangement centered between two silver Paul Revere candlesticks reflected in the high gloss of a Chippendale table. At the end of the dining room, lace inserts hung inside the three-sided bay window, defusing the harsh desert sun outside. The house had such a warm '40's feel to it that the first time I went over there, I expected to see Loretta Young come whirling out the kitchen door.

True to his word, Doc wasted no time having a wide porch built across the front of the house for his swing and two rocking chairs. By the second spring, vinyl siding covered every square inch of the pink stucco; the colonial windows were in -*and* a gable roof was added with two dormers. Anna had geraniums blooming all around what was now, a transplanted New England cottage. Since they didn't need all four bedrooms, Doc turned one into an office so he could spend more time at home. Anna moved his old roll top desk in next to his file cabinet and desk chair. While she got him set up in their new home, he unpacked his equipment at the office from the U-Haul, but being less organized than Anna, it took him four months to get things half-way situated. He had to do his moving in, in between the ranchers needing his services right away.

Each morning, he'd head out to take care of anywhere between one to fifteen head of cattle –sometimes more. It was over six months before he finally got around to opening the door to the backroom of the old building. The door wasn't padlocked, but the hinges were so rusted that it was hard to budge and creaked like something out of a horror movie. He got it about a third of the way open before hitting something heavy. After pushing on it a few more times, he put his shoulder against the door and shoved as hard as he could. He heard a box slide away and with that, the door opened and he stepped inside. He was immediately greeted by a jumbled mess of old medical equipment and boxes covered in decades of dust. Everything had been thrown about willy-nilly. Doc frowned at the disorganized chaos.

This kind of laziness really irritated his New England upbringing. Coughing from the dust storm, Doc fanned the air with his hand as he waded through the countless boxes stacked haphazardly on top of each other and knocked a few over. Having no idea what was inside them, he decided to give them a look-through before burning the entire lot. He pulled up a box and sat down, taking the lid off the one nearest him. Right away he saw that they were old medical records of all the people the doctor had ever treated. By now, Doc pretty much knew all of us out here and didn't recognize any of the names. Looking at the dates on the folders, he realized none of them were under twenty-five years old –so...all of these people were either living someplace else or deceased. He threw the files back in the box and grumbled, "Going through all this is a monumental waste of my time." He slammed the top back on, gathered the box up in his arms and took it outside to dump into the burn barrel. He made two or three trips before one of the boxes slipped from his grip, spilling its contents all over the floor. Cursing angrily, Doc bent down to pick up the papers. He absently looked at each one before throwing it back in the box, but when one caught his eye and he stopped.

The file had one name on it: Noreen.

Doc knew Noreen –and like the rest of us, found her "amusing" (-as he put it.) Noreen was an enigma to everyone, but no one ever tried to figure her out. Most of us thought it would be like trying to figure out the theory of relativity or unscramble eggs. However, *unlike* Einstein, Noreen was complicated in her simple mindedness.

Doc opened the folder expecting to find a lengthy history on her, but to his surprise there was only one page inside. He frowned and shook the file, but when nothing else fell out, his frustration merged with confusion. Sighing to himself, Doc took the one page medical record and sat down to read it. After he finished, a strange look came over his face and he slowly lowered the paper. The old G.P. had been a smart man and kept meticulous notes. Although there wasn't much for the former doctor to go on at the time she was brought in by her mother, he was able to accurately guess what was happening to Noreen. Thanks to him, his notes in the margins of the file gave Doc enough to piece together what a hell her life must have been.

CHAPTER THIRTY-TWO

I've known Doc now for a few years and along with Harley, consider him one of my closest friends. And I know him well enough to know that he doesn't like <u>or</u> entertain gossip of *any* kind. That includes giving out information on anyone –and most *especially* if they're patients of a doctor. So for him to *ever* say anything private about someone is about as rare as a marijuana bust in Vermont. But he was perplexed by what he read in Noreen's file and decided to confide in me one afternoon. I could tell something was on his mind when he came in and sat down at the bar, but I wasn't sure until he looked at me and said, "Can I talk to you about something extremely private, Mac?"

I put down my towel and came over to stand in front of him. "Of course you can Doc, you know that. What's wrong?" I frowned. "It isn't Anna is it?"

He shook his head and said, "No, nothing to do with Anna…it's…about Noreen."

Doc explained how he was taking boxes of old medical files out to be burned when one slipped out of his hands. As he was picking up the papers and putting them back in the box, he came across one with Noreen's name on it. She was only six or seven at the time, but her mother came in one day, wanting him to do a full exam. The doctor, whose name was George Lewis, was surprised to hear that it was the little girl that he needed to see, because the mother was in far worse shape than the child. Her face was a mass of scars, one eyelid drooped, and it was painfully obvious that the woman had had her nose broken many times. Her left leg was a good two inches shorter than her right, causing her to limp freakishly when she walked. From the grotesque way the bone protruded against the skin, he knew the leg had been broken more than one time and never set. The woman was a living walking-around train wreck. But he did a complete check-up on Noreen as requested.

With the exception of being a bit malnourished, the child was in good health. He checked her heart and lungs, but when it was time to do the pelvic, she didn't seem shy or try to resist at all. He'd never known a female (adult OR child,) that didn't hate this part of an examination. She climbed up on the table without a word of resistance and said nothing when he gently spread her legs. *That* was highly unusual, but when he examined her, he instantly knew why she wasn't sensitive to having her pubic area looked at, and he was both furious and horrified at the damage he saw. Her undeveloped female organs were so torn up and scarred over that she would never *ever* be able to have children. She was a mess and he knew it had to have been going on for some time.

However, things like that weren't addressed in those days, so Dr. Lewis didn't know whether to tell her mother or not. But Noreen's mother, who'd been watching his face like a hawk through the entire examination, saved him the trouble. "She's been diddled, ain't she" she said, matter-of-factly. When he didn't answer, she sighed, "Don't make no never mind if'n you tell me or not; I know she has. Her father and his brother's been goin' in her room late at night when they both is so drunk they can't hardly stand up..." She buried her face in her hands and Dr. Lewis called his nurse to come in. He tried to comfort her as the nurse got a pill and some water, but she refused to take it and finally stopped crying on her own. When she got up to leave, the doctor said he wanted to see Noreen again. But her mother never came back -and that was the one and only time any doctor *ever* saw Noreen. Without any more visits, all Dr. Lewis could do was make notes in the margins saying he suspected the mother had suffered many, many beatings, as well as the child having to endure ongoing molestation.

The writing stopped abruptly at the end of the page and Doc turned it over. There were two more entries on the back, but they weren't about Noreen; they were about her mother. The old doctor detailed a brutal beating she got one night from her husband. The beating was beyond anything she'd ever taken before and from what he'd heard, the woman was in bad shape. Somehow though, she managed to get away from him after he passed out, leaving Noreen there. Dr. Lewis felt sure that she must have been hurt to the point of death to go away and leave Noreen. He was positive that if there had been *any* way possible they both could have escaped, they would have. All his entries were dated, but Dr. Lewis's very last entry skipped over a year before telling about some hikers finding human remains scattered out in the desert. The bleached white bones had been out there for some time –and they were female.

The authorities gathered up what they could find and the skeleton was sent to the medical examiner in Houston; a man Dr. Lewis knew. He wrote asking that a copy of his examination be sent to him when he finished, explaining that the person might have been from around these parts. When he received the final report, the medical examiner noted that every bone in the skeleton's face was broken, along with a fractured neck and both old and new breaks in her right arm and leg. But it was the last part of his report that was the most disturbing of all. She'd still been alive when she reached the spot where the hikers discovered her skeleton; however, the countless fang marks in her bones told what happened next. The smell of blood had attracted coyotes by the pack and whatever chance she might've had ended then and there.

Everything in the old doctor told him it was Noreen's ma -and he hoped she was already dead by the time they got to her.

CHAPTER THIRTY-THREE

And that is how I came to know about that part of Noreen's life. But what none of us knew after that point was that her mother's absence left the little eight-year old to take the full force of her father's wrath. When he found his wife gone, he beat Noreen within an inch of her life and where he could intimidate her mother, it was a newer, stronger child that took his belt across her back. She's cried all her little girl tears the night her ma left and hatred hardened her against any pain he tried to inflict. No matter how long or hard he beat her she refused to shed one tear. She'd seen this bastard destroy her ma and her only purpose in life now, was to survive and destroy the son-of-a-bitch.

The law required that she go to school, so there wasn't much her Pa could do about that, but he never figured on Noreen being smart enough to learn what she was being taught ...along with a few things she wasn't. School was the best thing in Noreen's life. For six hours a day, she could control her destiny with no restraints. Naturally, all the girls at school hated her, but she could give a rat's ass. She rose above the rejection of her female classmates, who thought of her as "white trash," and passed by every one of them with her nose just as high in the air as theirs. She found her female counterparts pathetically stupid and comical –and sensing her contempt for them, they hated her all the more. Always thinking they were better than she was, they didn't realize that all the sexual molestation she'd taken was making her develop faster. She started her period before she was ten and although it gave her pain beyond words, by the age of fourteen the pendulum of life began to swing in Noreen's favor -big time. She shot up to five foot ten and began to blossom in all the right places. At fifteen she was the sexiest girl in this part of the southwest and by sixteen her figure was legendary.

Noreen had an irresistible hardness that attracted boys to her like honey. The girls were positively green with envy and she purposely wore clothes one size too small; along with developing a slow exaggerated walk to tease (or annoy) anyone who watched. Since Noreen was considered cheap and easy, she decided to make it pay off. While she may have been cheap, she sure as hell wasn't free and before long, she'd turned her sensuality into pure profit.

Noreen's father and uncle also were aware of her maturing body, but she had youth and strength on her side now and they couldn't have their way with her anymore; which, to her delight, enraged her father. He considered her, his private stock and threatened to kill her if he even so much as caught a boy LOOKING at her.

It was this threat that gave Noreen the perfect finish she needed on her plan to get rid of him.

Shortly before her seventeenth birthday, her father became adamant about her quitting school. Noreen knew it would only be a matter of time before he found a way, so it was time to put her plan into action. She'd had three years to formulate it, but now that it was time, she hoped she could pull it off. If it were successful, then the eventual downfall of her father would come in the form of a new boy at school by the name of Jared.

Noreen had seen Jared for the first time in her sophomore year. He played right guard on the football team and was as dumb as he was huge. At six feet five, two hundred and seventy-five pounds of solid muscle, he was a human locomotive—*exactly* what Noreen needed. Like every other boy at school, Jared was crazy about Noreen and openly drooled after her. Knowing this, Noreen flirted unmercifully with him; always careful never let him have his way with her. It drove him absolutely *crazy* to know that every boy in school could have her except him.

To further manipulate him into total submission Noreen made it a point to run into Jarred during class change. It was a moment Jarred lived for. She'd saunter up to him, back him into a corner behind the lockers and rub her huge breasts up against him. He'd almost pass out from pure pleasure when she'd cradle his crotch and press her hot lips to his in a kiss that was pure nuclear meltdown. In his uncontrollable excitement, he'd fumble madly trying to grab her breast, but she'd back away, skillfully holding his hand by the wrist, then smile coyly and slowly shake her head. "Uh, uh, Jared," she'd whisper hotly. "Mustn't touch."

Still holding his hands, she'd kiss him on the cheek and leave him with a rock hard hard-on that all the books in school couldn't hide. On these days he was always late for class. *Very* late.

Some said it was Noreen's prick teasing that made Jared the football great he became. He was a killer on the field and every opposing team in the state hated coming up against him. By his senior year, Jared was the greatest high school defensive lineman in the Southwest. His records for yards gained still stand today. He made All State, All Conference, and All American.

...And every girl within a hundred miles wanted him.

But all Jared lived for was Noreen -and all Noreen cared about was using him to her best advantage. Her constant teasing went on year after year with Noreen stepping it up the last year. Everything depended on perfect timing and she was just waiting for the right moment. Then one day during class change, Noreen backed Jarred into his usual corner. By this time Jared was out of his mind with desire and starting to get mean. He grabbed her around the throat and growled, "Not *this* time, baby." In the blink of an eye, he reversed their positions, holding her firmly against the wall with his hand still around her throat. He said, "You been stallin' me long enough! I ain't takin' it anymore! Either you'n me git together or I'll see you one night-"

Noreen smiled. It was time.

"You're so very right, Jared," she whispered sweetly. "In fact, why don't you come by this Friday night -that is...if you don't have other plans?" Looking him straight in the eyes, Noreen opened her lips and ran her wet pink tongue slowly over them, knowing he would *not* take no for an answer when he got her all alone. Jared starred at her tongue like a cobra mesmerized by a rat. Unable to believe his ears, he took his hand away. "W- What time?" he asked, finding it hard to breathe. She leaned in, pressing her breast into his chest and letting her fingers lightly touch his crotch. He was hard instantly."Is eight o' clock good for you?" she purred. (Hell, *three* o'clock would've been good for him.) His mouth was so dry he couldn't speak, so he nodded like crazy. She closed her eyes and was about to plant a kiss on his hungry lips, when the bell rang and Noreen left with a wink.

The fish had been reeled in and landed.

CHAPTER THIRTY-FOUR

Friday evening finally arrived. Noreen sat in the living room filing her nails, wearing a terry cloth robe and pink curlers. The heavy robe was stifling in the summer heat, but she didn't want to wear anything that might tip her father off that she was going out. She'd planned this night for too long and didn't need any of his craziness screwing it up. Night after night, she had lay in bed carefully planning her "date" with Jared. The timing *had* to be *exactly* right. She went over everything once more in her mind: Today was Friday and yesterday was the first of the month. Her father always went out on Friday night, but the first of the month was double insurance, because he got his government check and he never missed the chance to show off in front of his drinking buddies when he had money. But for some reason, he didn't seem to be in any hurry to go out tonight. With his feet splayed out in front of him, he was sitting on the sofa guzzling a bottle of gin he'd found somewhere. Thank God the bottle was almost empty.

Looking over at her, he belched loudly and she knew nothing good was on his mind. She didn't want to do anything to set him off, so she ignored him and continued filing her nails.

"You think you're so high an' mighty sittin' over there, don't'cha!" he slurred. Out of the corner of her eye, she saw him reach down and rub his crotch. Squeezing himself obscenely, he yelled, "Think I can't take you right now? Huh, DO ya?" She fought to stay calm by covering her anxiety with cold indifference, but every fiber of her being was on full alert. "You little bitch!" he snarled. "I'll *teach* you to ignore me! I'm comin' over there an' rippin' that robe off ya...then I'm gonna get me some'a that pussy you been givin' away. Hah -you thought I didn't know, didn't ya. Well, I know. I know everything, ya li'l slut." Throwing the now empty bottle on the floor, he staggered to his feet and unzipped his pants. The sound raked over her last nerve like fingernails on a blackboard. He chuckled and pulled out his penis. Taking a step in her direction, he waved it at her. "This is what you want, ain't it," he laughed. "Yeah...them boys can't give ya what a *man* can!" Noreen stopped filing her nails and threw her head back with an ugly laugh. Then she stopped laughing abruptly and looked at him with narrowed eyes. "Take one more step," she said in a low deadly voice, "and I'll cut off your *manly* joke of a pecker and cram it down your throat so fast, you won't even bleed for ten minutes." She glared at him with piercing eyes cold as steel, while casually slipping her hand into the pocket of her robe. Without taking her eyes off him, she pulled the filet knife out with all the ease of melted butter. Seeing the sharp blade made his hardening penis deflate like a balloon, and scratching his grubby cheek thoughtfully, he said unconvincingly, "Ah ain't scared'a you!"

"Then c'mon," she said. "I'd like nothing better than to cut your balls off. I ain't like ma, ya know. I'll kill ya!" She meant it --and he knew it. He stood there for a moment not knowing what to do. Noreen narrowed her eyes at him." Don't you have some place to be, *old* man?"

His face darkened with rage. "Meybe I do an' meybe I don't! An' meybe I'll jest stay *here* tonight."

"Shit," she thought. "I gotta back off before I screw this up." She shrugged nonchalantly. "Suit yourself...but you're gonna get awful thirsty." She knew if she planted that thought in his burned out brain, he'd think about it a minute and knowing there wasn't any booze in the house, he'd get up and leave. He was so predictable -like that dog she'd heard about in school that drooled every time some guy rang a bell. His face turned beet red with anger, making even more sweat roll down his neck. "I'll go out when I damned well want to," he yelled. "Ain't NObody gonna tell me what'ta do in my OWN house!"

"Careful, *old* man –you don't wanna give yourself a stroke." (She hoped he would stroke out with all that unspent money still in his pockets.) She glanced around the living room. "An' you call this shack a house?" That pushed him over the edge. He came at her, but Noreen was ready and with all the skill of a professional stripper, she slowly uncurled a long leg. Her robe fell open exposing the limb all the way up to her thigh. He stopped dead and stared openly as she uncurled the other leg and pushed herself up from the chair. He swallowed hard. God, he *hated* her for making him so damned crazy and not being able to have her. Even in hair curlers, she was beautiful.

Noreen loved having this control over him. She *wanted* to antagonize him and reveled in his torture. If she'd had the physical ability, she would've wrung every last drop of desire out of his filthy body then stomped on it, leaving him a quivering mass on the floor. Moving towards him like a cat, she flexed the fingers holding the knife before slowly winding them one-by-one around the handle. Her eyes glowed menacingly with pure hatred and each step made him quiver. The knife...the danger...it was all so exciting -but it also scared the pee out of him. When she was less than a foot away, she curled her hand tightly around the handle and gripped the knife close against her chest. She was a demon ready to strike at the slightest provocation.

He put on his hat and backed out the door. As the screen door banged shut, she doubled over in laughter -his pecker was still hanging out. Then she stopped laughing and hurried out on the porch to see if he was really gone. After making sure he was nowhere in sight, she ran back to her bedroom tearing the curlers out of her hair. She was just pulling on her dress when she heard the steps of Jared coming up the front porch. She stopped what she was doing and her eyes went to the old wind-up clock next to her bed. It was only twenty-two minutes past seven. Damn! She hadn't planned on Jared coming *early*.

Shit! Noreen couldn't *believe* they hadn't run into each other.

CHAPTER THIRTY-FIVE

With his heart in his throat and flowers gripped firmly in his hand, Jared walked across the porch. It was too hot for a suit and his armpits were already soaking through his coat. The shirt was choking the life out of him and rivers of sweat ran down his face soaking the collar. He wanted to take the damned thing off; it was worse than his football uniform -bulky shoulder pads and all. He tugged hard at the damp collar before knocking on the screen door. When no one came to the door he knocked again, but still got no response. Afraid that he'd been stood up, he peered through the torn screen and saw a fairly neat but shabby living room. A quilt tried to hide the sagging couch while a threadbare rug barely covered a scarred wooden floor. The only source of light came through the badly tilted shade of a lamp next to the couch. Other than that, it was dark and empty. He shuffled his feet, sighed, and knocked again.

Noreen heard him the first time, but kept him waiting, wanting to milk every bit of anxiety she could. When he knocked for the third time, she picked up a silver hairbrush and slowly ran it through her hair. The brush was her most treasured possession. It had belonged to her mother. She held it a moment before laying it down then she stood up for one last look. Having spent as much as she dared out of her savings on a cheap (but extremely flimsy) white peasant dress she'd found in a catalog, Noreen looked beautiful. The dress was made in Mexico from an almost transparent gauzy cotton material with lots of heavy cotton lace around the low cut bodice. She instinctively knew white would make her look virginal and irresistible -especially since it was *all* she wore. Noreen also knew she'd probably never wear this dress again -but if things went right, *once* would be all she'd need.

Again, a knock came from the front door –but this time it was more insistent.

"Coming, coming," she called casually. Squaring back her shoulders, she took a deep breath and said softly, "Tonight is for us, Mama. It's payback an' *boy*! IS that old bastard gonna PAY!"

Noreen left the bedroom, making sure to walk past the lamp in the darkened living room. The lamp had been left on solely to silhouette her body and Jared watched her glide towards him with a tightening in his chest. God, it was like she had nothing on. She stopped inside the screen door letting him take in the full effect. Maybe it was because they weren't in the usual surroundings of school that made the night turn magical, but Noreen looked so stunningly gorgeous that his already stressed hormones went into overdrive.

"H-Hello, N-Noreen," he gulped. The screen door screeched when she pushed it open and walked out into the moonlight. "Hello, Jared," she said in a low voice. "It's nice to see you. I was afraid you wouldn't be able to...come." She smiled at the double meaning of her sentence.

Suddenly remembering the flowers, he looked down at his hands. "Here. These...are for you." She took the flowers, which were half dead from the death grip of his hot sweaty hand. Noreen recognized the "flowers" from the weeds that grew around her house, but said nothing about it. She brushed them past her nose and smiled. Jared watched, unable to move. Her breasts were clearly visible in the moonlight and her nipples stood out pink and hard against the filmy whiteness. Noreen didn't give him time to recover as she moved in for the kill. She reached down and taking his clammy hand in hers, asked, "Would you like to come over here and sit in the swing?" Moving closer, she batted her long lashes. "It's so...*hot*...indoors," she said, enunciating the word. Still unable to move, Jared's Adam's apple bobbed up and down as he swallowed. He nodded and she led him to the swing. After they sat down, Noreen gently pushed it back and forth with her foot. She spoke to him, but he didn't hear a word. Her voice was like soft wind chimes and the sound of it made his spine tingle. It was absolutely all he could do to keep from raping her. "So," she was saying, "how do you like..."

"Noreen," he blurted out. "I-I'-"

Knowing he wasn't able to hold off for another minute, Noreen turned and pulled him to her. Her tongue gently wound its way around his and the hairs on the back of his neck stood up. Lord God –where had she learned to kiss like that? The sensation sent tiny convulsions through him. Noreen was aware of how little it would take to get Jared to the point of no return, but she had to pace things and keep total control. It was imperative that she unleashed Jared at the precise moment of her father's return. Her whole plan depended on her making sure he caught them in the act. But Jared was getting worked up too fast and it was taking every bit of her strength to control him. As Noreen grappled with him, she wondered where her drunken asshole of a father was. If he didn't get here soon, the "Raging Bull" would be finished and she'd have to kill the bastard herself. Jared was turning into a wild man and she was getting annoyed with all this bullshit. His hands flew out of hers every time she grabbed them and she wondered how much longer it'd be before she'd have to deck him.

Just as Jared had her pinned up against the chain of the swing, Noreen got a glimpse of someone coming towards them through the shadows of the trees in the moonlight. As soon as she recognized it was her old man, her heart quickened and she let go of Jared's hands. "Thank God, it's Showtime," she thought."

Her sudden cooperativeness startled him, but Jared was so thrilled at having his hands free that he grabbed her around the waist. Excited beyond all reason now, he pulled her down and Noreen helped by sliding under him until their pelvises were exactly face-to-face (so to speak.) Before he had time to react, she took his face in both hands and kissed him hard. A fire surged up his loins and he groped under her dress -which was magically up around her waist. Noreen relaxed and spread her legs wide open, wrapping them around his hips and thrusting her pelvis upward. She heard the zipper of his pants open and felt the throbbing heat of his rock-hard penis hit her leg. Grabbing his butt with both hands, Noreen pulled him to her and whispered, "Now Jared!"

Meantime, Jared was still reeling from finding out Noreen didn't have any panties on. And he *NEVER* expected the sensation he got when his fingers touched her naked skin. (Also he'd never known a girl who didn't wear panties.) While he fumbled around, Noreen saw her father weaving his way up the steps. "Don't fuck around, Jared," c'mon-do it!" Noreen took a quick glance over at the steps. Her father was just putting his foot onto the porch. Noreen screamed angrily, "<u>DO</u> <u>IT</u> <u>NOW, JARED</u>!"

Her use of the "F" word was the final inflammatory straw. Ripping the zipper off its track, Jared pulled his pants apart and lined his penis up for a touchdown. Heaven was just this close when it hit the fan. Her father heard her voice and growled, "Noreen, is that you?" When he saw them lying there on the swing, he went ballistic. He raced across the porch and yanked Noreen out of Jared's arms by her hair. He backhanded her across the face four or five times so hard it drew blood, then he roughly threw her down the steps. She fell off backwards landing hard in the dirt, but felt no pain. "WHAT'D I TELL YOU, GIRL, IF'N I EVER FOUND YOU FUCKING SOME BOY!" he screamed.

With his prick still standing at full attention a horrified Jared stared at Noreen on the ground. One second she was underneath him, the next, she was lying at the bottom of the steps with fresh blood down the front of her now bunched-up white dress exposing a triangle of jet black hair. (Noreen may have been a blonde, but she didn't come by it naturally.) This was too much. Jared quickly ran his hand through his hair trying to think of something. His confused hormones now surged with white-hot anger mixed in with unrequited passion. He wasn't sure what to do; it was like being on the football field with the score tied and thirty seconds to go for the Championship. For just a split second, he looked around for his coach to give him the next play.

But as far as Noreen was concerned, he was a stupid ox and she was getting pissed at his inaction. "What the hell good is he to me if the idiot just sits there and doesn't DO anything?" she thought angrily. She balled up both hands in the dirt; time was passing, damn it –along with this small window of opportunity. If her father suddenly caught wind of what she really had in mind, he'd dash into the house and get his shotgun. Then things would be... Noreen couldn't even bring herself to think about what they'd be.

It *was* true that Jared was slow witted, but he was so dumbfounded by the sudden turn of events that he was unable to react to the situation. Refusing to let anything ruin her carefully laid plans for this night, Noreen knew she had to think of something fast to light a fire under that muscular ass of his. Although her father was nowhere near her Noreen screamed, "No, NO! *Please* Jared, *help* me –don't let him hit me again!" Lowering her face, she wailed loudly and started crying fake tears. Hearing that, Jared lunged out of the swing. His feet barely touched the porch as he flew off tackling the man with all the bone crunching horror of a locomotive. Before the older man had time to get air back in his lungs, Jared picked him up over his head and body slammed him to the ground. The two of them rolled around in the dirt between two rusted out Fords, but her father was no match for the younger stronger boy. When he tried to get up, Jared quickly fell to his knees and pinned him down. Straddling him, Jared pounded the son-of-a-bitch without mercy. Noreen's eyes sparkled in the darkness as she watched, taking sadistic delight in every bone-crushing blow. Blood splattered everywhere like a wet sponge as Jared beat her father to a pulp. He was in a blind rage now that *nothing* could stop –and Noreen didn't want it to.

The fight was so intense that it was over in less than twenty minutes. When Jared was finally spent, he got up and gave the old man one final kick to the ribs, leaving him in terrible pain and gasping for breath. Noreen got up to her knees and pushed the hair out of her eyes. A little smile crossed her bloody lips as she looked at her father lying there in the moonlight. She'd never seen anything like Jared. He'd stomped, body slammed, and beaten him beyond her wildest expectations. Noreen had waited a lifetime to see her father finally *know* what it was like to be on the receiving end of a beating. His crumpled body looked like it had been hit by an eighteen-wheeler and she hoped the bastard was dead.

Jared came over and picked Noreen up in his arms. Putting her arms around his neck, she whimpered softly and nuzzled her head against his shoulder. He tenderly carried her up the steps into the house, never seeing the smile on her lips.

CHAPTER THIRTY-SIX

Jared didn't kill Noreen's father, but he did put him in the hospital for six months—in a full body cast no less. Noreen never visited him, so naturally when he finally got out he wasn't surprised to find that she was long gone -along with his shack -which she burned to the ground just before she left that night with Jared.

The day after they left, Noreen married Jared in that white bloody dress and never looked back.

I met Noreen for the first time about two months after I opened this place. I knew nothing about her past *or* present much less that she'd ever been married, so not knowing about Jared, I have no idea whatever happened to him. She just showed up here one night and has made it her home ever since. From the git-go the only two things I know about her, are that she is the most aggravating woman I've ever met and that she hates all women. Harley was right when he said Noreen *wasn't* going to take to Sam -and I wasn't looking forward to the night she walked in and saw her. I must have been out of my mind to let Sam talk me into hiring her to work here.

I tried to put it out of my mind, but it was like waiting for the "other shoe" to drop. Every time the door opened my anxiety level went up until sure enough, one night Noreen sashayed in. The door swung open and she walked in with her "rock 'n roll" hips swaying in demand that everyone stop and look. She reminded me of the opening shot in "Saturday Night Fever" with John Travolta. All that was missing was the Bee Gees singing "Stayin' Alive."

Like the reigning Queen Bee she was, her very presence commanded everyone stop what they were doing and swivel around to see her. As she strutted past her "public, Noreen waved her four-inch blood red nails with big smile and "Hey y'all." I could see her blue day-glo metallic eye shadow from clear across the room. The cheap jacket she wore made out of bunny fur made her shoulders look like Joan Crawford. Noreen finished off this Savadore Dahli nightmare with a red micro miniskirt over black fishnet stockings covering mile-long legs in thigh-high hooker boots. Completing this ensemble was a bright yellow t-shirt that tried to contain her huge breast. Noreen had a body that looked like Frank Frazetta himself designed it, so it didn't much matter if she had any fashion sense. (Or any *other* kind, for that matter.) And I'm not a big fan of killing animals for any reason other than necessary -especially not for their fur, so when I saw that jacket I wanted to rip it off her. She came straight over to me.

"Hi ya, Mac. Miss me?"

"Like hemorrhagic fever," I answered.

"Yeah, well, gimme a...tequila and...uh, what goes with tequila?"

"Salt works well," I said irritably.

"Nooo, no salt. Gotta watch my figure so others will." She found that terribly hilarious and died laughing.

"You're such a riot," I said dryly. "And since when do you drink tequila, anyway?" I wanted to know. Adjusting her fanny on the stool, she ignored my question and smiled, "Like my new coat?" I knew she was fishing for compliments and stood there with a glass in my hand waiting for her to make up her mind what she wanted to drink. "Not particularly..." I said.

"Why??" she frowned.

"Because," I said, "NO ONE looks good in dead animal skin!" (Then I recalled the image of Raquel Welsh's first poster.) "Okay," I conceded reluctantly, "with *one* exception maybe."

"Screw you!" she snorted, "I think it's beautiful -an' where's my drink?" I leaned over and slammed the glass down on top of the bar. "Listen, you twit! Do you have ANY idea what they do to animals to get their fur?" Without waiting for an answer, I proceeded to tell her all about steel traps, poachers, China's disregard for ALL animal life throwing in drift nets, vivisection, and making damned sure to end with a very vivid picture of the annual baby seal massacre.

Her face went ashen.

"STOP IT!" she cried. "GOD, you are the BIGGEST, meanest, liar, Mac!" She looked down at the coat like it was alive.

"Yeah, right!" I huffed. "And little animals just LOVE to be bred for their fur; having a white hot rod shoved up their ass while they're still alive so they can be skinned."

She stared at me horrified. "*WHY* are you making this up?" she yelled. "N-Next you-you'll be tellin' me that-that...people eat HORSES or somethin'."

"They do."

She frowned. "You are a seriously sick man, Mac."

I picked up the glass again. "Noreen," I asked tonelessly, "what do you want to drink?"

"A gin fizz," she answered sarcastically. "If I ain't killing anything." I was taken back; not by her sarcasm, but by her order. She'd never ordered a gin fizz before. Ignoring both, I said, "Okay...one margarita coming right up."

"Hey, I didn't order that," she protested. "I said I wanted a gin fizz! I changed my mind on tequila. Its cactus juice and I ain't killing no cactus."

"You DON'T have a CLUE as to what a gin fizz *IS*!" I shouted. "And I do NOT have any eggs to make one with -IF I ever was going to make one at all -which I am NOT!"

"You don't make it with eggs," she argued. "You make it with some pink stuff!"

"Yes, you DO," I argued right back. "A gin fizz takes raw egg whites!"

The color, both artificial and real, drained away from her face. "Raw?" she gulped.

"Yeah...aborted, fuzzy little chicks," I frowned.

"W-Well, w-why is it pink?" she asked weakly.

99

"Coloring, Noreen," I said. "Like your face."

I stopped yelling at her and took a deep breath. I knew I was just doing it because I dreaded the real problem -which magically appeared when Sam came up to the bar just then and called out an order. "I need two Jack Daniel's straight up and four Coors with heads on 'em," she said.

She had her head down looking at the napkin she'd written the order on. She held the napkin up and squinted. "Oh yeah, and one tequila –an' make it a double so I don't have to keep goin' back."

And there it was -the end of Life as I knew it. Noreen's head swiveled around like a rocket. Her eyebrows shot straight up and she honed in on Sam like a SCUD missile. I held my breath and quickly gave Sam her order. She walked away without ever noticing Noreen. Watching Sam like a hawk, Noreen's overly massacred eyes bored holes into Sam's back as she walked away. Snapping her head back to me, she narrowed her eyes and gave me a look that made the blood freeze in my veins. "*WHO* the hell is THAT?" she demanded hotly.

I didn't answer right away and she said, "I wanna know who that is, Mac!"

"Yeah -and I wanna know if we'll ever see Connie Chung again," I retorted without much conviction. I tried to sound blasé, but The Moment of Truth had arrived and I was standing on Ground Zero. There weren't any single females above the age of ten around here so Noreen pretty much cornered the market, but now Sam was a threat to her Queen Bee crown. And Noreen *hated* competition. "*WHO* IS SHE??" Noreen demanded again. I hesitated, giving serious thought to telling her I had no idea, but knowing that wouldn't work, I said, "Oh, just somebody I hired to wait on tables. It's just temporary," I repeated, "you know, not anything permanent." (I excel in redundancy.) Noreen shot daggers at me and my eye began to twitch. "It's my place, Noreen," I said, in between winking at her. "An' if I want to hire someone to help out, I will."

I tried to sound defiant, but Noreen didn't back off one bit. She glared at me with such venom I thought the twitch would become an all-out epileptic seizure. I knew she was about to erupt when thank God, Doug Metcalf roared up. I was never so glad to see anyone before in my whole life. "Doug!" I beamed, "Doug, Doug, *DOUGIE*! It is SOOO GOOD to SEE you, ol' friend...what'll ya have, buddy? Just name it! Anything at all...it's on th' house!"

Doug looked at me like I'd lost my ever lovin' mind, but as long as I was supplying free booze, he didn't question it. "Hi ya, Mac...uh gosh, I-I'm glad to see you too." He looked over and grinned at Noreen, who stuck her nose up in the air. Looking back at me he said, "Uh, gimme a double Jack Daniel's and a Coors Light."

"DON'T push it, pal," I mumbled under my breath, but his attention was already back on Noreen.

"Hi ya, Noreen! Where ya been, baby? I been lookin' everywhere for ya."

"Busy," she sniffed impassively. I gave Doug his order as he frowned at her obvious indifference. He took a long sip of J.D. and didn't say anything else, but I knew he wasn't giving up yet. The two of them sat there in total silence until the band struck up a slow dance. Doug jumped off his bar stool. His leather jacket creaked like –well, like a leather jacket. "Let's DANCE, Noreen!" Grabbing her by the hand, she tried to jerk away but he held on tight. He hadn't seen the object of his burning love in over three weeks now and his hormones were NOT going to be denied any longer. Reluctantly, Noreen got up, tossed down her drink while boring two holes in my skull. "I'm not finished with YOU, Mac," she warned.

"Yeah," I sighed. "I figured that."

I watched them go out on the dance floor. Doug took her in his arms and pulled her to his chest. He whirled Noreen around the dance floor with his left arm pumping her right one up and down like an oilrig. They looked like one unit welded at the chest with four be-bopping legs. Apparently this form of dancing is known only to Doug, a few cavemen, and a guy I went through ninth grade with. I was watching the spectacle with all the fascination of a train wreck, when Sam's voice interrupted. "Hey, Mac -you asleep?" she asked. "I called out my order twice-what's up?" I absently wiped at my mouth with the back of my hand. "Uh, sorry Sam, I didn't hear you -what'd you want?" She called out the order again. I nodded and got her drinks. I set them on her tray and she asked if I was all right. (Of course I wasn't "all right." I wanted to bolt out the door and run as far away as I could, but escape was totally out of the question.) "Yeah," I said. "I'm fine." She nodded and left again.

Amazingly, Doug managed to keep Noreen out on the dance floor for the next forty-five minutes.

I watched closely and wondered how much longer it'd be until Sam accidentally got too close. Like every predator, the female of the species is the most deadly. Noreen wasn't going to wait for a formal introduction before she struck-all she'd need was opportunity; which simply meant Sam only had to wander within hair pulling distance.

CHAPTER THIRTY-SEVEN

Thankfully Sam managed to stay out of Noreen's reach and the night passed without incident. But I knew things weren't over. Two days passed without Noreen coming in and I sighed in relief. Maybe she was in a charitable mood and Doug had scored after all.

On Tuesday, Legrand surprised me when he came in around noon. I hadn't seen him in all weekend and wondered what happened with the trailer I wanted to buy. "Hi Mac, sorry to take so long in getting back to you about th' trailer, but I had to run up to Houston for three days." He came up and sat down at the bar. I got him a beer. "Thanks, I need this after three days up there. Houston has th' absolutely worst traffic on earth."

"No problem, Legrand. Did you ever get in touch with the guy?"

"I did," he nodded. "Real nice guy, too. Name's Mason de Witt. He's a Cajun from just outside New Orleans."

"An' did you ask him about th' trailer?"

He nodded again. "Yep, an' he said to tell you you can have th' whole thing for eight thousand –furniture an' all."

"EIGHT thousand," I cried. "That's crazy!"

Legrand finished his beer and got up. "'Specially when you consider it's practically brand new an' cost over sixty *without* th' furniture. I think they soak ya for another twenty when you want it furnished."

"Listen, Legrand," I grinned. "Get him in here asap an' let me write that man a check. He can take it right across th' street an' cash it."

"So, you got th' money an' don't need me?" I nodded. He slapped the bar and said, "Good for you, Mac. I should be hearin' from him in a day or two. I'll send him right over when I see him." After he left, I stood there in disbelief. If the trailer was anything like Legrand said it was, eight thousand was a steal and I was thrilled to know I could afford it. I'd saved everything the bar had earned, mostly because there wasn't anything to spend it on out here and I never went anywhere. A stranger came in Friday afternoon and introduced himself. "Hi, I'm Mason de Witt," he said, shaking my hand. I grinned. "Mr. De Witt, it is so damned nice to meet you –can I get you a beer or somethin'?" He shook his head. "No thanks, I'll be leavin' these parts next week an' I gotta get on back an' pack up all the equipment. I just came by to meet you and see when you'd like the mobile home delivered."

"Anytime you can get it here," I smiled.

"An' where do you want it set up?"

"About ten or fifteen feet behind th' bar?"

"Okay," he nodded. "But it should be set up about twenty feet away. You got a septic tank?"

"Yeah," I nodded. "I just need to run a line into it from the trailer once it gets here."

"Sounds good," he said. "I'll have my guys bring it 'round after next weekend. It's th' earliest I can get a truck out here to move it -is that all right?"

"Anytime that's good for you, is fine with me."

"Then I guess that's it...unless you can think of anything else?"

"Can I give you the check for it now?" I asked.

"Sure...or you can wait 'til next week."

"I'd rather do it now. You can cash it at th' bank across th' street. Eight thousand? Right?"

"If that's agreeable with you," he said.

"Mister de Witt," I grinned, "it is more than agreeable! I feel like I should have a mask an' gun while I write out this check."

"Believe it or not," he laughed, "you're doing me a great favor taking it off my hands. Th' Department would only sell it for ten cents on the dollar an' of course I have to turn th' money over to them, but it's a real nice mobile home. It has carpeting, a big bay window in front an' although it only has one bath, its got a separate shower from the tub. Th' master bedroom is huge and takes up th' whole back end of the place."

"I can't wait! See you next Monday." I handed him the check and he stuck it in his pocket.

"I won't be here Monday, but my guys will," he said, shaking my hand. "Pleasure doin' business with ya, Mac –an' enjoy your new home."

"Thank you, Mason!"

I was so excited that I called Legrand right after he left. I told him I'd paid for the trailer and it would be here a week from Monday. Legrand said he'd be here to help get it set up and tie in the plumbing to the septic tank.

"Will th' septic tank be large enough to take care of th' bar an' th' trailer?" I asked.

"Yeah, I put in th' largest one I could figurin' you'd want to do somethin' like this one day."

"Great...let's celebrate over a beer later."

"See ya in an hour," he said and we hung up.

CHAPTER THIRTY-EIGHT

A week later, the trailer arrived just as Mason said it would.

Legrand brought his guys over to help get it off the truck and between all of us, we got it tied down just before the sun set. It was well after dark by the time the truck left and too late to tie into the septic tank, so Legrand said he'd be back the next day to do the plumbing. The guys were beat and I told everyone to come inside -drinks were on the house. I threw the keys to Legand and told him to play bartender until I got back. He asked where I was going, and I told him to take a look at my new home. He told me it wasn't quite ready for anyone to go in yet, but I said I didn't care –and running up the makeshift steps, I opened the door. Inside the small foyer, a hat rack hung on the wall next to a coat closet with little table for your keys. I went in the living room -and just like Mason said there was a bay window at the end. The carpet and drapes were a nice shade of green. The living room faced west towards the mountains and dark wooden mini-blinds covering the floor-to-ceiling bay windows had been tilted to defuse late afternoon sunlight.

The living room was bigger that I'd expected and the walls were drywall instead of the old wood paneling. A plain square end table sat next to an overstuffed chair with a lamp and two books on top. I wondered how they plugged in a lamp out in the middle of the room and saw a socket built into the floor. Ingenious. The living room had been painted a light terra cotta to match the rust orange sofa, while the dining room was sort of Army khaki green. I liked the idea of dry wall. The painted walls made it feel like a regular house. A window in the fairly good-size dining room faced south towards Mexico. A single red shaded light fixture hung over a green Formica table. The lamp's red shade looked nice with the window's simple red curtains and the khaki green walls. The kitchen was just beyond the dining room and had no windows and had been painted bright sunny yellow to compensate, I guess. The kitchen was long and not very wide, but it had all the appliances; a stove with oven and four burners, and a microwave overhead. Three bright red and yellow Mexican pottery canisters sat on top of butcher block Formica counters next to a double stainless sink. The counters were so spotlessly clean that I, for a brief moment, wondered about Mason. Maybe he was a closet cook who wanted to be a French chef. Noticing a dishwasher in between the stove and the refrigerator, I took a peek inside out of curiosity. Mason had never used it. Smiling, I closed the door, no longer worried about his manhood. Opening the overhead cabinets, I found dishes, glasses and bowls all neatly stacked inside. In the drawers, I saw a full set of flatware, a set of knives in another, and a few pots, pans, and skillet in the cabinets underneath. It was clear that Mason must've never eaten here. Can't says I blame him; I hate cooking for myself. I left the kitchen to go check out the rest of the place.

The trailer had two bedrooms –one for guests and the other the master. The spare bedroom was located at the end of the carpeted hall next to the bathroom. The bedroom wasn't very big, but had a window to keep it from feeling totally claustrophobic and I knew the builders had kept it small for extra footage in the living room and master bedroom. However, it was plenty big enough to hold a twin bed and small chest of drawers comfortably if I decided to turn it into a guest room. The bathroom was plenty big and conveniently located in between the spare bedroom and the master –which was on the end. There was a window over the tub, separate shower stall and wrought iron linen rack over the toilet. Across from the toilet were two sinks beneath a pair of mirrored medicine cabinets. The walls were wallpapered in a light beige and pale green geometric design.

I saved the master bedroom for last -and wasn't disappointed.

The bedroom was furnished in mission-style furniture, insuring that I could easily spend the next two-thirds of my life in here (and if it wasn't two-thirds, I'd make it that.) The focal point was a queen size bed centered beneath five windows going all the way across the back end of the trailer. The windows had no curtains; only dark sage-green mini-blinds. To the right of the bed was a nightstand with a clock and lamp. Across from the bed, three extra-large drawers occupied a simple wooden bureau, with a picture hanging over it of three cows grazing in a meadow. I could almost feel the soft cool grass beneath my bare feet. Everything in here took me back to my Amish roots and seemed to welcome me. Somehow Mason had even found a handmade quilt to go over the bed; which I couldn't believe he'd leave, but was glad he did. The quilt's squares of many colors were the very thing that made this room come together.

The closet was another surprise; there was plenty of room for my clothes and more. I was anxious to move in and wanted to do it tonight, but had to wait for Legrand to hook into the septic tank -unless...hmmm. There *was* a back door in the hall just across from the bathroom; I *could* sleep here and just open the door if I... Nah, what was I thinking? I shook my head and went down the hall to go meet the guys inside the bar. As I locked up, I couldn't believe the change of direction my life had taken and thought about something my father used to say. He'd say, "Mac, if you want to make God laugh -just tell Him your plans." I didn't understand the meaning of that until now. I looked back at the way I *thought* my life would go, only to see it end up in near death. No, this was the way to go. There wasn't a drug in the world that could make you feel more incredibly alive than having your life straightened out -and your very own home.

CHAPTER THIRTY-NINE

I thought it would take Legrand longer to tie into the septic tank, but he finished digging the drain and hooking up in less than two hours. However, he did come up with another problem I hadn't thought of. "What about electricity?" he asked.

"Right, I forgot about that," I said. "How do I get it on?"

"It shouldn't be a problem," he said pointing to the pole for the bar. "We'll just run a line over to that pole from the trailer, but you'll have to call the electric company and tell them about it. They'll wonder why the sudden spike in power an' have to come out an' put in a separate meter."

"And is that gonna cause me problems –like having no permit for this thing?"

"Just tell them how you got it from D.O.T. There should be one on it already."

I nodded and asked Legrand if he'd like to come in and see the place.

"Yeah –let's have a look see," he said and I unlocked the door. I took him all through the trailer and showed him all the things Mason had left for me, like dishes, flatware and pots and pans. Like me, he loved the colorful walls, bay window and especially liked the master bedroom. "Man, I cannot believe what a deal you got on this thing."

"I owe it all to you, really. In fact I owe you–"

He held up his hand and cut me off. "Don't start thankin' me, Mac. Everything I've done has been something' you needed and I knew how to do. For whatever reason, I strongly believe that God puts us where we're needed to help each other."

"Yeah, but I haven't done anything but take. I can't ride a horse or round up cattle or wire a fence. But, if you ever need a lost cause war fought…I'm your man."

Legrand smiled. "I'll bare that in mind."

When we were outside again, I asked, "Don't I have to have some sort of tag for this thing?"

"Already has one," he said squatting down and pointing to the frame underneath the bay window. "See? There it is." I bent down to look and sure enough, there it was.

Standing up again, Legrand said, "I'll call my electrician and have him come out to take care of wiring you up soon as possible. He stays pretty busy so you may not have any electricity for a while."

"Whenever he can," I said. "As long as I have a working bathroom now, I'll move my clothes and shaving gear in after work tonight. It'll be a relief to let Sam have th' whole storeroom to herself."

"You mean you been sleepin' in there on th' floor all this time?"

I shook my head. "Not *in* there, but just outside."

"Say –where is Sam, anyway? I ain't seen her around..."

"She caught a ride with Harley after he mentioned that he had to go into one'a th' border towns for some special fencing wire. She needed to get away an' I was tied up out here, so th' timing was good."

"And you been sleepin' on th' *floor* all this time? Man, your back must be killin' you."

"Let's just say, that queen size bed is sure gonna feel good."

"Yeah, I imagine it will," he said. "What'll you do if you need a light?"

"By th' time I close up, all I wanna do is hit th' hay, but I have a battery powered Coleman lantern I can set next to the bed in case I need it."

"A Coleman is okay -just don't light any candles." I assured him I really wasn't a "candle kind of person," and we said goodbye and I opened the bar.

CHAPTER FORTY

I was at the cash register when somebody yelled that there was a bus outside. I looked up and saw six guys troop through the front door, wearing enough sequins to dazzle the city of Seattle. Right off, I knew they were Country and Western musicians. You can always tell by the way every lock of hair is firmly in place, like they own stock in the hair spray industry. (Rock musicians do their hair with a Waring blender.)

Country pickers are as comfortable in a roadhouse as warts on a toad and came in like they owned the place. Like gods descending Olympus, they smiled at the folks gushing over their arrival, and although we get them in here on a regular basis, everybody is still awed by their presence. My pathetic little band proudly moved over to make room, always ready to give up their stage. (They were as star struck as anybody.)

About the same time they came in, Noreen came in angrily arguing with Doug on her heels. I could see she was already in a bad mood and frowned, not wanting to go through the third degree with her on Sam again. She hadn't noticed the musicians yet, but I knew as soon as she did, Doug would be history. Meantime, she came straight over to me. "Where's that girl?" she demanded. "You get rid'a her?"

"Well, why don't you just get right to th' point, Noreen? Don't beat around th' bush –what's on your mind?" She narrowed her eyes in a hard stare. "You fire her, Mac?"

Of course I hadn't fired her. In fact, Harley had dropped Sam off around 4 o'clock that afternoon and she was over on the opposite side of the room taking care of customers. I was about to tell Noreen all that when loud music blasted through the room, drowning out my voice. Since it's a fact of physics that two things can't occupy the same space at the same time, my lips moved but you couldn't hear one word. Which was lucky for me, because Noreen wasn't even looking at me anymore.

As soon as that first chord vibrated the walls, Noreen's head swiveled around like a mongoose. The instant she saw all those gorgeous men on stage, her face lit up and she forgot all about me, Sam <u>and</u> Doug.

I whispered, "Thank you, Lord." There were enough good-looking musicians in this group to keep Noreen's one-track mind busy for the rest of the night. Ever predictable where men are concerned, I KNEW she'd burn up her one brain cell trying to decide on which one to take home with her for the night. And sure enough, before you could say, "Yeehaw," Noreen was *gone* and I was off the hook. In the meantime, Doug had been talking to someone sitting next to him. When he turned around and saw the empty bar stool, his face went ashen. He looked around for her, but by the time he realized she had split without so much as a goodbye, the crowd had the gap closed behind her like the Red Sea. His eyes darkened and he got deathly quiet. His romantic plans had, once again, been ripped off. He slowly turned back to me and I didn't like the look. Usually, Doug is an easy-going guy and I don't know why Noreen loved tormenting him so much. He was above average looking, but to my limited knowledge she never let him touch her. I suppose she ignored him because he had nothing -and she'd had enough of nothing. He never showed much interest in money and was totally content to sleep under the stars in his old bedroll. All he wanted out of life was his bike, the open road and the dream of Noreen riding along with her arms around him. Unfortunately, it just never occurred to Doug that there was NO way Noreen would ever hook-up with him. As far as their goals were concerned, he really WAS from Mars and she was from Venus, although I'm not sure they EITHER one of them had any defined goals. Maybe Noreen didn't know where she was going yet; but she sure as hell knew where she wasn't going.

I looked at Doug and couldn't help feeling sorry for him. I knew just how fast our little dreams could turn into big nightmares. I slammed a glass down on the bar and said, "Here, have double...no -a *triple* Jack." I picked up the bottle and started pouring.

His face turned to stone. "No thanks, Mac," he said darkly. "Not this time..."

"Look Doug, why don't you just let it go," I said, setting the bottle down. "Noreen is Noreen...nobody's ever gonna rope an' brand her. That's just th' way it is. Don't beat yourself up over it."

He didn't answer. Instead he zipped up his jacket and pushed his way out the door. I watched him leave and sighed.

Then I finished pouring the bourbon and drank it myself.

CHAPTER FORTY-ONE

The place was packed and the band was really cooking when I saw it was going on 2:30. I don't know where the guys found girls, but about half of them had dates. As the guys stood in front of the stage with their lanky arms slug around their date's shoulders or two-stepped around the dance floor, I couldn't help but notice that they all looked like Brenda Lee -except one who looked like Sally Field.

I was glad to see everybody so happy and was raking in money as fast as I could pour. Since we've got no city or county codes to adhere to, I let things ride until first light started to peek through the knotholes in the walls. Morning had broken and I sent word up that drinks were on the house and to come on over. It took three more songs before they reluctantly wiped the sweat from their brows and put down their instruments. They came over to the bar and sat down. The audience followed right behind them and packed in three deep. If I got just fifty cents for every time the word "great" was used, I could have retired for the rest of my life.

It wasn't until I was pouring seconds that I realized I hadn't seen the guitar player. I looked up and down the bar, but when I didn't see him, I said to the bass player, "Ain't one'a you guys missin' –where's th' guitar player?" The bass player shrugged indifferently and turned his attention back to some cowboy who was buying the next round. I continued pouring drinks and drawing beers until I looked up and saw the guitar player standing in front of the stage having, what looked to be a deep conversation with Sam. I frowned. The rat. I wondered if he was trying to impress her...being a musician and all. My mood was now as dark and brooding as Doug's. What the hell could he be talking to her about? Whatever it was, Sam kept shaking her head no, like he was asking her something. Suddenly, my eyes widened. Dammit! Was he HITTING on her?

I didn't like this! I went over to the bass player again and said, "Your friend is over there talkin' to my waitress. Is he some kind'a rock 'n roll Romeo?" My tone made it clear I wasn't just making conversation and he was smart enough to pick up on it. He raised his eyebrows and turned around to see what this girl looked like that had me so riled up. Turning back again, he shook his head. "No...Travis is happily married and pretty much keeps to himself when we're on th' road." He picked up his drink. "I'd say he was just talkin'," he shrugged.

"Oh yeah?" I said. "Looks more like he's hittin' on her."

"So what if he is –you married to her or somethin'?"

"Watch your mouth, buddy," I warned. The bass player frowned at all this aggravation and turned around on his stool again. He took a quick glance and started to turn back before doing a double take. "Holy cow!" he cried. "I *flat* DON'T believe it!"

"WHAT?" I demanded. "Don't believe *what*?"

"Man, THAT'S Sammi Jo, Travis is talkin' to. I just FLAT don't believe it!" He called out to the others. "HEY GUYS—look over there, it's Sammi JO!" He jumped off his barstool and hurried off, leaving me to wonder what the hell. "HEY!" I yelled after him. "Come BACK here! How the hell do *YOU* know Sam?" All the musicians turned around. Seeing Sam, every last one of them left their drinks and jumped up to follow after the bass player. The scene looked like a high school reunion between the football team and their favorite cheerleader.

I stood behind the now-empty bar and watched every damned one of them hug Sam with great endearing warmth until I couldn't stand it any longer. I threw the towel down and went over to find out what the hell was going on. Sam saw me coming and pulled away. She told everyone she was sorry, but she had to go. They all protested, but she shook herself free and hurried towards me. Nobody made any attempt to follow after her, but now they all looked as confused as me. I got halfway across the dance floor before she looped her arm through my elbow and spun me around. As she dragged me away from the group, it hadn't escaped me how skillfully she was maneuvering me back to the bar. I said, "Nice intercept, Sam -what's going on?"

"Uh...oh...nothing's going on." she said, making that nervous little gesture women do to the back of their hair. "Just some old friends -what a surprise, huh?" I cocked an eyebrow as she picked up the pace. "Oh, yeah. That's the word, all right...a real surprise." When we reached the bar, I waited for her to let me in on it, but she untied her apron and placed it along with her tray, on top of the bar. To my total shock, she offered no explanation and said good night.

"W-Where're you going...?" I frowned.

"To sleep. And since this is Saturday, I'm off for th' next three days."

She turned to leave but I grabbed her by the arm. "Hold it! If you think I'm gonna wait three days for you to tell me who those guys are, you're *crazy*." She gave me a stony look. "Don't do this, Mac. I'm not in the habit of explaining a damned thing about my life to *anybody*."

My blood was beginning to boil and I guess I was gripping her arm harder than I realized.

Her eyes cut into mine. "Let go of my arm, Mac," she said in an icy tone. I knew it wasn't a request and let go. "Look," she said, rubbing her bicep, "this doesn't concern you. Believe it or not, I had a life before I came here."

"Yeah, an' you ran away."

"I also told you I didn't wanna talk about it! Why are you acting like a jealous teenager?"

Her words hit me like a slap in the face, but she was right; I *was* acting like a jealous teen-ager. Even I couldn't believe my actions. I looked down at the floor. "You're right," I nodded. "I am acting like an idiot. I'm sorry. See you Wednesday." I didn't look at her as she walked away. When I heard the storeroom door close, I looked up again and wondered what the hell had just happened and why I even cared.

CHAPTER FORTY-TWO

True to her word, Sam didn't come in for the next three days and I was left with a million unanswered questions. I also knew damned well that when she did come back, she still wouldn't explain anything. Wednesday evening, she was back to work like nothing ever happened. The customers were still all fired up about the weekend's unexpected concert, but not one word was spoken about it by either of us. Ever.

All that was five weeks ago...and I hadn't stopped thinking about it for one second.

CHAPTER FORTY-THREE

In all that time, I hadn't seen hide nor hair of Noreen and figured she was off again with somebody. Not that I missed her. She'd be back in here soon enough raggin' about Sam. It was just a matter of time until the other shoe dropped on that subject. Noreen was like rabid pit bull when she got hold of something that displeased her -and another female displeased her. So it wasn't a surprise when I heard the door open one afternoon and a voice rake over my back like shards of glass in cold water. "Hi ya, Mac." I turned around and noticed she was smiling like she'd just won the lottery. Could she have forgotten all about Sam? Could I be so fortunate?

She slid her tight little ass across the barstool. "Hello, Noreen," I said warily. "You wanna drink?"

She toyed with her hair and nodded. "Yeah, gimme a margarita."

I fixed her margarita, adding a little extra tequila to help her stay in a good mood.

"I just assumed you didn't want salt with that," I said.

"You assumed right," she answered. "Makes me bloat." I started to ask her what did she think the booze did, but knowing how her brain works I kept my mouth shut.

She sipped on her drink and I said "So, what's got you in such a good mood today?"

She set her drink down and proceeded to tell me where she'd been, showing me the jewelry and new boots her latest sugar daddy had bought her. Finally she got around to Sam. She ordered another margarita and looked around the saloon. "Where's that girl?" she frowned. "I don't see her. She finally wise up an' leave?"

"Okay, Noreen," I said, "let's just go ahead and get this over with. I don't usually defend myself in any decision I make; especially when it concerns my own property, but I know how you feel about this place, so I'm gonna try to explain it to you so that pea-brain of yours can understand." Without waiting for a response, I plowed straight ahead, telling her all about how Sam came in, passed out, and how Doc told me she couldn't be moved, so I nursed her back to health with a lot of help from Juan's mama and ending with how her coming to work here just sort of "evolved."

(I had to explain "evolved.")

The look on her face told me that none of this was sitting well.

"So," she sniffed, "how long is th' little tramp gonna be around?" I closed my eyes and rubbed my forehead. "As long as she wants, Noreen," I said. Opening my eyes again, I added, "And it ain't up for discussion, so get used to it." I was fed up with this whole thing and was about to tell her to get off my back, when two cowboys came in. They came up to the bar and ordered draughts. While I got their beers, the door opened and Doug came in. His face lit up when he saw Noreen and he headed straight over, pulling up the barstool next to her. He must have forgotten their last time in here because he smiled and asked, "Hi baby, what'cha drinking -a margarita?"

I took a deep breath and waited for the poisoned barb of sarcasm I knew was coming.

True to form, Noreen slowly lowered her glass and glared at Doug. Raising a dark thin eyebrow, she said, "No, you weasely little insect...its antifreeze to thaw me out, but it ISN'T working, so beat it-and I mean that literally!" If her words stung, he didn't show it. Instead he folded his hands across the bar and smiled at me. "Yo, Mac, how you been?"

I shrugged. "You know –not good, not bad. Can I get you somethin'?" His cheeks flushed beet red and he shook his head. I knew he didn't have any money but didn't want to ask. "Listen," I said, making up an excuse to give him a freebee without making it obvious. "I got some new beer th' supplier wants me to try. He says he needs to know what th' customers think about it –you feel like helpin' me out by tastin' a glass or two?"

He raised his head and smiled. "Sure, Mac. I'd be glad to."

I got his beer while Noreen continued to ignore him. They both sat there in silence until Doug asked, "So where'd you disappear to th' night you left me sittin' here -you know -that night them sissy musicians came in." And there it was –I was right back to that night again -damn it.

I picked up Doug's empty glass and re-filled it. He thanked me, then turned back to Noreen. She sipped her drink and stared straight ahead. "You took off with one'a them guys, didn't you," he said angrily. Now it was Noreen's turn. She set her glass down and smiled. "Yep, the drummer." Closing her eyes, she said dreamily, "And he was FANNNNTASTIC!" All the blood drained from Doug's face. He glared at Noreen with murderous intent as she went on. "Drummers have the MOST fantastic rhythm and never lose the beat." Her saying that was bad enough, but when she held her arms up and gyrated, Doug blew. He stood up so fast that he knocked over his barstool and the two cowboys turned to look from the other end of the bar. Doug grabbed Noreen by the arm and yanked her around to face him. "You're a no-good slut!" he growled. At that the cowboys got up, but I held up my hand and shook my head. They nodded reluctantly and sat back down.

Meantime, Noreen equaled his icy glare without batting an eye. "Take-your-hand-off-me, you cockroach," she said evenly. The acid in her voice made it clear that she meant it, and Doug slowly removed his hand from her arm. (Actually, I think Attilla the Hun would've let her go.) She stared him down. "Don't you *EVER* do that again mister. You don't OWN me! NOBODY owns me, you *GOT* that!"

Defeated, Doug looked down and nodded.

"Now, GET OUT OF HERE," she screamed.

Like I said before, Doug is an easy-going guy. I wanted to say something in his defense, but he was so beaten down his shoulders slumped and he turned to leave. "Wait a minute Doug," I said. "Before you go, tell me what you thought of th' beer?" Without turning around, his voice broke when he said, "T-Tell your guy it tasted exactly like Coors," –and he went out the door.

I knew then that he'd seen through my ploy on the free beer and it killed me to see how embarrassed and broken he was. Noreen picked up her glass then suddenly started to laugh. Setting her glass back down, she kept it up 'til tears trickled down her face. I was so damned angry at her for destroying Doug like that, that I wanted to slap the crap out of her.

"Did you see th' look on Doug's face," she giggled. "God! It reminded me of my old man's th' night Jared -." She stopped in mid-sentence and her smile disappeared. "Never mind," she finished.

CHAPTER FORTY-FOUR

I wondered who the hell Jared was, but didn't ask. After what Noreen had done to Doug, the last thing I wanted to know about was some other poor schnook she'd castrated. At the moment, I was so mad at Noreen that I couldn't speak. I got down a glass and poured myself a stiff double to keep from strangling her.

By my second re-fill, I'd calmed down enough to hatch an idea. I looked at Noreen, who was on her third margarita, and wondered if I could pump her for some information. Since she'd hooked up with the drummer, I figured he might've said something that would shed some light on this thing with Sam. I strolled over and said nonchalantly, "So, you took off with the drummer from th' group that night, huh?"

Always glad to brag on a conquest, she lit up and said, "Yep...an' he really *was* fantastic."

"Who were those guys –did he happen to mention where they were from?"

She shook her head.

"Well, how come he didn't leave on th' bus with th' rest of them that night? How'd he get to spend a couple'a days with you –didn't he have to play th' next gig?"

Again she shook her head. "No, he was just sittin' in with them on their last date. Their regular drummer was out with the flu. Some agent had him meet them on th' road in his own car, so he didn't ride on th' bus."

I knew less now than before I asked and nodded to hide my disappointment. By her fifth margarita, Noreen's happy mood was back – and thinking I was still interested, she chatted on and on about how great her one-night-stand was as I washed glasses and tried not to listen. Everything was going along on an even keel when the back door opened. My eyes nearly came out of their sockets and I stopped what I was doing as I watched Sam come in with Freeway. "Oh, no," I whispered. "Oh no, no, no!" Sam came straight over to the bar and pulled out a stool two away from Noreen. Freeway curled up beside her on the floor. "Hi, Mac, would you please give Freeway some water?"

Noreen was lost on planet airhead and didn't notice Sam's arrival until she heard the sound of her voice. Turning to look in her direction, her blue-green eyes flashed and narrowed like Snow White's wicked stepmother. I swallowed hard. "Uh, hi Sam." Glancing at Noreen, I added quickly, "I'd like you to meet Noreen." Sam smiled warmly. "Well now, right nice to meet'cha, Noreen," she said, extending her hand. Without taking it, Noreen replied coldly, "Yeah, ain't it." Puzzled by her indifference, Sam looked at me and withdrew her hand. She rolled her eyes like, "Who's THIS nut?"

I cleared my throat loudly. "So...you been out with Freeway?"

She nodded. "Yep. We climbed them big rocks 'way out by that old dry lake bed."

I nodded absently. "Yeah, it's nice out there. Wanna beer?"

"Sure -make it a Michelob Light," she said.

I left to get a mug out of the freezer, getting back as soon as I could. I didn't want to give Noreen any time to start trouble. I set Sam's beer down on the bar then got a bowl of water. Keeping an eye on Noreen, I handed the bowl to Sam and she set it down for Freeway. While she was bent over, Noreen asked hotly, "You married?"

Sitting up again Sam glanced at me then Noreen. Raising her eyebrows questioningly, she said, "Noooo, why?"

"Well, why not?" Noreen demanded. "You gay or somethin'?" I buried my head in my hands. This was not going well. Finally I looked at Sam and tried to change the subject. "You don't work tonight, do you?" Sam said no, but she'd be around if I needed her to. Noreen spoke up. "Excuse me, but am I sitting here, or *what*?" she demanded hotly. Surprised by Noreen's outburst, Sam looked at her. "Is there a problem?" she asked just a tad too sweetly.

"You bet your sweet ASS there is," Noreen shot back.

Noreen was wearing the unfortunate bunny jacket along with her jewelry and new boots. I mention this only because I noticed Sam's look of distain when she saw the fur.

"Well," Sam smiled, still looking at the wretched jacket. "Enlighten me." Noreen turned to me and I explained. "That means, tell her what's on your mind, Noreen"...and my life, pathetic as it was, flashed before me. But Sam was getting into this. She propped her elbow on the bar and cupped her hand around her chin. "And whereEVER did you get that charming coat?" she asked sarcastically. "It reminds me of the lampshades Hitler was fond of making. Although, I never knew why..."

115

Again Noreen turned to me and I just shook my head. "You don't want to know," I mumbled with a wave of my hand.

"You think you're hot stuff, don'tcha, missy?" Noreen spat.

"Missy???" Sam wrinkled her nose in stunned surprise. "Good lord, are you related to John Wayne?"

Noreen was becoming incensed –which is *never* good. She drew herself up to her full height and yanked the bunny jacket tighter around her body. The good news is that she was still seated, but I knew the volcano was only a bunny hair away from erupting. Without saying a word, I turned around and calmly took down the largest water glass I had. I filled it three quarters of the way with the strongest bourbon I could find.

Noreen's comebacks always got lamer and lamer when she didn't know what the hell the other person was saying. I couldn't remember a time when Noreen didn't control the situation -like with Doug, but I also couldn't ever recall her ever coming up against another woman like this. And I knew if push came to shove, she'd solve ANY problem with brute force if provoked...and Noreen was easily provoked. "Let's see..." Sam said thoughtfully. "I like to see if I can guess what kind of work a person does by the clothes they wear." I winched and moved as far in the background as possible, gulping the 80 proof bourbon down without stopping until the glass was empty. "You're a hooker in Hollywood," she smiled.

Sucking the last drop out of the glass, I started to pray. At first, Noreen was confused. She thought it was a compliment because Sam had used the word "Hollywood;" but it wasn't long before she connected the word "hooker" had also been used in the same sentence. Her overly mascaraed eyes flashed and she squeezed her glossy red lips together until they turned white. I watched Sam's smile fade, as the two of them honed in on each other like two warhead missiles. Neither said a word but so far, Noreen was still sitting down –which was a <u>good</u> sign. Staring at Noreen's black ringed eyes, Sam shrugged and looked away. "Or maybe I'm wrong and you're not a hooker. Maybe you're a raccoon."

That did it. Noreen slammed both her hands on the bar (NOT unlike a raccoon, I noticed.)

With daggers coming out of her eyes, Noreen huffed, "*Nobody* talks to me like that!"

I'd never seen her so furious, but Sam didn't back down. Unruffled, she said evenly, "I didn't know you served raccoons in here, Mac, but it's all right with me as long as they tip well."

Noreen jumped up and drew back her fist. "YOU wanna TIP?" she screamed. "I'LL give you a tip!" Uh, oh. Noreen had launched. I grabbed her arm just as the booze did its job and numbed my body. Good thing too, because Noreen's swing missed Sam and did a 360, letting me have it right in the face and breaking my nose. As I hopped all over the place yelling, "OWWWW," Sam stood up and said, "Well, I can see you're busy Mac, I'll come back another time."

"DON'T YOU DARE LEAVE!!" I screamed. I was in dire pain, but I knew that if Sam tried to go anywhere, Noreen was going to make damned sure she did it by leaving a great big chunk of her long black hair behind. Blood ran down my arm as I held my bleeding nose with my left hand and again grabbed Noreen's arm with my right. Her talons were extended about four inches from Sam's head. I yelled, "STOP IT, Noreen," ducking just in time to miss her next roundhouse punch. It whizzed over my head, barely missing me by three inches. "Stop it, RIGHT NOW!" I ordered from the safety of my cooler. Then I heard the rear door slam. Still holding on to Noreen's wrist with an iron grip, I slowly raised my head to bar level. Sam was long gone and I heard the engine of my old Ford truck crank up. I sighed. It didn't take a genius to find my keys over the visor. I swore under my breath and looked at Noreen. "You satisfied now?" I asked.

She just sniffed indignantly.

"Instead of breaking your arm, I'm gonna let go ONLY if you promise to behave yourself, you *got* that?" She blinked at me with all the innocence of a baby lamb. "Uh huh," she nodded, sitting down on her stool like she was a gen-u-wine lady. In a little girl voice, she said, "Thanks for standing up for me, Macky." Still holding on to her wrist, I put my bloody face smack in hers and I yanked her to me. "Are you CRAZY, Noreen?" I screamed. "I wasn't STANDING UP for *YOU*, you dizzy tit! I was trying to keep a fight from breaking out. A fight I don't WANT or NEED in MY place! And LOOK at what YOU DID TO MY NOSE, you, you-God, Noreen, I don't know *WHAT* you are! You're just plain NUTS, you know that?" Still gripping her wrist, I looked at her arm and let go by practically throwing it in her face. Her eyes clouded up and her lip trembled like she was going to cry. "And DON'T pull THAT crying crap on me, either," I warned. "I am in NO mood for it, so don't even THINK about it!" I was breathing hard. The booze had worn off and my nose was really starting to hurt. Without saying another word to her, I wrapped some ice in a towel and marched straight to the end of the bar. Holding the towel as close to my nose as I dared, I ripped the receiver off its hook, dropped in a quarter and dialed, hoping Doc would be home. When the phone stopped ringing, I heard his voice. "Hello?" he asked pleasantly.

"Yeah, Doc-it's me, Mac. Can you possibly come over here -like right now?"

"I s'pose so," he answered. "Something wrong with Sam?"

I was exasperated. "No," I said irritably.

He tried again. "Then is it Freeway?"

I looked down at the floor and blinked tiredly. "Nooooooo," I said evenly. "It's not Sam and it's not Freeway."

"Then, who is it Mac?" he asked.

"Dammit Doc-it's ME!" I said loudly. "Does everybody around here think I'm made of stone, or somethin'?"

Doc let out a laugh. "Well, there ARE some around here who think you have rocks in your head," he chuckled. "Especially since hiring Sam-but I digress...okay Mac, what's wrong?"

Without going into details, I told him I thought I had a broken nose.

"Good lord, Mac," he exclaimed. "Just how the devil did you break your nose?"

I took a deep breath. His previous statement about hiring Sam wasn't making this easy.

"Twenty minutes ago," I sighed, "Noreen met Sam."

"Oh, ho,ho,ho," Doc chuckled again. "'Nuf said-I'll be right there."

I hung up with all the agony of defeat and went back to Noreen. "I am REALLY PISSED at you, Noreen!" I fumed. "I went through the whole Vietnam war without getting injured and now, you've managed to do something the ENTIRE N.V.A. couldn't!"

"I'm real sorry, Mac," she said softly. "I meant to hit that girl."

"That doesn't make it hurt any the less," I frowned, "and I *should* 86 you from here for the next six months!"

"What does 86 mean?" she blinked. Just then, the door opened and Doc came in.

"That was quick," I said. He walked up to the bar and dropped his little black bag on the counter. "No traffic, he grinned. "Besides, I had to see this for myself. Hello, Noreen -you do this to Mac?"

"I didn't mean to," she answered as Doc adjusted his bifocals to take a closer look at my nose.

"Is it broken?" I asked.

"Yep," he nodded. "About all I can do for it is put some tape on it and hope it straightens out."

He taped it and when he finished, I felt like an elephant. "Here are some pills for the pain -but best thing you can do for a broken nose is try to stay off it as much as possible."

He laughed and Noreen giggled.

"Ha. Ha," I said tonelessly. "Man, you're just full'a jokes tonight, aren't you."

Doc turned to Noreen. "So, I hear you've met Mac's newest addition to the bar."

She stopped giggling and glared at me. "Yeah," she said.

"*Don't* start, Doc," I warned, looking straight at Noreen. "And if you know what's good for you, you won't say ONE word about Sam or Doc'll be puttin' one of these on YOUR nose."

Noreen shifted on her stool and frowned, but didn't say a word.

"Well gee, Mac, you're no fun," Doc said. "Guess I'll just go on back home and finish my crossword." Doc snapped his bag closed and turned to Noreen. "Sam's mighty pretty," he whispered loud enough to be heard in San Antonio, "but you're still the Queen Bee." He smiled and walked out. "You're a troublemaking old goat," I called after him. But his ploy had worked; Noreen was beaming. "He is NOT an old goat!" Noreen shot back. I feigned anger, but secretly I was pleased that he'd magically smoothed her overly made-up feathers. Noreen got up and gathered her things. "Oh NO, you're not LEAVING?" I said in mock sorrow. "So SOON?"

"Just can it Mac," she answered, sliding off the stool. "I gotta life, ya know?"

"Well, thanks a MILLION for dropping by and ruining mine," I said sarcastically. "If you're ever in the neighborhood be sure to stop in..."

Noreen was halfway to the door when she stopped and slung her purse over her shoulder. She turned around just far enough to give me one of her famous Lana Turner grins. "Oh, I'll be in the neighborhood. And I WILL drop in -count on it!" Then she winked at me and opened the door.

As she sashayed out, I heard dark jungle drums with each swing of her ample hips. The demented voo-doo Queen was back. I didn't know if Noreen was incredibly dumb or smart as a fox. I only knew the woman was dangerous to my body's well-being in an undefined way. I opened the bottle of pain pills, popped two in my mouth and downed them with more bourbon. Not a good idea, but at this point if they killed me, they'd be doing me a favor. Twenty minutes later, I didn't care if Noreen ever came back or not...I was in love with the whole wide world.

CHAPTER FORTY-FIVE

I don't remember going to bed that night, but when I woke up the next morning, my head was splitting and my nose hurt like hell. I knew I wouldn't be opening the bar anytime soon –if at all. I sat up too suddenly which sent my blood pressure through the roof. Falling back on my pillow the down feathers sent shock waves through my head. I groaned and lightly touched my head-which I thought was out further than it actually was. The day's events came flooding back as I vividly recalled the encounter between Noreen and Sam-and how I ended up the only one wounded. Damn that Noreen. She was a one-woman wrecking crew.

My nose was throbbing like a kettledrum and hurt worse than when I woke up. I reached over and got my pain pills off the night table. I shook out two, swallowed them without water then eased my head gently back on my pillow and let out a long sigh. There are a number of things that I don't do well, but being an invalid is number one.

I pulled up the quilt leaving my arms outside and folded my hands over my chest. After lying there for a minute or two, I wondered what time it was and looked over at the clock next to the bed. I frowned. It was only 8:30. I couldn't remember the last time I'd been up this early.

I stared at the ceiling until the pills kicked in and I fell back to sleep. A few hours later, the noonday sun came blazing through the overhead windows because I'd gone to bed and forgotten to lower the blinds-which wasn't too surprising given the shape I was in. The bedroom faced due east so the unrelenting sunlight was assaulting every last one of my senses. Barely awake, I covered my head with the other pillow and groped for the cord. Soon as I felt it, I pulled hard and the blinds dropped with a metallic clank. Satisfied to have the room darkened, I drifted back to sleep unaware that my right wrist was still hung up in the cord.

CHAPTER FORTY-SIX

My intentions were to sleep the day away and open the bar only if I felt like it later that evening. It felt good to just goof-off. Between the pills driving the pain away and my nose being a legitimate excuse, I felt I was perfectly within my rights to snuggle down into my *wonderfully* soft pillow and dream the day away. That was the plan anyway.

I was in a *deep* sleep when I first heard the banging. Thinking it was a dream, I tried to make it disappear, but the noise just persisted to get louder. When I finally woke up enough to realize it was coming from the front door, I rolled over on my back and flung my left arm out to the side. "God," I sighed, "WHY is this happening to me?" The banging continued until I couldn't stand it any longer. Sighing loudly, I tried to throw the covers off with my right hand, but my shoulder wouldn't budge. Wondering what the hell, I looked up and saw my wrist looped through the cord. "Damn," I mumbled, giving my arm a good yank. The blinds flew up on one side like an accordion and my pupils "boinged" down to the size of pinheads in the one o'clock sunlight. "Dear God, I'm *melting*!" I cried.

Wondering why the simple act of getting out of bed had to be so complicated this morning, I managed to get untangled and throw the blanket off. I snatched my robe from the back of the door and stumbled down the hall mumbling like a blind man with Terrets (sp?) Syndrome. Halfway down the hall, I tripped on nothing and stubbed my toe. Between it and the pills wearing off, my nose started hurting worse than ever. By the time I reached the front door, everything from head-to-toe hurt like hell and I yelled, "You'd damn well BETTER NOT be a Jehovah's Witness!"

"I'm not," a muffled voice said from the other side. "I'm Mormon." I unlocked the door and saw Sam standing there. She was smiling until she saw my face then her look turned to one of horror. I hadn't seen what I looked like yet, so I frowned and asked her what was wrong?

She said, "Oh my God, Mac...your face!"

"It's just a broken nose," I shrugged. "The bandage makes me look like an elephant."

Sam hurried up the steps and came inside. "No...it isn't the bandage. Have you taken a look at yourself this morning?"

"No, why?" She closed the door and led me over to the sofa. "Here, sit down, I'll go find a mirror."

"Don't bother. I don't have one. Just the one in the bathroom."

"Then get up and come with me." She helped me up and into the bathroom. I took a look in the mirror and gasped, "Good lord...I can't believe this!" I had two horrendous black eyes separated by a huge bandage. I touched my face lightly and whispered, "I look like I lost to Holyfield in the ninth round. Just *wait'll* I get my hands on Noreen!"

"*Noreen* did this?" she asked incredulously.

"The woman is a one-woman special forces," I frowned. "If we'd had her in Vietnam, they wouldn't'a stood a chance an' th' war would'a ended a hellava lot sooner!"

"Damn," Sam said, "I'm sure glad she missed *me*!"

I looked at her from the mirror. "Oh yeah, better I look like this, than you, right? *This* was *intended* for you!" I yelled, pointing at my nose. Sam looked sheepish and said, "I'm sorry, Mac, I didn't mean it the way it sounded –and I know it was meant for me. I never saw it coming until you grabbed her wrist. It sure never occurred to me that she actually connected with your nose, much less breaking it."

"An' you didn't bother to stick around to find out either, did you?" I said angrily. "I just hope you filled the gas tank after you got done with my truck!"

Oh...that," she said quietly.

"Just where'n th' Sam Hill did you go?" I demanded.

"Nowhere. Just drove around out to the desert for about three hours."

"*Three* hours?" I cried. "Now you damned *well* had better put some gas in."

"Th' truck has plenty of gas," she said. "I only drove out and back. Mostly, I just sat out there looking at the stars and listening to th' coyotes. It was so peaceful that I just sat there for a whi-" suddenly my knees buckled and I grabbed the edge of the sink.

She grabbed me under the arm. "Mac! What's wrong?"

"I need to get back in bed," I whispered. "I feel a little dizzy an' my nose is really killing me."

"C'mon," she said. She guided me back to bed and pulled the quilt over me. Picking up the vile of pills from the night table, she asked, "Are these for pain?" When I nodded, she wondered, "How often do you take them –it doesn't say on the bottle."

"I know. Doc left them for me. I 'spect they're horse pills so he doesn't label them. I'm to take 'em about four hours apart whenever I need." I winced as the pain sharpened. "I've taken 'em before."

She looked at me questioningly.

"They're harmless," I grimaced, closing my eyes and rubbing my forehead. "He won't give his animals anything too strong, unless it's an injection for a specific purpose like serious injury. Doesn't wanna take a chance on hurting or killing one. "

Sam opened the vile and shook out a pill. "I think I know what these are," she said. "They're mostly codeine and you're right, they aren't too dangerous if you aren't allergic or don't abuse them."

I opened my eyes, I said, "Well how 'bout giving me one before this pain puts me into th' stratosphere?"

"You got any milk?" she asked.

"I think so, why?"

"I'm going to get you a glass. You're supposed to take these things with food –be right back"

Oh great. A nurse. (I didn't bother telling her I seldom ever took them with anything.)

Sam retuned with the milk, which really didn't appeal to me, but I washed down the pill with it just to make her happy. "Okay," she said, taking the empty glass. "I'm gonna go an' let you get some sleep. Don't worry about anything, I'll open th' bar tonight."

"An' what if Noreen comes in?" I frowned.

"Then I'll *close* the bar," she laughed. She tucked me in before letting herself out and I drifted off to sleep not caring one way or the other.

122

CHAPTER FORTY-SEVEN

It was a surprise seeing Sam, but the real surprise was the milk. It made the pill work a hundred times better and I made a mental note to remember it when I took the next one. I slept the rest of the day, waking up around nine. Forgetting I had no electricity yet, I reached over and turned on the lamp. It didn't come on of course, and the house was dark. The only light coming in came through the blinds from the security light outside the bar. Sitting up, I turned on the Coleman lantern and took it into the kitchen. I wanted some hot soup, but when I opened the cabinets, the only things in there were a can of tuna, a box of instant mashed potatoes and some saltine crackers -no soup. Sighing loudly, I grabbed the saltines and took them with me into the living room. I could hear faint sounds of the jukebox coming from inside the bar as I ate in the semi-darkness. Everything seemed normal, so after I finished the crackers, I went back into the kitchen for the lantern and a glass of milk. Taking them back to the bedroom, I got in bed, took a pill with the milk and didn't wake up again until morning. If I hadn't been asleep, I would've never been so bored in all my life.

I only spent a day and a half in bed before I had all I could stand of lying around and went back to work. My nose had eased up a lot after the first day so I didn't need the pills until later in the day and at bedtime. I was behind the bar taking inventory, when Sam came in wearing a pair of jeans and a long fringed leather jackets over a white tee shirt.

"Nice jacket." I said.

"Thanks," she grinned.

"I've always liked th' fringe."

"Me too-the longer, the better, but I bet you don't know what th' fringe is for, do you?"

I stopped writing. "No," I frowned, "I never really gave it any thought, but if I had to come up with an answer, I'd guess it was some kind'a Indian decoration." I went back to my inventory.

"Yeah, everybody thinks that -an' th' Indians probably *are* th' ones who came up with th' idea, but it was adopted by th' cowboys...and I bet you don't know who th' first cowboys were either, do ya?" I turned around to look at her. She raised her eyebrows and shrugged. "Well, you *are* a Yankee..."

"Even us dumb Yankees know you smart-aleck Texans were th' first cowboys," I frowned. Sam laughed and shook her head. "No...we weren't," she smiled. "Th' Mexicans were."

I sighed. "So, now that I got my Texas History lesson 101 for the day, was there some point to the fringe question?"

123

"Oh yeah, th' fringe," she said. "Well, I s'pose it is just for decoration now, but a long time ago when cowboys ran into rain on long cattle drives, these leather jackets soaked up water like a sponge," she explained, "There wasn't any way to dry it so th' fringe beat out th' water as they rode along. Pretty neat, huh?" She leaned up on the bar and squinted. "Wow, your nose sure is purple lookin'." She reached out to touch it and I slapped her hand away. "Don't *DO* that!" I cried. "WHY does EVERYBODY have to TOUCH something that hurts like hell?"

"Sorry, does it hurt bad?"

"Well it sure'n hell doesn't hurt good," I frowned. Sam giggled and tried to stifle it with her hand. "Somethin' funny about this?" I asked.

"No, no, it's just that-"

"What," I frowned.

"Well, you seem like such a reasonably intelligent person that...um..."

"What?" I said threateningly. "An' you better make it good."

"That you wouldn't end up with a broken nose," she finished.

"I'm *not* intelligent," I huffed. "An intelligent person is somebody who can listen to th' William Tell Overture without thinkin' of Th' Lone Ranger." I turned back to my inventory and she asked what I was doing. "Takin' inventory, I need to call in some beer orders."

"Yeah," she nodded. "We're just about outta Coors Light." A few seconds later, Sam got around to what was really on her mind. "By th' way, just WHO IS this Noreen?" she asked. "She's a real *loony*, ya know that!" Before I could answer, she sat up straight and said, "Oh no, don't tell me she's your girlfriend."

"*Hardly*!" I sniffed.

"Then who is she?"

Sam's question had me genuinely stumped. Like Yellow Fever, Noreen was something you couldn't describe; you had to experience it. I put down my pad and pencil and scratched the back of my head. "I don't really know how to explain her," I began. "I guess every little town in the U.S. has a "Noreen. She's not a bad person, she's just...Noreen." And while it was true that most of the time she aggravated the hell out of me, it was more like a little sister aggravates an older brother.

I'd seen her do countless little acts of kindness when she didn't know anyone saw her; stuff like move a turtle off the road so it wouldn't get run over, or slip somebody twenty bucks without ever asking for it back. If they did try to pay her back, she'd deny doing anything like that to her dying day.

...And I'd never once known her to ever exhibit one shred of self-pity. Not an ounce.

CHAPTER FORTY-EIGHT

I didn't want to oversell Noreen, but for whatever weird reason, I felt it was important that Sam know there was a good heart buried under all that cheap clothing and outrageous make-up.

I rubbed the back of my neck and said, "I can't say that I really know anything about her, except that she's one of th' few people who was actually born and raised here on the outskirts of town. And I don't think she had much of a life as a kid."

"What makes you say that?"

"Well, for one thing, just look at this place," I shrugged. "It's not exactly a great place for a kid to learn how to interact socially with others. I mean it's a *ghost* town for God's sake."

"Does she have any brothers or sisters or other family?"

"Like I said, I don't know anything about her other than her comin' in here, but I've been around long enough to know how to read people. That's how I knew Noreen was gonna take a swing at you. She's got a low boiling point and you were already over th' line just by bein' female."

"Yeah, she's pretty hard to read through that hard exterior."

I got two mugs out of the cooler and poured us a beer. "True, but it ain't bulletproof an' every once in a while, I see somethin' in her eyes that makes me think Noreen's known a lot of sorrow in her life, an' maybe God finally balanced the scales by giving her one really perfect thing -her body. It's the only thing that she has complete control over on who gets close to it."

"Is she you know- a hooker?"

I shook my head. "No, she's not a hooker...not in the usual sense of the word. She doesn't...um, "take on" anybody unless she likes 'em in some small way." I looked at her and squinted. "Does that make any sense?"

"I guess so...okay no, not really," Sam frowned.

I shifted my weight. "Yeah –didn't think so. Okay, let me put it this way; even though she IS a female, it's my opinion that Noreen's had to live with other females constantly reminding her that she's "White Trash," until she pretty much hates anything that ovulates --which means YOU."

"Maybe," Sam shrugged. "But I haven't ever met anyone I couldn't make friends with," she said, "if I wanted to."

"Well, trust me on this one; you'll never get close to her and I strongly suggest you keep your distance. As you can see, she's half-cocked anyway an' has a wicked right cross."

"And I have an award winning left hook," she sniffed.

I glanced at her with a half-smile. I could just imagine Sam punching somebody's lights out. "Does that mean you wanna become her best friend?"

"No, but it does mean I can take care'a myself."

Just then the door opened and Harley walked in. He waved and came over, pulling up a stool next to Sam. They exchanged warm hellos and talked about the weather. He complimented her jacket then ordered his usual beer and bourbon. After he finished, he got up and put on his Stetson. "That was short -you leavin' so soon?"

"Yep, gotta turn in early. Won't be seein' ya for a couple of weeks. Gotta round up some strays."

"Well, I'll be here –an' by th' way, thanks for not asking...you know, about my nose."

Without turning around, he just waved and said he already knew all about how it got busted.

"WHO told you?" I yelled angrily. "*Doggone* it, it was Doc, wasn't it!"

He grinned and went out the door.

"Damn it," I muttered. "Is *nothing* personal in this town."

CHAPTER FORTY-NINE

Sam wanted to know if I needed her to work that night and I said that it would most likely be slow, due to the roundup Harley had mentioned. She then asked if she could take Freeway for a ride in my truck and I told her she knew where the keys were. Around 6:30, Legrand came in for a beer and to tell me the electrician would be out here by the first of the week, then like Harley, he left after only one drink. I didn't see another soul until around 9:15, when Doug came by looking for you-know-who. Thank God, I was able to tell him I hadn't seen her. He looked disappointed, but instead of leaving like usual, he sat down and ordered a beer. When he asked what happened to my nose, I told him Noreen did it and he grinned proudly like she was Mike Tyson or something. By 10:45, there wasn't a soul in the place so I went ahead and locked up without even bothering to clear out the cash drawer.

If I made eighteen dollars all night, I would've been damned surprised.

The next two weeks went by agonizingly slow. There wasn't a soul around thus making the place a *real* ghost town. Without anything to keep her occupied, Sam stayed in her room doing whatever it is that women find to do -or making short trips in my truck with Freeway. I worked the bar alone, washing and re-washing everything in an attempt to keep from going crazy from boredom and lack of customers. The only good thing to happen during that time was the electrician finally showing up and getting my power on in the trailer. I could at least watch television after closing.

Two weeks later, the cowboys returned and on Friday night, they piled in here like they'd miss the bar as much as it had missed them. My band was gleefully back on stage and played like they'd been practicing. A *lot.*

The bar was again alive with music, laughter, and lots of drinking. Most of the cowboys had dates and everyone was in great spirits, so what happened later on was like it was ordained by Destiny. It'd been a while since the last busload of entertainers had been by and around nine thirty, one pulled in. As soon as they heard the air brakes, everyone got up to run outside and see who it was. I'd gotten over being impressed by these buses long ago and stayed behind the bar, but after a moment, I heard so much commotion that I finally had to go outside. I walked across the veranda to see a colossal custom built shiny black bus with blacked-out windows, parked facing the wrong way next to the curb. A pair of glistening white eagle wings very similar to the Harley Davidson logo were painted on each side. In the center of the wings big red swirly letters trimmed in gold read, "Hank Fairfield."

I gasped, "Oh my God," and almost genuflected.

Hank Fairfield was THE biggest entertainer alive. If Elvis were still among us, Hank probably would've given even *him* a run for his money. He was a true Texan; as well as probably being the most loved and worshipped entertainer anywhere -just like Elvis.

Suddenly, the door hissed open and everybody stopped talking. After five long seconds of silence, the musicians began to pour out. They paraded past all the little Brenda Lee dates of the cowboys, sending them into a frenzy of clapping and jumping up and down like cheerleaders. Then the great man himself stepped out and smiled. He gave a tip of his black Stetson to the crowd and they went ballistic. I'd seen him on television, but I was not at all prepared for how big a man he was. He was HUGE. His black boots added three inches to his already six foot seven height. I guessed his weight at about two eighty, but from the way he filled out his special made Nudie suit, he was two hundred and eighty pounds of solid muscle.

As he breezed past me, he said, "Howdy," in a deep friendly voice. Then he stopped, came back to me and removed his hat. He took my hand and said, "Judgin' by that apron you got on, I'd say you're the proprietor of this here establishment -am I right?"

I blinked several times, unable to speak. The man TOWERED over me. I had to bend my neck back as far as it would go to look up at his face. Since I couldn't speak, I just gulped and nodded. "Wellll, right glad ta meet'cha," he said evenly. "We're on our way back to Dallas, but we gotta gig up in Houston tomorrow night and we're runnin' a little ahead of schedule." He kept pumping my hand (which had all but disappeared in his,) while I kept nodding like an idiot. "Th' boys git bored when they ain't workin', so when we saw your place, we wondered if you'd mind us stoppin' in to wet our whistle and well, maybe try out a coupl'a songs on your stage?"

Would I *MIND*? My head was spinning so fast I thought I'd faint. "I-I'd be mighty proud to have you in my place, Mr. Fairfield," I whispered, trying to sound as Texan as possible. He gave me a friendly slap on the back with his ham hock of a hand, knocking all the wind out of my lungs. "That's *mighty* neighborly of you, podner," he grinned.

"S-Sure thing, (cough, cough,) M-Mr. Fairfield," I wheezed.

He took off his Stetson and strolled through the door, after ducking first. I followed him inside like a zombie. The noise was deafening and I hurried behind the bar, calling to Sam as I passed her. "Sam!" I yelled. "Can you BELIEVE it? HANK FAIRFIELD is here in MY dump of a place!"

I was so excited that I never noticed how deathly white her face was, or that she was probably the ONLY person here that was NOT impressed by Hank Fairfield's appearance.

CHAPTER FIFTY

Again, I was the one legged man at an ass kicking contest. I could NOT keep up with all the orders and finally had to ask one of the guys if he could come back and take care of just the beer orders. But even with his help, the orders kept coming in and I was barely able to keep up with the margaritas and other mixed drinks. In fact, I was so darned busy that I never looked up once, so I didn't notice when Sam put on a dark Stetson hat. By the time I did notice, I just figured she'd taken it off some cowboy's head as a gesture of getting in the swing of things and didn't give it another thought.

Hank's band went up on stage while he sat at the bar and had a double Wild Turkey on the rocks. In my whole life, I don't ever remember being so impressed by anyone (-other than my father and maybe John Wayne,) but I was really star-struck by this man. Everything about him seemed larger than life; the relaxed way he sat on the barstool, the engaging smile he had for everyone -even the manly way he picked up his drink. He *was* John Wayne from head to foot.

He finished his drink and I had to shout to be heard over all the noise. "Can I get you another Wild Turkey, Mr. Fairfield?"

"Only if you'll call me Hank," he answered with a grin.

"You got it, Hank," I nodded, feeling like a fourteen year old school kid as I poured a triple over fresh ice and setting it in front of him on a clean napkin.

"You always this packed?" he asked.

I shook my head. "No-weekdays are just locals who come in to drink beer and shoot a little pool. I do a little better on weekends, but I ain't never seen it like this!"

"This is a dynamite place," he said, admiringly. "You don't see many like it anymore. In fact, closest ones I can think of would be the auditorium in Meridian, Mississippi or a dance hall over'n Greenwood, Texas." He took a look around. "This looks a lot like one'a them ol' saloon's from 'way back."

"It was built in the 1800's."

"Great balls of fire -how in th' world did you ever find it?"

"By accident. It was so rundown that I got it for a song, too -oh crimney, I meant that as a figure of speech."

"I knew what you meant," he laughed. "And I congratulate you on your excellent purchase. Too bad I didn't find it first. But Ah gotta admit, Ah never knew this place even existed, an' Ah've lived in Texas all mah life." He took another sip of his drink and looked around the bar. "Yeh," he smiled. "This here is th' kind'a town you might'a found Wyatt Earp and his boys, in."

I nodded. "Th' folks here are mighty protective of its seclusion, so unless you stumble on it by accident, I don't know that you'd ever find it."

"That what you did –stumble across it?"

I'd worked hard to put those days behind me and said, "Yeah –you could say that."

"Sounds like there's a story behind that statement –maybe one good 'nuf to make a country song."

"There's a story behind everything," I said, looking away.

"Ya know," he sighed wistfully. "Ah reckon there is at that."

He took a sip of his drink and let it drop.

Wiping his mouth off with the back of his hand, he said, "I shore wouldn't mind having somethin' like this of my own, one day." He tipped his hat back and mopped his forehead. "Yeah," he sighed. "With a place like this, Ah could come in off th' road. Have th' audience come to me an' save expenses."

"Not a bad idea, "I smiled.

"Jest name your price if'n ya ever wanna sell an' Ah'll..." Just then, his band finished playing and the audience started clapping in unison and chanting his name. The skin around his eyes crinkled when he smiled, making his smile even warmer. "Ah do believe it's time for me to earn my keep," he said, downing his drink. He gave me a wink, stood up and adjusted his Stetson then walked towards the stage. Stepping into the lights, his suit shot out a blinding kaleidoscope of colors. He waved his Stetson at the audience with one hand and slid the mike off its stand with the other. The crowd went wild. I thought the damned roof was going to explode into the sky. With no one at the bar now, I started to pick up all the empty glasses and did a double take. Noreen had slipped in unnoticed and was standing right up front looking up at Hank like he was a Texas T-bone and she hadn't eaten in a year.

He noticed too, and winked.

CHAPTER FIFTY-ONE

Absently touching my bandaged nose, I narrowed my eyes and whispered, "Oh no-when the hell did she come in?" I looked for Sam and seeing that she was busy on the far side of the room, I prayed she'd stay out of Noreen's line of sight. Looking back at the stage, I was relieved to see that Hank's being here had her too focused on him to give any thought to any other female.

No, to Noreen's way of thinking, there was plenty of time to get back to Sam.

Hank was a-once-in-a-lifetime opportunity -and she never missed and opportunity.

Hank had the kind of voice that gave you goose bumps. As I listened to him sing Willie Nelson's, "Seven Spanish Angels," it amazed me to no end, how one human being had the natural ability to create such spellbinding magic, but between his voice, six foot seven inch Texas Ranger frame -and that *suit*, Hank had it in spades. When he finished the song, the crowd erupted into applause and screams, but he ignored the adulation and looked over his shoulder at his band. A hush fell over the room as they nodded and the drummer called out "*one-two-three-four.*" Like a well-oiled machine they went into "The Boogie Woogie Boy of Company B." The stage rocked. Hank had the audience in the palm of his hand –along with Noreen. He flirted with her until she was about to go out of her mind. Twenty minutes later, he stepped off the stage and looking straight into Noreen's eyes, took her in his arms and started singing one of my favorite songs called, "Easy Lovin'." The crowd parted as they slowly danced across the floor. I shook my head; if *anything* in this world could kill Noreen, this would do it! (I knew mirrors, garlic, and crucifixes, sure didn't work.)

Hank crooned, *"Eeeeeeeasy* lovin'....*soooo* sexy lookin'" into the microphone over her shoulder, while Noreen closed her eyes and wrapped both arms around his neck. Infusing her body into his, she looked like a teenager on prom night. Seeing her like this made it impossible for me to stay angry at her –until I touched the bandage on my nose and the dark reality of who we were dealing with set in. I hoped Hank knew what the hell he was doing. Noreen never let go of anything once she had it in her hot little grasp –and right now, she had Hank in the strangle hold of a python. He may be used to dealing with groupies, but Noreen wasn't like any species known to mortal man.

I wasn't Catholic, but I made the sign of the Cross and sighed, "You're on your own with *this* one, pal."

Sam came up to give me an order, but I couldn't hear what she said. When I asked her to repeat it a little louder, she glanced nervously over her shoulder towards the stage. Turning back to me, she kept her head down as she said, "I need six beers!" I couldn't see her face under that hat and thought it a little odd that she wanted to wear it. I also couldn't help noticing her surprising lack of enthusiasm about Hank being here tonight. Everyone else couldn't contain their excitement, but she looked annoyed as hell, like she wanted to crawl into a dark corner and disappear. Maybe it was the way she kept her back to the stage, but for some reason her lack of enthusiasm stirred my curiosity. She never once looked at Hank or the band.

I got her the beers but watched her as she left. Sure enough, when she got close to the stage lights, she moved like a shadow, trying hard to avoid being seen. It was obvious that she was making damn sure to keep her head down. NOW I knew why the Stetson. It *was* to hide her face.

But...*why?*

CHAPTER FIFTY-TWO

Suddenly, memories of the last time musicians were in here came flooding back. They sure knew Sam but she never would explain how. Was this a similar situation? *No* –it couldn't be! Hank Fairfield was too big! This man was a living legend! NO WAY he was going to know some little waitress serving drinks 'way out here in this podunk tumbleweed place. I snickered at the absurdity my paranoia was inferring. (Or is it "implying"?)

After two hours on stage, Hank said, "We're gonna do ONE more, then we're headin' for th' bar!" Soon as he finished his last song, he handed the mike to one of his musician, bowed and stepped off stage taking his time strolling through the crowd, shaking hands with the swarm around him. When he made it to the bar, he took off his Stetson and laid it down alongside him. He picked up a napkin and mopped his brow. "Whew," he sighed. "Thanks for th' use of your stage."

"Are you kiddin'?" I said. "Thanks to you, I'll be a legend in this town from now on."

He threw the napkin in the trashcan then reached in his hip pocket for a big white handkerchief to wipe his whole face. I silently admired the full thick head of dark hair and absently ran a hand over my own thinning crop. Was no end to my envy of this man?

Stuffing the damp handkerchief back in his hip pocket, he said, "Well, if you ever wanna repay me, you can sell me this bar."

"You got it," I smiled. "How 'bout a drink?"

"Lord yes! It gets damned hot up there under them lights in this suit!" he complained. "To say nuthin' 'bout how danged heavy this mother is to wear. Some of these suits can get up to eighty pounds -did you know that?"

I raised my eyebrows in genuine surprise. "No, I never realized."

"It's like takin' off a suit of danged armor at night –oh, an' make that drink an icy cold Coors, will ya, please?"

"With a Turkey back?"

His eyes twinkled. "Ya talked me into it," he nodded.

I set his drinks down as he asked, "Say, who's that little wildcat I was dancin' with?"

"Wildcat is right," I said, leaning on my elbows across the bar. "Her name's Noreen, and she's th' one who did this to my nose!"

"Ho, ho," Hank chuckled. "I wondered what happened, but I think I'd have to come up with a better story, if'n a girl broke MY nose."

"Not around here, you wouldn't."

"She go with anybody?"

"Yes," I answered.

"Who?" he frowned.

"ANYbody," I shrugged.

"Well, that would explain it, then," he smiled.

"What's that?"

"She whispered somethin' in my ear while we was dancin'. Nearly made me swallow the mike."

I stood up. "I don't EVEN want to know what it was," I said holding up both hands. "But I WILL say this; whatever she promised you, believe it. She CAN deliver!"

"Wellll," Hank said, picking up his beer with a wink. "In that case, I CAN tell ya it involved a very inter-rest-ing time standing up in a phone booth."

"Did she happen to mention," I whispered, "that the phone booth has uneven parallel bars?"

Now both eyebrows shot up and he turned around to take another look at Noreen. Turning back, he said, "Hmmmm, maybe I should'a thought about this before lettin' my bass player get there first. Not that he's going to," he said, finishing off his drink. "We gotta split in fifteen minutes. Houston's still a long ways up th' road."

"Well then..." I said, refilling his beer. "Have one for th' road-I mean it ain't like you're drivin'."

"Not only that," he grinned, "but I got a bar on board that makes yours look downright puny, son."

"I just bet you do, too!" I grinned back. Twenty seconds later, Hank slammed his empty glass down and turned around on his bar stool. "LOAD UP, guys," he hollered. The guitar player played a few bars of "On Th' Road Again," and everybody started hustling.

Hank stood up and put his hat back on then stuck his hand out and said, "It was right nice ta meet'cha, Mac -you take care'a that nose now, ya hear? Best thing ta do, is to stay off it."

I picked up his empty glass and wondered if everybody on earth knew that same idiot advice.

As he headed for the door, I noticed Noreen nuzzling the bass player's ear. The guitar player came up and said, "Come on, Stevie, we gotta hit th' road." Without taking his eyes off Noreen, "Stevie" nodded and picked up his case. He put his arm back around Noreen's waist and they walked towards the door together. However, Stevie wasn't paying any attention to where he was going and slammed smack into Sam, who had her back to them as she picked up empties from the tables. Her Stetson fell off and she jerked around angrily. "Why don't you watch where-" but her voice stopped in mid-sentence, as she and the bass player stared at each other. Suddenly, he dropped his case and grabbed her in his arms. Swinging her around, he yelled, "Ohmigod! Sammi Jo! Sammi Jo!"

My jaw dropped as I watched her struggle to get out of his grasp. Noreen was as stunned as I was and I threw down my rag knowing the look on my face was the exact same as hers. Forgetting all about Noreen, Stevie yelled for the guitar player to run and get Hank, but he was already on his way through the door. Before you could blink twice, Hank was back inside demanding, "Where is she?" (I didn't know a man that size could move so fast.) He kept asking where Sam was and the guitar player pointed, but Hank was already halfway there. He hurried towards Sam, pushing Noreen aside and knocking her on her ass. Noreen quickly got up with blood in her eyes and ready to kill. Oblivious to what he'd just done, Hank grabbed Sam in both arms and lifted her off the floor. He whirled her around three or four times before he set her down and stared straight into her eyes. Holding her up by her slumping shoulders, he cried, "My GOD, Sam, it *IS* YOU!"

There wasn't a trace of happiness on her face as Hank buried her in a bear hug.

Rocking her back and forth like she was a precious rag doll, he said, "Good God, I've looked everywhere for you, girl! I thought Ah'd lost you for good this time, baby." Meanwhile, Noreen had regained her balance from where Hank had knocked her down and erupted with all the force of Vesuvius. Noreen was livid, but no one paid her any attention -which just made her all the madder. Shoving everyone aside, she plowed through the middle of the reunion. Stopping in front of Hank, she sputtered, "YOU two-bit rhinestone cowboy!" Hank tightened his grip around Sam as Noreen pushed him in the chest. "Just WHO do you think you are that you can make a fool outta me!

Hank had his mouth open, but before he had a chance to respond, she turned to Sam. "An' what th' hell are *YOU* –some kind'a groupie? I ain't liked you since I first laid eyes on you! You just need to get your stuff and go on back to wherever you came from -this town don't *need* another idiot woman in it!"

Oblivious to how that came out, Noreen missed the puzzled look on everybody's face. But Hank turned ashen -and I swear I thought he was going to take Noreen and throw her through the mirror on the other side of my bar. He was barely able to contain himself, as he said in a low voice, "You best shut that big mouth of yours, little lady...'cause if SHE don't hit you, I sure as hell WILL!"

Almost as tall as Hank, Noreen didn't back down an inch and yelled right back. "SAVE IT *cowboy* for somebody that threat might *actually* work on!" As they faced each other like two pit bulls, Sam broke loose from Hank's grip and pushed them aside.

"Just get out of my way," she fumed, "–*both* of you!"

Pissed at being discovered, she stormed across the dance floor like a nazi war criminal. Still waiting to see who would blink first, Noreen suddenly broke eye contact with Hank and turned her attention back to Sam. Poking Hank in the chest, she said, "I'll get back to you cowboy-but right now I got somethin' to take care'a first."

Sam's walking away was just too infuriating for her to ignore and Noreen hurried after her, screaming, "Don't you *DARE* walk away, you floosie -who th' hell ARE you that every one'a these musicians KNOWS YOU?" Sam stopped dead in her tracks as Noreen came up behind her, calling her every name in the book. I was wondering why Sam didn't walk away when I saw her relax, take a deep breath and square back her shoulders. Without saying a word, she turned around and coldcocked Noreen so fast, that nobody saw it coming. I blinked unbelievingly and watched Noreen go down like a bag of wet cement. Brushing her hands together, Sam stepped over Noreen's unconscious body and continued up to the bar. Slapping her hand on the counter, she ordered double bourbon on the rocks –and I gave it to her without *any* hesitation.

CHAPTER FIFTY-THREE

She sat down, but didn't pick up her drink. Instead, she stared at the glass, slowly turning it in her fingers. Hank came up behind her and took off his Stetson, laying it on the counter. Pulling out the bar stool next to her, he said, "It's damned good to see you, Sammi Jo."

When she didn't acknowledge his presence, Hank looked at me and said, "Ah'll have another Coors if'n ya don't mind, Mac. Looks like we're gonna be here awhile."

I got his beer and he nodded as I set down in front of him. Looking at Sam, he said, "Ah see you still got that wicked right cross." She glanced up at me then quickly lowered her eyes again.

"An' Ah seem to remember you also gotta mean left hook," he said, rubbing his cheek in fond memory.

I stared at them both in stunned fascination. Cocking my head, I leaned back against the cooler and crossed my arms over my chest. From the day she first came in here, I knew she was running from something -or somebody -and from the way he looked at her, it didn't take a rocket scientist to see that Hank was that 'somebody.' Although Sam's life was her own and she'd not seen fit to include me in it, I found this revelation disturbing. I knew it shouldn't have bothered me, but it did and I felt my shoulders slump. I'd grown a lot fonder of Sam than I'd allowed myself to admit. Hank put his hand over hers and I felt myself get unreasonably territorial when she didn't try to pull away. Finally, she did pull away and picked up her drink. "Here's to you findin' me," she said tonelessly. "Cheers."

She threw her head back and drank the bourbon down in one swallow and wiped her mouth with the back of her hand. "So...what now?" she asked.

"You know what," he answered congenially. "You're comin' back with me." He took a swallow of his beer and set the mug back down before running his fingers through his thick hair. "Th' bus is right outside-Ah'll wait while you go get your things together."

I stopped breathing and waited for her answer. After what seemed like an eternity, she said, "No," -and Life coursed through my body again.

Hank's brows came together. His smile disappeared and it was obvious he didn't like being defied, but as quickly as his smile disappeared, he relaxed and it returned. "Still stubborn as a mule, eh," he sighed. "Well, we'll jest see about that."

Sam turned to face him. "I'm not th' same little girl you can push around, Hank. I've got things *I* want to do and they aren't always what YOU want to do."

He thought about it for a minute then said, "Ah can *make* you get on that bus, ya know."

She rubbed the back of her neck. "There *was* a time that you could do that," she said. "But I wouldn't try it now." She stopped rubbing her neck and looked at him with a smile across her face. There was no humor in her eyes-just a warning. Hank met her eyes with the same unwavering gaze and I wondered if he was going to throw her over his shoulder. I knew if he did, I'd want to intervene, but -there was that thing about him being three times bigger than me.

"I'm not your property, Hank!"

Finally, Hank nodded and said, "Aw right, Sammi Jo. Ah reckon it's time you had a little space, so Ah'm gonna give it to ya. Ah'm a patient man, but don't take advantage of it –and until you can find a good lawyer to untie us, you *are* comin' back." He looked at me. "Ya gotta finish somethin' before you can start somethin' new, ya know."

Now Sam was angry. "That's not right, Hank! You know I was young and excited and didn't fully understand what I was doin when we-"

"Regardless," he went on, "it's legal an' binding an' without a good lawyer, there ain't a thing you can do about it. Jest remember-Ah found you this time an' Ah'll find you next time." His tone made it clear that he wasn't messing around and Sam pushed her glass towards me. "Don't give yourself any gray hairs over it; I'm not going anywhere."

I refilled her glass as Hank said, "Ah ain't worried."

Wrapping her fingers around the glass, Sam stared tiredly into space. "You're so damned sure of yourself, ain't you!"

He shrugged and finished what was left of his beer. "Ah ain't got time to argue," he said. "It's getting' late an' we gotta hit th' road –what do Ah owe you, Mac?"

"Not a thing, Hank. Not a thing."

He stood up, reached into his pocket and pulled out a wad of bills thick enough to choke a horse. Taking a hundred dollar bill from the roll, he slapped it on the counter. "Thanks for everything, Mac," he said. He picked up his Stetson and turned to Sam. "Ah'll be in touch," he said, and with that, he put it on and walked out the door. Five seconds later, I heard the closing hiss of the door and two seconds later, the big diesel engine roared to life.

Ten seconds later, there was nothing left of his being here but exhaust fumes.

CHAPTER FIFTY-FOUR

I looked at Sam with puzzled curiosity and waited for her to say something, but when she didn't, I asked, "So, you wanna tell me what that was all about?" Sam was rubbing her forehead with a tired, worried look, but as soon as I asked the question, those beautiful blue eyes turned hard as granite and she said, "No, Mac, I don't." Before we could say anything else, Noreen moaned and sat up, holding her hand to her jaw. "W-What happened?" she groaned. Sam picked up her drink and finishing it, got up from the bar. Giving me a hard look, she turned and headed for the storeroom without another word. As she passed Noreen, she said, "Put some ice on that jaw an' you'll be fine."

I got out a towel and filling it with ice, took it over to her. She held it against her jaw asking, "What th' hell happened?"

"You got knocked on your sweet ass, that's what," I told her. She looked confused. "By who?"

"Sam," I answered. "...And it's "whom.""

"*WHAT*???" she cried. "How th' hell did *that* happen?"

I helped Noreen to her feet and sighed, "It happened when your jaw ran into Sam's fist."

CHAPTER FIFTY-FIVE

I sent Noreen on her way and closed up. It had been one of the most extraordinary nights of my life and by the time I finally crawled in bed, I was exhausted. After turning out the light and rolling over on my side, tired as I was, I couldn't stop thinking about the night's events. Granted, Hank Fairfield showing up was spectacular, but it was nothing compared to seeing Sam knock out Noreen. I couldn't keep the smile off my face. Then I got around to what was really on my mind. I wondered what the story was between Hank and Sam. Clearly they had a history. I couldn't get it out of my mind that they might be married or at the very least, 'heavily involved.' Whatever the story was, it was a long way from being over. Only something unresolved brought out what I saw tonight. And just what the hell was *my* interest in all this? I kept asking myself that question like I was the one that had the answer. Fatigue finally won out and I drifted off without coming to any conclusions.

I showered and shaved the next day having completely forgotten all about Noreen. But when I opened the back door, there she was, sitting at the bar and mad as a hornet. Her left cheek had already turned deep crimson purple and her eye was swollen shut.

"It's about *time* you showed up, Mac!" she cried. "Just LOOK at me, will you!" She was hopping mad and getting more so by the second.

"Just how th' hell did you get in here this morning, Noreen?" I frowned.

"You forgot to lock th' front door," she yelled angrily. I looked at the door and sure enough, I'd clean forgot to lock it before I left. I went behind the bar to put on the coffee.

"Well, what do you want so early this morning?" I asked.

"I wanna know where that waitress of yours is, so I can have a 'word' with her about that sucker punch last night."

"Forget it, Noreen...besides, you asked for it."

"*SURE!* Take up for HER," she spat, taking a look around the bar. "Where *is* she, anyway?"

Getting out my coffee mug, I said, "Still asleep, I imagine." I held up the coffee pot. "You want some?" She shook her head no and I poured myself a cup. I went outside for a paper then came back in and sat down at the bar –hoping to read it and drink my coffee in peace.

"Are you just gonna ignore me?" Noreen sniffed.

"I'm gonna try..." I said without looking up, and she yelled some curse at me (and any future children I might have.) I put down the paper and asked her what she wanted me to do? She wasn't sure, but she thought I should do *something*. Sighing, I said, "Noreen...do you recall last night at *all*? Do you remember Hank Fairfield coming in and you getting all pissed off at Sam because he knows her? Do you remember pushing Sam to th' point that she knocked your lights out?"

She frowned and halfway nodded.

"Well then, why're you here-you wanna rematch or somethin'?" I picked up the paper and muttered, "Look, just go on home, okay? I've had enough excitement for one week."

That did it and she exploded. Now I dropped the paper and rubbed the splitting headache that was forming in my frontal lobe. I'd hoped Sam's fist had knocked some sense into her last night, but as I listened to her rant, I knew nothing had changed. Finally, I growled, "Damn it Noreen, I liked you a whole lot better unconscious." With that, she stood up and stormed out the door, vowing to take her revenge with or without my help.

I picked up my paper one final time and tried to finish the sentence.

When I hadn't seen hide nor hair of Sam by early afternoon, I decided to knock on her door and see if she was all right. I had the feeling that she wasn't there, so I opened the door and went inside. I was astounded. Everything was so nice and neat.

She had moved her bed under the window in the center of the room, placing two small bright red end tables with matching yellow lamps on each side. The bed itself was perfectly made up with bright orange, yellow, and lime green pillows thrown across a brown chenille bedspread. Black curtains covered the window. She had even painted the walls a soft yellow.

Good lord- when had she *done* all this?

I suppose I had expected to see her sitting crossed legged on the floor brushing Freeway or something, but when I didn't -it hit me! "Wait a minute!" I frowned. Freeway was gone -and SO was my truck. I vaguely remembered not seeing it when I opened up, but Noreen's presence had me so distracted that it didn't sink in until this very moment. I briefly wondered if she went to Houston -and stopped right there. I wasn't going to let that kind of thinking start taking over what was left of my fragile sanity. Besides, if she wanted to see Hank, she could've left with him last night on that rolling hotel.

I closed her door and went back to the bar.

It was almost five o' clock when I heard my truck pull in. Glad that she was back, I watched the back door in between wrestling a keg of beer I was trying to tap. When I saw the door open, I told myself I was just relieved she made it back with my truck in one piece, but it rang hollow. She and Freeway came up to the bar. "Hi ya, Mac," she smiled. "Need any help with that?"

"Thanks, but I've just about got it, now," I told her. "What's up? You sure left outta here early this morning."

"I did," she nodded. "Wanted to get an early start to Gentry's Appliances over in Mesa."

Wiping my hands off on a towel, I asked, "You mean that place down by th' border about thirty miles from here?" She nodded. "Harley showed it to me that day he took me out while you guys set up your new mobile home." (So *that's* where she got the things to fix up her room.)

I didn't mention anything about seeing her room and said, "I never been over to Mesa –is it nice?"

"It's just a small town of about 1,200, but yeah, it's nice. Mostly dirt farms owned by Mexican families."

"So, what took you over there so early *in-my-truck* this fine day?"

"Gentry's was having a sale on washing machines and T.V.'s, an' I got one."

"Which one -washing machine or T.V.?"

"Th' T.V. stupid."

I smiled. "You'd'a done better with the washing machine. The closest local stations are up in Houston and th' reception sucks out here. I can't get much on mine, even with that big antenna Legrand put up outside. Besides, I could'a used a new washer an' you could'a watched th' clothes go 'round an' 'round." She gave me a dirty look. "Yeah, right. I got a small 13 inch with a built-in V.C.R. I can set it up near my bed and watch movies-which is infinitely more interesting than watching your dirty underwear slosh around." (I wondered where she got the money to do all these things, since I knew I sure didn't pay her much, but didn't ask.)

"So, you buy any good movies?"

"It'd be kind'a stupid of me not too, wouldn't it?"

"Any John Wayne?" I asked hopefully.

"NO!" she said.

"What?" I cried. "No westerns? You un-American or something?"

"Don't be ridiculous, Mac. I bought every Bette Davis video they had – along with any other old black and white classic I could find. I really lucked out too. I found, "Double Indemnity," "Casablanca," "Stella Dallas," -and even found a rare copy of "The Portrait of Dorian Gray." "Oh yeah," she added excitedly. "And "Mildred Pierce" with Joan Crawford."

I frowned. "Except for "Casablanca," I never even heard of any of those."

She sighed. "*Why* am I not surprised?"

"Hey -just what kind'a guy do you think I'd turned out to be if I watched *those* movies as a kid instead of good ol' western shoot-outs?" I batted my eyes factiously and she frowned. "I'd think you're just what you are: loony and disturbed."

"Okay, who told you?" She rolled her eyes and let out a long sigh. "Can we please get back to movies?" she asked. "I'm excited about finding the Bette Davis videos in case you hadn't noticed."

"What a surprise," I said, "Mexicans like Bette Davis. Must be the eyes…"

She glared at me. "I don't know if they even *know* who Bette Davis is," she said.

"No? Then, how come you found some of her movies?"

"Gentry's has a little bit of everything. I think they're an outlet store for things that don't sell elsewhere. When I asked th' manager if he had anything with Bette in it, his face lit up and he pulled out a whole collection from underneath th' counter somebody had ordered, but never picked up. I guess I was just in th' right place at th' right time."

Welllll," I grinned. "Aren't you lucky?"

"Stuff it, Mac, or I'll go back and buy you the entire Barbra Streisand (sp?)Bette Midler collection."

CHAPTER FIFTY-SIX

In the weeks that followed, my nose healed and Doc removed the bandage, thus making my face fifty pounds lighter and improving my eyesight vastly. Noreen hadn't been around in over a month and I attributed her absence to my nose healing faster. Sam was more relaxed too without Noreen hanging around.

Adding to all this pleasantness, the end of summer was drawing neigh and the nights were getting cooler. After the sun set behind the Rockies, a light wind would pick up and blow all the day's heat away. It was on one such evening, that Sam left the bar to take a shower and watch a movie in her room. I was trying to figure up the week's receipts, when I suddenly heard her let out a scream. Frightened out of my wits, thinking that she'd been attacked by some psycho rapist hiding under her bed (unlikely as *that* was,) I jumped off the bar stool and rushed back to her room. I threw open the door, but she wasn't in there, which was confusing until I heard the shower still running. I ran to open the bathroom door just as she came running out...naked.

I don't know which one of us was the most shocked. Unable to move, we stood there staring wide-eyed at each other, until she screamed and ran back inside, slamming the door. I turned beet red and stammered, "Gosh, Sam, I-I am so sorry -*please* forgive me! When I heard you scream, I didn't think-I just...just..."

She didn't come back out of the bathroom for about five minutes, and I thought she was probably so embarrassed that she'd NEVER speak to me again. I started to leave when she finally opened the door and came out. She had a towel around her, but it was a small cheap one I'd picked up somewhere and barely covered her. She held her arm across the top to keep it from falling off.

I didn't know what to do or say. Her breasts overflowed the top of the towel and her legs seemed to go on forever. I'd been fighting these feelings for her ever since Hank showed up and seeing her like *this* was NOT helping the situation *one* damned bit.

Logic told me in no uncertain terms that she had something very tight with Hank -something that was *not* finished yet. However, my body didn't want to hear logic, so clearing my throat, I asked, "Uh, why-why did you scream?"

"There's something wrong with the water heater," she answered. "Halfway through my shower, the water turned ice cold." I scratched the back of my neck. "But it's a brand new water heater. Legrand put it in when he did the plumbing."

"I know, but that doesn't mean there wasn't something wrong with it when it got shipped."

Hmm, that was true. "Okay, I'll get my flashlight an' go see what I can find."

I turned to go when she grabbed my wrist and let go of the towel. I blinked in total disbelief and watched it fall to the floor. "S-Sam?" I whispered. I bent down to pick it up for her, but she put her foot on top. "Leave it," she said softly. Unable to think or breathe, I stood up again and she led me over to her bed. Throwing back the chenille spread, she crawled in and turned out the light, as I suddenly discovered what it felt like to fall weightlessly through space. She lay back on the pillows and her long dark hair fanned out over the white pillowcases like a mermaid. Still holding me by my hand, she looked into my eyes then pulled me to her and kissed me with such magic that I melted in her arms like a spineless blob.

CHAPTER FIFTY-SEVEN

After that, I couldn't get out of my clothes fast enough -and the instant I wrapped my arms around her body, I knew there would be NO turning back.

Maybe I'd spend the rest of Eternity in Hell for this one moment, but I would *do* it *gladly*.

I no longer wanted to figure her situation out; I just wanted to hold her –be with her. I buried my face in her hair, letting myself get lost in its fragrant softness. Her velvety skin was like nothing my fingers had ever touched before and it set me on fire. I could tell she felt the same way. She wrapped her arms around my neck and continued to kiss me in a way that spoke volumes.

I always believed intimacy should be drifted into gradually, but when you find that 'special someone' -you don't want to 'drift' –you want to run headlong towards her. I'm not talking about one-night stand attractions that end in meaningless sex; I mean a real desire to spend more than just a moment with that person. Sex is like fast food, where making love is akin to fine cuisine and a delicate wine -to be savored and enjoyed slowly. Our lovemaking was like that. Her desire for me was as healthy and strong as mine was for her. Neither of us showed the first signs of tiring and we made love over and over. Her body rose up every time, to meet mine with the same urgency.

Hours later, we lay in each other's arms without saying a word. There wasn't anything _to_ say and words would have been anti-climactic- (excuse the pun.) I also couldn't get over how *she* made the first move. (I was a hater of Women's Lib, but I could get behind *this* rule.) I was happier than I'd ever been in my life. I didn't have a care or worry in the world -that is, until I felt the first pang of guilt creep in like an evil fog. It wasn't subtle either, oh *nooooooo*, Hank's face just appeared in front of me as vividly as if he'd been standing there in person. I frowned and silently told him to go away, but he just stood there with an accusing grin. I looked over at Sam, who was sleeping with a guilt-free smile on her face.

I looked back and damn it, there he was...still grinning at me. The bastard.

CHAPTER FIFTY-EIGHT

I did *not* sleep well that night. I *should* have, but I didn't, thanks to Hank stealing all my joy.

However, Sam woke up smiling the next morning and turning over to me, she said, "Good morning, handsome." Hank was still there, so I resisted the urge when she wrapped her arms around my chest and nuzzled my ear. But when she slowly moved her leg up mine, I squeezed my eyes together and silently groaned. Then she kissed my neck, sending a chill down my entire body -and I rolled over and kissed her while practically crushing her in my arms. (Thankfully, Hank had to decency to disappear and we made love for the better part of the morning.)

Finally, I sat up on my pillows and said, "Sam...we gotta talk. I'm confused as hell. I mean there is *no* doubt how I feel about you, but where did all this come from on your end?"

She sat up, pulling her knees up under her chin and wrapping her arms around them, she let out a long sigh. "I...don't know, Mac. Last night, well, just seemed *right* for us. When we ran into each other –you know –outside the bathroom, something happened that I cannot explain. You startled me when you saw me naked, but I wasn't angry or embarrassed. It was like there was no one else in the world, but us." Sam rested her chin on her knees and looked straight ahead. "I don't know if it was the way you turned your head in the light or what, but the damndest feeling of wanting you suddenly came over me, and I knew if I denied it, it would be the biggest mistake of my life."

I listened, but all I could think of was, "Maybe I WON'T fix the hot water heater if *this* is what a cold shower does." (Dumb, I know, but that's what came to mind.) And yet, I kind of understood what she was saying. It's just that I never expected it to actually happen.

Oh sure, I'd fanaticized about us, but...there was a BIG leap between fantasy and reality.

Naturally, I wanted to talk about Hank and why she was starting something, if he was still in play. But I knew if I brought Hank into this now it would ruin things -which his standing at the end of our bed was already doing. Sam turned to me. "Look, Mac," she said. "I don't know where this is going. I don't even know where I'm going. All I know is I have strong feelings for you, and I don't want to wake up an old lady some day with the regret of never knowing what it was like to make love to you. I've already got enough regrets at *this* age."

My heart leaped at the word "love" then dropped when I realized what she said sounded like a one-time thing. "God, Sam, I hope this isn't just a fling –something to press in your Book of Memories. Because if it is..."

"No, Mac, it isn't and please don't spoil it by trying to turn it into something cheap and sordid." I took her in my arms. "That's not even in the same universe with last night –which is why I was hoping it *wasn't* anything like that." She put her arms around me and laid her head against my chest. We didn't say anything for a few minutes and then I said, "Last night was the most wonderful night of my life, Sam." She lifted her head and a smile spread across her face. "Mine, too, believe it or not."

"But Sam, I gotta know I'm not in this all this alone. I'm not a smart enough guy to play this game. We've started something an' I wanna take it all the way. So -where do we go from here?"

"I don't know. One day at a time, I guess." I still wanted to talk about Hank, but I knew I'd just have be patient and decided to save it for another time. "Okay," I nodded. "That's fair enough." We got up and I left her to get dressed, while I went to check out the hot water heater.

The water heater had a broken thermostat connection, so I called Legrand and explained the problem. He said, "I'll be over to check on it this afternoon,"

"Fine, I'll have a cold one waiting."

An hour later, I was wiping off the bar when Legrand walked in. "I thought you were comin' by sometime late this afternoon," I said. "Yeah, I was, but I got a free minute so I came on."

"Well, c'mon over an' have a beer first." He pulled out a barstool and sat down and I set his beer in front of him. He took a long thirsty draw then wiped his mouth off with the back of his hand. "Man, that's good -nothin' hits th' spot like a cold beer." Looking at me, he said, "You know, your water heater is less than six months old an' still under warrantee."

"Yeah?"

"Did you find out what's wrong with it?"

"Thermostat, I think. A broken connection or something."

"Hmm, yeah, sounds like it might'a happened in shipment. I'll go take a look soon as I finish this." He finished his beer and we left the bar.

"It is a broken wire to th' thermostat, but I wanna check it over to make sure that's all it is."

He went over the water heater with a fine-toothed comb, checking everything twice before he seemed satisfied, then knelt down and wrote the serial number down on a piece of paper. "Let's seeeee, this is an 80 gallon, right?" He scratched his head and asked, "Why'd we put in one so big?"

"Because of the bar an' two bathrooms."

Standing up again, he said, "Okay –that should do it. I'll call soon as I get back to th' store."

As we walked back to the bar, I asked, "Now for th' sixty-four dollar question -how long will it take to get it here?"

"In today's space age, I'd say about a month, or longer" he sighed.

"WHAT???" I yelled.

"Or I can send one'a my guys up to Houston…it'd be faster and cheaper."

"Do that…meantime, Sam can use the shower in th' trailer

"Okay." He put the piece of paper with the serial number in his pocket. "I'll call the supply house in Houston an' if they got th' part, I'll send one of the guys up tomorrow."

"Okay –an' I'll pay for th' gas."

"You bet your sweet ass, you will!" He laughed, but I knew he wouldn't charge me and I'd have to force the money on him. When we got back to the bar, two strangers were standing there in suits and sunglasses. One was taller while the other was short and muscular. I looked at Legrand and we both frowned.

"Hello," I said, suspiciously. "Can I do something for you gentlemen?" Neither one smiled as the taller of the two reached into his coat pocket and pulled out his wallet. Opening it, he flashed a badge, but I noticed it wasn't a cop's. "I'm Michael Shannon," he said. "Are you McIntyre ?"

145

"Yeah, I'm Mac," I frowned, trying to see his eyes behind those dark glasses. "What's this all about?"

"I'll ask the questions, if you don't mind," he answered curtly.

"Well, I DO mind," I said, just as curtly. "You ain't a cop, so what do you want?"

"I run a private detective agency out of Ft. Worth," he said evenly. "I've been hired by someone to find this woman." He held up a photo of Sam. "You know her?

"Why are you looking for her?" I asked, tightly.

"It's a private matter and I'm not at liberty to say. Have you seen her?"

"Maybe-but I'm not telling you a damned thing, so just beat it before I call th' law." (We had no law -not even a sheriff, but I was hoping he didn't know that.) He did and gave me a smart-aleck smile. "Why don't you just *do* that, Mr. McIntyre," he said smugly.

Shit.

We stood there glaring at each other in stalemate. Finally I broke and sighed. "Okay, I know her. She came in here a few months back and didn't look so good. Ends up, that she was sick. I kind'a nursed her back on her feet an' she took off again. Haven't seen her since." I was lying through my teeth and he wasn't buying any of it. "Really?" he said-and without taking his eyes off me, he tucked the photo back in his coat pocket along with his wallet and badge. "Okay, have it your way," he smiled, (reminding me of a cobra.) "I'm <u>very</u> good at what I do, Mr. McIntyre. I know she's still around here somewhere- which means *I'll* be around until I find her." I felt his cold hard eyes bore holes in my skull from behind the dark glasses before he turned and walked out with his 'shadow' following behind him. I didn't know who 'Silent Bob' was, but I figured he was the 'muscle' if things got out of hand.

The door closed behind them and I looked at Legrand. "What'd'ya make of that?"

He shook his head. "I dunno," he frowned. "But th' guy gave me th' creeps."

"Yeah, me too."

"Could Sam be runnin' from th' law or somethin'?" he wondered.

I shot him a dirty look and he threw up his hands. "Hey – you were thinkin' it, too."

"Yeah –well, Sam wouldn't know how to be an outlaw if her life depended-"

I stopped -didn't most people run from the law because their lives *did* depend on it? "Look," I said, running my hand through my hair. "Don't mention a word of this to *any*body –okay? If Sam's in trouble, I gotta help her. It can't be anything serious –I mean, it just *can't*-"

146

Legrand put his hand on my shoulder. "Never mind, Mac. I understand...and don't worry. I won't say a word to anybody."

He started for the door then stopped and turned around. "But let me know if there's anything I can do to help," he said sincerely. "I know some great underground tunnels down by Hidden River that run all th' way to Mexico."

I said, "Thanks, old buddy," and he waved.

Soon as he was gone, I stood there in the dead silence and wondered what the hell to do.

CHAPTER FIFTY-NINE

I went back to Sam's room. She was still in bed, reading a magazine. Looking up, she asked, "I heard voices –who were you talking to?" Not wanting to tell her about the detective, I scratched my head and said, "I thought I left you to get dressed."

"You did, but I haven't got a shower to get into, so I decided to stay here until you got back." She yawned and stretched. "So, what's wrong with th' water heater –an' who was that you were talking to?"

"Broken conection to th' thermostat –an' just some suit that was lost an' askin' directions to Houston."

She frowned. "He *must* be lost if he's 'way out here...and that broken thing means no hot water, right?"

"Right."

"Well, I gotta take a bath or a shower or something!" she said. "How long is gonna take to fix?"

I decided to have some fun with her. "About a month," I said with a straight face.

"A *month*??" she cried.

"Maybe longer."

"<u>OOOOOOOOH</u> *NO!!*" she yelled, throwing back the bedspread.

"That funky stuff might be all right for you guys, but there ain't NO way I'm going to go through *ONE* day without a bath!" She jumped out of bed to go past me, but I grabbed her by the shoulders and said, "Hey, hold up! Just where do you think you're going?" She struggled to break free. "I'm going to take *your* truck and find a motel," she frowned. "One that has a big, *clean*, bathtub with *plenty* of hot water!" I pulled her to me and laughed. "I was only kiddin' you, Sam. Legrand is going to go up to Houston tomorrow and pick us up a new thermostat. We'll have hot water by th' weekend." She jerked away and glared at me. "Th *weekend* -and just what the hell am I going to do, TODAY?"

"Well, I've got th' trailer...why not go out there an' use th' shower?"

"Yeah, I guess I can do that..." Sam took her towel and soap out to the trailer. Twenty minutes later, she came back in looking like a drowned rat. Her mascara was running down her face and her hair was sopping wet...and she was mad as a hornet.

"What th' hell happened to YOU?" I asked.

"Your shower...THAT'S what!"

"What...?"

"I turned on the water, got it just right and got in the tub."

"...And?"

"And just as I got all soaped up, the damned cold water pipe broke and sprayed me straight in the FACE! There is water ALL OVER the bathroom; the place is flooding like th' Titanic!"

"Great," I mumbled.

"So, NOW what am I gonna do?" she huffed.

"Look, I've got an idea, c'mon outside." Sam looked at me warily, but reluctantly followed me out the back door. I showed her the horse trough. "It's sunny and warm today –at least 90 degrees. I can fill that up and you can use it to take a bath. You know, like a swimming pool." Sam relaxed her face, but she *wasn't* smiling. She stared at the horse trough for all of a split second then turned and headed for the back door. "Me 'n Freeway will call you when I get checked in," she said, slamming the door behind her.

Knowing I was beaten, I sighed and got out the hose. I was filling the trough, when Sam came out with Freeway, a suitcase -and MY truck keys. She said, "I think there's a little motel outside Mesa. I'll call you with th' number in case you need your truck." Walking over to the driver's side, she opened the door and threw the suitcase in. Climbing in with Freeway and slamming the door behind her, she turned the key in the ignition. As the truck idled, she leaned her elbow out the window and said, "Have a nice time in your horse –thingy." And with that, she put the truck in gear and roared out of here.

I stood there feeling like 'Magnum' after Higgins took away the keys to the Ferrari –AND the wine cellar.

Meantime, my trough was overflowing and I shut off the hose. Stepping back out of the puddle, I tore off my clothes and grumbled, "To hell with her. This is a perfectly good bathtub –so what if the water ain't hot?" I got in without giving it a second thought and gasped as my balls disappeared into my stomach. Easing down into the painfully icy water, I made a mental note to ask Sam if I could maybe take a shower once she got checked into the motel.

After I got acclimated to the water and scrubbed myself clean, I got out and toweled off. I grabbed my shirt and jeans and pulled the plug on the trough to drain. When I was dressed, I went inside and found a card lying on top of the bar. I picked it up and saw that that asshole Shannon had left it. I fingered it and wondered again why the hell he was looking for Sam. Just then the door opened and two cowboys came in. I put the card in my shirt pocket. They sat down at one of the tables over by the pool table and yelled for two Coors. I nodded and brought them over. We shot the breeze for a few minutes then I waved and went back to the bar. I no sooner got back than the front door opened and Juan came in. My face lit up, as he came over with his ever-present baseball cap perched on top of his shiny black hair. "Hola, Senior Mac," he beamed.

"Where you been, boy?" I smiled. "Haven't seen you in a while."

"Si. I am in the school."

"Oh yeah, I forgot about school –so, how is it? You leaning anything?"

He nodded. "My English she ees muy mucho gooder."

"The word is 'better' –not 'gooder," I corrected.

"Oh, yes –'better.' Gracias, Senior Mac."

I got him a coke and asked how his family was then he asked how Sam and Freeway were. Everyone was fine and he sipped on his coke before asking, "I need to sweep, today –yes?"

"You know where th' broom is," I said. He finished his soda then hopped down and went to the broom closet.

An hour later, Juan had every corner swept out and the floor looking spotless. I gave him ten dollars and he left for home. The rest of the afternoon segued into a slow quiet evening. Sam called from a little motel she found just outside Mesa to give me her phone and room number. I told her to have a relaxing bath and I'd see her after Legrand got the hot water working again.

Another month went by and soon, we were in the middle of October. Talk around the bar turned to the holidays and the families that would be coming out. I didn't see any more of Mr. Shannon, but that didn't mean he wasn't still lurking in some dark corner somewhere.

I'd all but forgotten about Hank Fairfield when one afternoon the phone rang. I was in an unusually cheerful mood until I heard his voice on the other end. "Howdy, Mac, this is Hank –how're y'all doin' down there?" My throat constricted and burned like hell, but as soon as I was able to swallow again, I said tonelessly, "Hank -what a surprise..."

"Bet y'all thought Ah forgot all about ya, didn't ya?"

"Uh –yeah-I mean, *no*, no, of course not."

Knowing the next question out of Hank's mouth would be him wanting to talk to Sam, I glanced around for her...and sure enough, he said, "Sam around?" I wanted to tell him she wasn't, but knew it would be a stupid thing to do, so I said, "Sure. She's on the other side of the room though, I'll have to call her over."

"Thanks, Mac."

I laid the receiver across the top of the pay phone and signaled for her to come over. She saw me and excused herself. "What is it?" she asked, when she reached the bar.

I pointed to the telephone. "It's for you. It's Hank."

Her smile disappeared and she gave me a quick look before she went to answer the phone. I didn't want to hear their conversation, so I stayed at my end of the bar, wiping my hands over and over until they were raw on a bar towel. I KNEW this call was going to come one day... Twenty minutes later, Sam hung up and came down to me. I threw the towel down and looked at her. "So?" I asked evenly. "How's Hank?"

"He's...fine," she answered, without looking at me. "He wants me to come to Houston for th' weekend. He needs to talk to me."

I didn't say anything and she looked up. Shrugging my shoulders, I said, "So...go. I don't own you." It was a jackass thing to say, but I was pissed, hurt and worried as hell, and I'd be damned if I was going to make her stay if she didn't want to. "You gonna take th' truck-or do you plan on not coming back?" (The 'Moment of Truth' was here and I held my breath.)

"Of course, I plan on comin' back," she frowned angrily. "What kind'a question is that?"

"Under th' circumstances, a damned reasonable one, I think."

"Yeah," she sighed. "I guess it is."

It was half a day's drive to Houston and Sam left out of here early Saturday morning in my truck. There wasn't much to say before she left, so I stayed inside and watched from my bedroom window. Since she didn't take Freeway, I held on to the strong belief that she really would be coming back. I told myself that I had to let her go. She needed to work something out with Hank and if what we had was real, she'd be back. We couldn't have anything with him in between.

I'd seen time drag before, but *never* like I did that weekend.

Saturday night was unusually crowded and I stayed busy, but seemed to move in slooow motion. My band played about a dozen new songs and everyone was having a great time. They didn't have a care in the world and how I envied them. Around 9:30, Noreen walked in. She came up to the bar and sat down. I'd been trying not to think about Sam and Hank, so I was almost glad to see her. (If *anyone* could keep my mind of things, it would be Noreen.)

"Hi, Mac."

"Hello, Noreen."

"Gimme a margarita, will ya?" She looked around the bar. "An' where's that waitress of yours tonight?"

"Why –you wanna apologize to her for th' last time you were in here?"

"Not hardly," she frowned. "I just thought maybe you'd wised up an' fired her."

"I haven't –an' I'm not going to, so get used to it."

"Whatever," she waved. "So-where is she?"

Setting her margarita down, I said, "You must have radar, Noreen, because Sam's not here. She's up in Houston with Hank Fairfield for th' weekend."

Noreen's eyes flashed and a dark frown crossed her face. She picked up her drink without saying a word, but by her third margarita, she was loose enough to start yapping about Sam. "She's up in Houston, eh?" she said. "What's th' deal? I thought you an' her was"

"Was what," I glared.

"Ain't you worried that she's with that dude?"

"I don't wanna talk about it with you, Noreen, so just shut up and drink your tequila."

She giggled. "She's makin' a fool outta us both –maybe all *three* of us, countin' Hank."

Noreen's acid words were <u>not</u> helping the situation *one* bit. I knew she was insensitive to everybody's feelings but her own and usually made allowances for her stupid thoughtlessness, but I was on dangerously thin ice here. "Look," I said. "Just button it or I'm gonna throw you out."

"Awww, what's th' matter Mac? Broken heart?"

"What would YOU know about a heart -much less, a *broken* one, you dizzy tit?"

Noreen fluffed her hair and said nonchalantly, "This conversation bores me."

"Good –then change it!!" I cried, just as somebody called out, "Hey, Mac! How 'bout a couple'a beers over here?" I stood back and pointed my finger at Noreen. "YOU just better straighten up, Noreen. I mean it." I got the beers and walked down to the end of the bar.

As I set them down, one of the cowboys asked where Sam was, and the misery started all over again.

CHAPTER SIXTY

I was an emotionally exhausted wreck by the time I heard my truck pull in Sunday night. Her return didn't end the anxiety either- it just heightened it. Part of me was so glad she was back, but the other part was scared to death to hear what she might have to tell me. I was drying a glass and watched the back door open with my heart in my throat. Waving to me, Sam came up to the bar and gave me a kiss on the cheek. I'm naturally suspicious, so her good mood could only mean ONE thing. "Have a nice weekend?" I frowned. She handed me the truck keys and nodded. "Not bad. Hank played to a standing-room-only crowd."

"I didn't know he was there to do a concert," I said stiffly.

She looked at me and grinned. "Well, why else would he be there?"

"To see you, because he didn't wanna come here."

She laughed. "No. He had a sell-out concert to do."

I wanted to know what happened *every second* she was gone, but wasn't sure I'd believe her if she said nothing. Still, I went ahead and asked, "So, what happened between you 'n Hank?"

"Nothing happened," she shrugged, innocently.

My jealousy was getting the better of me and I almost came unglued when I heard those words. I thought instantly, "Yeah, I'll just *bet* it didn't."

But I held it together and asked instead, "Oh, really -then, why did he want to see you?"

"He just wanted to talk to me about some business concerning th' ranch," she said.

The <u>ranch</u>?? **What** ranch?

Sam noticed my confusion and said, "Our ranch just outside Dallas."

"*WHAT*??" I cried. "You live on a *RANCH*? With *HANK*?"

She nodded.

"For *how long*???"

"Gosh," she said, "forever."

THAT did it and my eyes bugged out of my head! After trying to hold it together all weekend, I exploded. "<u>YOU</u>! LIVE-ON-A-RANCH!!!" I screamed. "WITH HANK!" I paced up and down the bar, holding both sides of my exploding head. Finally, I stopped and looked at her.

"**WHAT** are you *doing*, Sam? Is this some kind of cruel game you're playing –because if you're trying to kill me, you're SUCCEEDING!!"

She held up her hand to stop me from ranting and raving. "No –<u>wait</u>, Mac! You don't understand! Let me explain –Hank and I are-"

"*STOP* IT, Sam! Just <u>stop</u> it *right* there. I've had all I can take. I'm done. Enough!"

I threw down my towel and walked as fast as I could from the bar, slamming the back door on my way out. If she was going to tell me that they were married or committed to each other, I did NOT want to hear it. I went to the kitchen and got out a bottle of bourbon from the cabinet. My last nerve was shot! My hand was shaking and tears stung my eyes, as I poured myself a stiff drink. I couldn't <u>believe</u> what I'd just heard. Sam and Hank. Living together. On a ranch.

And *she* thought nothing about it!

CHAPTER SIXTY-ONE

I couldn't even look at Sam for the next two weeks. Every time she tried to talk to me, I'd just turn my back or walk away. Needless to say, things became very strained between us.

Winter was now just around the corner and my heart turned as cold as the north wind that blew through the rafters. The only way I could stop the hurt was to stop feeling anything at all, and people began to notice. Harley was the first. He wanted to say something, but wasn't one to pry, so he just went on as if nothing was wrong. Doc asked if I was getting much sleep and when I said no, he asked if I needed something. I said, "Only if it's laced with cyanide."

November replaced October and Thanksgiving was less than a week away, when I got up one morning to find my truck gone. At first, I didn't give it any thought, but when I didn't see Sam *or* my truck by the next night, I started to wonder. If I hadn't had my head so far up my butt, I would have noticed Freeway was gone too, but I was too busy being pissed at her for keeping my truck so long. It was a slow night and when I still hadn't heard anything by closing, I went back to her room. As soon as I opened the door, the strangest feeling came over me. Although it was dark inside, I could tell *something* was <u>definitely</u> wrong.

I crossed the room and turned on one of the bedside lamps. The colorful pillows were scattered out across the brown chenille bedspread and the black curtains were drawn over the window. Her T.V. and videos sat next to her bed –just like always. Everything was perfect, but the room had an air of 'finality' about it.

I hurried over to her closet and threw the doors open. Empty hangers swung back and forth. Fighting back a rising panic, I searched the room for her suitcase. When I saw it was gone too, I felt physically sick and rushed to the bathroom to throw cold water on my face.

Water dripped down my neck, as I leaned on the sink and slowly looked up in the mirror. What I saw staring back shocked me. From somewhere in back of my skull, two sunken eyes stared out of two dark holes in a shallow unshaven face. I had become a wrath. Wiping my face off, I went back to her room. The hollow emptiness was like she'd never been here.

By now, I knew Freeway was gone too and seeing her little dog bed was more than I could take. I sat down on Sam's bed and let out all the tension of the past nine weeks. Ten minutes later, I wiped my eyes and saw a folded piece of paper lying next to the T.V. It was addressed to me and recognizing Sam's handwriting, I quickly grabbed the note and unfolded it.

It said:

> *Dearest Mac –*
> *We were on our way to finding something really special but ever since Houston, things have deteriorated between us -and I guess I can see how they would. They say hindsight is 20/20, so by the time I realized that I'd handled this all wrong, you were unwilling to listen, and now I don't think you'd believe a word I said.*
>
> *I wish you'd given me a chance to explain, but...maybe this way is best. Lately, things have taken such a left turn that I feel the only thing left to do is give us some space.*
>
> *Of course, Freeway is with me and I promise to take good care of her.*
>
> *As for us, well, maybe later on down the line, things will work out and we'll be together again. Meanwhile, please don't think badly of me –or Hank. He really is innocent in all this and all I can say is, trust me, things aren't always the way they look.*
>
> *I guess there's nothing else to say, except that you'll find your truck at the bus station in Houston. The keys are over the visor.*
> *-all my love,*
> *Sam*
> *p.s.*
> *By the way, Hank told me he hired a private detective four months ago out of Ft. Worth. His name is Shannon and if he hasn't shown up already, don't worry about it. Since Hank found me on his own Mr. Shannon is no longer in the picture."*

"Shannon!" I whispered, reaching into my pocket and pulling out his card. I tore it up along with her note, and threw the pieces in her wastebasket.

She'd never be coming back and to believe it would be a waste of my life.

CHAPTER SIXTY-TWO

Sam was gone.

Freeway was gone.

...And my truck was sitting somewhere up in Houston.

I closed the door to Sam's room and headed back to the bar. If *ever* there was a time to get soused, this was it. Grabbing an unopened bottle of bourbon and a glass, I sat down at the bar to do some serious drinking.

With the loss of brain cells comes blissful blackness, so the last thing I remember was pouring the last drop of bourbon into my glasses (-there were two of them by then.) Sometime the next morning, it felt like a billion killer bees stinging the tar out of my face. I tried to fight them off, but they kept coming in waves. I woke up enough to find myself lying on the floorboards behind the bar and Noreen straddled across my legs. She was shouting for me to wake up and slapping me with both hands. I grabbed both her wrists and yelled, "STOP it, Noreen! My GOD, woman, you're killing me -an' what are you doing on top on me?"

"Oh, Mac," she sighed. "I thought you were dead."

"Well, I'm not, an' my face is burning like a red-hot poker."

I happen to glance at Noreen and did a double take. Her lips were black and so were her nails.

"What th' hell happened to your face?" I scowled. Spreading out ten black claw-like fingernails, she said, "This is the latest color called, "Death Grape" -you like it?"

"Uge -you look like an apprentice carpenter who had a bad first day on th' job!"

"So, what happened?" she asked smugly. "Your waitress knock YOU out too?"

"No, you idiot, I drank too much last night. Look, I need to get up, so get off me."

"Here, let me help you," she said, backing off my legs. I cringed at her offer, but I sure wasn't in any shape to make up by myself. Rubbing the back of my neck, I sighed, "Okay, if you can just help me out to my trailer, I'll get into bed and sleep th' rest of this off."

I THOUGHT she'd take my hand and help me up, but noooooooooo, not her. I no sooner got the words out of my mouth, than Noreen had me slung over her shoulder like a sack of potatoes and we were out the back door with my head bobbing like a bobble doll. It took every one of my mental powers not to throw up.

She carried me up the steps, through the front door and down the hall where she *threw* me across the bed. I felt like a Mallard duck who'd just made a bad landing and tried to move, but Noreen flipped me over -and in the blink of an eye, had my pants off. With only my skivvies to protect what little self-respect I had left, she threw my legs under the blanket and covered me up to my chin. "There, Mac," she said with soft motherly concern. "How's that?" -and she actually patted me on my head. Pushing her hand away, I muttered, "Don't ever have kids, Noreen, unless they're born with reinforced titanium spines!" I glanced over at the clock on my nightstand to see what time it was, but the hands kept melting together like a Salvador Dahli painting.

I gave up trying and asked Noreen what time it was. "It's...let's seeeee, uh..." she squinted. "It's...uh..."

"Just tell me what numbers the big and little hands are on," I frowned. She picked up the clock and brought it about two inches from her face. "It's eleven thirty."

I always suspected she was nearsighted, but too vain to wear glasses.

This confirmed it.

Noreen left and I drifted off to sleep, waking around three in the afternoon. I got out of bed, stumbled into the bathroom and immediately threw up. Five agonizing minutes later, I dragged my sick sorry ass over to the tub and climbed my way back up on my feet. Opening the medicine cabinet, I took out a bottle of aspirin and caught a glimpse of myself when I closed it again. My eyes were internally hemorrhaging and both cheeks were a vivid shade of purple. I was pretty sure shaving was going to be excruciating and decided to hell with it. I got in the tub and took a long hot shower before getting dressed.

CHAPTER SIXTY-THREE

I got my truck back, thanks to Legrand taking me to a Greyhound bus stop. I caught the bus to Houston, found my truck right where Sam said it'd be and drove it back.

Thanksgiving came and went, along with Christmas and New Years. Soon spring had the entire desert in bloom. By Summer I only thought of Sam on that hot day in July when she first came into my bar –and life. Then winter was here again and a whole year had passed since she left. I never heard one word from her in all that time and eventually gave up hope of ever seeing or hearing from her again. I knew she and Hank were together on their ranch in Dallas, and tried not to dwell on it.

In time, my life settled back into the old routine. Noreen was thrilled to be the only female holding court in my bar again and never mentioned Sam's name. For as dizzy as she is, I think deep down she knew how I felt about Sam and didn't mention her because she didn't want to look like she was rubbing it in. (And probably because she knew I'd 86 her from the bar for life if she did.) Doc and Harley didn't mention Sam either, although I'm sure they often wanted to know if I'd heard anything. They loved her and Freeway as much as I did and had hoped everything would work out between us. I didn't listen to country music as much these days and when Hank came out with a new release I refused to put it on the jukebox -even after it went to number one.

One day, I was behind the bar and switched on the radio. I put it on the public radio station to listen to some classical music, which thanks to my mother, I learned to enjoy as a kid. I was listening to a beautiful opera, when the door opened and Noreen came waltzing in. Seeing Noreen while listening to opera is akin to trying to relax on a bed of nails. She pulled out a stool and I cringed as she raked it across the floor.

"Hello, Mac," she smiled, wiggling her tush over the barstool. "What's that you're listenin' to on th' radio?"

"It's opera," I answered, expecting her to say something stupid, but she said, "Oh my gosh, I **LOVE** opera!" I thought I was hearing her wrong and said, "You *what*?"

She grinned and said, "I *love* opera."

"Oh c'mon, Noreen -I don't believe you. Opera is so *heavy*." (If Noreen understood opera then life, as I knew it was over.) But she insisted that she "loooved opera."

I knew stranger things were possible, but I was still leery when I asked, "Do you have any...particular favorite?"

She looked at me and blinked a couple of times. "There's only ONE opera, silly!"

I was taken aback. "Really -and THAT would be...?"

"The Black one, of course!" (The *Black* one??) Dear God in heaven, the dizzy-tit knew "Aida!"

Maybe I'd underestimated Noreen all these years; maybe she did absorb more than sunlight and air after all. I whistled. "Boy, I never would'a figured you to know Verdi—and I DO mean NEVER!" Then I recalled the elaborate costumes they wore in "Aida," and saw how she might be drawn to that particular opera -especially the eye make-up.

She leaned her elbow on the bar, cupping her hand around her chin. "Boy, you really are dumb, Mac."

"Whoa, Noreen! Just because you're a little knowledgeable about Verdi doesn't mean you can EVER call me dumb!"

She sat up. "Well for gosh sakes, Mac," she sighed. "<u>EVERYBODY</u> in the WORLD knows opera's last name isn't 'Birdie' -or whoever you just said!" -and she gave me one of those limp-wristed wave-offs women do when they think they know everything.

"Her last name is Winfrey -Opera Winfrey! An' she only <u>USED</u> to be heavy. She's been on this diet forEV-VER an' looks absolutely FAB-U-LOUS!" ...And without pausing for breath, Noreen went on to inform me that: "Opera HAS a television show in th' afternoons ya know, an' if you watched it instead of listenin' to her on th' radio, you'd know what she looks like!" Then she frowned, "An' what's up with that awful music she has on today?"

I blinked incredulously before raising an eyebrow and saying evenly, "Noreen. Get...out!"

When she asked "why?" -I felt my eye begin to twitch. I didn't answer and she sniffed, "Fine, I'll just go home and watch her on television." She got up with her nose in the air and indignantly headed for the door. But on her way out, she turned around and gave it one last shot. "Hey, Mac, wanna know what Opera's last name is backwards?" she asked.

"NO, I don't!" I hollered. "And if you tell me, I WILL throw this glass at you!" She turned and walked out, slamming the door behind her. "It's Harpo," she yelled from the other side.

I drew back my arm -then said to hell with it. No sense wasting a perfectly good glass.

Around six thirty, Harley stopped in. We got into a conversation about cattle and round-ups and I asked him what it was like to live on a ranch. He thought about it a minute then said, "It's hard work, but there's no life like it. It has its own rhythm an' its th' only life for me."

In that instant by the look on Harley's face, I clearly saw why Sam went back to Hank. That life had to be wonderfully fulfilling. I had nothing like that to offer her.

"Mac? You still with us?"

"Huh? Oh, sorry, Harley. I was just thinkin' about what it must be like." I looked at him and asked, "You ever own your own ranch?"

"Yeah, I had a small one a long time ago, up in Wyoming."

"Yeah?"

"You live on it by yourself?"

He shook his head. "No- I was married at th' time."

"*YOU* were *married*?"

158

He nodded, but I saw great sadness in his eyes. "About twenty five years ago, I was married to a Comanche woman. She was as beautiful and graceful as a doe. She had big warm brown eyes an' th' longest, straightest, blackest hair you ever saw."

"She must'a been beautiful, Harley –what happened to her?"

"One day, we had to go down to a cattle auction in Arizona to buy a bull. While I was busy getting' th' bull loaded into th' truck, some drunk took exception to a white man bein' married to an Indian. Before anybody could do anything, he pulled out a gun and shot her. She was dead before she hit th' ground."

I stood back and swallowed hard. "No!" I whispered. "What d-did you do?"

"I killed him with my bare hands," he said evenly. "I don't remember any of it, but I beat him to death. Ripped out his throat, gouged out his eyes an' broke every bone in his face, back an' neck." He picked up his beer and finished it. "Did seven years for manslaughter."

"*Harley*! " I whispered again. I was so shocked I couldn't speak.

He took a deep breath and letting it out, he said, "Funny thing is, I ain't a 'white man.' My mother was full blooded Apache." (I didn't know he was part Indian and wondered what the drunk would've had to say about that.) Finally, I said, "Would you like another beer?" He nodded and I got him a fresh draught. Wrapping his hand around the mug, he said, "I never talk about that, Mac...an' I'd appreciate it if we never did again." And that was the end of it.

CHAPTER SIXTY-FOUR

I have a color television over the bar that the guys watch football on sometimes. Its old and the reception isn't great but it does the job. I seldom turn it on unless someone insists, so it was off the day when one of the cowboys came running in. He was all out of breath and it took him a minute before he yelled excitedly, "MAC! Turn on the television, quick! Channel three."

Since we were only a week away from Thanksgiving, the bar was full and I thought he wanted me to turn on a football game. Always glad to accommodate a paying customer, I went over and switched on the set. It took a few minutes to warm up, but as it did, I heard Hank's voice talking to the audience and jerked my head towards the cowboy. "Are you OUT of your ever lovin' mind?" I yelled. "Do you have a death wish??"

"W-wait just a minute, Mac," he said nervously, "an' you'll see why I wanted you to turn it on."

"Yeah? Well, it'd *better* be good!" I warned. The set finished warming up and Hank's face came into focus, dominating the screen (-along with that suit of his.) He was saying, "Welcome, folks, to the "Orange Blossom Special." It's our Thanksgiving tribute to fall, families and good ol' country music. But right now, th' good people at "Butter Rich Biscuits" wanna say a few words about their wonderful products, but stay with us, 'cause we've got a Special Guest here tonight an' you ain't gonna wanna miss it." I tried to tune out the cornball show, but after eight thousand commercials, it was back on and Hank took center stage again, blinding the cameras with laser flashes from his Nudie suit (which was a deep purple "tastefully" trimmed in bright yellow and green Austrian cut crystal.)

After much fanfare, he opened the segment with his latest song (–the one I wouldn't put on the jukebox.) When he finished and the roar of applause died down, he asked for the stage lights to be dimmed. As he requested, the stage lights went down, (but his suit didn't.)

Standing alone in the spotlight, Hank quietly took off his Stetson. An expectant hush fell over the audience, as he said, "Ah promised y'all a very special guest tonight an' Ah aim ta keep my word." Looking down at his Stetson, he cleared his throat. "Ya know," he went on, "it's been a long time since this person stepped on stage an' Ah can tell ya –it's long overdue. So, without wastin' anymore time," he said evenly, "here she is, my sister, Miss Sammy Jo Evans."

Dead silence followed Hank's words, except for the glass I was holding shattering on the floor. Then along with everyone else at the bar, I watched the curtains part and a vision from heaven walked out. *Holy* cow! It <u>WAS</u> Sam! Only...it <u>*wasn't*</u> the Sam I knew.

She was stunningly beautiful. Wearing an off the shoulder rainbow sequined white taffeta gown, she looked like Cinderella. Her rich dark brown hair had grown at least ten inches and flowed past her waist. She had it pulled back in a long straight ponytail surrounded with a crown of white gardenias, and the only jewelry she wore was a large pair of cluster diamond earrings. She sparkled like a million dollars, but it was those beautiful cornflower blue eyes that shined the brightest -even out sparkling Hank's suit. I stared at the television while my mind tried to grasp what the hell Sam was doing on a stage in Nashville, Tennessee. I <u>knew</u> why Hank would be there, but -why Sam?

Hank came up to her and put a reassuring arm around her tiny waist, as she waited for the thunderous applause to stop. The audience was now on their feet giving her a standing ovation, and the pride in his eyes was unmistakable. After three very long minutes, Sam finally walked up to the microphone and removed it from the stand. A hush fell over the audience as they waited for her to speak.

"Thank you," she said in a voice so soft you almost couldn't hear it. "Thank ALL of you, very, very, much."

"It's been a long time since I was up here and I-I don't know..." (Her voice faltered and she began again.) "I don't know how to-to *thank* you for the way y'all have stayed so loyal to me throughout the years, especially this *last* one." She absently rubbed her eyebrow. "I kind'a got burned out a year or so back and had to just get away for a spell. Anyway," she went on, "one day I found myself at a little crossroads smack in th' middle of nowhere. It wasn't much more than a ghost town, an' I'm not exactly clear on how I got to such a Godforsaken place, but I met some very special people there who didn't have a *clue* as to who I was. And I loved it, because the irony is that I was also at a crossroads in my life. So, when I realized I was just another lost soul passing through, I had the time'n freedom to find myself. It was wonderful because the longer I stayed there the more I learned about life -and *my* place in it. So, I want to dedicate this song to *everyone* in that special place, but most especially to the man I love. I-I hope you're watchin', Mac." I thought about it for a moment then turned to Harley and asked, "She IS talking about me, isn't she?"

"No, I don't think so," Harley replied dryly, "Must be another guy named Mac that lives out in th' middle of nowhere."

"Just for that," I said, "you're gonna pay for th' next beer."

"Shhh," Harley frowned. "Will you please be quiet? I'm tryin' to watch a friend of mine."

I smiled and turned back to the T.V. as a hush fell over the darkened stage and auditorium. Then somewhere in the darkness, a steel guitar began to play and orange lights slowly came up behind a transparent curtain. Behind the curtain, musicians appeared in silhouette. As she waited for her cue, Sam brought the mike up to her lips –and suddenly, I KNEW who she was! I clamped my hand over my mouth as my eyebrows shot straight up.

OH, my GOD -WHAT a DUNCE I'd been not to recognize her. HOW *many* TIMES had I listened to her on the radio? She was Sammi Jo *Evans!* And she was *Hank Fairfield's sister!*

Who knew he had a sister –or that it was *Sam*? I almost fainted, but decided to do it after she finished her song.

"You know, I've traveled all over this green and growin' land...
And I've seen all there is to see...
But of all the things I've ever done...
What means the most to me...

Is to share all of it with someone."

"I've seen th' high mountains...th' valleys an' th' plains...
I've seen th' sky above, oh, so blue...
I've felt th' warm breezes...th' soft an' gentle rain...
But had no one to tell it to."

"So, I guess I'll keep on looking...
Until I find a love of my own...
Then maybe I can stop all this wanderin'...
And finally call one place home."

The lilting folk-like melody segued into another song; one that was stronger and faster. The audience picked up the beat and started to clap along as the entire band joined in.

"We passed through life...
Just the Devil and I...
Havin' a good time...
With no time to cry."

"The world belonged to me...
And my ego was solid brass...
I used my youth in so many ways...
Thinking it would last..."

"Then one night, while I was dancin'...
Th' music went strangely out of tune...
I looked around to see...
If anyone else heard it in th' room..."

"Hollow faces stared back at me...
I saw misery in all their smiles...
Suddenly, I felt cold and empty...
As the Devil mocked me all the while..."

"I was th' one who'd been so wrong...
When I played such a wicked part...
And that night I learned the real fool is,
The one who never has a broken heart."

The song went up another note and Sam took a step back. The music swelled to a crescendo of instruments in perfect harmony with the bass and drums being the driving force behind the melody. Sam brought the mike up to her mouth again.

"For a heart that can break...
Is one that <u>can</u> mend
To beat stronger than ever before...
When it falls in love again."

The tempo suddenly slowed. All musicians stopped playing with the exception of the harmonica, bass, and a Spanish guitar, as Sam almost spoke the last words of the song.

"The world ain't an easy place...
And it sure as hell ain't mine...
It's just a table we find ourselves...
In a banquet where the Devil dines."

"I wasted so many nights...
In the Game of One Night Stands...
With empty promises of love...
French kisses and boogie bands."

"Love is the only thing...
That you can't give away...
Because the more you try...
The more it comes back to stay."

The last note of the song was played by harmonica and steel guitar. They slid in seamless harmony through octave after octave until they reached the stratosphere. The camera panned away from her, as the spotlight closed in on her face and faded to black. When the song ended, there was a long stunned silence. Then the audience jumped to their feet in thunderous applause. I never saw anything like it; it was adulation mixed with pure love. A young boy came up to the foot of the stage with an enormous bouquet of white roses. She knelt down to take them and fresh waves of unrestrained applause rocketed throughout the auditorium.

They went to commercial, but when they came back the audience hadn't slacked up a bit. Finally Hank held up his hand and signaled everyone to quiet down. It took a while but when they did, he took the mike from Sam. "I also gotta little announcement to make," he said. Sam looked at Hank, like she was wondering what the hell he was up to. Hank and his dazzling suit, looked right into the camera. "My sister ain't th' only one to find what she's been lookin' for out there on them crossroads," he said. "Ah also found what Ah been lookin' for..." and the next words out of his mouth dropped the mother of all bombshells. "Lissen up Noreen," he smiled, "Ah'm comin' back for you," and he winked at the camera. "Because your roamin' days are *over*, you lil wildcat, an' Ah'm bringin' my sharpest spurs along with th' wedding ring."

Before I had time to react to *this* bazaar twist, I heard a loud thud like wet sand hit the floor behind me. When I turned around to see what it was, everyone was bent over like they were looking into a hole. I leaned over to take a look and saw Noreen out like a light for the second time in her life.

I rolled my eyes and sighed; these Fairfields sure had an effect on her.

CHAPTER SIXTY-FIVE

I didn't hear anything from Sam for two days and was about to go crazy. And I wasn't the only one who wanted to talk to her -everyone had a million questions that I had no answers for. By the third day, I was ready to get out Shannon's card and hire him myself when the phone rang. Soon as I heard her voice, I cried, "Sam, I am so *damned* glad to finally hear from you!"

"Mac, I'm really sorry to take so long to call, but it's been crazy as hell here. It's just a..."

There was a lot of noise on her end and I interrupted. "Can you speak a little louder? I'm having a lot of trouble hearing you."

"That's what I'm tryin' to tell you -it's a madhouse here. There's been a steady stream of phone calls and people in an' outta here ever since the show. I'm trying to pack, but it's just been one interruption after another."

"I thought you'd be on your way by now -what's th' hold up?"

"The record people are here wanting me to get into the studio right NOW and record th' song I wrote for you."

"Sam, that song is beautiful. Is that the first time you sang it?"

"You *heard* it, then?" she asked.

"Yes," I said. "It- it was..."

I was so overcome that I couldn't talk and closed my eyes. It seemed like light years since I'd heard her voice.

"Mac...?"

"Th' song was beautiful, Sam," I said softly. "I-I can't wait to see you–when will you get here?"

"Probably not right away," she sighed. "Hank's over there right now tryin' to talk them into giving us some time off, but I've been gone so long that it doesn't look like he's getting anywhere." She stopped talking and all I heard was noise from people in the room. When she spoke again she said, "I just looked over there to see how it was goin' and I can tell you right now, I *will* have to record th' song before I can leave."

"Shit!" I frowned. "What does that mean?"

"It means, I'll have to spend all this comin' week in th' studio before I get outta Nashville."

"Then, I'm comin' up *there!*" I shouted.

"No, sweetheart, don't do that. I'll be in th' studio until all hours of th' night, and too tired to even talk by th' time I get out. Just stay there -it's gonna be hard enough on me as it is."

I took a deep breath and let it out. "Okay," I said, reluctantly. "But I don't like it."

"Look," she said softly. "Soon as I do th' recording, my obligation here will be taken care of an' I won't have to come back for a while."

"Fine," I sighed. "But Sam, do you have any idea how hard it's been these past what –fourteen months -since you just up and left? An' why did you do that without sayin' goodbye or anything?"

"It's a bit complicated, Mac, but for one thing, I had the record company on my back. I have a contract that states I have to do at least two recordings –or more -a year. They prefer I write the song, but that isn't as easy as it sounds. I *tried* to write something, but just couldn't. Between that an' being on th' road, th' pressure built up until I was so exhausted that one night, I threw a few things into a suitcase an' ran away."

I'd never been in show business, but I could understand pressures. Stress, no matter what the source, had its breaking point on the soul, and hers couldn't have been any better or worse than that of someone who'd been in Vietnam. She was saying, "I was so burned out by th' time I walked into your place, that my mind quit thinking about -or remembering much of anything."

"Yeah," I said quietly. "I remember that day well. You looked like something th' cat dragged in and I feel like an idiot for not knowing who you were. Why didn't you tell me?"

"When I woke up from the fever, I didn't know where I was -or who *you* were either. I was so full of paranoia that I immediately thought you were somebody from th' record company who'd come to take me back. I thought your not knowing who I was, was an act. It took me awhile to sort it out in

my head, but when it finally dawned on me that you *didn't* know who I was
-well, there wasn't a *chance in hell* of me telling you. You were wonderfully
real an' I was so sick and tired of the ass-kissing star treatment, that I did
<u>not</u> want to risk *you* changing."

"I don't kiss anyone's ass," I huffed, indignantly.

"Yeah, I know that now, but I didn't back then. I felt so safe an' happy
out there, that I even enjoyed Noreen," she laughed. "Then Hank walked in.
I couldn't *believe* it, but th' second I saw him, I knew it was all over."

"So, instead of taking that opportunity to enlighten me, you just let me
think Hank was your "significant other." Great. Talk about losing your
mind..."

"I'm sorry, but I panicked. I felt like a cornered rat when I saw him and
figured he'd spill th' beans about everything, but thankfully, he picked up
on y'all not knowing who I was an' didn't say anything. He bought me a
little more time to get it together, but I could see in his eyes that he wasn't
going to let go on for much longer."

"Swell," I grumbled. "For over a year, I've about shot myself thinkin' I
did somethin' that made you just up an' leave."

"You...did," she said, cryptically.

"Was it just one thing –or is it more?"

"It's...complicated."

"And just *what* did I do?"

"Well, for one thing, you made me fall in love with you. I didn't realize it
until that night we spent together. The next day, I wanted to just let go and
fall head over heels."

My heart skipped a beat. "Then, *why* didn't you, Sam?"

"Because, I was afraid to turn loose. I just wasn't ready..."

I remembered my own life of torment and confusion over Jenny after I
came home from the war. I wasn't anywhere *close* to being ready for love
again either. "I...can understand that," I whispered. "It's painful to jump
into loving somebody if they aren't there to catch you."

She didn't say anything. Then she said, "Look, I have to go. Hank's calling
for me to come over an' talk to the record execs."

"Don't go, Sam. We've still got so much to talk about..."

"I'm sorry, Mac, but I have to. I'll call whenever I can," she said, and hung
up.

I put the receiver back on its hook and frowned. When I asked her what
I'd done to make her leave so suddenly, she avoided giving me the whole
answer. Falling in love wasn't the only reason she'd left and although I
didn't know what it was, I *did* know there was more.

CHAPTER SIXTY-SIX

Ever since Jenny's betrayal, love only meant one thing -horrible hurt and the bitterness of being alone; of giving your heart to someone only to have it shredded and thrown back in your face at the time you needed them most. But since hearing the words of Sam's song –and now talking to her, I felt like we were finally on the same page...and it was something I'd never experienced before. Marriage had *never* even been a *remote* consideration for me, but after Sam left, I realized I'd been living only half a life. She was what was missing in my soul. Without her, I'd never be complete. I wondered if she felt the same way and was thinking about it when the door opened and Juan came in.

"Meester Mac! Meester Mac!" he cried. "Meese Sam! She ees on the teevees last night."

I told him I'd seen her and asked if he'd like a coke? He nodded and jumped up on a stool. Taking off his baseball cap, he laid it on the bar and asked breathlessly, "She ees coming back?"

"She is," I nodded, "-and she's bringin' Freeway with her."

"Oh, I mees leetle Freeway," he cried. I was about to agree with him when the door flew open again and interrupted me. I frowned, as it slammed against the wall and Noreen came running in like the FBI was after her. "MAC!" she cried.

"For Pete's sake, Noreen -what th' hell's th' matter?" She ran up to the bar and had to gulp a few times before she could catch her breath. "Mac, have you heard anything from Sam or Hank?"

"Yeah," I said. "I just hung up from talkin' to Sam a few minutes ago - haven't you heard from Hank yet?"

She shook her head. "We've never talked, so he wouldn't know where to find me."

"Oh yeah," I said, remembering he'd only spoken to her the one time he was in here.

"Okay -so where are you stayin' these days? I'll tell Sam, so she can tell Hank."

"You know that old motel about a mile from here? I'm stayin' there."

I knew the place she was talking about. "You're stayin' in *THAT* old place?" I frowned. Everybody called it the "Bates motel," because it hadn't been in operation for decades and was so run down. "*Damn*, Noreen, does anyone actually stop in that creepy place an' rent a room for th' entire night without fleeing for their life before sunrise?"

"No, it's closed, but I know old Mrs. Deerfield and she lets me stay there sometimes."

I shook my head, unable to imagine *anyone* staying there. "An' you're okay with that? Man, you got balls, Noreen I'll give you that. That place is straight out of a Hitchcock movie. Does your room even *have* a phone?"

"*Yeah*, believe it or not -an' th' room is darn pretty nice. Every year, she has it fresh painted in pink paint and there's a little girl's frilly white canopy bed in there with white furniture, along with clean sheets, T.V. and electricity. "Course I gotta wash an' change th' sheets 'cause there ain't no maid service."

"Wait a minute -you mean, only *one* room is kept clean?"

She nodded again. "Uh huh. She said she keeps it like that for her little granddaughter –you know, just in case she ever comes to see th' poor ol' thing."

(The room sounded like something out of Cinderella's castle at Disneyland.) "My God, Noreen, Mrs. Deerfield must be close to 90 –don't you mean her *great*-granddaughter?"

No, that's what she always calls her - her "little granddaughter."

"Well, jeese –just how old is this granddaughter?"

"Forty two..."

I stared at her for a second then mumbled, "I hope the old lady isn't holding her breath..."

"So, when is Sam gonna call again?" she asked.

"I don't know –she didn't say. They gotta stay in Nashville for Sam to do a recording, then I guess they'll be comin' here. We didn't get that far in our conversation."

"Did she say anything about me –or Hank?"

"Like I said, we didn't get that far."

Her shoulders slumped and I knew she was as disappointed as I'd been for three days. "Look, if you give me your number, I'll give it to Sam an' Hank will call you."

"Do you really think he will?" she asked. "I mean, he could'a just been jokin' about what he said on T.V."

"Forget it, Noreen, Hank's not like that," I reassured her. "I'm positive Hank is a masochist and is in love with you -although, I can't for the life of me explain *why*. But he has a contract with obligations -and while I realize patience ain't your strong suit, right now, you just gotta be patient. Look, trust me –he *wants* to talk to you -and he *will* just as soon as he knows where to find you." Her face broke out in a big smile. She gave me the number and hurried off after saying goodbye. Juan scratched his head. "Mees Noreen ees mucho loco –si?"

"Si," I nodded.

I got myself a beer, refilled Juan's coke and was about to sit down at the bar when the door opened again. Harley and Doc waved, as I said, "It must be open house around here, today." Taking off his Stetson, Harley laid it on the bar next to Juan's baseball cap. "Yeah, we just ran into Noreen –or she ran into us, I'm not sure." He pulled out a stool and sat down, as Doc pulled out the one next to him. "What's got her so flustered?"

"Hank –what else? You guys wanna beer?"

"Sure," Harley nodded.

"An' what about you, Doc?"

"Yes, I'll have one too," he nodded.

While I got their beers, Harley asked, "So, you hear anything yet from Sam?" I nodded and told them all the latest news. I was hesitant to tell anyone that I was thinking about asking her to marry me, so when he asked what came next, I shrugged and said, "Just have to wait an' see." Juan got up and put on his cap. "Gracias for the coke, Meester Mac. I must bee leaving to go back to mi casa. Por favor to let me know wheen Mees Sam comes to here." I smiled. "I'm sure you'll know about it five minutes after she gets here." He waved and left us to our beers.

As I was about to take a sip, the phone rang. I got up to answer it and to my delight, it was Sam. "Hello, Mac. Sorry to have to hang up on you like that, but I had to go. I've got some time now, and wanted to call you back."

"I'm glad you did, Sam. We were just talkin' about you."

"Who's "we" –Doc an' Harley there?"

"They are an' we're all wondering when you'll be getting here."

"I go in th' studio tomorrow an' if I have a sane engineer, I should be able to knock this recording out in just a few takes without him having us re-do the damned thing 140 times just to rack up studio fees."

"Okay, let me know how it goes –oh, and one more thing before you go, can you get Hank to call Noreen?"

"Thanks for reminding me. He's been going crazy wondering how to get 'hold of her. Do you have a number where he can reach her?"

"I do. She was just in here giving it to me." I got out the number and gave it to her. "An' pleeeeeeeeease have Hank call her right now, or as soon as possible," I said. "She thinks this whole thing is a joke."

Sam laughed. "Yeah, so do I, but you wanna hear what's *really* funny? Hank is not only head over heels crazy in love with her for real, but he's gonna ask her to marry him."

"An' that's funny?" I said.

"Think about it. It'll make us in-laws."

My eyebrows shot straight up. "Oh God," I whispered. "I hadn't even considered THAT!"

She said, "Gotta run, I'll call you tonight, but if you don't hear from me, you'll know I'm still in th' studio." We said goodbye and I went back to sit with Doc and Harley. I was telling them what Sam had to say when it hit me. Her exact words were that Hank and Noreen would be our in-laws, and as *horrible* as that thought was, it was also <u>wonderful</u>. *That* meant she *was* thinking about *us* getting married.

CHAPTER SIXTY-SEVEN

We sat there quietly drinking our beers, each lost in our own thoughts.

"You know, Time is the fire we spend our lives in," I mumbled absently.

Harley and Doc looked at each other. "Where'd th' hell did you get that?" Harley wanted to know.

"I dunno," I answered blandly. "Some "Star Trek" movie, I think."

And for as silly as that statement sounded, it proved to be true. Time was, indeed, the fire I spent the next agonizing week in. I thought Sam would NEVER get the song done to her engineer's satisfaction. She had to spend five days going over and over it again until she said she'd lost count on how many takes he'd done. "The man is a sadist," she complained. Just when I thought I couldn't take it another minute, she called and said Hank was loading their things into the limo.

"You're coming in a limo?" I asked. "Holy cow, how come you're not comin' by plane?"

"Because Hank likes keeping his ass on th' ground. I think he's got a "Buddy Holly" complex and is scared to fly. Most singers here in Texas, do."

"Well, I don't care how you get here –just get here."

Later that night, Sam called from the car to tell me they were headed my way. I was so excited that I couldn't sleep and started to clean the trailer from top to bottom. Around 3 a.m., the place was spotless (thus satisfying my Amish roots,) so I took a shower, fell into bed and was asleep before my head hit the pillow.

It took two days for them to get here, but they drove without stopping for anything except gas, restroom breaks and to eat. Hank had called Noreen to let her know he was on his way and she'd been waiting with me since 2:30. The hours dragged by until I was positive all time had just plain stopped. When we heard a car pull up around 4:30, we both shot off our barstools and ran to the door. Reaching it at the same time, we were stuck in the doorway until I elbowed Noreen out of my way. Once we were free of each other, we stood out on the veranda and watched the driver get out and walk around to open the rear door.

Hank's big boot was the first thing out –followed by his enormous frame and Freeway. With a grin on his face, he grabbed my hand and said, "Mac, it's damn good to see you, ponder -and to be back here. God, I love this place." Noreen hung back while Hank shook my hand. I think she still thought this whole deal was just a big hoax, because it was the first time since my knowing her, that she looked like she didn't know what to do with a man. Hank opened his arms wide. "Well," he laughed, " –you just gonna stand there or are you gonna come give me a big ol' hug?" That broke her hypnotic spell and she couldn't run to him fast enough. He lifted her off the ground and swung her around. I turned my attention back to the limo just as the chauffer was helping Sam out of the car.

When she was all the way out of the car, he stepped aside and I could see that she had something in her arms, wrapped up in a blanket. "What's that," I asked, "–a wounded armadillo you found along side of th' road?"

"Not exactly," she smiled. "C'mon over here and take a look."

I went over and she pulled back the blanket. "Mac," she said, "meet your son, Matthew."

CHAPTER SIXTY-EIGHT

The tiniest face looked up at me and smiled. I looked at him then at Sam. She beamed with all the pride of a new mother and I felt every drop of blood rush out of my head -and that's the last thing I remember before waking up lying across my pool table with Sam hovering over me.

"I think he's finally awake," she said, holding a wet towel against my cheek.

"W-what happened," I whispered.

"You fainted, sweetheart. It was thoughtless of me to do this –I should'a told you about the baby, but I thought it would be such a wonderful surprise."

"Oh, it was a surprise, all right."

Sam helped me to sit up. "Are you disappointed?" she asked.

"Are you crazy?" I cried. "I think it's terrific –I just need time to adjust to all this new found happiness. An' what am I doin' on th' pool table?" Hank wrapped his arm around Noreen. "When you dropped like a sack of potatoes," he said proudly, "my little girl here threw you over her shoulder and carried you in."

I shot Noreen the most evil look I could conjure up. "Not again," I growled. "Damn it, I *hate* it when you do that, Noreen!"

"Hey!" Hank cried. "She can't help it if she's strong."

"Then put her in a circus," I frowned. "Just make her *stop* makin' me look like a fool."

Hank had his mouth open to say something, but I said, "And *don't* you say another word!"

Sam leaned over and put our baby in my arms. "No fool ever made anything this perfect," she smiled. "Noreen just wanted to help, that's all."

"Yeah," Hank agreed. "Sam couldn't lift you an' *Ah* shore wasn't about to carry your lilly white ass in, so Noreen rescued you, you ornery ungrateful cuss." I looked at Matthew and couldn't stay mad. "Okay, Noreen, you're off th' hook. But don't ever lay a hand on him, you Amazon."

"You mean, I can't *never* hold him?" she cried.

"Of course, you can," Sam said. "Mac is just kidding."

I said, "I am not," and Sam shot me a look. "Okay, okay...you can hold him, but *only* if Sam stands next to you." I reluctantly handed Matt to Noreen. She was surprisingly gentle as she took him from me. Her face softened in wonder and she whispered, "Oh Sam, he is just precious." When tears filled her eyes, I felt my heart soften. I never thought of Noreen as having an ounce of motherly instinct in her, but clearly a baby brought out *something* hidden and I was seeing her in a whole new light.

"It's time to feed and change Matt," Sam explained. "I'm going to take him and Noreen back to my room. It's been a long trip for him and he's gonna need a nap after he eats."

She took Matt from Noreen and looked over at the chauffeur who had been quietly standing in the far background. She said, "Jerry, would you bring in Matt's things, please?"

The chauffeur nodded and went out. Giving him a quick once-over, I saw he was a tall well-built man of about 35. He wore a gray chauffeur's uniform complete with short black leather driving gloves, gray cap and black visor. I couldn't see his eyes behind the mirrored sunglasses, but I could tell he was a no-nonsense guy.

As soon as the girls were out of the room, I asked Hank, "Where'd you get that guy –the CIA?" "Jerry? Naw, he's been with me for 19 years. He's ex-Navy Seal trained in all that shit they gotta learn –plus he has a course in counter-terrorist driving."

"Right," I frowned, " –like some terrorist is gonna be interested in you."

"Ah didn't *say* they *would* –Ah jest said he was *trained* in that kind'a thing. He's gotta black belt in that same karate stuff Steven Segal does. You should see him –he's faster than greased lightning."

"Yeah, and you exaggerate."

"You jest better hope you don't never see him use it."

I changed the subject and asked Hank what was really on my mind. "Listen, Hank, are you SURE you know what you're doin' - I mean, with

Noreen?" Hank's face grew serious. "Listen, ponder, this ain't mah first rodeo. Noreen's not a virgin, but she ain't a phony who tries to pretend she's one, neither. No, with her, what you see is what you get, an' I like that. She's th' real thing."

"Yeah, so's root canal," I said.

CHAPTER SIXTY-NINE

I have to admit, I wasn't completely convinced about Hank's love for Noreen, but it soon became clear that the two of them were a perfect match -he wasn't wrapped real tight, either. As for me, like anyone who comes in in the middle of a movie, I had a LOT of questions and needed some down time alone with Sam. After I hung a "CLOSED" sign on the front door with a big heart drawn around it, I asked Hank if there was something he and Noreen could find to occupy themselves for the night.

He winked. "Ah'll have Jerry drive me an' Noreen down to Mexico for a night of festivities. Ah'm *sure* we can find somethin' to do South of th' Border."

"Oh, jeese," I frowned, "this has International incident written all over it. Somebody ought'a call the Mexican government an' warn 'em that you two are comin'." Just then, Sam and Noreen came out of the bedroom. Hank told Noreen about their plans for the night and she headed straight for the limo. When they were gone, I turned to Sam and said, "If I'd known it was that easy to get rid of them, I'd have-"

"You'd have what?" she asked.

"I don't know," I shrugged. "But I'd have thought of something."

Sam smiled and picked up her suitcase. "I'm taking this back to my room," she said.

"You hungry?" I asked, and she nodded. "I'm famished," she said. "I'll get Matt and be right back." The three of us went out to my trailer, and while Sam took Matt back to my bedroom, I went into the kitchen to see what I could rustle up for supper. I opened the fridge and found an unopened pack of salami, some Swiss cheese and two ripe tomatoes, along with a jar of pickles and a six-pack of beer. Ten minutes later, Sam came out and we sat down to eat. The conversation was mostly about Doc and Harley, and how things had been around here. I really wanted to ask her about the past year and the birth of Matt, but since I didn't want to push her, I told her nothing much changed around here in the time she was gone. We finished eating and two beers later I took our dishes into the kitchen and put on some coffee. When it was ready, I brought it out to the table. As I handed her the mug, she leaned back and looked at me. "I guess by th' way you've been lookin' at me all night, you've got a lot of questions, don't you."

I was relieved when she said that and said, "Yeah, I sure do."

"Fire away," she smiled.

"Okay, how 'bout startin' with *why* you just up an' left here without a word to anybody?"

Sam looked down for a moment. "Because, the night we slept together, I got pregnant."

I was stunned. Then I said, "Damn it, Sam, why didn't you tell me?"

"Listen, Mac, I want to go back to th' beginning –back to th' day I walked in here, you remember that?"

"Like I could ever forget it," I frowned.

"The day I showed up, I was walking a razor's edge both physically and mentally. I'd been out on the road for sixteen months *straight*. I was sick of not knowing what day it was or what town I was in. They kept promising me some time off, but it never happened. After a while, th' pressure started to build 'n build until I felt like I was losing my mind. At first, I was furious nobody paid any attention when I said I was tired -then I just stopped caring anymore."

"Why on earth, didn't you tell them where to stick it an' take six months off for some R & R?"

"Because," she explained, "I have a recording contract that stipulates I have to do two recordings a year. They prefer we write our own stuff, but I couldn't write my own name anymore, much less a song. It didn't matter, they wanted something written and recorded, so they could get me *right back* out on th' road again to promote it."

She paused, then leaned back and sighed. "Such a vicious cycle. I was burned out and knew I had to get away, but before I had time to make any plan of escape, the damned Thanksgiving Special came up an' *that* did it! Th' sleeping pills I'd been taking stopped working and my hands started to tremble uncontrollably. I became a zombie. One night, I just packed my bag and left. I don't even remember doing it."

"So, what you're saying is, you were supposed to do the Thanksgiving Special *before* you ever showed up here two years ago?"

"Yes...we were already setting up for rehearsals."

"But, the Special aired *this* year."

"Yeah, there's a two year gap. With me gone," she said, "the Special had to be put on indefinite hold and suddenly, a whole lot of people were out of work. *Everyone* was pissed; musicians, stagehands and camera crew, along with other acts already booked. I was in a shitload of trouble. The record company was so furious that they told Hank to find me *fast*, so they could sue me before they shot me. Actually," she smiled, "there was a *long* line of people who wanted to kill me."

(I was beginning to understand the shape she was in when she got here, and why she had to go back and straighten it out.) "So, what happened when you finally *did* show up?" I asked.

"Mmm, let's just say the return of the prodigal daughter wasn't as forgiving as in the Bible. It was tense. However, when I got back, I clearly saw how screwed up my thinking had been when I left. Somewhere in my disturbed mind, I thought if I just stayed out here, it'd all blow over and I'd be forgotten. I'd call Hank someday and tell him where I was but-"

Her face darkened and her voice became angry. "I mean, you couldn't find this place with th' help of NASA, so what're the odds of him just happening to stumble across it?"

She thought about it and shook her head. "Maybe him findin' it *was* just fluke -or maybe it was Devine intervention –I don't know. But whatever it was, at *that* moment I realized how stupid my idea had been and there was no sense runnin' anymore. No matter how well you think you've covered your ass, there's *always* the element of the unexpected."

Sam picked up her coffee.

"That's gotta be cold," I said. "Let me get you a fresh cup..."

"No, thanks, this is okay."

"Okay, so how did you get them to drop th' lawsuit an put you back on th' show?"

"Well, after Hank left here," she explained, "he went straight to the record execs an' told them he'd found me -and as expected, they weren't impressed with the news. They were still were going to take me to court for breach of contract."

"So –what happened?"

"Besides singing, my big brother is a master at two things; guilt trips an' bluffing. With him, the two are interchangeable -if *one* doesn't work he'll use the other. He just reminded them of all the times they'd promised me time off -then said it was *their* fault I got burned out in th' first place. Of course, the executives didn't buy that for a minute –that is, until he casually mentioned that the press was interested in talking to me and knowing all about my absence. He said I could either tell the <u>real</u> story or...say that the record company had "arranged" for me to get away for a little well-earned rest. Especially," she winked, "if HE backed up th' story!"

"Hank is their number one moneymaker and he had 'em over a barrel, sooooooooooooo, after a short meeting, they said they'd drop all charges IF I came back *right* away an' did the Special, along with recording a new song AND keeping all my obligations...on th' road."

"How'd you find all that out?"

"I called Hank one night after you closed th' bar. By then, I was going into my second month, but, wasn't ready for anyone to know just yet. My biggest priority was Nashville. Something had to be done about the mess I'd left. I had to find out how bad the situation was and what to expect after I got back." She took another swallow of cold coffee. "Hank said I should c'mon back as *soon* as possible. If I did, the show would be back on again and things would smooth over...so...I took your truck and left. Sorry..."

"That was rotten," I frowned.

"Hey, this was my mess an' I had to handle it alone."

"I don't agree," I said sternly. "From th' night we slept together, you had me. And even though I didn't know you were pregnant, I had every right to know about Matt."

"You're right," she sighed. "An' Hank rode me constantly to pick up th' phone an' call you!"

"Then why *didn't* you?"

"Please, Mac, let's not fight about this. I did what I thought was best. Maybe I was wrong, but it's in the past now. We're together again–and that's all that should ever matter."

I sighed and gave up the argument. "That's true," I smiled. Then a light bulb went on. "Hey! The show still didn't come on that year –why not?"

"Because, nothing is ever as easy as I hope," she said. "I thought I could get back to Nashville an' get th' special done *before* I started to show. That way, I wouldn't have to tell the bosses and put up with more of their wrath. But, of course, that didn't happen. I was already going into my second trimester, so as soon as we started costume fittings, my seamstress noticed she was having to let the waist of my dress out a bit more each week. Alice has been making my costumes for over ten years and knew what the problem was immediately. She tried to help me hide it -until I finally told her to tell the record company, because I knew if she didn't, she'd lose her job."

"Why did it matter? Pregnant women work all the time today. Didn't Lucille Ball break that barrier?"

"Yeah, but Lucy didn't have an exclusively country audience. Maybe things'll get better in th' 21st Century, but in this day an' age, my being pregnant *and* unmarried still won't fly with country people. Since they're the backbone of my popularity *and* record sales, the execs wouldn't take a chance on offending even ONE person. So," she sighed, "th' Special was put on "hold" *again*...and I had to sit out th' rest of my pregnancy as a pariah."

I frowned. "Why in hell didn't you call me, Sam?"

"I thought we already went through this..." she said. "With everybody so mad about the Special being postponed, I couldn't take a chance on you hating me, too."

"God, Sam...I would'a been *anything* but mad! I would'a been th' happiest man on earth!"

"I realize that now," she nodded. "But I've made so many bad choices over the past two years that I decided not to make any more for a while."

"So, what'd you do for th' next five or six months -take up knitting?"

"Yeah, right. *Me*, knit. No, Hank got me a three-bedroom apartment along with some live-in help, which left me with nothing to do. So I spent the rest of my time eating pickles 'n ice cream an' worked on getting your song ready for *if* and when we *ever* did th' show."

I was about to ask about Matt's birth, when a loud clap of thunder shook the trailer.

"Looks like we're in for a bad storm," I said -and right on cue, another loud clap reinforced my statement. A second later, a scary flash of lightning lit up the windows and Matt began to scream from the bedroom. Sam stood up. "I better go in to him," she said, and I nodded. As she left the table, the skies opened up and raindrops the size of your fist rained down on the roof and pounded the windows. I decided on another cup of coffee and went into the kitchen.

I'd just sat down again when she came back with Matt. His face was red as a beet and crying loud enough to wake the dead. Sitting down in her chair, Sam rocked him gently in her arms. Slowly, he stopped crying and fell back asleep. Looking at me, she put her finger to her lips and whispered, "I'm going to take him back to bed."

When she came back to the table, she was frowning.

"What's th' matter?" I asked.

"How am I going to get back to my room in all this rain?

"You don't. Stay here in my room and I'll take th' couch."

"But everything I need is back there. There's Matt's diapers, my purse, and-"

"Tell me what to get an' I'll go." Another brilliant flash lit up the room and she looked nervously towards the window. "I don't know, Mac. Nobody should go out in this."

"I'm not made of sugar," I laughed. "I won't melt."

Turning back to me, she said, "Yeah, but you know what they say about sinners an' lightning...maybe you ought not chance it."

"So, don't stand close to me," I smiled.

I went to the front door and got my rain slicker out of the hall closet. I put it on and Sam held the door open while I ran out into the pouring rain. Once I got inside the bar, I found her purse on the bed with Matt's diaper bag alongside on the floor. I grabbed them and ran back out in the storm again. She opened the door just as I ran up the steps. "Here," I said, shaking water off and handing her the purse along with Matt's diaper bag. "Is that everything?"

"Close enough," she nodded.

After I hung my dripping slicker up on a peg by the door, we headed back to the bedroom. I got my pillow and blanket and started to leave when she came over and put her arms around my waist. "You sure you don't want to sleep in here with us?" she asked seductively.

"Oh, my naïve little Princess," I said, softly. "There is *nothing* I'd like better, but if I get in that bed, sleep is th' *last* thing you'll get." Wrapping her up in my arms, I leaned down and kissed her long and hard. Afterwards, she said breathlessly, "Let's get a nursery in here as soon as possible!"

I winked at her and said, "Its number *one* on my list."

CHAPTER SEVENTY

Next morning, I woke up early. Still half asleep, I threw back the blanket and stumbled into the kitchen, cracking my toe only once on an end table. Ignoring the excruciating pain, I put on the coffee, hobbled back to the couch and pulled the blanket up over my head. I had no intention of falling back to sleep, but...you know what the road to Hell is paved with, and forty-five minutes later the smell of coffee woke me up. A little smile spread across my sleeping face as I my eyes fluttered open. Yawning, I sat up and stretched, wondering how *anyone* functioned without coffee first thing in the day. Once again, I stumbled into the kitchen. I got out the biggest mug I owned and filled it with the black steaming hot liquid. I drank my first cup standing right there then re-filled the mug and took it back to the couch. All was quiet at the other end of the trailer, so I sat back on my makeshift bed, sipping and staring off into space. As soon as the magic elixir reached the cognizant part of my brain, I went into the dining room and opened the blinds. The sun was out in all its glory. The sandy desert had absorbed the rainwater like a dry sponge and everything was already bone dry.

I was on my third cup of coffee, when Sam came out of the bedroom. By now, I was wide-awake and annoyingly chipper. I smiled and said, "Good morning, sleepyhead."

"Oh shut up," she growled. "It's unnatural to be so cheerful this early."

"I'm not cheerful...I'm on my third cup of coffee."

Her eyes widened. "Oh God. Coffee. Where is it?"

"In th' kitchen –want me to get you a cup?"

She waved me off and followed her nose towards the coffee pot.

"Matt still asleep?"

She nodded and put her finger to her lips. Just then, the phone rang and we both jumped.

"Oh great!!" she frowned, wiping up spilled coffee. I set my mug down and ran back to the bedroom, hoping to get there before it woke Matt. Grabbing the phone on its second ring, I turned away from the bed and said hello. "HI, podner!" Hank boomed, nearly splitting my eardrum in two. I jerked the receiver away from my ear and frowned. "I know you're in Mexico, Hank, but I can hear you fine –no need to shout."

"Jest wanted to call an' let y'all know me'n Noreen are a little hungover, but soon as we can git it together, we'll be back there by early afternoon."

"You mean you're *not* in jail?"

"No," he laughed. "But it ain't 'cause we didn't try…"

"Th' Mexican police must be an understanding lot," I said. "Or did you bribe your way out of trouble?"

"Actually, me'n Noreen found somethin' else to do instead of gittin' neked an' jumpin' in some fountain. But it still involved a lotta tequila.

"Really?" I asked, skeptically. "Well, don't bother tellin' me what it was."

"No, no- *that* came later. No, this is somethin' else –somethin' that involves you guys, too."

"Okay, as long as it doesn't involve the four of us on a trapeze, what is it?"

"Tell ya when we get back -bye!" click.

I hung up the dead receiver and went back to the living room.

"Was that Hank?" Sam asked, knowingly. I nodded and she said, "Did he wake up Matt?"

"No, I got to it before he woke up."

"So- are they in jail?"

"He says they aren't."

She smiled. "Amazing."

"They're comin' back sometime this afternoon –an' he has a "surprise.""

"God, I hope he didn't buy us a hotel," she frowned. "Or a pony for Matt."

"A hotel…?" I said.

"With Hank, you never know."

CHAPTER SEVENTY-ONE

The limo pulled up in front of the trailer sometime between noon and one o'clock. I was in the shower and heard Hank telling Noreen to leave the bags alone and let Jerry bring them in. I got out and dried off, then got dressed and went out to the living room. Jerry was sitting at the table in his chauffeur's uniform, having a soda. He got up when I came in. "I hope you don't mind me taking the liberty of getting a soda from your refrigerator," he said. "Miss Sam told me it would be all right."

"Oh course I don't mind, Jerry, but wouldn't you rather have a beer?"

"He doesn't drink," Hank said.

Looking at Hank then back at Jerry, I said, "You do drugs, then."

"NO dummy, he don't do drugs, neither," Hank growled.

"You mean to tell me," I asked incredulously, "he's worked almost two decades for you, and he doesn't drink or do drugs?" Looking back at Jerry again, I said, "I know -you must be insane already –right?"

"Jerry is a Buddest –he meditates."

"He'd have to," Sam said, "with all th' waitin' around he does for you."

Hank shook his head and said, "Come over 'n sit down an' lissen to th' plan me 'n Noreen came up with while we was down in Mexico." Sam shrugged and we followed him over to the couch. As soon as Hank sat down, he picked up my blanket. "What th' hell is this?" he asked. "Don't tell me you had to sleep on th' couch last night. What'd you do –piss mah sister off *already?*"

"No stupid, we had a bad storm and I slept out here, so she and Matt could take my room."

"Yeah, well if that's true, y'all need to get a nursery." I jerked the blanket away from him. "I *know* that, genius. Now, what's this great plan you came up with?"

He settled back and put his arm around Noreen. "Well, since Christmas is less than three weeks away," he said, "we got ta thinkin' that we all should get married as soon as possible an' head up to Dallas to stay at th' ranch for th' holidays. Like a honeymoon."

Sam's eyes lit up and she jumped out of her chair. "OH, Hank!" she cried. "*That* is a wonderful idea!"

My God! Hank had actually come up with an intelligent idea. I had given the idea of marriage a lot of thought and wondered how to approach Sam about it, but this was the perfect solution. Now, I looked at her. "You *did* hear the part about us getting' married, didn't you?"

She threw her arms around me and nodded. "Oh YES! YES! YES!"

My face was turning blue from the stranglehold she had me in, before she let go of my neck and turned to Noreen. "Noreen!" she cried. "Let's go back an' check on Matt while we plan th' wedding." Noreen gleefully agreed and followed Sam to the bedroom, leaving Hank and me to talk.

"So?" he smiled. "What'd'ya think?"

"I can't believe it," I said. "I've been trying to think of how to ask Sam about getting' married and this is perfect. All that's left is, where an' when?"

Hank called Jerry into the living room. "Jerry will drive us to Houston, where we'll check into th' hotel at th' Galleria on Westheimer. We'll take things from there after we get settled in."

"What about th' rings -shouldn't we get them before the wedding? Or do you propose to use one'a your cheap cigar bands?"

"Everything we need is right there at the Galleria. Jewelry stores, men's tailors, shoe stores, florist, Bridal shops -an' mah cigar's ain't cheap."

"*Bridal shops*? You're planning on it being a *big* wedding? Are you crazy? I thought we'd keep it low-key and go to city hall."

"You don't really know women at all, do ya buddy. Hell- they're WOMEN! A'course they're gonna want a big wedding with all th' trimmin's."

"And I suppose that means Noreen intends on wearing white?" I frowned.

"Yep!" he said. "Jest as white as they make!"

"Terrific," I sighed. "Well, if anybody could curdle the color white…"

"What's that?" Hank laughed. "You think my li'l darlin' should wear a scarlet wedding gown? Cause if ya do, maybe Sam should get one too – "*Daddy*."

I had no comeback for that and said, "Ya know -now that you mention it, white is a nice color. I like white. Tell Noreen she should *definitely* wear white…as white as they make!"

"I thought you'd see it that way," he laughed. Looking at Jerry, Hank said, "Be ready to leave outta here tomorrow, Jer."

"What time, Mr. Fairfield?"

"Noon –that should put us into Houston before dark."

"Very good," Jerry nodded. "I'll be ready."

He said good-bye and I waved to him as he went out the front door. Turning back to Hank, I said, "Where is he going –does he have a place to stay?"

Hank shrugged. "Ah don't know. He may drive back down to Mexico far as Ah know."

"What kind'a boss are you?" I frowned. "Don't you care if he has a comfortable place to stay?"

"Jerry knows this state like th' back of his hand. He's got a million places to go…an' he's been with me long enough to know he has th' freedom to do it, as long as he's back here when Ah need him."

181

"So, you don't care if he stays in a brothel…"

"Nope, jest as long as he's back in time," he said. "But Ah know Jerry, an' he ain't gonna stay in no whorehouse. Jerry's got more quality women stashed around Texas than Ah can keep up with. An' everyone of 'em would give up their left elbow to be with him."

I raised my eyebrows in surprise. "No kiddin'?" I said.

Hank smiled. "Ah've seen one or two, an' believe me, they have class up th' wazoo. Each one of'em makes Miss Universe look downright homely. They're gorgeous beyond words."

"Who's gorgeous beyond words?" Sam asked, as she came in the living room with Noreen and Matt.

"Why, you two, of course," he smiled. "Who else?"

Sam handed Matt to Noreen and sat down. "So-what's the plan?"

Hank told her about leaving for Houston the next day and she said, "Good. The sooner we get to th' ranch, th' better."

I frowned. "Uh…what about the getting married part?"

She laughed and leaned over to kiss my cheek. "That," she said, "is already done in my heart. A wedding is just to keep us in good standing with God."

CHAPTER SEVENTY-TWO

That night Hank and Noreen slept in Sam's old room. Sam, Matt and I kept the same arrangements as the night before. Before going to bed, I packed a suitcase with enough clothes, socks and underwear for three or four weeks, then I called Doc and told him we had decided to go up to Hank and Sam's ranch in Dallas for the holidays. Before hanging up, I asked him to tell Harley to spread the word that the bar would be closed for the next month. I didn't want to tell him about the wedding plans because I knew it would hurt him not to be there with us.

After we hung up, I called Legrand at home and told him essentially the same thing, adding that the keys to the bar and trailer would be under the overhang on the first post to the right facing the bar. I told him to open up anytime he wanted –and maybe a few hours in the late afternoon for the holidays. I knew he'd want to be with his family on Christmas, but I suggested he might open it the week after for New Year's. "Just post a note on the door sayin' what hours you'll be open," I said. "If you decide to do it."

When I hung up from talking to Legrand, I felt like I'd covered all my bases and could leave without worry. I kissed Matt and Sam good night then went out to the couch.

Next day, Jerry pulled up in front of the trailer at high noon on the dot. While he loaded the trunk with our suitcases, I went around the house checking to make sure that everything was either turned off or shut tight. Noreen helped Sam with Matt and Hank stood around smoking a cigar and supervising. Twenty minutes later, we piled into the limo and headed for Dallas by way of Houston.

Sam held Matt, Hank held Noreen and I held Freeway.

CHAPTER SEVENTY-THREE

The first leg of the trip was spent in high spirits. We were looking forward to our weddings and spending the holidays together. The girls chattered endlessly about going shopping, while Hank and I just listened and smiled. Things were going along great until Sam's face suddenly turned white and she said, "Oh, no…"

"What's wrong?" I frowned. "Did we forget something?"

"I just had a *terrible* thought," she said.

Hank leaned up. "What is it, Sis?"

"If th' press gets wind of all this," she said, "it'll turn into a three ring circus."

"Shit," Hank muttered. "You're right."

"How th' hell could they find out," I wanted to know.

"They hang around city hall like vultures," Hank growled. "They'll know two seconds after we take out th' license."

I'd forgotten in the eyes of the world, I was marrying a "celebrity." "Crap!" I frowned. "That's a sobering thought." Then I brightened and said, "Hey, maybe they won't find out."

Hank and Sam looked at each other and said in unison. "Ah…ignorance is *such* bliss."

After that, it was like a pin pricked a balloon, letting out all the air. With this dark cloud hanging over us, all conversation ceased. We quietly stared out the windows until one-by-one the rhythm of the road lulled us to sleep. We slept for the rest of the trip and just before dark, I felt the limo slow, hit a slight bump, and come to a stop. My eyes fluttered open enough to see we were under a canopy with enough lights to rival Las Vegas. Jerry got out and was met by a young man wearing a dark blue uniform pushing a large brass luggage cart.

Hank was first to break the silence. "Looks like we're here," he yawned.

Like zombies, we got out of the car and followed the bellboy into the lobby. Jerry drove off to park the limo. At the desk, Hank told the clerk he had two adjoining suites reserved on the top floor. Since Matt was cranky, he gave Sam our key card first so she could go on ahead. After checking in, we took a private elevator to the top floor. I opened the door to the suite and was blown away by the view. With over 1,800 square feet and windows overlooking all of Houston, I felt like I was on top of the world. There was even a Jacuzzi big enough for ten people.

I didn't want to appear like a country bumpkin, so I said, "Is this the biggest one they have?"

"No, ours is bigger," Hank, teased, just as Jerry came in with the brass cart holding our luggage. He pushed it past us and took the suitcases to the bedroom. Hank unlocked the door between the suites and Jerry took their luggage in. When he finished, he asked, "Will that be all, Mr. Fairfield?"

"Yeah, Jer -jest see that th' limo is tucked away some place safe in that garage downstairs."

He nodded and touched the brim of his cap. "Already taken care of, Mr. Fairfield."

"Thanks...an' here's the key card to your room. It's on the floor just below us."

"Very good, Mr. Fairfield...and what time will you need me tomorrow?"

"Do you know where city hall is –'cause Ah wanna get over there bright 'n early."

"Yes sir, I know exactly where it is-what time would you like to leave?"

"Be out front by eight thirty so's we can git there first thing when they open up at nine."

Jerry nodded and said good night. After he left, Hank suggested that we have a drink before hitting the hay and went over to the well-stocked bar. He poured himself a bourbon 'n branch and a tequila straight for Noreen. I joined Hank in a bourbon over the rocks and Sam had a white wine. Soon as everybody had their drink Hank lifted his and said, "Here's to us".

CHAPTER SEVENTY-FOUR

It was still too early for me to go to sleep, so I asked Sam if she wanted to watch some television after we got in bed. She told me she was going in to take a shower first, but agreed to a little T.V. after she got out. The hotel had provided a crib for Matt and he'd fallen asleep before his head hit the pillow. Needless to say with things so quiet and romantic, I had a *better* idea for Sam after she came out of the shower and slept very little that night. But bright and early the next morning, I was woke up from a very contented sound sleep by a loud knocking. I was pissed as I opened the door and the bellman wheeled in an enormous table with everything from coffee and eggs to sausage, waffles and pancakes. "What th' hell?" I muttered. "I *didn't* order this."

The bellman explained that Hank had sent up the huge breakfast, saying that he'd wanted to make sure we were awake and well fed before we left. "I should'a known," I grumbled.

An hour later, we came down to the lobby to find Jerry waiting for us at the front door. He wasted no time getting us to city hall and we arrived with fifteen minutes to spare.

Sam hadn't remembered to make arrangements for a sitter, so we had Matt with us. He was still sleeping, but she woke him to give him a bottle while we waited for nine o'clock to roll around. When the doors opened at 9:01, we got out and went inside. There wasn't anybody else around, but Hank checked out the lobby and restrooms for reporters anyway. Soon as he was satisfied there weren't any, we got the licenses and were about to leave when a clerk asked Hank to step into his office. Hank was annoyed, but smiled pleasantly. "Prob'ly wants an autograph. Y'all go on to th' car...Ah'll jest see what he wants an' be right out."

We went out to wait for him in the car, but after twenty minutes went by and Hank still hadn't come out, I said, "Look, I know Hank has trouble spelling his name, but this is ridiculous."

Sam looked at the door. "I agree," she frowned. "Something's wrong."

Forty-five minutes later, Hank finally came out and got in the car. Jerry started the engine and pulled away from the curb. "Damn, Hank," Sam said. "What took so long?" He didn't answer, but when we were about a mile down the road, Hank leaned back and put his arm around Noreen. While we waited for him to tell us what happened, he said softly, "Honey...why didn't you tell me you were married before?"

All the blood drained out of Noreen's face and she stared straight ahead with eyes as big as saucers. Hank rubbed her arm until finally, she lowered her eyes and whispered, "It-it was a long time ago. I was only eighteen an' I-I..."

She buried her face in her hands and sobbed. "I-I wanted to tell you, but was afraid you...you wouldn't want me anymore." Her body convulsed, as a lifetime of tears poured out of her soul. Hank gently took her hands away from her face and wrapping her in both his arms, pulled her close to him. I felt tears sting my own eyes and looked away.

"Don't cry, precious," he whispered. "That shit don't make no nevermind to me. Ah only needed to know cuz there's a record of th' marriage, but there ain't none for a divorce. Th' clerk caught it just as we was leavin.'"

Noreen wiped her eyes and looked at him. "That's cause there ain't any papers for a divorce," she said. "He was just a boy I knew from high school. His name was Jared an' I-I don't even know what happened to him after I left seven months later." Suddenly fear wrapped its icy fingers around her heart. "Oh, God, Hank-does this mean we can't get married now?" He shook his head and pulled her closer. "Naw, baby girl, we're gonna sho'nuf git married. Ain't nuthin' gonna stop us, neither."

I leaned up and asked, "*Really*? And just how'd you pull *that* off?"

"Well, when Ah finally found out what all th' ruckus was about, Ah made up a story about Noreen's house burnin' down. Told him there wasn't nothing but ashes left. Problem solved."

"*That* won't explain why papers aren't on file with th' court," I frowned, wondering if he realized just how close to accurate his story was. Hank smiled again. "True, but soon as I saw the name of the li'l ol' town Noreen got married in, Ah knew it'd been hit by a tornado thirteen years ago. Plumb destroyed everything. It's impossible for anybody to ever find *any* records on ANY *thing*."

I sniffed. "Yeah, but city hall LOVES to be assholes. If they know she was married, they *can* keep you from getting married if there's no proof of a divorce." Hank settled back with his arm still around Noreen. "Ah reckon you're right," he grinned. "But they don't seem to mind so much when you got a wad of cash."

And at that, we all sat back and smiled...even Noreen.

CHAPTER SEVENTY-FIVE

Back at the hotel, the girls wanted to go shopping, so Hank and I took Matt up to my room and ordered lunch. While I changed him, Hank called room service. Thinking this was going to be a piece of cake, I got out a fresh diaper and powdered his bottom like I'd seen Sam do. Next, I tried scooting the diaper under his butt, but he bucked so much that it bunched up and wouldn't co-operate. I turned him over on his side, but he rolled back before I could get the diaper in place. This went on for about five minutes with me getting nowhere. Finally, I yelled for Hank to come help. He came in a minute later with a bourbon in his hand and growled, "What? Ah'm trying to watch John Wayne."

"Never mind that, put down your drink and come over here an' help me get this fool diaper on."

"*Boy*, you mean you can't put that diaper on a li'l baby?"

I turned to glare at him while trying to wrestle Matt. "That's *exactly* what I'm saying," I frowned. "But since you seem to be such an expert, YOU do it," and I threw the diaper at him. He caught it without spilling his drink, but gave me a dirty look. I stood back with my arms crossed over my chest, knowing damned well, he didn't have any more of a clue about babies and diapers than I did. After setting his drink down, Hank turned the diaper around a few times and scratched his head.

"What's th' matter, genius –can't you figure it out, either?"

"This ain't like a guitar -which is th' front an which is th' back?"

I said, "I think those sticky tabs go in front, but I can't figure how you're supposed to get th' dang thing *on* -he won't lie still long enough for me to scoot th' diaper under his butt."

I went over to help him just as I heard the key card in the front door. The girls came in and finding nobody in the living room, Sam yelled, "Hey-where is everybody?"

Hank and I looked at each other and said, "They're *back* -thank God!"

Sam came into the bedroom. "There you are," she said. "What's going on –did you feed him yet?" Hank gave her the diaper and picked up his drink. "Hell no! We been tryin' to figure out how th' hell you put this damned thing on for over an hour," he growled, as he stormed out of the room.

"He exaggerates," I frowned. "It's only been half an hour. But how th' hell *do* you get it on?"

She said, "I don't know how *you* two idiots were trying to do it, but it's really very simple," and I watched as she took both Matt's ankles in her left hand, lifted his lower body and slid the diaper effortlessly underneath him with her right. Laying him back down on top, she simply removed the protective backing from the two tabs and taped the diaper together in front.

"See? It's simple." The entire thing didn't take ten seconds and it was at that moment, that I conceded women *were* the more intelligent of the species. We men lost the race by light years. Women could take over anytime they wanted.

"Now that he's changed, watch him for me while I go warm up his bottle, okay?"

I nodded and watched her leave for the kitchen, still trying to digest the mysterious ways of women –and diapers. When she got back with Matt's bottle, she picked him up and rocked him in her arms while she fed him. He grabbed the bottle in both of his tiny hands and pulled on the nipple like he was starved. It didn't take long for his eyes to close after he finished and she laid him down for his afternoon nap. As she pulled the blanket up, I noticed how much he'd grown. "He looks bigger," I said.

"He is. Before you know it, he'll be going off to college."

College??? Holy cow, I hadn't thought about that and wondered how the hell I'd be able to afford it. "Gosh," I muttered, "I hadn't even considered *that*, yet."

"Don't worry about it now," she smiled. "It's still a long way off."

"Yeah but, I need to be ready for these things," I protested.

"He may not even want to go," she shrugged. "He may decide to be a musician –or go into the military. Why don't we just wait an' let him decide?"

"Or maybe he'll become a chauffeur," I frowned. "That seems to be a lucrative business."

Back in the living room, an explosion had taken place. Noreen was opening boxes and spreading stuff all over the sofa, while Hank sat there and watched her with all the happiness of a father watching his kid on Christmas morning. "Man, your credit card must be smokin'," I told him. "You girls buy out every store?"

"Nooo," Sam answered, picking up a white satin high heel. "I didn't see anything, but Noreen found these to go with her dress –once we find it."

"Yeah, an' I found *these* for th' honeymoon," she said, excitedly holding up a black see-through lace camisole with matching thong. "And these to go with 'em." She reached down into the pile of boxes and pulled out a pair of long black lace opera gloves with 18 inches of blood red fringe running down each side. Hank's face lit up and he happily inspected her purchase, while I looked at Sam. She whispered, "You should see what I made her put back," and wiggled her eyebrows like Groucho Marx. "Where'd you find them –"Strippers 'R Us?"

"No, we found 'em in a little place called, "Fredrick's of Hollywood."

"Yeah, a.k.a. "Strippers 'R Us" an' I just hope you didn't buy a matching set."

"Actually, I did," she said. "Got it in white though -thought it was more tasteful

"*What*?" I cried, and she busted out laughing. "I'm kidding, Mac."

I was relieved to hear it, but also a little disappointed.

CHAPTER SEVENTY-SIX

Room service brought our lunch. Hank had done overkill on ordering and there was more than enough for all of us.

It was over coffee that Hank brought up the subject of the wedding. "Ya know," he said, "we gotta do this gettin' married a.s.a.p. Christmas is jest aroun' th' corner an' it's a long drive to Dallas from here."

"I agree –what do you suggest?" Sam asked.

"Ah'll have Jerry call city hall today an' make us an appointment soon as possible."

"City hall? What happened to having a big wedding?" I asked.

"We'll have to do that later, right now, we need to get her done an' hit th' road."

I knew he was right. "But," I frowned, "we've all still got things to do to get ready."

"Then we better hustle."

Sam looked at Noreen. "You ready to go do some more shopping?" Noreen eagerly shook her head and they both got up from the table. Looking over at me, she asked, "Are you going out?" I nodded, and she looked at her brother. "What about you?"

"Nope, Ah'm stayin' right here an' watching a football game."

"Then you'll be here until I get back and I can count on you to watch Matt?"

"Yep," he grinned, and turning back to me, Sam asked, "Where are you going?"

I rubbed my hand over my chin, feeling the stubble. "Well, I need to do a little shopping myself." She nodded and waved on her way to the door with Noreen. After they left, Freeway came over and put her paw on my knee. I took what was left of my sandwich and gave it to her. Suddenly it dawned on me that I'd been so busy, that I hadn't been taking her out. "Good lord, I haven't taken Freeway out since we got here!"

"Yeah, I noticed th' poor li'l thing dancing cross-legged across th' floor a few times, an' that's why I been havin' Jerry feed her an' take her out three times a day."

I patted her on the head. "Poor little Freeway; I forgot all about you. Can you ever forgive me?" She licked my hand (-the one with the sandwich) - and I said, "I'll take that as a "yes."

Hank stood up, flipped his lighter open and lit a cigar. "Th' Cowboy's game starts in twenty minutes –what're you going shoppin' for?"

"I thought I'd go look at some wedding rings," I said, sliding my chair back. "You wouldn't happen to know where I might find a good jewelry store, would you?"

"There all over th' place, but ask at th' desk," he said, turning on the T.V. "An' look fer somethin' big an' sparkly for Noreen. Price don't matter."

"*What*? You want *me* to pick out *her* ring for *you*?"

"Well hell, boy, you're marryin' mah sister, ain't ya –that shows you got good taste. 'Sides, Ah ain't no good at that stuff, so if you see somethin' ya think she'd like, get it for me."

I rolled my eyes and mumbled, "Crimeny, do I have to do *everything*?"

CHAPTER SEVENTY-SEVEN

I got off the elevator in the main lobby and asked the desk clerk where I might find a good jewelry store. He directed me to the third level. I thanked him, took the escalator up to the third floor -and there it was, right in front of me. The store looked pretty pricey from the outside, but it was nothing compared to the inside. When I stepped through the beveled glass doors, my feet sunk into a four-inch thick carpet so plush it felt like I was walking on a cloud.

The entire store was one color; pale mauve. Mauve rug, mauve water-stained silk on the walls, mauve jackets on the clerks -I was enveloped in mauve.

The store was opulent and inviting. The center of the room was dominated by a seven-tiered oval-shaped chandelier hanging over three display cases. The cases were arranged in an even larger triangle, taking up three quarters of the floor space. The glass tops were completely bare except for a lone Tiffany lamp sitting off to one side. The lamp's large umbrella shaped glass shade of red, gold, green and turquoise, gave the store its only shot of color. Everywhere you looked, the store quietly screamed of money, but the true decadence was what was in the display cases. Diamonds of every shape and size blinded you with their sparkle.

I expected the store to be relatively empty and was surprised to see it was a beehive of activity. Immaculate customers in Armante suits bought seven figure baubles like price meant nothing. Not one of the five clerks in attendance seemed anxious to wait on me, so I wandered over to one of the display cases -painfully aware of a security camera tracking my every move. I tried to look as dignified as possible, but it would take more than the faded jeans and a western shirt I wore. Hoping to get the attention of one of the clerks, I leaned over the counter, but it was like I was invisible. Thirty-five long minutes passed before I finally noticed one guy standing against the back counter. I looked over and yelled, "Hey! A little help here, please?" The snotty little clerk considered it as he took his time coming over. When he reached me, he asked coolly, "May-I-*help*-you?" -sounding ridiculously insincere. I said, "Sure," and pointing to a ring I had my eye on, completely missed the look of disdain. He unlocked the back of the case, took out the ring and reluctantly handed it to me. Seeing that it wasn't exactly what I had in mind, I handed it back and asked to see what else he had. He raised an eyebrow and made it a point to sigh loudly as he showed me ring after ring. After what seemed like an eternity to both of us, I told him none of them were what I wanted.

Finally, he asked, "And just **what are** you looking for, sir?"

I scratched the side of my cheek. "Well, I'm not rightly sure," I smiled, "but look at it this way, now we know what I'm not looking for."

"How *very*...**true**," he spat. I tried not to laugh as I said, "C'mon...we got two more cases to look through." We moved down to the next counter, where my eye caught a large diamond encrusted band accentuated in rich dark amethyst. This ring was like nothing I'd ever seen before and stood out from all the rest. I leaned in for a closer look. The width of the band was wide enough to cover half the finger, but what really made it unique was a fine thread of gold that wound its way through the stones like a slender vine. I looked up. "This one," I said.

"Ah, yeeees," he said icily. "You have *surprisingly* marvelous taste!" I frowned at the left-handed compliment, but let it slide. He pulled out the ring. "THIS..." he beamed, holding it up like it was the Holy Grail, "Is THE Crown Jewel of ALL our rings."

I could just see this on Sam's beautiful hand and I wanted it so bad, I could taste it. Feeling the weight of every cent I'd saved up in my pocket, I was absolutely confident that I had more than enough to buy it. "It's just what I'm looking for -how much is it?"

I *knew* the question was a mistake the instant it left my mouth. This was the kind of store where if you had to ask, you couldn't afford it. He stood back and taking a soft clean cloth out of his pocket, carefully cleaned off the stones before holding it up to the light. A sly smile crossed his lips, as he slowly moved it around catching every sparkling facet. I was completely mesmerized and he knew it. "Isn't it exquisitely BREATHTAKING?" he whispered. "This is something only a Queen should wear."

I ran my fingernail nervously over my eyebrow, knowing damned well, that I had just given away one of the most powerful "tells" you could give a salesperson. I'd showed him my hand by asking how much the ring cost and his whole demeanor had changed instantly.

Knowing he now controlled the situation, he continued to describe *everything* about the ring. It was agonizing. "You have EIGHT carats of the highest quality pave diamonds, here," he explained, pausing just long enough to let it sink in before going on. "And see here?" he pointed, thrusting the ring in my face. "EACH one of these diamonds is TWENTY THREE points of blue white perfection! And see these stones here? THESE stones here are **not** amethyst, as one might think; oh *nooo* -they're Alexandrite."

I had no idea what Alexandrite was and mumbled, "They look like amethyst..."

He glared at me like I was a member of the Gump family and sniffed. "Hardly! THIS quality of Alexandrite is a "one-source" stone, found only in Russia. The mines were played out decades ago and now stones of *this* color and magnitude are very rare. Why, there are over SIXteen carats of *fully* cut Alexandrite in this ring." Suddenly he inhaled sharply, smiled and closed his eyes. I didn't know if his medication just wore off or if he was having an orgasm. After a moment, I loudly cleared my throat and he blinked a few times, resuming his speech as if nothing happened. "This ring is an estate piece believed to have come from the Romanoff family itself! There just ISN'T another ring like this in ALL the world." I was *convinced* that each word of this rhetoric raised the already astronomical price by hundreds of dollars and opened my mouth to stop him from going on. But, he wasn't finished. "The Alexandrite stones are channel set, while the diamonds are recessed prongs -and just *LOOK* at the way this delicate vine of gold weaves its way through the stones."

I was getting tired and knowing I'd already made an ass of myself by asking the price, decided to throw all caution to the wind and ask again. "Yes, yes," I said, "but what I really want to know is, how m-"

"We know for a fact by the mark here on the inside," he interrupted, "that this ring was hand crafted by one of the FINEST jewelers in all Europe -LEGENDARY, in fact. And do you know *how* you can tell Alexandrite from amethyst?" Without waiting for a reply, he went on to inform me. "You can tell by the way it changes color in natural sunlight. Indoors the stone is an incredible deep purple while outside, sunlight turns it a sort of odd greenish-purple color."

He smiled wistfully. "Wouldn't it be SOMETHING if this had once adorned the hand of the Czar Romanov's wife?"

"Not really," I sighed, "since the Romanov's were slaughtered by the Bolsheviks. And I don't really care if all the stones were hand set by chimpanzees! You and I both know, I already *want* the ring –so HOW MUCH it is?"

"Do you realize," he said sternly, "that you have almost a quarter troy ounce of EIGHTEEN karat gold here?" He hefted the ring in his hand for emphasis. I looked at my watch and sighed, "Okay, you win. I thought th' damned ring was for sale, but since you're so freaking attached to it -you keep it!" I was almost to the door before he cried, "Wait!" and I smiled to myself.

I went back over to him, still convinced I had enough money to buy the thing. "Then tell me how much it is!"

He looked me up and down for a moment, then said, "Are you *sure* you want to know -because we don't provide oxygen to walk-ins if you faint." I reached over the counter and grabbed him by his over-priced tie. "Why you arrogant little snot," I growled, smashing his face down on the glass.

"Oh, dear God!" he croaked. "Its- its -*one hundred* and *ninety* **thousand** dollars!"

My heart froze and I let go of his tie. Straightening up, he readjusted his clothing, while waiting for me to start breathing again.

Finally, I whispered, "You're kidding!"

He squared his shoulders and daintily put one hand over the other like a little girl. Giving me an insolent smirk, he raised one eyebrow and said, "No sir. I assure you, I NEVER kid about something like THIS." **SNAP**! The trap was sprung. He had me, and I would have rather fallen through an open manhole than ask the next question. "Well, do-do you have anything-" I gulped, "-that's a-a little cheaper?" Looking outrageously superior now, he jutted out his chin and said coldly, "Cheaper? We don't *DEAL* in chea-"

Suddenly, he stopped talking and stared over my shoulder. I figured he was through humiliating me and started to leave with my tail tucked between my legs. Before I turned away though, I happened to notice the contemptuous look on his face was now completely gone. At first, I thought he'd found a small spark of human compassion in that cash register heart of his, until I noticed he wasn't even looking at *me*. I quickly turned around to see who he *was* looking at and saw Hank standing there in the doorway. The little clerk darted around the counter so fast, that he almost knocked me down. "MIS-TER *FAIRFIELD*!" he twittered. "Ooohh MY, it is SO good to see you -come right IN!"

Hank removed his Stetson and walked in. "Howdy, son," he grinned, draping his arm around the excited little man's shoulders and gently steering him back to me. "Don't let me interrupt a sale." The clerk laughed. "Oh, I don't think this gentleman is buying," he snickered. "I think he was just looking." ("Oh crap," I sighed to myself, "will this humiliation ever stop?") Hank grinned like he knew just what I was thinking and said, "Is that true, sir -are you "jest lookin'?"

I gave the clerk my dirtiest look. "Much as I HATE to admit it," I glared, "I guess I am."

Hank put his Stetson on again and took the ring out of the clerk's hand.

"Well -let's jest take a look see here..." he said, holding it up to the light. "Whoa," he whistled, "now THIS here's a hunk'a ring!"

"So's th' price."

"Hmm, izzat so...an' jest how much you reckon a ring like this runs?"

Beads of sweat popped out on the clerk's forehead, as I glared at him defiantly. "Go on an' tell him," I said evenly. He looked away and pulled a handkerchief from his front breast pocket. Nervously mopping his face, he said, "Uh, well, it-its one hundred and ninety thousand, Mr. Fairfield. But of course, if **YOU** were interested in it, I'm positive we could work something out." Without batting an eye, Hank said, "That much, huh?" And holding up the ring again, he looked at me. "She sho' does sparkle pretty, don't she?" he grinned, reminding me of Andy Griffith. Then like lightning, he closed his fist over the ring. He was all business now. "Okay, let's talk turkey, son...jest exactly how much IS a ring like this gonna cost me?"

The clerk looked at me, then Hank -then hurried behind the counter. His fingers were a blur, as he crunched numbers for a full minute before asking, "One hundred and twelve thousand...?"

"Tha's quite a drop in price," Hank said, shaking his head. "But Ah know you can do better than that." Hank smiled and winked at the clerk, whose face looked positively green, as he went back to his calculator. Five long sweaty minutes later, he looked up hopefully and swallowed.

"H-How about- e-eighty-five thousand...?"

Hank stared at the ceiling before shaking his head again and again, as he refused offer after offer. Still the clerk wouldn't give up and continued to work feverishly on his calculator. Finally, he looked at Hank. "W-Would...s-sixty-five thousand...be acceptable?" he whined. "It's a true antique, Mr. Fairfield. It-It belonged to the Russian Czar Romanoff's wife."

Hank studied the ring closely. "Hmmm, izzat a fact?" he muttered. "Well, shoot son, Ah don't know nothin' about them people over there in Russia, so Ah'll take yer word for it -but even so, it still seems like an awful lot to pay for a dead woman's ring," and turning to me, he asked, "What'd'a *you* think, mister?"

The price was now in my range of affordability and I said, "I don't know, but it seems like a fair price for something as beautiful as that is. And besides, he's sellin' it to you, so my opinion don't count..."

"Yeah," he winked, sounding more and more like Andy Griffith, "but you like it, don't'cha."

"Oh yeah," I nodded. "I like it a lot."

"Ah bet you wanted it for somebody REEEEL special --huh?"

"As special as they come. In fact, one'a her smiles can outshine that ring any day."

Hank grinned from ear to ear. "Wow! *That's* special," he said. "Then sixty-five thousand ain't a lotta money -right?" -and before I could answer, he looked at the salesman. "Tell ya what ya do," he said. "Make it fifty eight,

194

an' you can throw in another one just like it." The little guy turned an even deeper shade of pea-green and I thought he was going to fall out right there on the floor. "Fifty eight thou...?" He closed his eyes and swayed. "A-And you...you want a-another one..." he coughed, "j-just like it." Hank shrugged. "Or as close as ya can git. That is, if we can come to terms here on th' price." And turning to me, he asked, "You don't mind, do ya, sir?"

"Be my guest."

The clerk held on to the counter with one hand and took out his handkerchief again with the other. "I'm sorry, Mr. Fairfiled, but I-I don't h-have another one like it," he said. "That ring is a one-of-kind estate piece – however, I'll *gladly* show you what we...what we DO have."

Hank ran his hand behind his neck non-chalauntly (sp?) like he was buying a prize steer. "Oh, don't trouble yerself, son. I think I'll jest let this fella here pick out something. He seems to have mighty good taste, don'cha think?" The salesman looked at me, then rapidly blinked at Hank. "*You* want *this* man to pick out another ring?? For...*you*?" It was painfully clear that the guy was starting to unravel, but Hank wasn't quite ready to let him off the hook just yet. "Ah do...an' by th' way," he smiled, "PLEEZE tell me you would'a sold this man that ring for th' same price as me."

Barely able to contain himself, the salesman croaked, "Of course."

"Okay then, guess we're 'bout finished here," Hank said, turning around and heading towards the door. When he got halfway across the room, he added, "Oh, an' put both'a them rings on my bill, ya hear?" The clerk's face went totally blank and his head dropped for just an instant before looking up again and asking, "Did you say, p-put them *BOTH* on *YOUR* bill, Mr. Fairfiled?"

"Yep, sho' did, son," he waved.

I watched Hank walk out and silently reminded myself to never get in a cut-throat poker game with him. Then turning back to the clerk, I sighed, "Okay so, where were we?"

The guy stared at me. "Who *ARE* you?" he demanded.

"Oh...I ain't nobody," I answered modestly. "But by this time day after tomorrow, I'll be his brother-in-law. I'm marryin' his sister."

"Y-You're marrying Miss Evans?"

I nodded and he made a little squeaking noise before clamping both hands over his mouth.

"You got any'a that oxygen around you keep for special occasions," I asked. "Like maybe, this one?"

Just then the manager came over. "Is there a problem, Harry?" he smiled. "I saw Mr. Fairfield in here a moment ago and wondered if everything was satisfactory?" Harry's hands were still clamped firmly over his mouth. "Harry...?" the manager frowned in concern.

I spoke up. "Uh, yes...everything is just fine. Harry's been taking very good care of me an' my brother-in-law."

The manager raised a questioning eyebrow. "You are Mr. Fairfield's in-law?"

"Well...I-I will be day after tomorrow," I nodded. A smile broke out on his face. "Well," he said good-naturedly. "Congratulations sir, and please accept our best wishes." He shook my hand then turned to Harry. "And Harry," he instructed, "whatever price you quoted Mr. Fairfield and this man, knock twenty-five percent off." Harry jerked his head towards the manager. "B-But, sir," he croaked. "I've -I've..."

"Don't argue with me, Harry," the manager said affably. "Give the man the discount."

Harry watched the manager walk away like a man condemned to the gallows and closing his eyes, he broke out in renewed perspiration. "I am dead," he moaned.

"Relax," I smiled. "Just leave it the way you'n Hank agreed on ."

His eyes popped open again and for the longest moment, I thought he was going to pass out from relief. "Oh," he panted, "thank you, thank you, THANK you, sir! You have *no* idea HOW much I appreciate that! If I extended the twenty five per cent to you after what I've already done...well, I'd be out of a job." Suddenly the blood in his face drained away and his eyes grew even widener. "Oh dear God! I never should have said that!"

I patted his shoulder. "Look, just treat th' next guy that comes in here a little nicer, okay?"

Mopping his brow, he nodded vigorously. "Oh, yes sir, I will –and if I was the LEAST bit rude or-or abrupt earlier, I *sincerely* apologize."

"Forget it, it's over 'n done with. C'mon, let's just get back to business. You heard Hank; he needs a ring too. It's gonna be a double wedding, so show me what else you got -and make it gaudy." He looked confused. "Gaudy? Wh-What exactly IS gaudy, sir?"

I looked up and down the counter until I spotted a ring twice as big as Sam's and loaded with enough diamonds to choke an elephant. I pointed to it. "That one comes close -although it's still in too good'a taste...I guess you fellas just don't deal in gaudy."

"N-No sir, I don't think so," he said and taking a quick glance to the left and another to the right, he leaned over and whispered, "But between you and me, this one IS known as "tacky." And raising an eyebrow, he nodded as if we were co-conspirators. "Why Harry," I said with genuine surprise. "I do believe you have a sense of humor." He smiled at the compliment and taking the ring out, handed it to me. The ring would have knocked anybody's eyes out and sparkled like game night at Yankee Stadium. "Its perfect!" I said, "Give me the bottom line on it."

"That one goes for one hundred and fifty four thousand," he said, "but I can go a little lower than I did on your ring without losing my job."

"Well, we don't want you to lose your job -you just got your membership into th' human race. But, tell me something –does it have a story like mine does?"

"No, it was commissioned by a sheik for one of his many paramours, who believed bigger is better. A rather large paramour, apparently," he sighed. "However, for whatever reason, he never came back for it and it isn't something that appeals to the normal crowd. The diamonds are of the highest quality and there is NO doubt of their authenticity, but let's just say that it would take a woman of, umm, rather large stature to wear this and carry it off successfully."

I laughed out loud and threw my credit card down. "That's Noreen, all right!"

Harry picked up the credit card and handed it back to me. "Um, Mr. Fairfield was clear that these were to go on his account."

"Oh, yeah," I said. "Well, can you put mine on this?"

He shook his head. "I'm so sorry," he said sincerely, "but we don't take that one –do you happen to have an American Express?"

Now I shook my head. "Fraid not."

"Too bad, however, there may be something my manager can do, let me call him."

He picked the in-house phone and called the manager, who came right over and said pleasantly, "Hello again. Do you need my help here?" Harry nodded and quietly explained the problem of my undesirable credit card. When he finished, the manager picked up my card and nodded. "It's true that we don't ordinarily take this one," he said. "There's nothing wrong with it, of course, it's just that we prefer American Express. However, in some cases -like this one, we *do* make exceptions. We'll gladly accept your card, Mr.-?" he glanced down. "...McIntyre." Then he smiled and handed my card to Harry saying, "Harry, run this through with Mr. McIntyre's purchase."

Harry left and turning back to me, he said, "By the way, I don't believe we've been properly introduced, Mr. McIntyre; my name is, Maxwell Fielding." He shook my hand again and smiled once more. "And again...all our best wishes to you and your bride."

"Thank you very much," I said. "You've been most helpful -I won't forget it." Harry came back with my credit card and the manager excused himself by saying, "Please let us know if we can ever be of service to you again in the future."

Handing me my card, Harry asked, "Would you like separate receipts?"

"Yeah, if you don't mind."

"Very good. I'll be right back with them."

When he came back with the receipts, I saw why they'd happily made an exception on taking my card. Even before taxes, the total for Sam's ring was enough to feed the Dallas Cowboys for a year. This was the largest thing I'd ever put on my card and I asked, "Did you have any trouble getting it to go through?"

Harry said, "Oh, no sir. Approval was instantaneous."

Well...that was a surprise. I signed the store's copy, and Harry said, "Here are your rings. I put Mr. Fairfield's on his personal account and here is his receipt." I thanked him and put both in my pocket, then said goodbye figuring I'd better get out of there before VISA discovered just how many zeros were on my charge.

CHAPTER SEVENTY-EIGHT

The girls still weren't back when I got to the room. Hank was watching the end of his football game, but got up when he saw me. "Hey," he grinned, turning off the television. "Did you have any trouble findin' us somethin'?" I sat down next to him on the sofa and took the rings out of my pocket. I showed him the one I got for Sam first and he said. "Yeah, Ah knew you had good taste. That's a beaut."

"An' thanks to you, I could afford to buy it -although just barely."

"They always jack up th' price in these fancy stores," he grinned. "An' Ah love to play hardball with 'em. It's one'a th' perks to bein' famous that Ah actually enjoy."

"Do you go in there a lot? They seem to know you real well."

"Ah stop in from time to time to pick out somethin' for somebody's birthday or some li'l filly that's been real nice to me." He suddenly glanced up and cleared his throat. "Uh, 'course that's all in th' past – you know, back when Ah had free range."

I grinned and he quickly changed the subject. "So, what'd you find for Noreen?"

I opened the other ring box and he let out a long low whistle. "*Holy* cow," he said. "THAT is *some* ring." He took it out of the box and stared at it. "It'll sho' nuff blind ya -you think she'll like it?" he asked.

"Oh yeah, she'll like it all right. She'd like it if they were cubic zirconium." I reached into my pocket again. "An' here's th' receipt."

He looked at it and said, "Where's your ring? I told 'em to put them both on my account."

"I know, but I wanted to pay for Sam's ring and after you got th' price into my neighborhood, I was able to put it on my VISA."

Hank frowned. "They don't take VISA," he said.

"Not ordinarily...but I guess since you're gonna be my brother-in-law, they made an exception. If VISA doesn't pay off," I smiled, "they'll come after you."

"Yeah, probably," he sighed.

"I just hope you know what you're doin' getting hitched to Noreen - that ring you bought cost enough to feed two Third World countries. Even after they dropped th' price."

Tucking the ring into his pocket along with the receipt, he said, "Ah knew it was th' right thing when she told me all she needed was me an' a plain gold band."

"Wait a minute," I cried. "A plain gold band? That isn't like Noreen!" Then it dawned on me. "Well, what'd'ya know," I whispered. "Noreen's in love. And I thought that was as rare as Amish slam dancing."

Hank sat up and clasped his hands together. "Ah may seem like a bumpkin," he said. "But this ain't mah first rodeo. If there was th' slightest doubt in my mind that Noreen didn't love me, Ah'd be usin' her just as much as she'd be usin' me. A good time would be had by all- no harm, no foul. But Ah know she's come from a hard life an' all Ah want to do is make her happy."

"Well," I sighed. "You've seen something in her that th' rest of us missed, but I gotta admit, she's different since she met you." I looked at Hank. "Has she ever told you anything...about her childhood?" I asked.

"NO, an' Ah won't never ask either -an' if *you* know somethin' about her childhood, don't tell me. Ah don't wanna know nuthin' before Ah came into her life."

"I don't know a thing about her before she started comin' in th' bar," I shrugged. "Far as I know, she never existed before then. Besides, I had my own problems..."

The conversation wound down and we sat there for a moment, then he asked, "You hungry?"

I said, "I am starved," and he got up to call downstairs and order us something to eat.

While he was on the phone, I got to thinking about the crossroads and wondered how things were back there. When Hank came back to announce that lunch would be here in twenty minutes, I was so lost in thought, I didn't hear a word he said. He repeated that lunch was on its way and when I still didn't say anything, he sat down and shook my shoulder. "Mac –did you hear me?"

I blinked. "Huh –what?"

"Where were you, boy –what's on your mind?"

"I –uh, nothin'," I said, shaking my head.

"Don't bullshit me," he said. "Spit it out -what's botherin' you?"

I gave up and told him. "It's just that, well...it doesn't seem right for us to be getting married without Doc an' Harley bein' here, too."

He started to say something when the door opened and Jerry came in with Freeway. Taking off her leash, she ran over and jumped in my lap, licking me all over the face.

"Hello, Mr. Fairfield," Jerry said. "We've been out for our walk and everything is taken care of for the day -would you like me to take her out later tonight before you go to bed, Mr. Mac?"

"That would be appreciated, Jerry," I nodded, "-and thanks for taking care of her for me."

"She's a pleasure, sir," he smiled. "I'll return for her after 8 p.m." As he started for the door, Hank got off the sofa. "Hold up a minute, Jerry," he said. "Ah need to go over somethin' with you." Jerry waited for Hank and they both went out in the hall. Closing the door behind him, Hank said in a low voice, "Where's Arte?"

Jerry answered, "He's in Stephenville with Tyler." (Tyler was Hank's bass player.)

"Okay," Hank said. "Ah want you to call him tonight an' tell him Ah need him to drive th' bus down to th' crossroads an get Mac's friends, Doc an' Harley. Bring 'em back here a.s.a.p. Ah want 'em here *before* th' wedding – got that?"

"How do I find this Doc and Harley?"

"Oh, yeah," Hank said thoughtfully. "I forgot you never met them. Okay, Doc is the local vet around there. Ah don't know his last name, but Ah'm sure you won't have any trouble findin' him, an' when ya do, he'll tell ya how to find Harley. Now, get a rush on, boy. We ain't got any time to waste. By th' way, is th' bus with Arte, or did he leave it here an' drive up with Tyler in his car?"

"I'll see to it that everything is taken care of, Mr. Fairfield -and yes, he took the bus to Stephenville." He turned to go when Hank grabbed his arm and stopped him.

"Listen, when Arte gets back here, you check 'em into this hotel, but put 'em on th' third floor an' *don't* tell a soul they're here –ya got that?"

"I understand perfectly, sir." He turned to go again and again Hank stopped him. "One more thing, Jerry...make sure Arte knows he has to go tomorrow. He only has two days to get there and back here. Now, once they're here, you get them to city hall *before* you come back for us an' make sure you don't let *anybody* see 'em. This is a surprise an' Ah'm goin' to a lotta trouble to make sure it stays that way –you got that?" He nodded and

200

headed for the elevator just as the doors opened and room service pushed a table out. Jerry got on the elevator and just before the doors closed, Hank told him to call as soon as he talked to Arte. Then turning back to the waiter, Hank smiled and opened the door for him. "Lunch is here!" he yelled. Hank signed the check and we sat down to eat. We were just having coffee when the girls came in with a bellboy pushing a cart loaded down with packages. A few fell off and Sam helped him pick them up after asking him to put everything on the sofa. Throwing her purse down on one of the chairs, she turned to us. "Hi guys."

"Hey, sis."

"How's Matt –he give you any trouble?"

"Naw, th' little booger slept most all day."

"Great," she sighed wearily. "I hope he'll sleep long enough for me to catch my breath before he wakes up and I have to feed him." The bellboy finished unloading the packages and he left after Hank tipped him. "Speaking of food," I smiled, "you girls hungry?"

"No," she said, "we grabbed a bite while we were out." I looked over at the sofa. "No kiddin'-and just when did you have time to eat?"

"We found time, smarty pants."

"Looks like you bought out th' mall. What'd you buy –can I see?"

"Don't you dare look," Sam warned. "Y'all can't see anything until we get married."

Noreen looked at Sam in disappointment. "Can't I even show Hank what I got?"

"NO, Noreen -it's bad luck. Now give me that package, I'm gonna put it away with mine."

Clutching her package tightly in both arms, Noreen pouted, "Don't you trust me?"

"Not even a little bit," she said, taking the package away from her. Noreen started to protest, but the phone rang and Sam picked it up. After saying hello, she said, "Hold on," and held the receiver out to Hank. "It's for you -it's Jerry." Hank threw down his napkin and almost knocked over his chair getting up from the table. "Just hang it up in here, sis, Ah'll take it in your bedroom." Sam hung up the phone as her brother hurried past her. I picked up a clean cup and asked if she wanted to join me in a cup of coffee. She sat down and said, "So, you do any shopping?"

"Mmmm, maybe," I said cryptically.

"Oh yeah?" she grinned. "What'd'ya buy me?"

"Uh uh, if I can't see what you bought, you can't see what I bought."

"Oh yeah? Well, you better hide it good."

"Thanks for th' warning," I smiled.

She was still trying to weasel it out of me when Hank came out of the bedroom and said he had to go meet Jerry down in the coffee shop. Sam looked at him. "Why do you have to go meet Jerry right this minute?"

"Because," he sighed, "Ah gotta talk to him about some last minute details."

"Like what?" she frowned.

"Like our date an' time at city hall, for one thing," he lied.

"Yeah, how's that comin' -you got us anything yet?"

"Uh -not yet, but Ah'll let ya know when Ah come back," he told her on his way out the door.

"I hope he gets us a time around 4 in the afternoon," she said, shaking her head.

I looked at her. "You getting excited –or cold feet?"

She smiled mysteriously, "I GUESS you'll just have to wait an' find out, huh?"

CHAPTER SEVENTY-NINE

We were sitting there for another forty-five minutes before Matt woke up and started to cry. Sam set her cup down. "Guess he's awake now an' hungry," she sighed. "At least he gave me a chance to catch my breath first." She got up from the table and left for the bedroom. Another half hour passed before she came out again. "I'm gonna have to break down an' buy him some new clothes soon as all this is over," she said. "He is growing like a weed." I was reading the paper and looked up. "He doesn't wear clothes, does he? I mean, all he does is sleep, eat and –you know."

"He needs new jammies and some play suits," she explained. "He'll be crawlin' all over th' place and all this sleeping will be a thing of the past."

"I can hardly wait," I said.

"Me too," she sighed. "I'm starting to feel old just thinking about trying to keep up with him."

When Hank walked into the coffee shop, Jerry was sitting at a table over in the corner away from the rest of the customers. There was a tall glass of iced coffee sitting on the table. Hank hurried over and Jerry stood up. "I got you an iced coffee, Mr. Fairfield," he said. (Jerry never drank coffee.) After Hank sat down, he said, "So –what's up? Did you get Arte?"

"I spoke to him right after I left you," he said, looking at his watch. "He should be just about halfway there." Leaning back in his chair and running his hand behind his neck, Hank raised his eyebrows and let out a deep breath. "Damn, that's gonna be cuttin' it close," he said.

"True," Jerry agreed. "But if anyone can do it, Arte can."

"All right, just call me soon as he gets here."

Jerry nodded and getting up, Hank walked out without ever tasting his coffee.

When Hank came back to the room, Sam asked, "So? Did Jerry get us a day an' time?"

Hank frowned and mentally cursed -he'd forgotten all about that. "Uh, not yet," he said. "But remind me to call him in a little bit." An hour later, Sam reminded him to go call Jerry and he went into the bedroom again. When Jerry picked up, Hank said, "Listen Jer -Ah clean forgot to ask you if you got us a day an' time at city hall yet?"

"Yes sir," Jerry said, and he gave Hank the information. As he wrote it down, Hank said, "Holy cow, Jerry -is that th' *only* time you could get?" Jerry assured him it was and explained why.

"Oh boy! Sam is gonna hit th' roof when she hears this –an' Ah'm blamin' it all on you." He hung up and said a silent prayer. When he came back into the living room, Sam looked up hopefully. "Well –did you find out anything?"

"Yeah, Ah got it all right here, but you're not gonna like it."

"Why not?" she frowned.

"Because it's this Monday."

"**WHAT**?" Sam cried.

"Yeah –an' you ain't even heard th' worst part...it's at 9 a.m."

All the blood left Sam's knuckles, as she sat up and clutched both arms of her chair. Her face turned deep purple and she sputtered, "**NINE** a.m. – have you lost your ever lovin' **MIND**?"

She jumped out of her chair and ran over to her brother. "What is wrong with you, Hank?" she cried. "Not *only* is it the crack of dawn, but there is NO way we can get ready by then –we have to get our hair done, do our make-up and get dressed!" Sam paced back and forth and wrung her hands. "Lord, lord," she wailed. "I'll have to get up a **3 a.m.**" Hank put his arm around her. "It was th' only time available between now an' th' end of January," he said. "It's too near Christmas an' between being booked already and them closing for th' holidays, it was all Jerry could get us. An' th' only reason we got this time is 'cause some couple sobered up and cancelled their plans."

Sam pulled away from him and sat down again. "How will we get everything done?" she whispered. Then she sat straight up. "Our hair! Today is Friday –**how** are we gonna get our hair done before th' wedding?"

"Well, isn't there a salon here in th' hotel?" Hank asked.

"Yes, but you said the wedding is **this** coming Monday!"

Hank looked confused. "So?"

She was about to cry. "So, salons are **closed** on Mondays."

"Shit," he mumbled. Tears welled up in her eyes. "NOW what'll I do? I haven't time to do my hair *and* Noreen's, and still have time to get dressed."

"I have an idea," I said. "Call down to the salon an' ask if someone will work Monday."

Sam stared at me. "Do you realize they'd have to get here *before* sun-up?"

I shrugged. "Explain it to them an' see if they'll do it anyway."

"Men," she frowned. "You think everything can be fixed so easily." Then she got up and headed for the phone. "It's worth a try," she sighed. "But I ain't holdin' my breath."

CHAPTER EIGHTY

Sam made her phone call and returned looking somewhere between relieved and pissed off. "Okay," she said. "It took a LOT of begging, but I got a girl who's gonna come do it."

"That's GREAT, sis," Hank said, glad to be off the hook.

"I'm glad you think so, because it's gonna cost FOUR times as much an' YOU'RE payin' for it!"

"Uh, sure," he gulped. "Jest don't pick up any sharp objects 'tween now an' then, okay?"

With the "hair-do" problem straightened out, we were able to relax for the rest of the weekend. Saturday was spent with the girls taking care of last minute details, while Hank and I watched football. (At least he did -I read the paper and did the crossword puzzle.) Sunday afternoon, Hank was watching yet another football game when he got another call from Jerry letting him know that Arte had just arrived with Doc and Harley. Hank turned off the television and said he was going down to the lobby -and this time he didn't bother to give an explanation.

When he reached the lobby, he saw everyone waiting for him at the front desk. Doc and Harley looked relieved to see Hank, since no one had bothered to tell Arte why he was picking them up in the middle of the night, and both men were in the dark as to why they had practically been kidnapped by a stranger driving Hank's bus. Hank greeted them with a wave and a grin. "Ah'm so glad you made it," he said, slapping them on the back. Then he told the desk clerk he had two reservations for adjoining rooms on the third floor. "Ah, yes, Mr. Fairfield...just one moment." He found the reservations with no trouble and gave Hank their key cards. "Here you are, and I hope you will find everything satisfactory," he smiled.

Hank handed the cards to Jerry. "Y'all go on over to th' elevator," Hank told them. "Ah just need to speak to th' clerk 'bout some last minute business."

Doc and Harley walked over to the elevator to wait for Hank with Jerry. When they were out of ear shot, Hank leaned over the desk and said in a low voice, "Listen, Ah want you to see to it that they get everything they want or need –and do **not** send a bill up with anything they order. Everything is to go on my bill- understand?"

Clearly, sir," the clerk nodded. Hank stood up and smiled. "Good. An' if you run into any problems, make sure you talk to me personally - *NOBODY* else –got it?" The clerk nodded again and Hank walked over to the elevator. "Is everything all right?" Doc asked.

"Now that you two are here, things couldn't be better," Hank grinned.

The elevator doors opened and they waited while a few passengers got off, then they rode it up to the third floor. Jerry opened the door for them then went in and opened the adjoining doors. Harley looked around the room and whistled. "Wow –these are some digs," he said.

"Go take a load off, while I get us a drink," Hank said. He went over to the bar and picked up a bottle. "Hope bourbon is okay 'cause that's all they put in a Texas bar." He poured their drinks and after he gave everyone a glass, he sat down in a chair across from them and said, "Sorry Ah didn't git to give ya no advance warning about this, but it happened sort'a spur of th' moment."

Everyone settled back with their drinks and Hank began to tell them why they'd been asked to come. He explained that Mac had been feeling so lowdown and disappointed over them not being here, that he had the bright idea of calling Arte to go after them. "This whole thing is to be a surprise for Mac, so you guys gotta lie low."

"I think that it's a wonderful idea, Hank," Doc said. "Harley and I were also feeling very disappointed about not being here, but we understood that you people have been on a whirlwind ever since getting back to Mac's."

"Ah hope Arte wasn't outta line or anything with you," he said.

"Not at all," Doc smiled. "He was very polite and said he didn't know anything other than you'd called and told him to find us and bring us back here."

"Might be a good idea though," Harley said, "that if ya ever wanna do this again, to give us a head's-up first, 'cause your man woke me out of a sound sleep an' damned near got shot."

Doc nodded. "Yes, he showed up at my house after midnight and it was well after 2 a.m. by the time we left. But that bus of yours is amazing. I had no idea it had beds and everything one could ever need."

"Yeah," Harley chimed in. "That thing's like a five star hotel." Doc looked at him. "How would you know what a five star hotel is like?" he frowned. "Or *any* hotel, for that matter."

"Well," Hank said, standing up. "Ah'm just happy you're here, an' anything you want or need, just pick up th' phone an' call room service or ask Jerry, okay?" He left them with Jerry to answer any questions they had.

When Hank came back to the suite, Sam asked, "Everything all right -no last minute screw ups?"

"Everything's fine, sis. **Just** *fine*."

That night, Sam informed us that Hank and I would be sleeping down in his suite, while she and Noreen stayed in ours. We started to say something, but she held up "the hand" and said there was no use protesting, because we were not going to see them again until we came down the aisle. We didn't like it, but we reluctantly kissed the girls goodnight and left.

Monday morning started off in a blur. First, breakfast arrived, which no one could eat, then the hairdresser showed up a nerve wracking forty-five minutes late and Sam could not get Matt to settle down. He was so fussy that she had to rock him in her arms the entire time the girl worked on her. With her hair finally done, he'd calmed down enough for her to put him down and move on to doing her make-up.

Meanwhile down in our suite, Hank and I also got up early, but unlike the girls, we didn't have a lot to do and killed time by going through three pots of coffee until it was time to get dressed.

Back upstairs Sam was interrupted from doing her make-up by a knock on the door. Since she was still in her robe, she told Noreen she'd get it and went to the door. She opened it and a nice looking middle-aged lady smiled at her. Having no idea who she was, Sam said, "Yes, can I help you?" The woman said, "You must be Miss Evans, I'm Mrs. Franklin –Hildegarde Franklin, but please...just call me Hilda." Sam was confused. "I'm sorry, Mrs. Frank- uh, Hilda...but what can I do for you?"

"Oh dear," the woman said. "Someone forgot to tell you that I was coming, didn't they?"

"Tell me...what?"

"I'm a sitter from the hotel. I had a phone call from the manager two days ago, about sitting for your baby." She reached into her purse and took out a badge with her photo. "Here's my credentials," she said, holding it up. "You're getting married today, if I'm not mistaken?" Sam closed her eyes and slapped her forehead. A sitter. She had completely forgotten to see about getting one for Matt today. "Oh lord," she said. "I *completely* forgot about hiring a sitter," she said. "Who called the manager?" Hilda pulled a slip of paper out of her pocket. "A Mr. Jerry Lassiter," she said.

Jerry! Dear, sweet, thoughtful, Jerry. The man was uncanny. He never let any detail slip past him. "Please come in, Hilda," Sam smiled. "Jerry works for my brother and thank God, he thought to call." Hilda came in and Sam told her to follow her into Matt. "He's usually very good," she explained, "but for some reason, he's been crabby all morning, so you may have trouble with him today."

"That's all right," Hilda smiled. "Babies are very intuitive at this age. He's picking up your vibrations and is threatened by the confusion."

"Gee, I never thought of that," Sam said. "But it makes perfect sense."

Matt was sound asleep when they reached his crib. Hilda looked at him. "What a sweet baby," she smiled. "Oh, he looks like a perfect angel right now," Sam whispered, "but watch him - he can turn on you in the blink of an eye." Then she added, "Takes after his father."

They both laughed and Hilda said, "Well, I'm looking forward to spending the day with him."

Freeway heard their voices and came out from underneath the crib. Sitting at Sam's feet, Sam introduced them. "Hilda, this is Freeway, Matt's constant companion."

Hilda patted her head. "Hello, Freeway."

Sam looked at her watch and cried, "Oh jeese, it's going on 7:30! I've gotta finish getting ready. Can I get you anything before I go –some coffee or anything to eat?"

Hilda shook her head. "No, thank you. I've already had my breakfast and I've brought some knitting along with me to pass the time. I'm quite all right."

"Okay, but if you decide later on that you want something, you just call room service and have them bring it up." Hilda agreed and Sam went back to getting dressed.

In the bathroom, she picked up her lipstick brush again, but instead of applying the rogue, she slowly lowered her hand and stared at herself in the mirror. The reality suddenly struck her that from this day forward, things would be different. In less than two hours, her life wouldn't be exclusively hers anymore -and for better or worse, would be up to her and Mac.

Noreen walked in. "Hey -can you do me up in back?" she asked.

Sam blinked and said, "Sure –turn around."

******

Finally it was time to go. Hank and I got dressed then took the elevator down to the lobby, where Jerry was waiting for us. He had already taken the girls to city hall, then Doc and Harley, and come back for us. I still had no idea they were here as I blithely piled into the limo behind Hank.

CHAPTER EIGHTY-ONE

I was a nervous wreck by the time we got there and had to pee so bad, I thought I'd die. I didn't even wait for Jerry to open the door; I opened it myself and flew inside. I'd just made it to the urinal, when Hank came in. "You okay?" he frowned.

"Yes, mother, I just had to pee."

"Yeah, well, by that hundred yard dash you did, Ah jest wanted to make sure you weren't escaping out th' back door or nothin'."

I went over to the sink and washed up. "You're a riot, you know that?" I dried my hands and started out the door. "Uh, ya might wanna zip up, podner," Hank said. I grabbed my zipper and zipped up, as we went out to wait in the outer lobby for what seemed like an eternity. I nervously shifted my weight from one leg to the other and looked at my watch. "It's a quarter past nine, what's th' hold-up?"

"All ah know is, we gotta wait here 'til somebody comes out an' tells us when to-"

Just then the doors opened and a little man came out wearing thick glasses and a suit from the '40's with a shirt collar two sizes too big for his scrawny neck. "The ladies are up front and they're ready for you, now," he said. "Follow me, please." We did as he asked and as I pushed the door open, I whispered "Holly Mother of God!" and stopped dead in my tracks.

CHAPTER EIGHTY-TWO

Both women were visions in white. Noreen's white satin dress hugged her ample figure like a second skin. She turned to face us and a sleek fishtail train wound its way around her legs.

The low-cut "V" neckline of her gown fell off milky white shoulders into long tight sleeves ending in an elongated bouquet of Calla lilies. Her abnormally over-bleached blonde hair had been toned down and highlighted to a believable color, piled up loosely on top of her head with honey blonde tendrils falling around her face. Her make-up was flawless and she wore no veil; just three large white gardenias along the left side of her head. She was a *goddess*.

But if I thought Noreen was something, I couldn't breathe when I looked at Sam. World War Three could've dropped the Bomb on us and I wouldn't have been able to take my eyes off her. I recognized her dress right away; it was the same white gown she'd worn on their television special. And where Noreen's was long and sleek, Sam's was yards and yards of anti-bellum fullness and grace. She was a Barbie doll in a tight fitting bodice that made her small waist look even smaller. The white frothy skirt winked and sparkled like dewdrops from hundreds of tiny rainbow sequins. Her gown reminded me of one I'd seen in an old Bette Davis movie called, "Jezabel" designed by Orry Kelly -only she was even more stunning. Her hair had been pulled back in a long braid surrounded by a halo of slender white ribbon and baby's breath.

The girls were as different as brides as they were individuals. Noreen was a picture of Amazonian Art Deco while Sam was the fairy princess – and wars had been fought over lesser historic beauties. When I took my place beside Sam and she looked at me, all the angels in heaven must have wept with envy.

I was floating somewhere above the stratosphere when the Justice of the Peace began the ceremony. I didn't hear a word he was saying, until I felt a sharp elbow in my side and heard someone growl, "Wake up, dufus an' put th' ring on Sam's finger!"

I blinked and said, "Oh, sorry..." and reaching into my inside pocket, pulled out the ring.

As I slid it on Sam's finger, her mouth fell open but before she had a chance to say anything, the J.P. turned to Hank and asked him to give Noreen hers. He did and she went into cardiac arrest. Leave it to Noreen to bring the wedding to a screeching halt, as she held out her left hand and wailed, "Oh, my stars! Oh, OH, MY GOSH ALMIGHTY!"

"If you don't like it, Ah kin always take it back," Hank teased. Without taking her eyes off the golf ball size diamond encrusted ring, she clutched her bosom and cried, "Oh, no, you won't! You heard th' man –it stays on 'til Death, so don't you DARE try to take this off my finger!" Sam looked over and rolled her eyes when she saw the ring. "My God," she mumbled. "Is there a headlight missing from th' limo?"

"It IS a honker, ain't it," I beamed, proud of my choice in both rings.

"Hank always did have th' worst taste," she sniffed.

I coughed and looked up at the ceiling.

The J.P. had a lot more words to rattle off before he finally pronounced us husbands and wives. Then he said the magic words and turning to Sam, I took her in my arms and said softly, "Hello, Mrs. McIntyre." I kissed her and it was all over –we were married. We turned around to leave and ran right into Doc and Harley standing there. Both Sam and Noreen screamed, "Oh, my **God**!!!" I was speechless and it took me the better part of a minute to realize they were really there.

I gasped, "*Doc*! *Harley*! Is it really *you*? H-How-?"

"Hank sent someone after us night before last," Doc smiled.

"Yeah," Harley added, "said you wouldn't get married 'less we was here, an' since we couldn't be responsible for you not makin' an honest woman of Sam, we came up just to make sure."

I looked at Hank. "*You* did this? How?"

"You was all mopey," he shrugged. "So Ah had Jerry send Arte to go get 'em."

I was completely taken aback. Hank had managed to keep this from all of us. I couldn't believe it and didn't know what to say. "So **THAT'S** what all th' secret phones calls have been about between you an' Jerry." Sam said. "Yep," he nodded. "Well, that's a relief," she frowned. "I was afraid you two were cookin' up something really stupid."

"Like what?" he frowned.

"Like a hot air balloon honeymoon."

"Damn," Hank said. "What a **super** idea! Wish Ah'd thought of it."

"C'mon," she smiled. "Let's get outta here."

CHAPTER EIGHTY-THREE

Just when I thought the day couldn't hold any more surprises, we went into the lobby and a million brilliant flashes suddenly went off in our faces. Temporarily blinded, I pulled Sam close to me and put my arm up across my eyes. Noreen screamed and Hank angrily threatened to tear somebody's arm off. When my vision cleared, I saw the lobby was crawling with men behind flashing cameras that kept going off.

"W-What's going on?" I asked.

"Reporters!" Sam spat.

"Son-of-a-bitch!" Hank swore. "Ah should'a known we couldn't get away with it!"

There were so many of them in the lobby that they had the front door blocked off and we were unable to get out. Suddenly, an overly aggressive reporter weighing over 300 pounds shoved Doc so hard that he went down and disappeared amidst the crowd. To make it worse, in his careless rush to get a photo, he stomped on Doc's legs, as he tried to get over him. Like lightning, Harley stepped in and decked the bastard, knocking him ass over teakettle. Another reporter moved in quickly and grabbed for Sam. I pushed him away and drew back my fist, but missed hitting him and clocked the jerk next to him, dropping him like a bag of wet sand. Harley got Doc back on his feet and just as I thought a real fight was going to break out between all of us, Jerry pushed the door open, clearing a path by pinning several photographers against the wall. As he held the door, he yelled, "Hurry, Mr. Fairfield, I've got the limo running!" and we wasted no time scrambling out to the waiting car.

Once everyone was safely inside and the door was locked, Jerry got in behind the wheel. By now the limo was surrounded by reporters who dove for cover as he floored it. When we were a mile or two safely down the road, Hank leaned up and said, "Good work, Jerry."

"I tried to reach you before they did, but they swarmed in like locusts."

"Yeah, an' there's no stoppin' 'em when they're like that either," Hank said, before turning back to us. "Is everybody all right?" he asked. "What about you, Doc?"

We all seemed to be in one piece, but wondered how the news got out about our wedding. "Somebody from city hall either called them," he said, "or they sent somebody in to see if anything's goin' on -which they do periodically."

I was worried about Doc and looked at him. "You okay? You took a bad spill back there."

"Yes, yes, I'm fine," he smiled, but I knew he must have hurt something, because I saw him limping when we ran out to the car and he tried to hide the fact that he was rubbing his knee.

"What now?" I asked.

"We go back to th' hotel, have some supper then pack up, an' head for Dallas."

Harley said, "Not me...I need to head on back a.s.a.p."

"Same here," Doc nodded.

"Can't you *please* take some more time off an' go on to Dallas with us?" Sam begged. "There's plenty of room at th' ranch, an' I promise **ALL** reporters will be *shot* on sight!"

"I wish I could," Doc sighed. "But if an animal gets sick or dies while I'm gone, I won't ever be able to live with myself."

"Yeah, an' as y'all know, a ranch don't run itself," Harley said. "My bein' gone this long is too long."

"We understand," Hank said. "Ah'll arrange for Arte to take y'all back tonight, but first, we're gonna have a real nice supper up in th' suite to end this day proper."

CHAPTER EIGHTY-FOUR

Jerry let us off at a side entrance in the garage and we took the service elevator up to our suite. Once we got inside, Hank picked up the phone and called down to the front desk to ask if any reporters had been around -or *were* there now. "No, sir," the clerk informed him. "I haven't seen any reporters, but if one shows up, I'll be sure to notify you -will you be in this suite?"

"Yeah, we'll be here 'til around midnight, then we're checkin' out, so have everybody's bill ready for me."

"It'll be ready, sir."

"Good, now put me through to room service."

Without changing, Sam went right in to check on Matt. Hilda was holding him and looked up when she came in. "OH! *What* a gorgeous gown, Miss Evans...I mean, Mrs. -gosh, I don't believe I know your new name."

"McIntyre," she smiled. "Gee, but that's got a nice sound to it, doesn't it?"

"It does," Hilda agreed. "May I see the ring?" She showed Hilda her ring and the woman's eyes popped open. "Oooh my," she said admiringly. "I've *never* seen anything quite like it before."

"Yeah, it is a little over th' top, isn't it," Sam laughed. "So, how'd you and Matt get along?"

"We got along fine. He settled down after you left and your Mr. Lassiter came up to see if I needed anything. He also walked the little dog, so we were quite well taken care of."

"I am so glad to know that you didn't have any problems."

At that moment, Matt suddenly began to wave his tiny fists around and in the blink of an eye, he was wailing at the top of his lungs. "Not a one - until just now," Hilda said.

"Great," Sam sighed. "Well, it looks like I'm in for it tonight. Thanks, buddy."

Hilda stood up and put Matt in his crib. "Maybe not," she said, covering him with his blanket. She leaned over and slowly stroked his forehead. In moments, he was fast asleep.

"That is amazing! How'd you do that?"

"It's really very simple," Hilda smiled. "Rubbing the forehead causes the mind to relax. Our skin was designed to respond to touch and quite honestly, nothing feels as good as the loving caress of a loved one. It's especially comforting to babies."

"Hmm, I think I saw that once down in Florida when a guy rubbed the stomach of an alligator. The thing was asleep in two seconds."

"It's the same principle."

"So, we could end world war if we just massaged each other more?"

"Well, that's overly simplifying, but…you've got the idea," Hilda laughed. "Unfortunately, that can have quite the opposite effect on adults once they hit puberty, so for now, I'd stick to rubbing the forehead."

"Oh yeah…" Sam blushed, suddenly remembering the hundreds of massage parlors.

"By the way," Hilda added, "Matt was very hungry earlier and drank almost an entire bottle of warm milk just before you came in, so he'll most likely sleep for the rest of the night -unless you have to change him."

"Hilda, you are a *true* marvel," Sam whispered.

"Well," she said, picking up her knitting and stuffing it back in its bag, "if you're back for the night, I guess I'll call my husband to come pick me up."

"OH, don't disturb him -let Jerry drive you back in the limo."

"Oh, my, no," she answered. "I wouldn't know how to act in one of those. And besides, if I got to like it, it would spoil me for our old Ford Taurus – then my husband would get mad and before you know it," she laughed, "that limo ride would be the cause for a divorce."

Sam took Hilda's hand and smiled. "C'mon then, you can call your husband from th' living room." They came out of the bedroom and Hank asked how much he owed her. After Hilda told him, he paid her, adding an extra hundred. "Oh, this is far too much money," she cried, but Hank just closed her hand over the money and said, "Miz Franklin, you're worth every penny." Sam came over and hugged her, saying that if they got back to Houston, she'd love to have her take care of Matt again. Hilda nodded, then called her husband and said goodnight to all of us before going downstairs to wait for him.

After she left, Hank picked up the phone and called Jerry. "Hey, Jer," he said. "Listen, we're gonna have a little celebration dinner 'fore we leave. What'd'ya say, you come up an' join us?"

"Thank you, Mr. Fairfield -what time?"

"Room service said it'd take about an hour for prime rib. Ah know you don't drink, but maybe you'll make an exception this one time an' have a glass of champagne with us?"

"I'd be honored, Mr. Fairfield, but since I have to drive to Dallas tonight, I'd prefer to pass on the champagne. No offense, sir, but I wouldn't want to take a chance on anything happening today."

"An' none taken, Jerry. You're absolutely right. See you in about an hour."

CHAPTER EIGHTY-FIVE

I hated to see the girls go change out of their wedding dresses for dinner.

"Oh well," I sighed, "I guess, "All good things must come to an end," and Sam told me that that was the wrong way to look at it. "In our case," she said, "All good things are just beginning."

I liked that saying a whole lot better.

It took dinner a bit longer than an hour to arrive. Hank was starving and kept looking at his watch. After almost two hours, Hank was visibly annoyed and wanted to know "what was taking so damned long?" When the knock on the door finally came, I silently said a prayer for room service and hoped the hotel had hospital insurance. Hank yanked the double doors open so hard that it almost sucked the two waiters inside. Startled, they hurriedly wheeled in a large round table, apologizing for the long wait. I waited for it to hit the fan, but in spite of the threats he'd sworn earlier, Hank smiled and said sweetly, that he "didn't mind at all."

Although Hank had only ordered one prime rib roast, each end of the table held *two* standing rib roasts. Silver domes covered other dishes, but in the very center of the white linen tablecloth were three white candles surrounded in a blanket of white roses.

The men thanked him for his patience and without wasting another second, quickly went about setting everything up, turning down the lights and lighting the candles when they finished. The table was a masterpiece. Even Hank was impressed. He asked to sign the bill, but the waiters said, "No sir, Mr. Fairfield. This is on the hotel to wish you all the very best on your marriage, and say it has been our pleasure to serve you all these years." Ever used to being in control, Hank didn't know what to say. Finally, he said softly, "Tell everyone thank you."

The men turned to go, but he said, "Wait jest a minute," and reached into his pocket. Humility was new to Hank and to his way of thinking it only seemed natural to give something back. He took out four one hundred dollar bills and handed each waiter two. However, to their credit both men said, "No, Mr. Fairfield, this is our gift to you," and left before he could protest. Hank stuffed the money back in his pocket and said, "They think they're slick, but Ah'll just leave this at th' desk for 'em when Ah check out."

Sam looked at him. "Don't do that, Hank," she said. "It would spoil the gesture an' ruin everything. This is something that *they wanted* to do for us and you don't pay for a gift."

"Yeah, but-"

Sam went over to her brother and kissed him on the cheek. "No "buts." You're a goodhearted person, Hank, and the workingman's friend, but sometimes folks just want to show how much they appreciate you for being you. In a world that puts a price tag on everything, it's beautiful to still find some things don't have one...an' *this* is one of those times." Her words slowly sunk into his thick skull and Hank nodded. "How'd you git to be so smart, li'l sister?"

"I'm not positive, but I think it was sometime between birth and starvation –which is now," she laughed. "C'mon, let's eat!"

CHAPTER EIGHTY-SIX

When we sat down to dinner, the only person missing was Jerry. Hank called down to his room, but there was no answer.

"This ain't like Jerry to tell me he'll be here, then not show up, or call - or *somethin'*," Hank said. Sam looked worried. "I hope everything is all right," she said just as there was a knock on the door. Hank opened it and there stood Jerry holding a large pink box in his hands.

"Where th' hell you been, man?" Hank growled.

"I *am* sorry, Mr. Fairfield, but I wanted to get you a cake to celebrate your wedding -only there aren't any bakeries open at this time of night – excuse me, but is it too late to come in?"

"Oh, sorry, Jer...no, c'mon in." Jerry came in and set the pink box in the table. "This is all I could find and I had to go all over Houston to find it at an all-night grocery." He opened the box and took out a sheet cake decorated with pink flowers, blue balloons and green icing that said, "HAPPY BIRTHDAY, TIMMY."

We looked at the cake then Jerry, and he shrugged. "This was all I could find, except for one that said, "GOOD LUCK, THELMA, ON YOUR RETIREMENT. I guess she didn't retire..."

We stared at the cake again then broke out in laughter. Hank put his arm around Jerry's shoulder. "C'mon -we were just sittin' down to eat, an' Timmy's cake'll go good with coffee."

After dinner, we were stuffed, but we cut the cake anyway and toasted Timmy's birthday. Everybody fell into conversation over coffee and I asked Doc and Harley how the bar was doing.

Harley told me, "After Legrand closes up on Fridays and Saturdays, he goes over an' opens your place up from four 'til midnight. Then after church on Sunday 'til about 6."

Doc was listening and said, "He tried opening it during the week, but it was too much for him, so he opens it on the nights that bring in the most business and gives your band the chance to work."

"*My* band works on Sunday?"

"It's just practice, mostly, I think," Harley said. "Anyway, Legrand takes whatever money is left over after he pays them an' deposits it in your account over at th' bank."

I frowned. "That isn't what I told him to do. I wanted him to keep whatever th' bar made."

"Legrand isn't going to do that," Doc said, shaking his head.

"But," I protested. "That means he's running his hardware store, his cattle ranch, and my bar. I just wanted him to open it **if** he had time -I didn't want th' money!"

Harley shrugged. "Like Doc said, he ain't gonna do that. It's your bar – so, it's your money."

"God," I sighed. "I owe him for so much. I'll call him an' tell him to keep th' money."

Harley shook his head. "I wouldn't do that, if I were you."

"Why not?'

"Cause he'll just be pissed at me for tellin' you, then I'll be pissed at you -an' you don't want that." I looked at Harley and grinned. "Naw, I *sure* don't want that," I said, then asked, "What about Juan –has Legrand seen him?"

"Oh, yeah, he still comes by and Legrand pays him to sweep up on Tuesdays or Wednesdays for th' weekends –you know, to carry on th' tradition you started. When he wanted to know where you were, we explained to him that you were away in Houston getting married to "Mees Sam." That made him happy -just sez he misses you an' Freeway."

"It's probably Freeway more than me."

Then Doc changed the subject. "So, now I imagine you'll be moving to Sam's ranch outside Dallas. Have you given any thought to what you're going to do about the bar?"

And <u>there</u> it was; the question I'd been avoiding asking myself.

"I haven't thought that far ahead yet," I frowned. "My *plan* was to die right there on th' crossroads an' be buried out on the lone prairie." Hearing that, Doc sat back in his chair and rubbed his chin thoughtfully. "You know," he mused, "my grandmother used to say, if you want to make God laugh -just tell Him your plans."

CHAPTER EIGHTY-SEVEN

On that note, we fell silent and I gave some serious thought about having to give up the bar. Going to Dallas wasn't "just a possibility" –it was the natural thing to do. Ranch life would provide the perfect environment for Matt to grow up in. Animals and kids went together like salt and pepper. On the other hand, I'd poured my heart and soul into restoring the saloon, and along the way, not only found my salvation, but also some mighty good friends. While I mulled this over, Jerry stood up and excusing himself, left the table to go make a call downstairs to the desk. Hank pulled the champagne out of its silver bucket and said, "Y'all had better saved some room for champagne!"

"Hear, hear," Doc smiled. "I'm ready."

Hank stood up and popped the cork. After pouring everyone a glass, he looked at us and raised his. "To our new wives –and old friends!"

We had just finished when Jerry came back. He said, "I called down to the front desk to get a weather report and they said it's going to turn cold here tonight, but they're predicting snow flurries in Dallas." Sam's eyes lit up. "*Really*? Oh, I hope it does snow," she cried. "It'll mean God's gonna give Matt his first White Christmas!"

"How about reporters?" Hank frowned. "See any lurking around down there?"

Jerry shook his head. "No, I made sure to ask and the clerk said he hadn't seen any at all. I think if we move fast, we might get away before they find out we're still here." Hank set his glass down and said, "Sorry, folks, but it looks like th' party's over -time to pack up and hit th' road." Everyone let out a little moan and pushed their chairs back from the table. Turning back to Jerry, Hank told him, "You git a'hold'a Arte. Tell him to have th' bus gassed up an' ready for th' trip back in one hour –we gotta move fast!" Jerry nodded and wasted no time heading for the door. Hank followed him with Noreen in tow, but before they went out, he looked back with one last instruction. "Sis, you an' Mac be downstairs in twenty minutes an' be sure you bundle up Matthew good an' warm."

She nodded and we left for the bedroom. We were almost finished packing when she stopped and held up her wedding gown. "What's wrong?" I asked, and she sat down on the edge of the bed. With the gown crumpled in her lap, she sighed, "This whole day has been such a whirlwind that I haven't had a minute to stop and think."

"About what, sweetheart?"

"Well, for one thing," she sighed, "we don't have *one* picture of our wedding. Reporters showed up and ruined everything, and if it hadn't been for Jerry, we wouldn't have even had a cake-no matter *how* pathetic it was."

I suddenly realized how disappointing the day had been for her. I sat down next to her on the bed and took her hand in mine. "Yeah...I guess it *has* been disappointing, when you really <u>look</u> at it, hasn't it?"

She brushed away a tear and said, "Oh, don't get me wrong...it –it's just that a girl's wedding day is something she dreams of all her life and-"

"...And we didn't get to do it right in a church with friends and an *invited* photographer," I finished for her. She looked at me and nodded.

"Well, now that you mention it..." I sighed, "I guess we're just gonna have to do it again in a real church with a real photographer!"

Her face lit up. "OH, Mac –could we?"

"I don't see why not."

Sam jumped up. "That would be fantastic!" she cried, hugging her gown.

"Only problem I see is, do we know of a church?"

"I do!" she nodded. "The one Hank and I grew up in. It's a beautiful old stone church with four story high wooden beamed ceilings and *lots* of stained glass. It's the perfect place for the fairytale wedding I've always dreamed of."

"...And *I'll* get to see you in that dress all over again," I grinned.

CHAPTER EIGHTY-EIGHT

We finished packing and were only five minutes late meeting everyone down in the lobby. Hank had us checked out and the bill already on its way to his business manager. I carried our bags off the elevator while Sam balanced Matt in one arm and juggled Freeway's leash with the other. After I handed our luggage to Jerry, I took Freeway from her. Outside, Arte was ready and waiting by the curb with the bus's motor running. Doc and Harley were waiting to tell us goodbye. Sam gave them each a big hug and promised to bring Matt down to see them real soon. The night air had turned considerably cooler since the sun went down, and a light wind played with the hems of our coats as we climbed into the back of the limo. I was the last in and got the window. Jerry closed the trunk and got in behind the wheel. Hank took one more look around to see if he saw any reporters. When he was satisfied there weren't any, he settled back and told Jerry to start the car and head for Dallas.

As we pulled away from the hotel, Noreen cuddled up to Hank, resting her head on his shoulder. He put his arm around her and pulled her close, then laid his head back and closed his eyes. Sam rocked Matt while

Freeway curled up in my lap. Once we got on the highway, it wasn't long before the steady hum of the tires lulled us to sleep.

CHAPTER EIGHTY-NINE

Hours later, I felt the car slow down. It made a turn and tires crunching over gravel woke me up. I rubbed my eyes and looked out the window. We were on a narrow private road with oak trees on either side. The trees formed a leafy canopy over fences that ran parallel to the road. This had to be the drive up to the house. I leaned up to look, but we were still too far away. Glancing over to see if anyone else was awake, I saw that they were still fast asleep, although I didn't see how. Hank was snoring loud enough to wake the dead. He snored on the intake and sounded like a motorboat when he exhaled. Noreen wasn't much better.

Only Freeway was awake. I put my arm around her and the two of us watched out my window, as endless miles of rolling hills disappeared into far-off mountains rising up out of an ethereal ground mist. Their ridges touched the sky and made me think of my grandfather. Although the land was different here, mornings like this have a spiritual sameness everywhere. I leaned back in my seat and stared out the front of the limo. Never in my wildest imagination did I envision the ranch being this big. I couldn't see its vastness, but I *felt* it. I slowly stroked Freeway's head and thought about this new turn my life had taken. It was like a dream, and certainly a *long* way from where I was when I got back from 'Nam.

Suddenly Jennie popped into my head. Her betrayal had been the final nail in a coffin full of both personal and combat deaths. I didn't understand it at the time, but just as suddenly as she'd popped into my head, I understood why she'd been taken out of my life. God had a better plan. I thought He'd abandoned me, but He had been with me every step of the way, guiding me to this very moment. The limo slowed down and I looked up to see the house come into view.

...And *what* a house it was!

CHAPTER NINETY

I don't know what I expected -probably a modest little house or something 'way over the top, but man, was I wrong! This house was a sprawling single story home with a lived-in simplicity. Its unassuming air invited you to come inside, put your feet up and sit a spell. Jerry pulled up to the steps and got out. He went around to the trunk while everybody woke up.

"Looks like we're here," Hank yawned.

Noreen sat up and frowned. "Where are we?" she mumbled, rubbing her eyes.

Sam grinned. "We're *here!*" she cried loud enough to scare Matt, and he began to wail. She handed him to me and said, "Mac, take him for me while I get out."

"Then what?" I frowned.

"I'll take him inside and give him his breakfast, silly." She got out of the car and I handed Matt to her. Before she turned to go inside, she looked up at the sky. "The sun is trying to come out from behind the clouds, Jerry," she said. "I thought you said we were supposed to have snow." Jerry came around from the back of the car with a suitcase in each hand. "Yes, Miss Sam...we're supposed to have snow flurries, but they didn't say when." Sam shrugged and went up the steps with Matt, leaving me to get out and help Jerry with the rest of our luggage. He handed me two bags and picked up the last three. I followed him up the steps, across a wide spacious porch to the front door. The house had a high-pitched gable roof with the peaks at each end. The sides of the roof sloped down over the porch, shading it and five wooden rockers sitting in front of six wide airy windows. Baskets of ferns hung in between ten posts supporting the roof.

As I followed Jerry inside with the bags, my head just missed hitting the unusually low ceiling, and I wondered how many times Hank had knocked himself out here before learning to duck. But if I'd had any reservations about coming here, they all vanished. It was love at first sight and I was *home.*

CHAPTER NINETY-ONE

Jerry went on while I set the luggage down on the slate floor of the foyer. There wasn't any carpet –not even a throw rug by the entrance. A coat rack over in the corner with rain gear draped over it, told me why. The foyer was sparse except for a five by six foot oil painting hanging over a long rustic table. The painting depicted a large herd of cattle being driven through a blinding rainstorm. Intrigued, I went over for a closer look.

The sky was black and threatening and the wind whipped through the cowboy's slickers like a hurricane. Lightning flashed wickedly over distant mountains, as a hard rain beat down on both the drovers and the cattle. With water pouring off their Stetsons, the men lowered their heads against the wind and struggled to keep the frightened herd together. The picture was so real, that I felt the tight reins in my hands and clinched my fists.

Hank's voice came from behind me. "That's an honest-to-goodness Remington," he said, pointing to the signature. "See where he signed it?"

"If this is *real*," I said, "it's worth a fortune! Just where'd YOU get an authentic Remington?"

"This is just one of two paintings -th' other one is hangin' in th' living room. C'mon, Ah'll show it to ya."

I followed him down the step into the living room. We turned left, passing by a sofa table behind a leather couch and stopping in front of a stone fireplace. Another painting hung over the mantle. This one showed four or five cowboys around a campfire looking tired after a long day's ride. Firelight flickered against their faces, as orange-red embers spiraled into the clear night sky. Remington had such a remarkable talent for capturing the feel of the West, that I could almost hear the coyotes in the distance. "So, once again, where'd you get not one, but two Remington's?"

"From my granddaddy."

I rolled my eyes in exasperation. "Okay then, how'd your *grandfather* get them –he ride with Butch Cassidy or some other outlaw's gang?"

"Ah'm gonna *kick* your *ass*, you know that?" he frowned. "Just so happens, smart-ass, that somebody over at th' state capitol in Austin gifted 'em to him. Granddad was a big player in politics. He had a lotta pull in th' Texas Senate an' entertained higher-ups like th' governor, pretty reg'lar."

"Wow, *really*?" I said, in surprise. "My apologies."

"Great granddaddy came out here in th' early 1800's, an' our family is one of th' oldest to ever settle in Texas. He saw th' future in land an' bought up as much as he could at fifty cents an acre –which was a good chunk'a change back then. *Now* it costs a fortune just to keep up th' taxes."

"How much acreage did he acquire?" I asked, thinking it was probably only about a hundred or so acres.

"Th' ranch goes on as far as th' eye can see, for one hundred an' twenty miles."

"*WHAT*?" I cried.

"Yep," Hank said matter-of-factly. "It's a workin' ranch of course, so we've got about twenty or thirty thousand head'a cattle, but Dallas is movin' out this way faster'n a Texas tornado. Land developers are always tryin' to find a way to get this place."

"Well, if that's true, you got trouble. Those bastards are relentless – what've you done so far to hold them off?"

"Make *sure* th' taxes are paid an' call on some of mah family's old cronies up in th' state senate if they get too pushy."

"Must be expensive to keep a place like this," I said, sympathetically. "Damn land vultures…they're not above doing anything to get what they want –and it would take an act of God to stop them, even if you do have some political pull!"

"That's true -but something happened about ten years ago that insured they *wouldn't* be getting this place, ever –no matter *what* they did!"

"Did God Himself, come down and drive them away?" I kidded.

"Damned near," he said. "One day, Ah got a letter in th' mail askin' permission for some guys to come out here an' run some kind'a geo-thingamabob test. Ah didn't think nothin' of it, so Ah said okay. Well, they came out and poked around th' ground for about a month, an' damned if they didn't find oil up on th' north slope."

My face brightened. "Well, that's *great*! Now you can keep 'em from building their god-awful condos, or timeshares –or whatever. Oil trumps real estate developers every time."

"Yeah…but *then* th' damned oil company wanted to buy up all mah mineral rights!" he frowned. "Ah asked 'em if they thought Ah looked stupid."

I raised an eyebrow. "…And what did they say to *that*?"

Hank glared at me. "Ah told 'em they could drill all they wanted, wherever they wanted, as long as we kept th' land -AND twenty-five per cent of th' profits."

"Lord," I gasped. "You don't ever have to work again in your life!"

Hank laughed. "Ah don't work now," he grinned. "But naturally they wouldn't go for twenty-five per cent –or even twenty per cent…so we settled on five per cent and Ah keep th' land an' all its mineral rights, until such a time as Ah decide to do different –which Ah won't."

"Five percent -oh, you poor baby."

"Heartbreaking, ain't it?" he laughed. "But you shouldn't make fun of it, son. Now that you're family, it belongs to you as much as us."

I felt all the blood drain from my face. That was a staggering thought and the room started to look all watery. Hank pointed over to the couch and said, "You're lookin' a little pale there, boy. Why don't you go on over an' sit down on th' couch, while Ah go see if th' girls got any coffee made yet." He patted me on the shoulder and I sat down to think about what he'd just said. I wasn't used to being...rich. It was all too much for my pathetic money deprived brain to handle. To me, having money just meant I could order extra cheese with my hamburger. Before I could get a handle this sudden information, Hank came back and sat down on the other end of the couch. "Noreen's bringing us a tray out," he said. "Coffee was just perkin' when Ah went in."

He leaned back and pointed across the room. "See them two pearl handled six shooters mounted up there on th' wall?" he asked. "They belonged to mah great grandfather. He was fast as greased lightnin' with a six gun an' could knock th' eye outta a gnat at fifty yards."

"That's what I like most about you Texans," I sighed. "You never exaggerate."

"Well, we gotta git th' point across."

Noreen came in with a tray. She set it down on the glass top coffee table and that was the first time I noticed it was made from a wagon wheel. "I suppose this wagon wheel came off your great granddaddy's covered wagon when he came west," I said, again sarcastically.

"Yep, it sho' did," he nodded, with a twinkle. "Ah believe it was th' right rear."

"I was being sarcastic," I frowned.

"Yeah, Ah noticed, but sarcastic or not –you was right."

"And you *know* it came off the right rear –really," I huffed.

"Do y'all want any cream or sugar?" Noreen asked.

"Ah don't, sugar booger –what about you, Mac?"

"No, black is fine. By th' way, where's Sam?"

"She's in at th' kitchen table feedin' Matt," she answered. "You want me to tell her to come out here?"

I shook my head. "Don't bother her," I said. "I'll go in when we finish our coffee."

She nodded and smiled at Hank before she went back into the kitchen. He blew her a kiss and she giggled.

"Oh, lord," I said. "I think I'm gonna be sick if you don't stop with the newly-wed stuff."

He told me to shut up and handed me my coffee. We settled back on the couch and I said, "It must've taken years to finish a house this big. How long did it take to build?"

Hank looked around the room and said. "This living room, a bedroom an' a kitchen that caught fire, are th' only original parts of th' house. There wasn't no porch, entrance way, or dining room." He took a sip of coffee and went on. "An' there sure weren't no bathrooms."

"But this place is huge," I argued. "Did you add on?"

He nodded. "About two years after mah great grandfather finished building th' house, a woman who cooked for them spilled a pot'a grease across th' wood burning stove an' 'fore ya could blink, th' whole kitchen went up like a tender box."

"What happened –did the house burn down?"

"Mah grandfather managed to get it under control before it destroyed th' rest of the house, but it pretty much left th' kitchen in ashes."

"Anybody hurt?"

"Thankfully no, but they had to eat a lotta beans cooked over an open campfire, while he rebuilt it," Hank smiled. "And when he did, mah great grandmother had him make it bigger, which is what we got today."

"So who added th' rest?"

"That would be mah grandfather –an' my father. As times progressed, granddad's family grew an' they needed more bedrooms -so he had 'em added them on, along with plumbing later on. After he passed an' Dad took over, he modernized all th' plumbing an' Mom had him put in a washer, dryer an' dishwasher. So," he exhaled, "that pretty much brings us into th' 20th Century now."

"How many bedrooms?"

"Four, countin' th' master."

"I noticed the oak floors," I said, "–and what's the origin of the rug covering it?"

"There ain't a nail anywhere in these floors. Th' floorboards were cut by hand an' are all tongue an' groove," he said. "An' Ah don't know much about th' rug –except its Navajo. It's been here long as Ah can remember an' Ah jest never thought to ask where it came from, but Ah reckon mah grandfather picked it up somewhere over in New Mexico or Arizona. He was always interested in the Navajo an' Zuni tribes, so he'd visit their pueblos reg'larly, picking up whatever struck his fancy." I looked around the room, noticing quite a few Navajo clay pots and Zuni fetish dolls.

Seeing a doll in a display case, I got up and went over to look inside. A weird, almost evil looking doll with tree root arms and legs, stared back at me. "What's this one?" I asked.

"That's a Zuni fetish doll. Its made outta cottonwood root an' was used by th' medicine man in some kind'a secret ritual. In Indian culture, the doll is highly regarded to have a lotta spiritual power an' treated with respect. No one is really supposed to have one, but an old medicine man gave that one to him –after he blessed it, of course. Legend has it that they're strictly not to be touched, so Ah locked that one in that glass case. Ah ain't sayin' Ah'm superstitious, but Ah figure no sense pissin' th' li'l guy off."

"He kind'a gives me th' willys," I said.

"Me too," Hank nodded. "That's why Ah don't destroy him. He's rumored to come back an' get even with ya, if you try."

"What about burning it?"

"Shhh, lower your voice -he might hear you."

"Oh, for Pete's sake -it's a doll, you idiot."

"You *don't* mess with it, Ah told ya –it's got powers!"

I rolled my eyes and frowned. "Not to change the subject, but when I came in, I couldn't help noticing that the foyer ceiling is the same level as in here -but seems a lot lower."

"Yeah, when th' porch an' entrance were added, my father just continued th' living room ceiling out there. But when he raised th' entrance two feet, it *lowered* th' ceiling -which wasn't a problem for them," he laughed. "But he never accounted for having a son over six feet tall. As a teen, Ah got more bumps on mah head 'fore Ah learned to duck. Now, it's just a natural reflex."

He picked up the coffee pot and held it out to me. "Want any more coffee?" he asked. "If not, Ah'm going to go in an' check on Noreen. Ah wanna show her our bedroom, so we can get unpacked." I shook my head and told him to go ahead. After he left, I got up and went over to look at the grotesque fetish doll. Its twisted little arms and legs stuck out in all directions. The primitive face and beady eyes stared at me, emitting some sort of...eerie *power*. I turned away and sat down again. Hank was right - the doll was just plain evil. I sat there on the couch passively, not wanting to glance at the thing, but I was certain its creepy little eyes had me in their sight. I found being all alone in the living room unnerving and wished Hank would come back. After a while, I decided to get up and take our mugs back into the kitchen. I picked up the tray and started across the floor absolutely *positive* the doll was following my every step.

CHAPTER NINETY-TWO

Sam asked if anything was wrong when I put the tray down by the sink.

"No," I smiled. "The coffee was just a bit strong, I guess."

"Yeah, well, I'm not surprised. Noreen put enough coffee in to wake the entire State of Texas." She got up from the table. "I think Matt's had enough to eat."

"Anything I can do to help?"

"You can go find Jerry an' ask him to set up his bed. I'll put him down and get unpacked."

The phone rang just as I turned to leave. "I'll get it," she said, motioning me to go on. I went on and found Jerry out front with the hood up, leaning over the engine. I called to him as I went down the steps. "Hey, Jerry – everything all right?"

"Oh, hello, Mr. Mac," he said, standing up and wiping his hands on a rag. "Yes, everything is fine, I'm just changing the oil. Is there something I can do for you?"

"Yeah, Sam asked me to ask you if you'd put up Matt's crib for him? She wants to put him down for a nap."

"Certainly, sir. I'll be right in." He slammed the hood down and went to get the crib out of the trunk. I went inside, closing the door and turned around to see Sam coming towards me. She didn't look happy. "That was Hank's agent on the phone," she said.

"Oh? What did he want?"

"I don't know...he wanted to talk to Hank, but he's gone out to the barn to see Rusty, our foreman, so Sid said he'd call back."

"You don't seem too pleased about his call."

"I'm not. Christmas is just around th' corner, and Sid only calls when he wants Hank –or *me*, to go on th' road."

"Surely," I frowned, "he wouldn't send either of you out at this time of the year -*especially* since it's Christmas and you both just got married."

"Hah!" Sam laughed humorlessly. "You don't know show business."

The front door opened and Jerry came in with Matt's crib. "Which bedroom would you like me to set this up in, Miss Sam?"

She told him to set it up in her old room. He nodded and we went back to our conversation about the phone call. "So, what do you think the phone call means?"

Sam frowned, "I don't know for certain, but like I said, he's probably got something lined up for one of us –an' we haven't even had time to unpack." The back door slammed and Hank come through the kitchen yelling, "Where is everybody?"

"Out here," Sam called. He came in and said, "Rusty sez we got about a hundred new head since last spring."

"How'd you do that?" I asked.

"They were born during calving season," Sam answered, and looking at Hank, she said, "How's Rusty doin'?"

Hank nodded, "Same as ever –just glad we're home. Said for you to come on out an' see him." He went over to the desk and picked up a pile of mail. "Sez your horse needs a good ridin'." Sam and I exchanged glances before she said, "Uh, Hank...Sid called."

Without looking up, Hank continued to go through the mail. "Mmm yeah -say what he wanted?" She went over and stood next to him. "No, he didn't

-he said he'd call back." When Hank still didn't look up, Sam reached over and snatched the mail out of his hands. "Hank...you know as well as me why he'd be calling."

Hank turned to her with a big grin. "An' jest what do you think it means, li'l sister?"

"It means he has something lined up for one of us on th' road," she said, angrily.

He shrugged. "Ah don't think he'd do that," he said. "He knows we jest got married an' its Christmas. Maybe he just wants to wish us Happy Holidays..."

"Yeah, " she snorted, "that'll be th' day. Sid only calls when money is to be made. He doesn't celebrate Christmas an' it probably ain't even on his calendar."

"Aw, agents don't pay no never mind to that stuff when there's money to be made," Hank said in their agent's defense. "Sid's a good ol' boy an' we've made a lotta money together. 'Sides, he's your agent too, an' it's his job to keep us out there. He's jest doin' his job."

"Ya know," she huffed, "Just *once*, I'd like us to have a **normal** moment in life!"

Taking her in his arms, he said, "Define normal, sis." She let out a sigh. "I don't think I can."

Hank let out a belly laugh and squeezed her before letting go. Since show business was out of my element, I didn't know what to say, and there was a long gloomy silence, as I stood there like a bump on a log. Then an idea hit me and I said, "Hey –wanna go get a Christmas tree, Hank?"

"That's a damned good idea," he said. "And Ah know just where to find one. C'mon, Ah gotta get us an axe from th' woodpile an' th' keys to th' truck from Rusty."

"You're gonna chop it down, yourself?" I said, disbelievingly.

"Why not?" he shrugged. "It's a tradition 'round here, an' Lord knows, we got plenty'a trees." Sam's face lit up. "And I'll go up to th' attic an' get th' decorations while you guys are gone," she smiled.

Jerry joined us again in the living room. "Everything is ready for you, now, Miss Sam," he said. "Is there anything else I can do for you?" Shaking her head, she thanked him and turned back to us. "Go on Mac, I'll get things taken care of here, while you hunt us a Christmas tree."

"You don't have to say it twice," I smiled, kissing her on the cheek. I grabbed my coat and left with Hank out the back door, but as soon as he crossed the back porch, he stopped and yelled for Sam. She came running out. "What's wrong, Hank –you chop off your foot already?"

He shook his head and grinned. "Nope, jest wanted you to take a look up at th' sky."

She ran to the edge of the porch and looked up. Snow flurries fluttered down from the sky, landing lightly on her face.

"SNOW!" she cried. "Oh, Hank -that's a good sign -a *very good* sign."

"You didn't think Ah wouldn't order snow for you on Christmas, now did you?"

I looked at him and frowned. "Right," I huffed. "And do you walk on water, too?"

"Only if it's frozen," he grinned.

CHAPTER NINETY-THREE

Hank grabbed an axe from the woodpile and got the keys to a truck they kept there on the ranch, from Rusty. We drove out past a deep gorge that reminded me of a mini-Grand Canyon. Once long ago, rushing water cut its path through here, leaving the gorge after it either moved on or dried up. The area was now a lot of dry sagebrush and reddish-gold sand.

Hank smiled to himself as he drove over the rough terrain. He knew every tree, every stone, and every mountain out here. He could close his eyes and see every place he'd played, every stream he'd waded in, and every rock he'd climbed as a boy -and he could pinpoint the spot where he'd find the best Christmas tree. He drove on past the gorge until he came a thick outcropping of trees. Pulling up to the tree line, he stopped and we got out. Taking the axe from of the bed of the truck, I followed Hank into the woods as flurries of snow swirled around us like fine feathers. When he found the tree he wanted, I gave him the axe and stood back. He chopped it down and I helped him carry it out and load it in back of the truck. After we secured both the tree and the axe, I opened the passenger side door and asked, "Is that it?"

"That's it," he nodded, climbing into the cab.

On the way back, we passed a big river I hadn't seen on the way out.

"Did we come this way before?" I asked. "Because I don't remember that river, if we did."

Hank shook his head. "No, we're going back a different way. Thought you might like seeing this part'a th' ranch."

I turned back and looked out my window. The river's swift moving water cut a wide swath, raising the level of its banks four or five feet. Knee high grass grew all along the rim of the banks, and cottonwoods grew so close to the water that their roots showed through from where the river had washed away the dirt.

"That's a big river," I said. "Looks deep."

"Yeah, it's over fifty feet an colder than an ex-wife, Hank nodded. "Runs down from th' mountains windin' through here to meet up with th' Rio Grande somewhere further south."

I looked at Hank. "We got time to stop an' take a look at it?"

"Sure," he said, pulling over about ten feet from the river's edge. We got out and walked down to the bank. "Those tree roots look like their dipping their feet into the cool wetness," I mused.

"Ever hear th' phrase "Bourbon and branch?" he asked.

"Seems like I have," I nodded.

"Comes from what yer lookin' at," he said, pointing to the roots.

"Huh?"

"Long time ago, they used to dip their glass in th' water that ran just under th' tree roots for their bourbon," he explained.

"You just made that up," I sighed.

"Nope. Ah've known that since Ah was jest a tadpole."

I shrugged. "I guess that's as good an explanation as any."

"How far across is it?"

"Ah don't know –maybe twenty, thirty feet."

"Any idea how fast th' water runs?"

"Nobody 'round here was ever dumb enough to wanna go in an' find out."

"You can measure it from here on the bank, ya know."

"Well, say, that's somethin' *you* can do, city boy."

"I hate it when you call me that," I frowned. "One'a these days, Alice...to th' *moon!*"

"Ah know," he laughed.

We stood there a little longer and I watched as a large branch came towards us from upstream. In the blink of an eye, it floated passed us and disappeared from view in less than five seconds. I took a step away from the bank and looked up at the sky, noticing the snow flurries were getting thicker. I was about to say something when Hank asked, "You 'bout ready to head back?"

I nodded and started walking back to the truck, but turned around for one last look. I wasn't paying attention to where I was going and the next thing I heard was Hank yelling, "MAC! WATCH OUT! His voice startled me and I turned around just in time to whack into a tree.

"OOOWWWWW," I cried, grabbing my eye. Blood spurted out between my fingers and down my elbow. Hank came over to see what I'd done to myself and said, "I tried to warn ya, but it was too late." A deep frown creased his forehead, as he took my hand away. "Man, you really did a good job -you got about a three inch gash right above your eye." He squinted for a closer look. "Looks pretty deep, too," he added.

I grabbed a handkerchief out of my hip pocket and held it up to my eye. It was soaked in a matter of seconds. "Well," Hank sighed. "This kind'a wound bleeds like a stuck pig, so guess we better git you home an' take care of it 'fore you bleed to death." He helped me into the truck then went around and got in on the driver's side. "Can ya keep th' handkerchief up tight against th' cut?" he asked, and I nodded.

When we got back to the house, Hank threw the keys to Rusty and told him to bring in the tree for him. Rusty asked what happened and Hank told him I walked into a cottonwood. Talk about feeling stupid –I didn't even know Rusty and could just imagine what he was thinking.

I sat down at the kitchen table while Hank yelled for Sam to bring the first aid kit. She came in with it two minutes later and gasped. "MAC! What did you DO?" Hank took the kit from her and opened it, but before I could answer, he said, "Dufus here, walked into a tree," and looking at me, he said, "He's a city slicker an' don't know you're s'posed to be nice to trees."

I was fuming and if I could've done so, I would've shot him.

"WHAT?" she cried.

"It was an accident," I said. "We were down by th' river an' I wasn't looking where I was going."

"But how did you-?"

"I turned around to look at it once more while we were walking back to the truck, and next thing I know, this hostile tree jumped out and attacked me -which city trees *never* do! Look," I sighed, "can we just drop this whole thing?" Hank rummaged through the first aid kit. "All we got in here, is some butterfly sutures," he said.

"Whatever, just stop th' bleeding." He told me to hold still while he poured some peroxide on a piece of gauze and swabbed my cut –and none too *gentle* either. I frowned and jerked my head away. "Hey, take it *easy* there, Florence Nightingale!" I growled.

"Oh, stop being such a big baby," he said.

He finished cleaning my eye and put the butterfly stitches on then stood back and said, "You'll live, but it's swelling up nicely." I wanted to see how it looked before my eye closed completely and asked Sam if she'd get me a mirror. She came back with a hand mirror and I held it up to my face. "OH CRIMENY!" I cried. "My eye looks like Mick Jagger's lips!"

I dropped the mirror in my lap and glared at Hank. "And hitting th' damned tree didn't hurt as bad as *you* fixin' th' cut!"

"What a weenie," Hank huffed. "Maybe you'll learn to pay attention where you're goin' from now on." The screen door opened and Rusty came in with the tree. "Where you want this, Hank?" Hank went over to Rusty and looking at Sam, asked, "Where you want me to put it?"

"Good thing you didn't ask **ME** that question!" I said.

Sam told them to put the tree by the fireplace then sat down beside me at the table. "You okay?"

"Yeah," I said. "It hurts a lot, but I'll live."

"I'm afraid it's gonna leave a scar," she said.

I sighed. "One more ain't gonna be noticed."

I looked at the wall clock hanging over the sink. It was going on six o'clock already. "What's for supper?" I asked. "I haven't even looked to see what's here," she said. "Probably canned whatever-I-can-find."

I smiled. "I've eaten a lot of that -and besides, I love surprises."

I got up and started for the living room. "Where are you going?" she asked.

"To find some aspirin," I said.

CHAPTER NINETY-FOUR

Sam told me where to find the bathroom and I got the aspirin out of the medicine cabinet. I shook out three pills and swallowed them with some water, then went to check on Hank and Rusty in the living room. They had just finished propping up the tree. It looked a lot fuller than when Hank chopped it down. I went over to them. "Th' tree looks great," I said. "We did good."

"What'd'ya mean "we" white boy?" Hank said. "Ah did all th' work. You just walked into 'em."

Rusty stood up and stuck out his hand. "Hi, I'm Rusty."

He was a lot younger than I expected. I guessed him to be about twenty-seven and had Robert Redford rugged good looks. I shook his hand. "Pleasure to meet you, Rusty," I smiled, "–I'm Mac." His grip was firm but not bone crunching. "How's that eye?" he asked.

"It doesn't hurt as bad as my pride," I said. "I feel pretty stupid walkin' into a tree."

"That's because it was pretty stupid!" Hank said.

"Looks like Hank did a fair patch job on it. Only took two butterfly sutures, but it's already a nice shade of reddish-purple."

I nodded. "Yeah, Dr. Frankenstein did okay fixing me up."

"Dr. Frankenstein, eh," Hank said. "I seriously doubt even *he* could save that ugly mug."

"*Me*, ugly? Hah! You looked in a mirror, lately?"

"All Ah know, is you almost ruined a perfectly good tree out there today," he smiled.

"Don't let ol' Hank get you down," Rusty said. "He's not happy 'less he's riling somebody up. We don't pay no attention to him round here, but you're still kind'a new. You'll learn, though."

"*Him* get *me* down –that'll be th' day," I grinned looking at Hank. "I'm Irish an' we get even when you least expect it." Rusty put a friendly hand on my shoulder. "You're gonna work out 'round here just fine, Mac."

He cleaned up a few branches off the floor and we all three went back to the kitchen, where Sam had Noreen chopping onions and peppers to mix in with some fresh sausage she found in the fridge. Rusty came up to the stove and leaning over the frying pan, breathed in the mouthwatering aroma. Noreen smiled at him. "Hello," he said. "I'm Rusty." She nodded and said, "I'm Noreen," as she added the peppers and onions to the sausage. Moving out of her way, Rusty said, "I gotta get back to th' barn, but save me some of that, Miss Sam."

She winked at him. "How's lunch, tomorrow?" and Hank and I said in unison, "If there's any left." Rusty pushed open the screen. "You need to c'mon out to the barn soon as you can, Miss Sam. "Little Britches" misses you somethin' awful. He's been chompin' at th' bit now for a good while, waitin' on you to get back an' take him for a run." He started out, then turned back and said, "An' you come too, Miss Noreen. I got a fine horse for you –sweet'n gentle as a sunrise."

"We'll get out there, tomorrow, Rusty -give Britches a kiss for me, okay?"

Rusty looked doubtful. "I might brush him for you, but I don't think he'd take too kindly to me kissin' him." Sam laughed and waved, then turned back to her cooking. Noreen drained and diced some parboiled potatoes to add to the sausage while Sam added salt and pepper.

"How long 'fore that's ready, sis?"

"It's just about ready now," she said. "You can pour us each a glass of tea while I get th' plates."

"How about me -can I do anything to help?" I asked. "You could get the knives an' forks out of this drawer," she said, pointing to the silverware drawer. I opened it and took out the flatware. "What's Matt doing?" I asked. "He's lying in his crib staring at the hanging mobile while he tries to coordinate his hands with his feet."

"Sound amusing, but tricky," I said.

Sam turned off the stove and picked up the frying pan. "Its READY!" she yelled. "Everybody sit down." She set the pan down on a trivet in the center of the kitchen table and we all dug in. Forty minutes later, the four of us were relaxing over a hot apple pie that she'd found in the freezer and put in the oven just before we sat down to eat.

Noreen made coffee and brought the pot over.

Hank sat back with his second slice of pie and brought of the subject of someone named Rose. "Now that you got Matt to take care of an' Rose is gone, we're gonna need someone 'round here to help with th' cookin' an' cleanin'."

"Who's Rose?" I asked.

"She worked for our family for over thirty years," Sam explained. "But she's been more like a mother to Hank an' me, than a housekeeper."

"What happened to her?"

"Her husband had a stroke and she had to quit to take care of him full time, but Hank and I take care of all his medical bills, and pay her more than th' required retirement sum each month."

Yeah," Hank said, "she didn't wanna take it, but ain't no way we ain't gonna take care of her."

"And Rose is as honest as the day she was born," Sam added. "It'll be impossible to replace her."

"Yer right, sis –it don't look too promising."

"Problem is," I frowned, "Nobody wants to work these days."

Hank nodded. "That's true.

"People like Rose are a dying breed," Sam sighed. "She came from an old traditional Jewish family in the Bronx. She had good work ethics -and her chicken soup could cure anything."

"Same with the Amish up in Lancaster. Kids made fun of them and called them "Old School," but the Amish are loyal, honest, and as hard working as your friend."

"Amen" Hank said.

Sam got up and cleared the table. Noreen rinsed the dishes and ran hot soapy water in the sink while Sam left them to soak overnight. "I'll do these sometime tomorrow," she yawned. "Right now all I want is a hot bath and get into bed."

"Where's our bedroom? I'll go in and unpack our bags while you take a bath."

Wiping off her hands, she said, "Already done."

"When did you-?"

"While you were out smashing your head."

"I thought you were gonna go up in the attic?"

"Unpacking seemed more pressing, so I did it after I fed Matt. Hank can go up there tomorrow an' bring them down."

"Great," he scowled. "That's one'a my *favorite* things to do -thanks, sis. There must be forty-eight boxes of lights, tinsel, and other crap, for mah big feet to lug down them teeny tiny narrow stairs." Sam came over and patted her brother on the cheek. "If you get any crabbier, I'm gonna make you dress up like Santa Claus for Matt on Christmas morning." Hank threw up his hands. "Okay, okay, you win. Ah'll be *happy* to go up in th' attic. Just hold off on that old moth eaten Santa suit Dad used to wear. Besides, Matt's too young to know who Santa is an' seein' me in that suit could put him in therapy for years."

"We could get some'a them doggy reindeer antlers at Wal-Mart an' put 'em on Freeway," Noreen offered. We stared at her, speechless. Finally, Hank blinked and said, "Yeah, Ah like that idea a whole lot better."

CHAPTER NINETY-FIVE

Outside of the living room and kitchen, I hadn't seen any of the rest of the house. I followed Sam down a wide hall where the bedrooms were, glancing in each one as we passed. There were four or five of them -all large spacious rooms with windows that looked out on the front of the house.

Every one of them had queensize beds, except the last one. It had two twin beds.

"Hey," I said, "Why do all th' bedrooms have big beds in 'em except that last one?"

"Because, sometimes folks come to visit us with kids," she answered. "One day, that'll be Matt's room."

"How much further 'til we get to our room?" I wondered.

"We're down here on th' north end of th' house," she said. "Just a little further."

She came to a door at the end of the hall and we went inside. I let out a low whistle. "Say, John Wayne didn't happen to live here at one time, did he?"

"No, we just used his decorator."

The room must've been the master, because it was three times larger than the rest, taking up the entire end of the house. A rustic pine headboard rested against the windowless north wall and to my delight, the bed was a California king. On the other side of the room opposite the foot of the bed, two rockers sat on top of another Navajo rug in front of a fireplace stacked with logs. A door in the wall to the left of the fireplace went into a private bath with a tub and separate shower stall. The shower stall alone was the size of my entire bathroom back at the trailer. After checking on Matt in his crib, Sam showed me where the closet was with my clothes. She got herself a towel out of the bathroom and said she was going to take a bath down the hall, so I could have this one all to myself. I went into the enormous bathroom, striped down and turned on the hot water. As soon as steam fogged up the room, I opened the door and got in. The instant the shower hit my back I felt my body turn to putty. Letting the hot water do its magic, I closed my eyes and let out a long sigh -then worked up a soapy lather and soaped every inch of my head and body. With a seemingly endless supply of hot water, I stayed in for the better part of an hour and was right in the middle of "Jeremiah Was a Bullfrog," when Sam came in.

"I didn't know you were a Hoyt Axton fan," she yelled. I couldn't hear what she said and turned off the water. "What?" I asked, stepping out of the shower and grabbing a towel off the rack.

She had a towel wrapped around her and said again, "I didn't know you were a Hoyt Axton fan."

"Uh –I love Hoyt Axton, but...what's that got to do with taking a shower?"

She wiped off the mirror and got out her toothbrush. "Because you were singing one of his songs."

"No, I wasn't," I said. "I was singing, "Jeremiah Was a Bullfrog," by Three Dog Night."

"Mmmm, yes-and no," she said, dropping the towel and slipping on her nightgown. "That song was written by Hoyt Axton."

I stopped drying off and thought about it. "Are you *sure*?"

"No," she said, sarcastically. "I wouldn't know a *thing* about music. But since Hoyt's been a friend of ours ever since Hank got his first record contract - I'm *pretty* sure I'm right."

"Man, you should go on "Jeopardy."

CHAPTER NINETY-SIX

The following morning, Sam jumped out of bed and ran to the front window. Yanking the blinds open, she cried, "LOOK, MAC! It *snowed* last night!" She hurried to the closet and pulled out her clothes. Yanking a cranberry sweater over her head, she said excitedly, "Get up, Mac! I want to get out there!" I rubbed sleep out of my eyes and propping myself up on the pillow, looked out the window. It was a beautiful sunny day with about two inches of snow on the ground. For one instant, I was a ten year old back in Lancaster County. I threw back the covers and got out of bed yawning and stretching. "Okay...I'm up, now what?" I asked groggily.

"I'll fix breakfast while you bring Matt in th' kitchen -then I'll feed him, bundle him up, an' take him out to see th' snow."

She zipped up her jeans and sat down on the corner of the bed to put on her cowboy boots. Jumping up again, she ran to the dresser and wrapping a rubber band around her ponytail, headed for the door. "Hope you're hungry," she said, grabbing her coat on her way out.

"Hungry?" I mumbled, wondering how anyone could move so fast so early. I couldn't even think about food much before noon. I went into the bathroom to relieve myself and splash cold water in my face. After brushing my teeth, I shaved, dressed, and was just putting on my shoes when I heard her yell that breakfast was ready. I picked up a sleeping Matt from his crib and left for the kitchen. "C'mon, boy, let's go see what Mommy's got for us." He yawned and fell back to sleep in my arms. I wrapped his blanket around him and smiled. "You're my son, all right."

In the kitchen, Sam had the table set with everything from coffee to a platter of ham and eggs, to waffles and syrup. "Good *God*, Sam, do you think we're lumberjacks?"

Noreen was in there too. She brought a plate over with a stack of toast she'd made and set it down in front of me. I looked at her in wonder. "You're up early, Noreen," I said, picking up a piece of burned toast. "...And *so* domestic, too."

"I dunno," she giggled. "Must be th' country air." I sat down at the table with Matt. "Why –is it different from desert air?"

"Oh, shut up, Mac."

"Ahh," I smiled. "Now, there's th' Noreen I know and love. For a while, I was wondering if you'd had a personality transplant -or aliens had replaced you with a clone."

"What's *that* supposed to mean?" she frowned, moving the toast over next to the waffles.

"It means you've been so sweet here, lately...not like your old self, at all."

"Kiss my butt, Mac!" she said, just as Hank came into the kitchen. "That's a job you *best* leave to me, Mac," he smiled.

Her face lit up and she and threw her arms around him.

"Mornin', sweetheart," he said, patting her on the butt. He pulled out a chair for her and one for himself. Noreen poured his coffee while he wasted no time digging into the ham and eggs. "Man, this is great, sis," he said, in between mouthfuls. He picked up a piece of charred toast and was about to razz Sam, when Noreen smiled and said proudly, "I made th' toast!"

Hank shut his mouth and forced himself to take a bite. "Mmmm," he coughed, "deeelicious, darlin'." Sam was at the stove warming a bottle for Matt and said, "I'm glad you like breakfast, Hank, but I can't do this every morning, so you gotta find us a housekeeper -as *soon* as possible." Hank frowned, and I knew he had no idea where he was going to find somebody capable to do all the needed to be done around here. "Ah'll find somebody for ya by next week," he said. "Or right after Christmas, but 'til then, we jest gotta hang tough an' spread th' work around."

Sam came over with Matt's bottle and taking him from me, said, "Do whatever you gotta do, just do it quick. Here, Mac, I'll feed him."

"What about you?"

"I'll eat when I finish." She sat down across the table from me and gave Matt his bottle.

"Why don't you eat, an' let me feed him?" Noreen said, pouring her a cup of coffee. Sam shook her head. "No, I haven't had much time with him the past few days. I better do it before he forgets who I am."

I said, "Not to change th' subject, but I gotta call Legrand sometime after breakfast. He must think I've completely forgotten him."

Sam nodded. "That's a good idea –an' while you're on th' phone, I'll take Matt out."

"Fine," I said. "–and what plans do you have for us, today?"

"We're gonna go out to th' barn an' see th' horses," Noreen chimed in. "Right, Sam?"

"Yes. I promised Rusty we'd come out an' see "Little Britches," so maybe you'll go with us after you get off th' phone."

I nodded and she looked at her brother. "What're you going to do, Hank?"

He gave her a dirty look. "**AH'M** gonna be up in the *attic!*" he frowned.

"Perfect," she grinned.

CHAPTER NINETY-SEVEN

Right after breakfast, I called Legrand at the hardware store and he answered on the second ring.

"Legrand!" I said. "It's me, Mac –I'm so sorry I haven't called you before this."

"MAC! It's great to hear your voice."

"You must be ready to kill me for being away so long, but it's been a whirlwind ever since I left. This is, honest-to-God, the first chance I've had to call you."

"It's okay, Mac. You know this place, time moves slowly. Nothin' much has happened since you left."

"Well, it seems like it's flown by at th' speed of sound, here."

"Where are you?" he asked.

"At th' ranch just outside Dallas."

"Nice -what's it like up there?"

"Legand," I said. "You wouldn't believe it. I had *NO* idea..."

"Big, huh?"

"Would you believe me if I told you it's one hundred and twenty-something *miles*?"

There was a long silence at his end and I waited for it to sink in. "W-What...did you say?"

"You heard right. This place is huge. Hank's great grandfather bought up as much land as he could at –get this -fifty cents an acre." He built it into what it is today and they own land as far as th' eye can see -and then some."

"A hundred and twenty *miles* -I never *dreamed*..."

"Me either," I laughed. "And you've only heard th' half of it."

"There's more...?" he asked. "What is it –he own all of downtown Dallas?"

"Better than that, oil was discovered an' they got wells steady pumpin' out th' stuff."

"Son-of-a-bitch," he said. "You hit th' motherlode, boy!"

"I did that th' day I met Sam," I smiled. "Outside of her loving me an' giving me a son, I don't even count the rest."

"So, I guess you won't be comin' back, huh?"

"Sure I will," I said. "That bar is my baby an' all you guys are my friends. I can't just walk away."

"Seriously," he said. "You ain't comin' back, are you."

I drew in a long deep breath and straightened up, as a dull pain started to drill its way in between my eyes. "I am, Legrand, but it probably won't be until after Christmas."

"And then what?" he asked.

"That, my friend, is something I can't answer at this time."

Well, you know I'm here for you, if you need me."

"You still openin' the bar?"

"Yep, three days a week, like clockwork. "

"Listen, you don't have to do that. Just close th' door an' lock it. Everybody knows I'm away."

"I kind'a got used to it," he said, "It ain't all that bad...in fact, I find it a downright pleasure."

"Your wife is gonna kill you, you idiot."

"Honest –she's okay with it. She always liked you -you know that. Besides, spendin' time at th' bar, gives her more time away from me," he laughed. "And ME more time away from her findin' a million things for me to do. Hell, I don't even have to take out th' garbage anymore, 'cause I get home too late. If she'd let me, I'd try to buy it from you."

Feeling guilty as hell, I tried to think of something that would make him give up taking care of the bar, but I knew he'd rather die before admitting he was just doing this for me. "I don't know what to say, Legrand...but I DO insist that if you're gonna keep takin' care of things there, that you keep th' damned money. It can't be all that much, so do NOT argue with me. Besides," I laughed, "I got oil wells, now."

When I heard him laugh too, I felt the pain ease up in my forehead. "Okay...if it'll make you feel better. It ain't all that much, ya know –just a couple'a hundred a week –if that."

"Whatever it is, you keep it, okay?"

"Okay -sure."

"You seen Doc or Harley?"

"I have and they said they were at your wedding."

"It wasn't much of a wedding," I said. "Just some Justice of the Peace at city hall. But I had NO idea they were coming. Hank sent one of his guys after them to surprise me an' Sam."

"Yeah, they told me. Said some guy woke 'em up 'round midnight and put 'em on a private bus. They didn't even know it belonged to Hank, 'til th' next day."

"You *know* if I'd known about it, you'd have been there, too, but Hank didn't know, or else he'd probably have kidnapped you, too. He's crazy."

"Hey, lighten up Mac. I didn't mean to lay no guilt trip on you. I think it's great that they were there. Besides, one'a my girls was in a church play that same weekend an' I couldn't'a made it, anyway."

I said, "I don't know if you're lying or not, but I'm not kiddin' when I say you didn't miss much. Sam was so disappointed that we've decided to do it all over again for real, up here in th' church she grew up in –and THIS time, your whole family is comin'. Hank'll send his plane or bus, whichever one you want."

"Sounds great, Mac! When is all this gonna take place?"

"Well, we just got unpacked, so we won't have any time to plan th' wedding 'til after the holidays...maybe say, oh around th' end of January or sometime in February. By then, maybe Matt'll be big enough to be ring bearer," I laughed.

Legrand laughed, too. "And how is Matt?" he asked. "I never got to see him, but I heard about him from Doc an' Harley."

"Legrand," I said proudly," he is the most beautiful thing I've ever done. I never thought I'd ever have anything like him –*or* Sam."

"Being a father, myself, I know th' feelin' old friend, but let's just hope he grows up to look like Sam." And we ended the conversation on that high note, along with me wishing his family a Merry Christmas. Hank walked in just as I hung the receiver back on its hook -and the phone rang. I moved out of his way and he picked up the receiver.

"Yeah?" he said.

He listened for a few seconds then put his hand over the mouthpiece and mouthed, "It's Sid..."

I nodded and motioned that I'd be out in the living room, as he said, "Yeah, Sid, Ah'm still here..."

The conversation with their agent was not only lengthy, but heated as well. I heard Hank's voice yelling all the way from the kitchen. I couldn't make out what he was yelling about, but I knew he wasn't one bit happy about it, whatever it was.

I sat down on the leather couch and heard voices out on the porch. Sam and Noreen were sitting out there in the rockers with Matt. I picked up a magazine from the coffee table and without looking at anything, thumbed through the pages to kill time until Hank got off the phone.

Finally, the call ended and Hank came out of the kitchen. I threw the magazine down and sat up.

Hank paced back and forth, frowning and almost rubbing the skin off his chin. The anger on his face was unmistakable. "Uh, oh," I said to myself. "Whatever that phone call was about can't be good." He stopped pacing and I thought he was going to put his fist through one of the walls or worse, come over and do bodily harm to the nearest person –which happened to be me. While I waited to see which one it'd be, Hank came and sat down next to me. I think I flinched, but if I did, he didn't notice.

"Ah'm so danged mad, Ah could tear somebody apart," he said angrily, and I moved away a bit. "As you know, that was our agent," he said matter-of-factly. I nodded and when he didn't say anything, I took a chance and asked, "What happened –does he want you to go on th' road?" Hank's eyes shifted to glare at me, and he slowly shook his head. "No, not me," he said in a low growl. "It's Sam."

I sat straight up and cried, "**WHAT**?"

Hank grabbed my shoulder and said, "Listen, you can't say nuthin' to her about it! At least, Sid had th' good sense to talk to me first an' not her. He KNOWS Ah do *not* want her upset for th' holidays. This is y'alls first Christmas together an' Ah don't want *nuthin'* to spoil it, ya hear?"

I frowned. "But what does Sid want her to do –and *why*?"

Hank looked away. "He wants her to go on th' road for th' next three months."

"But WHY?" I wanted to know.

"Because, that song she wrote for you has taken off like a rocket an' doesn't show any signs of slowing down. We been too busy to notice, but its been at number one ever since it came out. Sam HAS to go on th' road."

THAT was when I discovered what a double-edge sword fame was. *Everybody* in the world owned you. Suddenly, I understood what Elvis must've gone through and wondered how he stood it for as long as he did. Shit. If I had to go through what these stars did, **I'D** be on drugs, too. Never again, would I fault *any* of them for dying early. So many put all their hopes and dreams in the shallowness of fame, that Death was the *only* way out. For them, it was better to go out quick than to live their fifteen minutes of fame only to be forgotten and have to live the life they tried so hard to escape, out in long obscurity.

Hank's voice was saying, "Mac? Mac? Are you listening?"

I blinked and said, "Oh, sorry, Hank –what?"

"Ah said, Ah bought a little time for her," he repeated. "Ah told Sid that if he called here again before Christmas was over, Ah'd not only quit, but Ah'd come down there to Nashville an' rip out his heart!"

"What'd he say to that?"

"He said he didn't have no heart, an' that Ah'd have to find somethin' else to rip out. But" Hank went on, "he promised he wouldn't call back." We sat there without saying anything for a minute -then I asked softly, "So...when does she have to leave?"

...And when Hank took his time answering, I took it to be another bad sign.

"She has to leave for Nashville three days after Christmas," he finally answered. "She's to be th' guest star at the Opry, opening New Year's Eve."

I slumped on the edge of the couch with my hands hanging limply in between my knees. Finally I sat up and asked, "Is there no way out of this?"

Hank shook his head –and that was that.

CHAPTER NINETY-EIGHT

Neither Hank nor I mentioned Sid's call.

Hank went up to the attic without one word of complaint and brought down every box of decorations he could find. Sam was delighted and dove right into them. "Why Hank" she smiled, "you've gone from Grinch to one'a Santa's helpers." She pulled the ornaments out one-by-one and they would've been unloaded much faster, if every piece she took out didn't have a story.

Finally, she came to the last one, finding the dreaded tangled ball of lights at the bottom. She pulled them out and said, "I know you're gonna flip your lid, Hank, but you're th' only one who can straighten these out." She handed the mess to him and he wordlessly began to untangle them. Confused by his passive demeanor, Sam watched him closely and I nudged him. "Say somethin' crappy about th' lights," I whispered, "before Sam wises up that somethin's wrong." He nodded and went into a tirade. "Damn these *lights*!" he yelled. "Ah get so damned tired'a this shit every year!" He threw them down in a fit of fake anger. "Why do we have to put these stupid things on th' tree anyway."

"Because," she said, picking them up, "the lights are the soul of the Christmas tree. Without them, the tree is lifeless and you might as well not even have one –and *don't* throw them, again!"

He glanced at me and shook his head. "You're right, sis" he said. "Ah didn't mean to be an ass. It's Matt's first Christmas and we have so little time like this with each other."

His words pierced my heart and I turned away before anyone saw my face. I thought this was going to be the happiest Christmas ever. Instead, it was going to be like watching the clock run out in the last quarter of the Super Bowl with the score tied.

CHAPTER NINETY-NINE

For the next few days, I was actually able to put everything out of my mind and enjoy the time we had left. Sam and Noreen took Matt with them Christmas shopping -hinting strongly, that we'd better do the same. They had Jerry drive them to a northside mall in the limo, while Hank and I took the truck to a separate mall. Sam's gift was easy. I got her a beautiful rose-gold cross with twenty-one of the most perfect blue-white diamonds money could buy. Hank bought Noreen a five thousand dollar gift certificate to Lord and Taylor's, and four five hundred dollar certificates to a Boot and Western Wear store for Rusty and the other three ranch hands. He said that those, along with healthy bonuses, would keep them happy for another year.

The night before Christmas Eve, everyone had all their shopping done and presents sitting under the tree. Hank had a fire going and we sat on the couch, trying to guess what was inside each gift. Noreen brought out a tray of eggnog and set it on the coffee table. It was like God was giving us this one perfect moment. Sam held Matt, who was surprisingly awake, and

Noreen played with him by wiggling her fingers at him. I thought she looked stupid, but he found it highly amusing. Suddenly, we heard footsteps on the front porch and then a chorus of voices singing, "God Rest Ye Merry Gentlemen."

We hurried to the front door and opened it. Standing there on the porch, snow fell behind nine teenage boys and girls dressed like they'd just stepped out of a Dickens novel. I was completely mesmerized - it was like being in an 1800's snow globe. The carolers broke into song again with, "Deck the Halls," "It Came Upon A Midnight Clear," "The Twelve Days of Christmas," and ended with my favorite; "Silent Night." We applauded when they finished and Hank thanked them personally for trudging up the two miles it took from the road to the house.

"Oh, we didn't walk," one of the boys, said. "We came in a sleigh," and he stepped aside to show us the one horse sleigh standing by the steps. I laughed, while Hank scratched his head and grinned. Noreen and Sam squealed and clapped their hands together saying they wanted to go for a ride.

The boy said, "Get in!" We looked at each other and racing down the steps, piled in the sleigh like giddy school children and pulled the blanket up over our knees. The boy got in and said, "Giddy-up, Mistletoe." The horse threw back his head, jingling the bells on his harness and we pulled away, leaving the others to wave to us from the porch. "No smooching, now!" someone called, and Hank yelled back, "NO promises!" As we headed down the drive, snow came down harder and thicker. It was a dry snow and already an inch covered the ground. From my boyhood days in Pennsylvania, I knew Sam was going to get that White Christmas, after all.

Sam huddled up to me with Matt and Noreen cuddled up to Hank. Suddenly, he broke out singing, "Jingle Bells, Jingle Bells," and we all joined in. Twenty-five minutes later, we were back at the house, not wanting to get out. "That was great," Hank beamed. "Ah ain't had this much fun since Ah was a boy!"

When the others came down the steps to gather around him, Hank asked them where they lived. They told him they lived all around the ranch on neighboring farms. "But your place is so big, you'd never know ours was anywhere around here," one boy laughed.

"An' do y'all go 'round singin' at Christmas, every year?"

The boy nodded. "Yessir," he said, "We do it for th' church. We're a youth group an we raise money for poor children."

"Well, we shore did enjoy it. Y'all made this feel like Christmas –thank you."

Hank reached into his pocket and took out -I don't know how much money, but I guessed it was in the four figures. "This is to show our appreciation," he said, "an' don't forget th' Lord –after all, it's His birthday."

The boy went pale and said, "Holy cow! T-thank you, sir!"

Carefully folding the money into his pocket, he wished us a Merry Christmas and everyone except one girl, clamored noisily back into the sleigh. She started to climb in when she stopped and turned around. "Excuse me," she said politely, "but aren't you Hank Fairfield?"

Hank looked at her and said, "Well...yes -an' no."

She looked confused. "Excuse me...?"

"Ah'm Hank Fairfield every day of th' year –except tonight," he smiled. "Tonight, Ah'm jest an ol' country boy who's grateful for what all th' good Lord has given him an' wants to be with his family."

The kids nodded, understanding perfectly. "Well, good night, Mr. Fairfield...and God bless you." We waved to them, as they drove off into the night singing, "Joy to the World."

Back inside, I whispered, "How much did you give them?" and he said, "Does it matter?"

CHAPTER ONE HUNDRED

The next day was Christmas Eve-day. The excitement started building from the moment Sam got out of bed and saw two more inches of snow on the ground. She dressed hurriedly, braided her hair and took Matt out of his crib. In the kitchen, Sam and Noreen fixed another lumberjack breakfast and when we sat down to eat she could not stop talking about the night before.

"Oh, remember Hank, when Dad wanted to give us an old-fashioned Christmas, an' he hooked up that horse of his to some ol' sleigh he got from one'a the neighbors?" He nodded and she went on, "Oh, Hank -this is turning out to be the **best** Christmas *ever*!"

I made a guttural sound in the back of my throat and Hank raised his eyes to give me a warning glare. We both knew her happiness was short lived, but he didn't want me to show it. Just as I regained some composure, she turned to me and said, "You know, Mac –I just know this is the beginning of a long, happy, life together." She leaned up and put her hand on my arm. "We're going to have many, many, more Christmas's like this!"

And that **did** it. My smile crumbled and I nearly choked on the boulder-size lump in my throat. Unable to stop the tears from welling up in my eyes,

Hank saw what was happening and saved me from making a complete ass out of myself, by reaching over to pick up his coffee and "accidentally" knocking his plate on the floor. It shattered loudly and Sam jerked her head in that direction. "Hank!" she cried, jumping up from her chair. "Are you hurt?"

He shook his head. "No, but Ah'm sorry 'bout th' plate, sis."

She bent down to help Noreen pick up the pieces. "Don't worry about it, it's just an old mismatched plate. No harm done."

While she was busy down on the floor cleaning up the broken plate, Hank looked at me and made a slashing motion across his throat, mouthing the words, "Stop it!" I nodded and sat back in my chair, as Sam stood up and walked over to dump the broken pieces in the trash. She came back and smiled. "See? That wasn't so disastrous."

Pushing my empty plate away, I cleared my throat a couple of times and tried to act casual. "Well, I guess Hank's elbow put an end to breakfast."

"I think everybody was done eating, anyway," she said. She gulped down the rest of her coffee and took her cup over to the sink. Noreen took my plate as I got up and pushed my chair back under the table. Hank stood up too. "Why don't you an' me go in th' living room, Mac," he said, "an' git outta th' way." He gave Noreen a kiss on the cheek and said, "Come join me, when you're through in here, okay lamb chop."

"NO peeking at anything under the tree," Sam warned.

We left the kitchen together and as soon as we were out of earshot, he roughly grabbed my upper arm and turned me around. "Are you out of your mind?" he spat. "You almost blew it in there! You *gotta* keep it together, Mac!"

I jerked my arm away from him just a roughly. "What th' hell do you think I'm tryin' to do?" I said angrily. "It's killin' me to see her so happy an' thinkin' she's got all th' time in th' world to enjoy it!" Pissed off now, I frowned at him and said, "Sam may be your sister, but she's my heart an' soul, and I can only *take* just so much!"

"Ah understand it's hard on you, Mac –*believe* me, Ah do -but you gotta think of Sam right now. Bite your tongue until it bleeds if ya have to, but **don't screw this up**. We jest gotta get through today and tomorrow…"

I nodded slowly. "Okay, okay. But, *you* gotta be th' one to break it to her!"

"It's better if Ah did it, anyway."

"When?"

"Not 'til day after tomorrow."

"Oh, God," I said. "The next twenty-four hours are going to be pure torture. It'll be like waiting for th' other shoe to drop –only in this case, it'll be like waiting for the blade to come down on my neck. I dread seein' how she'll take it."

Hank snorted. "She'll take it fine. She's a pro. She'll be pissed as hell at first, then she'll pack up her stuff an' say no more about it."

"How can you be so sure?"

"Because she's done it a thousand times before."

"Yeah, but she never had a husband an' son, before," and he didn't say anything to that.

Thirty minutes later, Sam and Noreen finished cleaning up the kitchen and came out to join us. "All done," she said.

Hank wrapped his arm around Noreen. "So, what're you two up to, today, sis?" he asked.

"We're going out to the barn," she said, pulling on her coat and gloves. "It's such a beautiful day, I'm takin' "Little Britches" out for a run in th' snow."

"Great idea," Hank grinned. "It's a perfect day for it." He looked at Noreen. "An' are you gonna go for a ride, too, my li'l dumplin'?" When she nodded, he asked her, "Have you ever been on a horse?" and she shook her head.

"Great," he mumbled.

"Don't worry about her, big brother," Sam said, patting his cheek. "I'll see that she gets on and off okay."

The girls' left for the barn. "Better stand by to call 911, Mac -this has disaster written all over it." Then he hit my arm with the back of his hand and said, "C'mon, let's go out there an' watch this fiasco. Ah can't wait to see if Noreen knows which end of th' horse is th' front."

"Since she knows what a horse's ass is," I said, "I'm bettin' she does."

"Since it's Christmas, Ah'm just gonna let that slide."

Rusty had "Little Britches" already saddled up and Sam was sitting on his back. She came up to us on the back porch. "Hey, you two," she smiled. "You wanna join us for a ride?"

"Naw, y'all go on," Hank said. "Ah got some last minute bills to go over."

I knew he was lying. He was really going to call Rose to see if she'd possibly be able to come over today and cook Christmas dinner for them. He'd told me earlier that he wanted to eat Christmas dinner in the dining room like a real family.

"Bills?" she cried. "On Christmas? Are you nuts?? What about you, Mac?"

"Maybe another time," I said. "I think I'm just gonna sit in front of th' fire an' catch up on my reading."

"Sounds dull –doing bills an' readin' a book, but okaaay."

Rusty brought Noreen's horse out of the barn and over to her. "She's all saddled and ready to go, Miss Noreen," he told her, as he helped her into the saddle. "And her name is "Buttermilk.""

Not wanting to waste any more time, Sam said, "C'mon Noreen, let's ride!" She grabbed the reins tight and leaned forward in the saddle, leaving Noreen and "Buttermilk" in her dust. Noreen watched Sam disappear over the horizon, then turned to Hank with a bewildered look and said, "Do you know how to make this horse go?"

Unable to control himself, he busted out laughing.

When he could talk again, he said, "Just sit up in th' saddle an' nudge her easy-like in the sides with your heels. Not too hard though –she's an old girl an' ya gotta treat her gentle. She hasn't had a saddle on her since th' late 70's...and Ah think it's been longer than that since she actually did any runnin'."

Noreen did as Hank said, but "Buttermilk" just stood there and blinked. Hank frowned and rubbed his chin. "Hmm," he mumbled. "Maybe she's retired." He called Rusty out of the barn, and said, "It don't look like "Buttermilk" is in th' mood to take anybody for a ride today," -or any other day, for that matter." Rusty ran his hand over her flank and smiled, "It *has* been awhile since she wore a saddle, so you could be right."

"Put her back in her stall an' give her some fresh hay, then get Noreen another one, okay?"

"Sure –anyone special?"

"Is "Bluebell without fold?"

"She had her colt last spring," he said, "So she's in fine shape –fact is, it'd prob'ly do her good."

Hank nodded. "Alrighty then, saddle her up -and why don't you go with 'em just to make sure everything goes okay."

"Sure thing, Hank –be glad to." Rusty led "Buttermilk" back to the barn and came out ten minutes later with a non-descript brown horse, alongside a saddled brown and white paint.

"Wow, what a beautiful horse, " I commented.

"That's "Apache." Hank explained. "Rusty roped him wild an' broke him hisself. Them two are joined at th' hip. Ah ain't never seen a more perfect match 'tween a man an' an animal. It's like they can read each other's minds."

"Where'd he find a wild horse?" (I was used to finding everything in a super market, so the very thought was foreign to me.)

"His sister lives 'way up in th' Sierra Nevada Mountains, in a little copper mining town called, Ely. They got what's called, "free range," out there. There ain't no law that sez you gotta fence in your livestock –which Ah think is dumb as hell -so horses, burros and whatever else has four legs, runs wild out there." Hank leaned up against a post and folded his arms over his chest. Making himself comfortable, he said, "Two years ago, he drove his truck out for a visit. His sister works at some local diner, so one day while he was killin' time up in th' mountains, he saw this big herd'a wild horses."

"Most of th' horses were brown or black, but this one Indian paint stood out. He sets his mind right then to catch him an' rode his sister's horse out every day for a week an' waited. On th' fifth day, they came by again. He lit out after 'em, but his sister's quarter horse wasn't trained. She didn't know knee commands or how to close in on th' herd. Rusty comes from a long line'a cowboys back in Montana and he can easily separate any horse from th' rest'a th' herd with a trained quarter horse, but without one, well, it ain't impossible –just harder."

Hank shifted his weight against the post. "So, Rusty kept a tight rein on his sister's horse with one hand an' got out his rope with his other. Without both hands free, he missed th' paint on th' first try, but got him on th' second one. Soon as the horse felt th' rope 'round his neck, Rust said he fought like a tiger. Now he's got a new problem; his sister's horse didn't know how to stop and hold her ground, so Rusty had his hand's full keepin' a tight rein on her, as well as trying to keep th' paint from slippin' his rope. He managed to do it, but that son-of-a-gun bucked and stiff legged so hard against the rope that his hooves plowed deep ruts in th' ground all th' way back. By the time Rusty got him in his sister's corral, that was one pissed off horse and things only got worse.

He took off runnin' 'round the corral, shakin' his head an' tryin' to kick down the fence, but ol' Rusty's as hardheaded as he is. He let him run hisself ragged, then bought a second-hand horse trailer th' next day an' drove him back here. Took two days to saddle break him, but by th' time Rust finished with him, that horse respected him an' they been best bud' ever since -and he's never hit "Apache." A deep frown crossed his face and I didn't miss the anger in his voice, as he added. "Rust knows you don't *never* gotta hit *any* animal! Ah'd fire any asshole that did, if Ah didn't hang him, first!"

"What happened to his sister's horse –didn't die of a heart attack, did she?"

"No, but Rust said it took over two hours to cool her down. He was concerned that she might'a pulled a tendon or something from runnin' her so hard, so he walked her for an hour to make sure she was okay, then he brushed th' sweat off her for another hour. Rusty'll stay up all night if he has to, until he knows an animal is okay."

"I remember reading somewhere in th' bible about a man being judged according to how he treats his animals," I said.

"When did *you* ever spend any time readin' the bible?" Hank snorted.

"Hey –I went to Sunday school every Sunday when I was a kid," I frowned. "Had to, or my grandmother would'a boxed my ears."

Hank dropped his arms and stood up as Rusty pulled Noreen alongside him by "Bluebell's" reins. "By golly, you're lookin' like a real cowgirl, sweetheart," he grinned. Rusty handed her the reins. Noreen looked unsure what to do with them as she took one in each hand. "No, Miss Noreen," he said gently, "ya gotta hold 'em both in your right hand, like this," and he showed her with "Apache's" reins. She shifted them to her right hand and asked, "What do I do with this hand?"

"It's just a free hand for holding on to th' saddle horn or restin' on your leg while you ride, but cowboys use it to hold a rope for ropin' cattle."

"Oh" Noreen said.

"Okay, if you're all set, Miss Noreen, I guess we can mosey along, now." She waved to Hank and off they went to find Sam. We watched them poke along over the hill then went back inside. Slamming the screen door behind him Hank said, "They're movin' so slow that Rusty'll probably fall asleep in th' saddle." I followed him through the kitchen to the living room, where he went straight over to the phone and picked up the receiver. He dialed Rose's number and waited for her to answer. As soon as he heard her voice, his face lit up. "*Hey*, Rose, this is Hank...how *are* you, sweetheart?" I went over to the couch and sat down while they talked. A few minutes later, he came over and joined me. "She's gonna come over," he grinned.

"That's great -but how's she going to leave her husband for that long?"

"Sadly, her husband passed away about a year ago. She said he had two more strokes and went into a coma after the second one. He spent the last month of his life in ICU without ever waking up from it, and then one morning, he just quietly passed away. Some ending huh, to a marriage of over fifty years?"

"God –it has to be lonely to spend your last years alone after a lifetime together."

We sat there for a moment then Hank looked at his watch. "Ah told her Ah'd be sendin' Jerry after her in ten minutes. Ah better go call him right now –wait here."

"So, did you invite her to have dinner with us –since *she's* th' one fixin' it?" I called after him.

"A'Course Ah did, you moron" Hank frowned. "But she already has plans to go to her daughter's house an' spend Christmas with her grandkids."

"Oh! So, she has a family!" I said to his disappearing back. Hank nodded then called Jerry and told him to come by the house before he went after Rose. Five minutes later, Jerry came in the front door, pulling on his gloves. "Hello, Mr. Mac, Merry Christmas."

"Hi, Jerry, same to you."

Looking at Hank, he said, "I'm going to get Rose, now, Mr. Fairfield."

Hank pulled out his wallet and handed Jerry his credit card. "Take her by th' grocery on th' way back -tell her to get whatever she wants for dinner tomorrow."

Jerry nodded.

"An' are you gonna be able to join us for Christmas dinner?"

Jerry shook his head. "Thank you, but I have plans with a lady friend over in Dallas."

"You sly fox," Hank laughed. "Well, just be sure to see me before you leave today, okay?"

"You gonna give him his Christmas present?" I asked after he left.

"Yeah –in th' form of a big bonus check. Figure he can use it to show his lady friend a real good time...an' maybe she'll return th' favor."

"I don't think Jerry needs any money for that to happen," I sighed. "He's smooth as Bond - *James* Bond."

CHAPTER ONE HUNDRED ONE

We were in the kitchen drinking coffee, when Jerry came in carrying a bag of groceries in each arm. Rose was right behind him. He set them down on the kitchen table and went back to the car for more. Hank cried, "ROSE!" getting up from the table and holding his arms out to her.

She was a small woman of about five foot four and didn't weigh a hundred pounds. She came over to him and he wrapped his arms all the way around her.

"Hank, you big ol' teddy bear," she laughed.

He held her at arm's length and said, "My God –you are a sight for sore eyes; let me *look* at you, darlin'!" and turning to me, he said, "Rose, Ah got someone here Ah want you to meet."

Pulling off her gloves, she smiled and unbuttoned her coat. Hank helped her take it off and she stuck out her hand to me. "Hello –I'm Rose." Taking her hand in mine, I noticed her eyes were the warmest shade of hazel. "Hello, Rose," I smiled, "I'm Mac."

"Are you in Hank's band?" she asked politely.

"No, Rose, Mac is Sam's new husband."

Her eyes widened and her jaw dropped open. "*What? H-husband*? Sam got *married*?"

"That ain't all," Hank grinned. "She's got a brand new baby boy, too."

"MY STARS – a baby? How'd that happen?" she gasped.

I looked sheepish as Hank said; "Ah'll explain everything, later –but right now, let's put you to work. It's been a coon's age since Ah had any'a your good cookin'."

He started taking groceries out of the twentysome-odd bags sitting on the table and said, "Oh, yeah –an' *Ah* got married too." It was all too much for her and Rose sat down. "Wh- *you* got married, *too*? What's happening to this family?"

"Can I get you some water or something?" I asked, and she nodded. I got her a glass of cold water and she drank it down in one gulp. "This is all too overwhelming...I'm having trouble digesting it." She looked at Hank suddenly, and said, "You're pulling my leg, aren't you?"

"Honest," I said. "It's all true –and a bit of a surprise to us, too."

She stood up and composed herself. "Well, you're just going to have to tell me everything, Hank Fairfield –and do *not* leave <u>one</u> thing out!"

Taking the turkey out of a grocery bag, she asked, "And just where *IS* Sam?" and carrying it over to the counter next to the stove, Rose bent down and opened a lower cabinet, knowing exactly where to find the roasting pan she was looking for.

"She's out ridin' her horse with mah wife, Noreen. Ah wanted to get you over here before she got back."

"So, she has no idea I'm here?"

Hank nodded. "Ah wanted it to be a surprise. These days, she has her so hands full with taking care of Matt –that's her son –that she doesn't have any time left over to cook a big dinner."

Rose put the turkey in the pan and pulled out the innards. Rinsing them off, she set them aside to make gravy with later. "I'm glad you called me, Hank. It hasn't felt right for a long time, *not* being here." She pulled a large knife out of the carving block and asked Hank to find the celery, onions, and herb breadcrumbs. He found them and handed them to her.

"To tell the truth," she sighed, "I haven't felt useful, since I had to quit to take care of Abe."

Rinsing off the knife, she dried it and began dicing the celery. When she finished chopping every bit of the celery into teeny, tiny pieces, she did the same to four onions, then opened the breadcrumbs and emptied them all together in a large bowl; adding warm water along with salt and pepper. As she made the stuffing, Hank cleared his throat. "Ah'm glad you brought that up," he said, "because –well, Ah wanted to talk to you about comin' back again."

She stopped making the stuffing and took a deep breath. "Oh, Hank, I'd love nothing more than to come back here, but I'm just too old to keep up with it, now," she said.

251

Kissing her cheek, Hank said, "You'll never grow old, Rose," and she brushed him off with a wave of her hand. "Oh -get out of here and let me cook," she frowned. "Go on, now –*scat*!"

"And you just better let me see that baby!" she called after him.

"Just as soon as Sam gets back," Hank smiled. "She'd kill me if she wasn't th' one to show him to you."

I was about to follow Hank into the living room when Rose grabbed my hand. "It is so nice to meet you, Mac -you've married into one terrific family."

I placed my hand on top of hers. "I know –I just don't know how I got so lucky."

"It isn't "luck," she said. "It's a blessing -just as it was a blessing for me to work for this family."

I started out again when I decided to take a chance and ask something. "Rose, what kind of people were Hank an' Sam's parents?" The words were no sooner out of my mouth than the look on her face made me regret the question. "I'm sorry," I said feeling like a fool. "It's really none of my business –it's just that the subject has never come up and –oh jeese, just forget I ever asked." I turned to leave and she said, "No –wait." She wiped her hands off on her apron and motioned me over to the kitchen table. After we sat down, she said, "You're family now, so..." and she paused to gather her thoughts. "What would you like to know about them?"

"Well," I sighed. "I don't want to pry –but I just wondered-"

"-what happened to them?" she finished.

"Yes."

"To begin with, their parents were good churchgoing people who taught the children the value of hard work, respect for others, as well as taking responsibility for their own actions. For all their money, they had their share of hardships and wanted their children to know what it was like to face them head on. Without going into every boring detail, I'll only say that Hank and Samantha had the best upbringing anyone could possibly have. They had good parents."

And I know good parents. I'm Jewish and was raised in a traditional Jewish tenement building back in Brooklyn, after my mama and papa emigrated to New York from Russia."

"My father worked hard for very little money and we lived a terribly poor life by today's standards. Mama stayed home to care for the family. She did everything from washing our clothes by hand in a washtub with a scrub board, to hanging them out our kitchen window on a shared clothesline that ran across to the adjacent building. She starched, ironed, and mended all our school clothes and papa's work clothes. She did all the marketing and cooking -and I learned how to cook by helping mama prepare the seder for Passover. All the food was prepared by hand and it could take up to a week to get everything ready -*if* we could even afford everything. Mama *never* stopped celebrating life and if there was nothing else in our home, there was joy and love."

"Excuse me just a second, Rose -did you say you grew up in Brooklyn?" She nodded and I said, "But Sam said you grew up in the Bronx."

Rose lowered her head and covered her mouth with the back of her hand. "Yes, I imagine she did," she nodded. "Sam always gets the two mixed up. She does the same thing with Philadelphia and Pennsylvania. Ever since she was a child she's done that. I remember one day she was telling me about the Declaration of Independence and said very matter-of-factly, "Rose, did you know that the Declaration was signed in Pennsylvania, Philadelphia -not Washington?" and Rose burst out laughing. "I still can't tell that story without laughing."

I listened to her tell about the Fairfield family and could just see a little Sam telling all about the Declaration of Independence. "Anyway," she went on, "one day they ran out of feed for the horses. It had been raining a lot and water got in the barn, getting the bags wet. Mold grows very fast on wet grain and has to be thrown out, because horses can't eat it without getting colic or other life threatening problems," she explained. "It was late afternoon, and still raining, so Mr. Fairfield asked Mrs. Fairfield if she'd like to ride along with him to the feed store. She knew the store was about twenty-five miles away and went along to keep him company."

"It wasn't at all unusual for her to go along -they honestly loved each other very much and tried to spend as much time together as possible. By the time they got to the store and the truck loaded with five fifty-pound bags of feed, it was almost dark."

I interrupted to ask, "Is that enough feed for all the livestock they have?"

"No, no, –they only needed enough to get through the next day. One of the ranch hands would've gone back and picked up the full amount they needed. Anyway, they started back with the feed loaded in back of the truck covered in plastic to keep it dry, when halfway home, the sky turned frightening dark and threatening. Lightning struck the ground all around the truck and a violent wind came up, making it almost impossible to hold the truck on the road –even with the extra weight."

"Meanwhile, here at home, a news bulletin came over the television warning people to stay inside because of flash flooding, and we all began to worry and watch the clock tick away the minutes. It got later and later and when they didn't come home that night, Hank –who was just nineteen, called the state police. ...Their truck was found in a gully eight miles away the next morning, upside down with them still inside." Rose's face cracked.

"It –was horrible. Sam was still in high school and very close to her mother, so…it was especially hard on her."

And there it was.

I swallowed the dryness in my throat, unable to believe how parallel our lives had been. We both had lost our family tragically and dealt with it in an unhealthy way.

"Are there any other questions you might have?" she asked kindly.

I shook my head and got up from the table just as Hank came in. "Mah God, Mac, Ah can't leave you alone with a beautiful woman for ONE minute!"

"True -especially one that cooks this good," I grinned.

"Yeah, but if you don't get outta here an' leave her alone, she ain't gonna never get no cookin' done."

I looked at Rose and sighed, "Well, we been found out -guess we'll have to call off th' moonlight swim, later."

She got up and said, "Oh, get out of here, the <u>both</u> of you."

CHAPTER ONE HUNDRED TWO

The sun had long gone down behind the horizon when I heard Sam and Noreen come in, laughing and giggling like two teenage schoolgirls. They hung up their coats by the back door and were still laughing when they saw Rose taking the turkey out of the oven. Sam stopped and looked at her like she was seeing a ghost. "*Rose?*" she whispered. Rose set the turkey on top of the stove and said, "Well don't just stand there, girl –come give me a hug!" Crossing the kitchen in two great strides, Sam grabbed Rose and smothered her with kisses. "Oh, my God, it is *so* good to see you!" She held her out and looked at her. "WHAT are you doing, here?" she grinned.

"Ah called her," Hank said, walking back into the kitchen.

"*YOU?*" she cried. "Oh, Hank –you *sweetheart.*"

"Yep, Ah knew if we had to depend on you two to cook dinner tomorrow, we'd be eatin' ham an' eggs –so Ah called an' asked her to come over."

"But that's not the only reason why I came," Rose said. "I heard my little Samantha had a baby and I wanted to see for myself."

"YES!" Sam cried. "And he is *beautiful!*" Then her smile disappeared and she said, "Oh, Rose, how is Abe doing?"

"He passed away a year ago," she smiled.

Sam's face fell. "I am so sorry to hear that."

"Well, don't be –Abe is out of pain now, and at peace. God bless his soul."

Noreen came over and said, "Mmmmmmm, I'm starving -*what* is that great smell?"

"Rose, this is Noreen, Hank's wife –and its tomorrow's dinner, so don't you dare touch ONE bite."

After introductions were made, Sam took a bottle out of the fridge for Matt and handed it to Rose. "It's time for me to feed my little poop machine, so will you warm this up for me, while I go get him?" She ran out of the kitchen without waiting for an answer and came right back with Matt. Hank looked up and said, "Ah think you just set a new world's record for the 440 dash, sis."

Rose gasped. "Ooooh, let me *see* that precious baby!" and she held out her arms. Sam handed him to her and pulling his wobbly little head back, Matt stared at her like she was Godzilla.

"He's less than a year old isn't he?" Rose smiled, and Sam nodded. "He was just born this last May." Rose cooed over him until he began to cry. "He must be hungry," she said, giving him back to Sam.

"Yeah, I'm sure he is," she said. Rose got his bottle out of the pan on the stove and looking out the kitchen window, noticed it was snowing. "Oh, look!" she said, handing the bottle to Sam. "It's snowing again."

She opened a canister and suggesting we all sit down, put on a pot of coffee. As soon as it was ready, she brought the pot over and for the next half hour, it was like old times sitting around the kitchen table with friends on a snowy evening.

Rose told us about Abe's last days, then Sam told her about the reverse order of Matt's coming into our lives before the wedding and Rose scolded them both for not letting her know so she could be there –even if it was at city hall. "Well, we can fix that," I said. "We're planning on doing it again in a real church before God and everybody."

Her face brightened. "Oh, wonderful –when?"

"Hopefully, sometime next February -and you can be our Flower Girl!

Rose said, "I'd better be!"

She got up and fixed us a platter of sandwiches for supper while she waited on two minced meat pies still baking in the oven. When the oven's timer bell rang, she took the pies out and then covered everything and put it in the refrigerator. "Okay –that's it," she said, untying her apron.

"It should taste even better tomorrow after sitting in the refrigerator all night." She looked at the clock and shook her head. "Good grief -it's almost eight thirty. I have got to get back and finish wrapping my presents for the grandchildren."

Little did we know that when that oven bell went off, it would signal the close of a great day.

A veil of sadness fell over us, and everyone got quiet when Hank went to the kitchen phone and called Jerry to bring the limo around to the back porch.

It was Christmas Eve, it was snowing – and it was time for Hank and Sam to say good-bye to the only present they really wanted.

CHAPTER ONE HUNDRED THREE

Christmas morning saw even more snow. I heard church bells ringing in the distance, as Sam bounced out of bed and got dressed. "Hurry up, sleepyhead," she yelled. "It's Christmas morning!"

She ran out, leaving me to try and push back the covers. I got one foot out and -that was as far as I got. I lay there for a minute then pushed the blanket off with my other foot. It was freezing and I groaned. I was married to an Eskimo. Sam kept the heat down around fifty-eight degrees at night and if I didn't have an extra goose down comforter, she'd be waking up to a frozen block of ice.

My breath hung in the air like a fog, but I managed to get dressed in spite of flapping my arms to keep warm. I made my way out to the living room where to my eternal gratitude, Hank was throwing another log on the fire he had going in the fireplace. The girls were sitting on the floor, pulling presents out from under the tree. I saw a tray of Danish on the coffee table with a big pot of coffee next to them. I plopped down on the couch and poured myself a cup. Noreen said, "Look, Mac is here –can we open our presents now?"

I sat back and smiled like waiting on me was a bit preposterous, but said, "Yes, Noreen –by all means, go ahead and open your presents."

I asked Sam where Matt was. "He's too little to bring out here," she explained, "so, I fed him and he fell back to sleep." She picked up a present and looked at the tag. "Here, this one's for you, Noreen." She handed it to her and picked up one with her name. Sipping hot coffee and nibbling a cheese Danish, I watched them tear into their presents. Noreen was ecstatic over Hank's shopping certificate...and *so* was Sam over hers. Hank didn't waste a lot of brain cells on being original.

He picked up a present from under the tree and threw it to me.

I said, "If this is a gift certificate-"

He just smiled.

I tore off the wrapping paper and opened the box. Inside was a nice pair of jeans and two western shirts, along with a hand-tooled leather belt and a big silver Navajo belt buckle. Before I finished checking them out, he threw me another present. This one was larger and heavier –and I was pretty sure I knew what it was. I tore off the wrapping paper, and sure enough, it was a pair of western boots. "Wow," I said.

Having never worn western boots before in my life, I took them out and put them on. They felt pretty damned good and fit perfectly, but I couldn't identify the material. "What kind'a leather is this?"

"Ostrich," Hank said. "Dyed ostrich -Ah was gonna have 'em dyed pink or orange, but decided on that there dark brown color at th' last minute."

"Thanks," I frowned. "And I've already got a *great* idea where to put these pointy toes."

Sam reached under the tree, looking for my present to her. Soon as she found it, she ripped off the paper and holding the box in her hand, said, "Oh, I just *love* presents in small boxes!" Then she opened it and squealed, "Ooooooooooooh, **MAC**!!" pulling the cross out. Noreen's eyes widened and she openly drooled over the diamonds sparkling in the firelight. "Where'd you *ever* find that, Mac?" she said, "I want one just like it."

"Forget it, Noreen," I frowned. "There's only *one* like it –just like Sam!"

Getting up from the floor, Sam came over and sat next to me. "Put it on for me, please?"

She pulled her hair out of the way and I hooked the chain. She turned around. "I'll never take it off," she swore -and the look in her eyes at that moment was all I needed for Christmas.

Her kiss blotted out everything and everybody, until Hank cleared his throat loudly and said, "Where in Sam Hill, is mah present –didn't none'a y'all git ME anything?"

Sam got off the couch and pulled Noreen up from the floor. "Sure we did," she said excitedly. "Its over here in the hall closet –you know -th' one we never use."

The two conspirators went into the hall, after telling us to stay in the living room. A minute later, they came back lugging something bulky and heavy -that clanked when they dropped it on the floor. Sam pulled off the blanket that was covering it, and Hank's mouth fell open. It was a black handmade Mexican saddle with matching bit, harness, and reins, trimmed entirely in silver.

Hank was dumbfounded and couldn't stop running his hand over the leather. Finally, he found his voice and whispered hoarsely, "Ohmigod, Sam -Ah...*always* wanted a saddle like this," and picking up the harness, he said, "There must be two hundred pounds'a silver in this outfit!"

"Not quite that much," she said, "but I did tell them to put on as much silver as they wanted to. I started to tell them to make it gaudy as hell, but...Mexicans do that naturally." She ran her hand over the smoothness of the silver. "And yet, everything comes out absolutely beautiful -like nothing else in the world."

"But Ah'd know this silver anywhere. It's pure Taxco silver!" he said, unbelievingly, and she nodded. "It is indeed."

"But where'd you find a rig like this? You sure as hell can't buy one already made!"

"I ordered it while I waited for Matt to be born –over a year ago. After Noreen came into the picture, she was stumped for a Christmas present, so- long story short -we went in on it together and had it shipped to Dallas through Roger."

(Roger, I discovered later, was the owner of a shop that sold boots, western wear and tack for horses –including saddles –but nothing like this one.)

"Jerry picked it up when he took us Christmas shopping at that mall three blocks away from Roger's store."

"Damn!" he said. "That's where Ah ordered Mac's boots from, but Roger never let on that he had a saddle for me –an' he can't keep a secret!"

"Unless, he knew I'd <u>kill</u> him if he told you about it."

"*Damn!*" he repeated.

"Well, you must be impressed 'cause you've run outta words," Sam said.

CHAPTER ONE HUNDRED FOUR

There wasn't anything that could possibly top the day.

Sam gave me a very classy heavy gold ring with an oval black onyx surrounded by diamonds. Noreen got Hank a black suede jacket to go with his saddle. The western-cut leather jacket had Indian beading on the yolk and fringe down the sleeves. It was such a classy one-of-a-kind garment, that I wondered if her taste had improved since she got married -or if Sam had picked it out.

All the presents had been opened and boxes and wrapping paper were scattered everywhere.

"This has been a wonderful Christmas," I said. "Now, how 'bout some breakfast?"

I got up and started towards the kitchen, when Hank held up his hand and said, "It ain't over yet, Mac. Sit back down –you too, sis. Me an' Noreen got one more thing."

The two of them left the room and Sam came over to sit next to me. "Wonder what those two have cooked up?" I frowned. She shook her head slowly and said, "I don't know…but I haven't entirely ruled out the hot air balloon, yet." Several minutes passed before they came back. Hank was carrying something in his arms and set it down on the floor in front of us.

It was an old-fashioned Amish cradle.

I stared at it and scratched the side of my face. Finally, I said, "This is an Amish cradle." (duh.)

Noreen clapped her hands and cried, "Yes!" and then looked at Hank with a big smile. "He knows what it is, Hank!" Hank rolled his eyes. "Yes, sweet potato," he sighed, "somehow Ah knew he would."

"Where did you find this –in an antique shop?"

"Got it back in Lancaster. Me an' Noreen wanted to get Matt somethin' for his first Christmas that he'd remember…his pa, too."

"How did you know where to find anything in Lancaster -have you ever been there?"

"Ah called the Chamber of Commerce there, dummy –how'd'ya think?"

I didn't have an answer.

I knelt down and ran my hand over the hand rubbed oak. The cradle was beautiful -and like everything the Amish made- the beauty was in their time honored practical simplicity. Suddenly, my childhood, my grandparents –and everything I'd tried so hard to distance myself from, came flooding back; and for the first time in a very long time, the memory was not painful. This was my first true Christmas.

A hood ran across the top of the cradle to shade the baby from sun and wind if he or she were outside. The only decoration on the entire thing was a folk-art heart painted in the center of the headboard. The cradle alone would have been more than enough, but there was also a tiny mattress covered by a multicolored baby's quilt with a white cotton pillow trimmed in hand tatted lace. "This might be one of the dearest things you've ever done, big brother," Sam said.

"It-it's something from *my* roots," I said in amazement. "I can't begin to tell you how much that means to me."

"Yeah, well…Ah'm glad you like it. Them Amish fellas gotta little shop back there that sells this stuff, so ah had 'em ship me one a.s.a.p. Came here 'bout a month ago by Fed Ex."

I nodded. "A special favorite with the women tourist are their quilts - they come from all over just to buy them. Occasionally, you can find a piece of furniture made by the men, but since the Amish do everything the old way, it takes three times as long. I'm very surprised you found a cradle that hadn't been snapped up." I turned to Sam. "Why don't you go get our son?" She hurried from the living room and came back with Matt. Sam put him down in the cradle and covered him with the quilt, which he took great delight in kicking off. Covering him again, she gently rocked him back and forth and couldn't stop gushing about how cute he looked.

Hank said, "Did Ah hear somebody say somethin' about gettin' some breakfast?"

Sam looked at her watch. "Well, yeah, I guess I could rustle up something, but I need to get dinner in the oven."

"What time do you want to eat dinner?" I asked.

"Rose said if I put everything in at 350 degrees, it should take about an hour...so around three?"

"Okay, sis –but only if you fix us some ham an' eggs in the meantime."

"I swear, Hank," she frowned, "you'd think you were helpless -fix it yourself."

"Okay," he shrugged, "but Ah don't know if you've ever seen a kitchen after Ah've had'ta cook in it." He looked at her with a straight face and said, "It's pretty ugly."

Sam gave up. "Oh, all _right_! I'll fix some ham and eggs -c'mon, Noreen." She went into the kitchen and Hank hollered after her, "An' make some more coffee, too."

I looked at him and said, "You're pushin' it, now."

CHAPTER ONE HUNDRED FIVE

Outside of glancing in on my way past it, I really hadn't seen the dining room. But now, I saw it was set for Christmas dinner with dishes, wineglasses, and silverware. Six matching chairs sat around a long highly polished mahogany table covered in a lace tablecloth. On each end of the table, a single silver candlestick held a single white candle. The room was large and spacious with *plenty* of elbowroom. An antique oak sideboard took up the entire space at the far end of the dining room beneath three large windows. The windows were covered in old-fashioned heavy lace curtains and a bouquet of fresh flowers sat in the center of the sideboard.

Hearing a sound behind me, I turned around to see Sam coming through a swinging door in the wall that connected to the kitchen. She was carrying a platter with the turkey.

"Oh!" she said. "I didn't know you were in here." She set the platter down in the middle of the table, and I asked if there was anything I could do to help. "You can bring in the salad and sweet potato casserole -I'm still waiting on the rolls to finish baking."

I helped bring out the food. "What about napkins?" I asked.

The oven bell went off and she pushed the swinging door open. "In there," she said, pointing to the top drawer of the sideboard. "I gotta go take th' rolls out," and she disappeared once more into the kitchen. I took out the napkins and after folding them next to the plates, lit the candles. Sam came back with a basket covered in a checkered hand towel to keep the rolls warm.

"Okay, y'all," she yelled. "Let's eat while it's hot -an' bring Matt in, in his cradle!"

When everyone was settled around the table, Hank bowed his head and said a prayer.

"Dear Lord, this is Your birthday and yet we are the ones who have gratefully received. For all You have given, we honor and thank You - amen."

We all said, "amen" and the dinner table became a beehive of laughter and talking as we dug in.

Rose had been right when she said everything would taste better today -or maybe it just seemed that way. We went through the entire sweet potato casserole, over half the turkey, all the rolls, salad, peas, and two bottles of wine. Dinner was perfect and we all complimented Sam on her "warming up" abilities. She got up from the table and after taking a bow, said thank you and went into the kitchen; coming back with minced meat pie in each hand. We sat back and groaned.

"Does that mean you can't eat any pie after I've slaved all day over a hot stove to make them?" With a roll still in his mouth, Hank shook his head and said, "We're stuffed, sis...but how 'bout a little later on with some coffee?" She sighed and took the pies back into the kitchen.

Noreen looked around the table and said, "Does anybody want anything else to eat?" I looked at her and wanted to ask what part of "we're stuffed" did she miss, but it was Christmas, so I kept my mouth shut. When we shook our heads, she got up and started stacking the dirty dishes on top of one another, while I blew out the candles and gathered up the dirty silverware. I was on my way to the kitchen when she said, "Here, Mac, give those to me -you go on out in th' living room with Hank."

I shrugged and handed her the knives and forks, then went out to the living room with Hank.

He didn't go over to the couch like I thought he would. Instead, he went to the foyer and opened the front door. "Let's sit out here," he said. "Th' sun's out an' it's warm enough to enjoy."

I followed him out to the porch and we sat down in the rockers. The bare trees cast long shadows in the late afternoon sun as it glistened off the tiny ice crystals in the snow.

"This is the life," I sighed. "It's like time stopped out here –no hustle, no bustle."

"Yeah…it sho' is," Hank smiled.

We were sitting there half dozing in the warm sun, when Rusty came running up on the porch like the devil himself was after him. Hank's eyes flew open and he sat up. "What's wrong, Rusty?" he frowned. Rusty quickly took off his Stetson. He was breathing hard and said breathlessly, "Sorry to disturb you, Hank, but I saw two cars stop down on th' road earlier. I had th' gate closed, so they couldn't turn in but they didn't look like th' types to let a gate stop 'em."

He was still breathing hard and stopped to catch his breath. "I didn't like th' looks of them" he said in between gulps for air, "so I saddled "Apache." They saw me comin' an' drove off before I could confront them, but -I know who they are."

Hank said, "Who are they?"

"Reporters."

"Son-of-a," he whispered.

He finally caught his breath and said, "What'd'ya want me to do?"

Hank thought about it a minute, then said, "Ah know it's Christmas, Rust, but keep a sharp eye out for them. Now that the bastards know we're here, they'll probably try to sneak back tonight."

Rusty put his Stetson back on and nodded. "I'll get th' other guys to help me stake out th' fence down by th' road –the only way they're gonna get in here tonight," he added, "is by helicopter." He hurried back down the steps and I felt my world crumble. I looked over at Hank. He was steaming -and I wasn't much better. Finally, I said, "Until right now, I was actually able to forget about -*things*, today." Hank didn't say anything, but I could see his mind was going a hundred miles an hour. I shut up and leaned my head back on the rocker. We sat out there without talking, until Sam and Noreen came out to join us with Matt. As Sam sat down, she said cheerfully, "Gosh, you two are awfully quiet –you *must* be stuffed."

Hank didn't answer and his lack of saying anything set off Sam's suspicions.

"Okay," she said, "what is it?"

I was *positive* he was going to tell her about Sid's call. But he didn't. Instead, he said, "Rusty spotted reporters down by the turn-in to th' house," and I slowly turned my head to glare at him.

"Damn it," she said angrily. "What are we gonna do?"

"Not much we can do long as they stay off th' property. Rusty's gonna keep watch down there all night." Sam looked angry and clutched Matt to her like a mama lion. If she was this upset by a few reporters, I dreaded to see what she'd be like when she heard the *really* bad news. She got up and said, "I'm going to take Matt back in the house."

Noreen watched after Sam with her normal confused wide-eyed stare - and I thought to myself that this was *one* time I envied her living on another planet.

CHAPTER ONE HUNDRED SIX

Hank still didn't tell Sam she was going to have to leave, and the later it got, the madder I got. But when it was time for bed, I pulled him aside and demanded hotly, "Just *when* are you planning on telling Sam about Sid's call?"

He said, "Ah guess now's as good'a time as any."

"Well *don't* rush into it," I steamed. "Maybe you can wait a little longer and spring it on her tomorrow, as you hand her, her bags."

"Okay," he nodded. "Tell her to meet me in the kitchen right now."

"Okay, but I'm going in there with you."

"No...Ah'm used to bein' th' bad guy, so it's better if you ain't there. Besides, no sense in her killin' both'a us. "

"Well, it's really swell of you to wait until we go to bed! Now, I gotta sleep with one pissed off woman all night."

"Oh shut up an' jest go git her, while Ah pour mahself a stiff drink."

Sam was putting Matt down in his crib and stood up when she saw me come in. "Oh, Mac, this has been the *best* Christmas, *ever!*" she smiled, coming over and putting her arms around my neck. I hugged her and it killed me to know what was coming, but...it *had* to be done. I pulled away and said, "Sam...Hank needs to talk to you."

She still had her arms around my neck. "Right now?" she asked and I nodded. "But, it's time for bed an' I wanna thank you for my present," she winked.

"Look," I sighed, pulling her arms away and holding her hands in mine. "Don't make this harder on me than it already is." She looked confused. "I don't understand, Mac...what's going on?"

I wanted to tell her so bad, but I said, "Just go meet Hank –he's waiting for you in the kitchen." She coolly took her hands away from mine and looked at me as she went to the door. Unable to meet her eyes, I stuffed my hands in my hip pockets and looked down at the floor.

I was brushing my teeth when I heard her voice all the way from the kitchen, followed by a loud crash -and another. Then all was quiet. I rinsed my mouth and hung up my toothbrush, then climbed into bed and steeled myself for the hurricane I knew would be blowing in any minute now.

I waited...and waited...and waited. When an hour went by and still no Sam, I threw back the cover and got out of bed. I crept down the hall to the kitchen, where I saw broken glass all over the floor and the back door standing wide open. Careful not to step on any glass, I went out the back door and stood on the porch looking for Sam or Hank. But there wasn't a soul around and I wondered if they'd been abducted by aliens.

I was about to go back inside and search the house when I heard a faint commotion. Unable to tell where it was coming from, I walked to the end of the porch and listened. It sounded like it was coming from somewhere in front of the house. I ran back to the bedroom and pulled on my new boots. Grabbing my jacket off the chair and putting it on over my pajamas, I hurried out the front door. On the porch and heard several angry voices coming from down by the front gate. I flew off the porch and started running in that direction as fast as I could. When I reached the main road, I saw four of Hank's men on horses chasing four men on foot. It was pure chaos and I frantically looked for Sam and Noreen in the darkness. I finally saw them standing together over by the gate. Two cars were parked on the other side with their doors open.

I ran to her, calling her name. "SAM, SAM!" When she saw me, she turned around and hugged me. "Oh, Mac," she said.

"*What* is going ON, here?" I asked.

"Reporters -they got in by climbing over th' gate, but they didn't know Rusty was waitin' for them, so all hell is breaking loose." She looked at me with alarm. "Where is Matt?"

"He's still in his crib," I said.

Just then, we heard a gunshot go off. I pulled her to me and said, "Does Rusty carry a gun?"

She shook her head. "NO! None of them do...only a rifle when they're out on the range!"

She pulled away from me and stated running towards the house.

"WHERE ARE YOU GOING?" I yelled.

"To get Matt –I don't want him up there all alone."

WELL, DON'T BRING HIM DOWN HERE! BOTH OF YOU STAY UP THERE!"

I started to go after her, but was trying to decide whether to do that or stay here and see if there was anything I could do.

While I tried to decide what to do, a man came up behind me and wrapping his arm around my neck, put a gun to my head. "Don't move, buddy, or I'll blow your head off!"

"Who th' hell are *you*?" I said, instinctively reaching up with both hands to pry his arm loose.

He tightened his grip and growled, "I said, *DON'T* **MOVE**!"

I stopped struggling and tried to think what to do. I'd never come up against a maniac with a gun before, so my knowledge was woefully lacking. I also never knew reporters to carry weapons or act like this. Hank and Rusty were busy fighting this jerk's buddies so they didn't know I was here, much less entertaining an armed jackass. I saw Rusty lasso one of the men. He quickly got off his horse and wound the rope around him so he couldn't move. Two ranch hands got the other two and Hank hurried over to help tie them down. The score was now Cowboys-Three and "Reporters"-Zero.

This didn't sit well with my hero and I heard him cock the gun.

"Looks like your friends don't care much what happens to you," he said. "They got my buddies, but they'll let 'em go fast enough when I blow your brains out."

"W-what are you doing?" I asked, feeling the muzzle push against my temple.

"Ventilating your skull," he said. ...And *there* it was! I about to buy the farm and all I could think of was this guy watched too many James Cagney films.

"Ya know -nobody talks like that anymore," I said.

"Shut up, wise guy," he ordered, and I got that creepy feeling –you know, the one where you're just one second away from having your brains blown out?

He whispered, "Say goodbye, asshole."

Shrugging, I did as he said and said, "Goodbye, asshole."

Feeling the gun's pressure increase against my head, I closed my eyes and thought about Matt and Sam, and how wonderful my last day here on earth had been --and that maybe Sam's having to leave *wasn't* the worst thing in the world after all. But, just as I felt his finger start to tighten on the trigger something bazaar happened. A shot rang out and *he* disappeared. One second he was there, the next –he was *gone*. Totally baffled, I wasn't absolutely sure I hadn't been killed and ran my hands all over my head and up and down my body to check for blood. When I didn't find any, I was at a complete loss -until I saw Jerry. He had my tormenter down on the ground with his arm straight out, twisted at the wrist like a pretzel. The jackass probably would've screamed too, if Jerry didn't have his knee on his Adam's apple. (I'd never thought of the knee as a deadly weapon before.) Jerry picked the guy up and holding him against a tree, turned to me and asked, "You all right, Mr. Mac?"

"Y-yes, I think so," I gasped, rubbing my neck. "Thank you, J-Jerry."

He handed me the gun. "You might want to hang on to this to give to the police. I'm sure it isn't registered." The guy kicked and squirmed, but Jerry's arm didn't budge an inch –and he wasn't even sweating.

"Ya know, Jerry, I can see why Hank pays you so much," I said, putting the gun in my coat pocket. "But quite frankly, I don't think it's enough and you should ask for a raise –a **BIG** one."

CHAPTER ONE HUNDRED SEVEN

Rusty and the other ranch hands brought the prisoners up to the house. Tied up from shoulder to waist, Rusty made them walk all the way while Jerry brought us back in the limo. When we got back to the house, Hank went in to call the sheriff. I hurried in to find Sam on the couch holding Matt. Wrapping paper and boxes were strewn all over the floor, as a reminder that it was still Christmas -but it no longer seemed like it. The fire had died down, so I threw some more wood on it then sat down with Sam. We heard a car pull up in the driveway and two doors slam. Hank said," That's Frank an' his deputy –Ah'll let 'em in."

Hank and the sheriff were old high school buddies. They had gone from ninth grade through graduation together. They'd both played football and been popular with the girls. Hank invited them inside, leaving the door open for Rusty to bring in the "reporters." They all stood in the foyer, while Hank explained what had taken place. After the sheriff wrote it down, he went out to the car and ran the names. When he came back, he took off his glasses and said, "These guys aren't reporters, Hank, but...I think you already guessed that."

"Well, what th' hell are they, then?" Hank frowned.

"They're a bunch of punks that somehow found out where you live and told one'a them supermarket rags, that they could get pictures of y'all."

Hank looked disgusted. "What charges can you pin on 'em?"

"Well, let's seeeee," the sheriff said, putting on his glasses again. "There's trespassing, of course, assault an' battery...aggravated assault -so far, we got a nice list of felonies."

I stood up and reaching in my pocket, I said, "Got something else you might be interested in."

I walked over and handed him the gun. "One of 'em had this on him and was all set to shoot me too, when Jerry showed up an' ruined his plans – thank God."

Sam sprang up from the couch. "MAC!" she cried. "Oh, sweetheart, I should've never left you alone out there."

I put my arm around her. "Hey," I said, " -you did th' right thing comin' back here."

"Hmm, this little item just tacked on two or three more charges," he said. "Attempted murder, carrying a concealed weapon and th' gun is probably unregistered –which is another felony."

"Can't ya come up with any more than that?" Hank growled.

"Um, maybe false imprisonment –"

The guy who tried to kill me cried, "FALSE IMPRISONMENT?? How th' hell do you figure that?"

The sheriff looked at him. "I don't figure this man stuck around voluntarily, while you held a gun to head. Seems to me your arm held him against his will –that's false imprisonment."

"Oh, *man*! " he screamed. "You can't do that!"

"Watch me," the sheriff smiled. "Well, Hank, if there's nothing else, I'll take th' gun and these four back to lock up. You gonna press charges?"

"Hell YES, Ah'm gonna press charges -you ever know a Texan that *wouldn't*?" The sheriff shook his head and said, "This has been quite a haul, y'all," and looking at his deputy, said, "Okay Tyler, put th' cuffs on and load 'em up."

His deputy handcuffed the morons, then marched them down the steps and threw them none too gently into the back of the squad car. After making sure they were secure, the sheriff got in and called, "See ya, Hank," before driving off.

"Yeah, Frank –an' call me when you're ready for me an' mah lawyer to go forward on this!"

He waved to the sheriff until his taillights disappeared down the drive. When he came back in the house, his whole demeanor had changed. He closed the door and said, "Mac, Ah'm sorry you had to go through that business with the gun."

He came over to me and looked me straight in the eye. "Ah had no idea you were even down there," he said, "and this thing got 'waaaaay outta hand when a gun was brought into it!"

He wasn't joking and looked genuinely concerned. "Sam an' me was having that little discussion in th' kitchen when we heard a lotta shoutin' down by th' main gate," he explained. "We both lit outta there to see what all th' noise was about. When we got down to th' road, we saw Rusty tryin' ta keep two cars from crashing through th' gate." Hank shook his head thoughtfully. "Noreen showed up just about th' time Ah jumped in th' middle of everything."

I nodded. "I heard you and Sam in the kitchen -well, I heard *Sam* anyway," I shrugged, "but then it got real quiet and I went in to see if everything was all right. When I saw th' back door standin' wide open, I knew something was wrong."

"Ah never saw you come down –when did you get there?"

"Soon as I saw th' back door open and heard the commotion, I started running. I got there just before Rusty lassoed that guy."

"That's when we were in th' thick of it."

"Yeah, and I got to watch the whole thing with an arm around my neck and a gun gouging into the side of my head."

Hank was visibly upset. "I heard a gunshot –was it at you?"

No, Sam and I heard it too. She took off running back to the house as soon as she heard it, because Matt was back there alone and none of us knew where the shot came from."

"Then how did YOU end up with it pointed at your head?"
"Well, th' guy was already pissed off beyond reason when he came up behind me -but when you captured all his cohorts he *really* got mad! And I can tell you, when I heard that gun cock-" ...I sucked in a deep breath and didn't finish the sentence.

"How come you ain't dead -was he bluffin'?"

"Oh, no - he *was going* to shoot me all right. I felt his finger tighten on the trigger."

"Well, what *happened*?"

"Just when I thought it was all over, he –just wasn't there!"

"**What**?"

"Yep, Jerry came up behind him and yanked his sorry ass to th' ground, just as he pulled the trigger. Fortunately, the shot went wild. Sam was *right* when she said Jerry is worth every penny you pay him."

Getting up from the couch, Sam came over to us. She looped her arm through mine. "Mac...I-I don't know what to say...if I lost you..."

I kissed her cheek. "Don't think about it, my love. I'm here and that's all that matters."

"Man, Ah gotta have a talk with Jerry," Hank said.

"You might consider giving him a raise too."

"Lissen, if you keep that up, *Ah'm* gonna shoot you," Hank frowned. "He already makes more in a year than Ah do." Then he looked at Sam. "You still mad at me for not telling you about tomorrow, sis?" he asked.

She looked at her watch. "It's almost one o'clock," she sighed, "and I'm too tired to be mad at anybody –so, no."

Hank touched a dried blood mark on the side of his head. "Ah'm glad to hear that, because you damned near gave me a concussion in th' kitchen."

"I missed you by a mile," she said, picking Matt up from the couch. "If I was "gonna git you, I'd'a <u>got</u> you –an' it wouldn't'a been your *head*! You'd'a been walking funny for th' rest of your life." Freeway was lying on the couch beside Matt and raised her head when Sam picked him up. "C'mon Freeway," she said. "Let's go to bed."

Hank went over to the bar and pulled out the bourbon. "Ah'm gonna have a double before Ah hit th' hay –how 'bout you, Mac?"

I shook my head. "No thanks, I'm with Sam -all I want to do is get some shut eye."

We said good night and left Hank to his bourbon. When we got back to the bedroom, I couldn't ignore how worn out Sam looked, but didn't say anything. She got out her nightgown and I crawled into bed. "By the way," I asked, "what did you throw at Hank to get all that glass all over the kitchen floor?" Pulling the nightgown over her head, she mumbled, "A glass... followed by another glass." She climbed in bed next to me and slipped under the covers mumbling something about "missing him the first time."

I leaned over to kiss her good night, but as soon as her head hit the pillow, she was gone. The day had taken its toll and all the fight was out of her.

I smiled and turned out the light, never dreaming I'd be thankful to some two-legged jackass for almost "ventilating" my skull.

CHAPTER ONE HUNDRED EIGHT

The following morning, it was still dark outside when I opened my eyes and stared at the ceiling. An unexplainable oppression bore down on my chest, making it hard to breathe. I didn't understand why I felt this way, but my subconscious knew- Sam was leaving in a few hours. With sleep now impossible, I folded my hands over my chest and stared at nothing for the next hour. First light crept silently around the blinds, then full morning. I eased out of bed and opened the blinds. It was cold as ice in the room, but

I didn't feel it. The snow was still fresh, but marred now by countless footprints of last night.

Last night -what a stupid, dangerous encounter that had been. I was taking the whole thing 'way to calmly, but it didn't seem important in the face of Sam leaving. I closed the blinds again. It was only six thirty –too early to wake Sam and besides, I wanted her to get as much sleep as possible.

I slipped on my slippers and robe and went out to the kitchen. I put on the coffee and fixed some toast while I waited for it to drip. When it was ready, I took the toast and coffee over to the table and opened the back door. I sat down and wrapped my hands around the warm mug, listening to the crows caw noisily outside. No matter how cold and numb you are, that first swallow of hot coffee always warms the body and soul. I wasn't thinking about anything in particular and other than the noisy chatter of the crows, the house was quiet. I felt like the only person in the world...and it was depressing as hell.

I got up from the table, pushing the screen door open and walking out on the porch. The sun wouldn't reach this side of the house until late afternoon, so last night's chill still hung in the shadows.

The barn was about fifty yards away from the house, give or take a yard. Rusty was out in the corral, grooming one of the horses in the sun like nothing ever happened last night. The other ranch hands were busy pouring feed in their buckets or pitching hay. Rusty looked over my way and waved when he saw me. I smiled and waved back. I envied them; the life of a cowboy was so carefree –no decisions to make, no sad goodbyes, no keeping up with the stress and worry of the world...just the same predictable routine every day.

I liked predictable routine.

Suddenly, I missed my quiet little bar back on the crossroads. Things had been so non-stop hectic that I hadn't had time to think about my life back there. I thought about the saloon, its opera boxes –and my little band on Friday nights. I thought about the day I first saw Sam and smiled, remembering how pathetically ratty she looked. I remembered the night Hank's bus pulled up out front and how excited I'd been. So many surprises...but maybe the biggest surprise was that Noreen would end up MY sister-is-law!

What a journey Life was. I started out in Amish country, traveled halfway around the world to lose a terrible war in a strange land, lost my girl to my best friend, lost my family to death and lost my home to "bank" robbers. And just when I gave up on this whole stinking mess, I'd found Sam –or maybe she found me. Whichever way it happened, I done something I swore I'd never do; fall in love -*and* leave the saloon. But I did

270

fall in love and left to come here and start a life with Sam. She was what gave my life meaning -without her, I could find nothing to hold on to. We'd made Matt together –and *together*, we were a whole unit. She was the glue that held us together.

I felt as homesick as Sam must have being away, and maybe one day I'd feel this was home too, but this morning, it was as strange to me as the moon.

I was sliding head long into self-pity and had to stop before I ended up in a strait jacket. I tried to think of something else to take my mind off this soap opera.

Suddenly, I remembered I hadn't talked to Doc or Harley since Houston. I'd meant to call Doc's house yesterday after Christmas dinner, but forgot all about it after last night's events. I turned around and yanked the screen door open. I hurried inside, setting my half empty cup on the table and ran to the kitchen phone. I looked at the clock as I picked up the receiver. It was just going on eight –Doc might still be there. I dialed his number and counted ten rings. I was about to hang up when I heard his voice.

"DOC!" I cried. "It's me, Mac! Merry *Christmas*, old friend."

"Mac!" he said, sounding delighted. "It is so good to hear from you! I was afraid you'd abandoned us po' folk down here for the big city life of Dallas."

"Never!" I laughed. "In fact, I haven't even seen Dallas, except for a mall Hank took me to when we went Christmas shopping."

"Well, Harley and I thought you'd forgotten us. He spent Christmas Day with me, and even stayed late hoping you'd call."

"Thanks, Doc, now I really feel crummy," I frowned. "Believe me, I wanted to call, but contrary to what you may think, it hasn't been all good news here."

"What's wrong, Mac? Nothing to do with Sam or little Matt, I hope."

"Not in the sense you mean. We're all fine, but Hank got a phone call from their agent just before Christmas to tell us that Sam's record is doing so good, she has to go on the damned road."

"For how long?"

"Indefinitely."

"Well, when does she leave?"

"Today...in a few hours." I purposely didn't tell him about the brouhaha here last night –nor did I mention my close encounter of the deadly kind. I not only didn't want to cause him any undue alarm, but I wanted to forget it ever happened.

"Listen," Doc was saying, "as luck would have it, I'm just on my way over to Harley's right now. He's got a sick steer he wants me to look at. I'll tell him about your call and explain why you didn't get to call us on Christmas."

"Thanks, Doc –I'd appreciate that."

"How is Hank? And Noreen? How is she taking to all this"

"Noreen is Noreen," I said. "Just the other day she got all huffy about something she heard on T.V. that she took to be racist."

Doc sounded amused. "Really, what was it -a news program?"

"No, nothing that intelligent. It was a commercial. She heard something about "not mixing whites with coloreds" and didn't realize they were talking about laundry."

"Bless her heart," Doc laughed. "Noreen will never be a rocket scientist."

"She'll never be an earthling."

"I hate to hang up, Mac, but I have to get over to Harley's. I'll see if he can come over for supper tonight and maybe you could call us back, say – around seven?"

"You got it, Doc! Til seven –see ya." We hung up and I felt a world better.

I heard feet shuffling behind me and a voice growl, "What're you doin' up so early?"

Hank came in with his robe all-askew and his slippers on the wrong feet. He had a two-day old beard and rubbed his eye. "Who're you talkin' to on th' phone," he yawned, "an' is that coffee, Ah smell?"

"Doc –and yes." I answered.

He got out a mug and poured himself a cup. "How is ol' Doc?" he asked. I had my mouth open to answer him when the phone rang. Hank frowned. "Now who th' hell could that be this early?" He went to answer it, taking his coffee with him. It was Sid, checking on Sam. He wanted to know if she was ready to leave today. "Hell, no, she ain't ready to leave!" Hank said. "It's just th' crack of dawn an' she's still asleep, you money-grubbing s.o.b.! Don't you *never* sleep?"

Ignoring Hank, Sid told him he was sending a car after her at one o'clock to take her to the airport. Hank hung up and brought his coffee over to the table. Sitting down across from me, he scratched his head and said, "Ah should'a stayed outta show biz an' tended to cattle ranchin.'"

He took a swallow then set his mug down. "If it was me that had to go, Ah wouldn't mind in th' least. Ah'd take Noreen along; Jerry'd drive an' we'd be together. But you got a family an' it ain't right for Sam to be th' one that has to go on th' road for God knows how long."

I nodded, but didn't say anything.

"Ah don't know what's worse," Hank sighed, "bein' a success or a failure. Each one comes with its own price tag."

The "Blues" were coming back, so I got up and poured us another cup of coffee. "You want anything else –like some toast?" I asked. Hank shook his head and I took the empty coffee pot over to the counter. I turned around to go back to the table just in time to see Sam walk in. Ordinarily she was a half-asleep zombie, but this morning, she had her hair brushed and was fully dressed –and although she looked like she'd just stepped out of "TEXAS WOMAN" magazine, she still looked tired.

"Well, good morning," I smiled. "Would you like some coffee? It'll only take a minute to put on another pot."

Without smiling, she nodded and looked at Hank. "What time will the car be here?"

"Cuttin' right to th' chase, huh?" Hank said. "How'd you know Sid called?"

"I heard th' phone ring while I was getting dressed -who else would call this early?" She raked a chair across the floor as she pulled it out.

"It'll be here at one o'clock –you all packed?"

"I'm dressed, ain't I?" She sat down and leaned back with her arms crossed. "He say where I go after Nashville?"

Hank shook his head. "He'll give you th' itinerary after th' show."

"Dare I hope it'll be mostly in and around Texas?" she said.

Hank looked at her. "Realistically speaking –no."

I brought the coffee over along with a mug. Sam looked as resigned to her fate as Ann Bolen did to hers. I set the mug down and filled it. After taking a few swallows, she said, "You still haven't found anyone to help out around here, have you, Hank? It was more of an accusation than a question.

"No Sam," he sighed patiently. "Christmas was just yesterday. Between it and th' Battle of San Jacinto in our front yard last night, Ah haven't had time to even give it another thought."

"So *who's* gonna take care of Matt without me here –huh-answer me *that*, Hank!" she demanded.

"Ho, boy –here it comes...Mount Vesuveius," he said, rubbing his forehead. "Ah *knew* you were actin' way too calm!"

I said. "I'll take care of Matt, sweetheart. Don't worry about him, I'll change, bathe, and feed him. He'll be fine until Hank can hire somebody fulltime."

Sam got up, slamming her chair back under the table. "I'm not going!" she steamed. "Let Sid sue me –I don't care, but I'm NOT leaving my son, alone."

Hank got up and put his hands on her shoulders. "Settle down, sis. Ah got somebody trustworthy in mind, IF they're available."

"WHO is it?" she wanted to know.

"Trust me, Sam –it's somebody you won't have a worry about."

Her face lit up. "Is it Rose –is she gonna come back?"

Hank looked at me then Sam. "Uh, no, honey –it won't be Rose."

"Then I'm *not* going!" she said, crossing her arms defiantly over her chest.

Hank said, "Ah guess this would be a Mexican stand-off, if we was Mexican"

"I mean it, Hank –I am **NOT** going!"

Throwing his hands up, Hank leaned back and sighed. "Okay, Sam –you win. Don't go. Hell, this is a free country an' nobody can force you. Go unpack...Ah'll call mah lawyer an' we'll just go to court."

"Fine," she sniffed, and walked out of the kitchen.

I watched her leave then looked at Hank with my mouth wide open. "Are you crazy?" I said.

Hank shook his head. "Nah," he said, "Ah know mah sister an' we go through this every time she don't wanna do somethin'."

And taking a swallow of now cold coffee, he grinned as he said, "She'll go."

CHAPTER ONE HUNDRED NINE

...And she did.

Come one o'clock, the car arrived and Sam was waiting on the porch with her bags packed. She kissed us goodbye and got in without another word of protest. I watched the car until it disappeared and then turned to Hank. "I would'a never believed it," I said.

"Happens all th' time," he grinned.

I heard Matt crying from the open front door. "Guess it's his lunchtime," I said, going in.

I got his bottle out of the refrigerator and warmed it up in a pan of water on the stove like I'd seen Sam do. His bottle was ready in less than three minutes and taking it in to him, I spent the next forty-five minutes bathing him, powdering and changing his diaper, and finding his flannel p.j.'s. As I pulled the top over his head, I said, "This is a piece of cake, buddy. Mommy would be so proud of us." He looked at me like he understood every word and I poked his tummy. "You're gonna be a big tough cowboy, some day – you know that? Pretty soon, we're gonna have to start feedin' you steak." He giggled and Freeway cocked her head. "And you're a good nursemaid, Freeway," I told her, patting her head. She wagged her tail. Matt giggled and squealed as he tried to clap his hands together. He was such a happy baby (–spastic –but happy.)

He was clean, changed, and fed now -and smelled *soooooo* good. I sat down in the rocker and rocked with him until I saw his eyes close. Easing out of the chair, I gently put him back in his crib and covered him up with his quilt and blanket. Freeway took her place under his crib and I quietly tiptoed out. Back in the living room, Hank was sitting at his desk, going over some bills. He had his glasses on and looked like a professor of Western History. When he saw me, he took off his glasses and threw them down on top of the bills. He rubbed his eyes and sat back in his chair. "So how's mah little nephew?" he asked.

"Good as good an' growin' like a weed." I looked around and said, "Where's Noreen?"

"She's working on somethin' for me," he said.

"Anything harder than unscrewing the lid off a jar?"

"About the same level of difficulty."

"Okay, that takes care of her for the rest of the day," I said. "What're *we* gonna do?"

Hank got up, came over and patted me on the shoulder. "Ah thought it might be a good time to give them boots an' jeans Ah gave you for Christmas, a workout."

"I have NO idea what that means -and am afraid to ask."

"It means it's time you saddled up an' went for a ride."

"Now wait just a doggone minute," I frowned. "It's been decades since I was on a horse."

"It's like ridin' a bicycle," he assured me. "You don't forget how –now, go get dressed an' meet me out in th' corral."

He left me standing there with a *bunch* of reservations.

CHAPTER ONE HUNDRED TEN

I changed clothes and met Hank out at the barn. He was talking to Rusty when I walked up.

"Hi, Mc," Rusty grinned.

"Hi, Rusty –how are you, today?"

"I'm just fine –Hank tells me y'all are going to take a ride, today."

"I don't know..." I frowned.

"Don't lissen to him" Hank said. "Saddle "Diablo" an' bring him out for Mac."

Rusty's face went a little pale and he said, "You sure you want me to saddle *him*?"

"Why?" I asked hysterically. "What's wrong with him?"

Hank said, "He's our best horse an' nothin' for you to worry about." Turning back to Rusty, he said, "Yeah, go ahead an' saddle him for Mac." I couldn't swear to it, but I thought I saw Rusty cross himself as he went back in the barn. I paced apprehensively and looked at Hank, hoping to see some clue of the evil brewing. I just *knew* he was up to no good, but he never let on.

Five minutes later, Rusty came out with the blackest horse I'd ever seen. His coat, mane and tail were black as the Ace of Spades -and he wore Hanks silver saddle.

"Wow," I whispered, "that horse is beautiful –and you're gonna let me ride in your new saddle?"

Yep," he said, taking the lead rein from Rusty.

I was so impressed, that I didn't notice the wild look in "Diablo's" eyes - or the way he threw his head up and down while snorting fire and pawing at the ground. Hank held him steady as I put my foot in the stirrup. The second my foot went in the horse backed up violently, forcing me grab hold of the saddle horn and hop around on one leg. Hank got him to settle down long enough for me to swing my other leg over his back, but once I was in the saddle, Hank handed me the reins and the horse took off at neck breaking speed. He didn't walk or canter –he went from zero to ninety in the blink of an eye -and for the next two hours I held on, as he took me through barbed wire fences, snow filled gullies, ice cold creeks, and damned near killed me with low lying tree branches.

Forget the reins –I held on to the saddle horn for dear life.

I had NO idea where we were or how to get back, but fortunately, the horse did, and we flew into the corral just before sunset. I had twigs in my permanently swept-back hair and mud in my teeth. My legs were locked onto the horse's sides so hard Rusty had to practically pry me off.

"How was your ride?" Hank asked innocently, as Rusty held me up.

"That…was…the…most…terrifying…thing…I've…ever…gone…through, " I gasped. "And I've been to Vietnam." I glared at Hank, "And YOU could've told me, that "Diablo" stands for "Angle of Death!"

Hank and Rusty exchanged glances. "You gotta tell him, Hank."

"Tell me what?" I gasped, still clinging to Rusty for support.

"Diablo" is Hank's horse," Rusty said. "No one has ever been able to ride him, *but* Hank."

"Well, I got news for y'all –I *didn't* ride him."

"Yeah, but you stayed on," Rusty said admirably. "No one's ever done that before, either."

Blood started to flow in my veins again as the G-force subsided and I felt my Irish temper rise.

"That killer horse belongs to you?" I huffed.

"Yeah, he does," Hank smiled. "An' he pure hates everybody –even me."

"I'm going to kill you," I swore. "I don't know *how* yet...but I am. It could be poison, a gun, or some other method, but I'm gonna *get* you, Hank!"

"Oh, stop bein' such a drama queen, you little weenie."

"And I'm going to make it an *especially* horrible death if you don't stop calling me that!"

Rusty said, "You should get a medal for ridin' "Diablo," Mac –an' making it back in one piece."

"Yeah, well...I'll be satisfied if I can just make it to the grave yard," I said as I tried to walk a straight line back to the house.

CHAPTER ONE HUNDRED ELEVEN

I soaked in a hot, hot, bath for an hour and when I got out, Hank gave me double bourbon. I took it over and sat down in an overstuffed chair in front of the fire, and when the glass was empty I had another. When I'd reached two sheets beyond "mellow," I said, "So what's for supper?"

He said, "Leftovers, Ah guess," and I made a face. "Uge...can't you come up with something else?"

"Maybe," he shrugged, noncommittally. I didn't like the sound of that and suddenly had a terrible thought. "You <u>CAN</u> cook...can't you?" When he didn't answer right away, I asked him again. "Hank...? You know how to cook...right?"

He shrugged again. "How hard can it be?"

"Oh God," I muttered. "We're in trouble."

We went into the kitchen and I waited while Hank went through the cabinets. He found two jars of spaghetti sauce and a large package of unopened spaghetti. "How's this?" he asked and I smiled. He nodded and got out a medium size pan to dump the spaghetti sauce in. He turned the stove on "high" underneath the pan, and then opened the spaghetti. Filling a big pot with water, Hank put it on another burner –then took my drink from me and upended the glass. "Ah need this more'n you," he said, waving the empty glass under my nose. "Well, don't just stand there; go git me another one."

I went out to the bar and brought the bottle back. I could see this was going to be one of those nights where it might be best to be drunk.

When the sauce began to bubble, I commented on how good it smelled, and was impressed until the water for the spaghetti began to boil and he looked at me. "How long you think Ah should let th' pasta cook?"

"I don't know -thirty minutes??"

"Sounds about right," he nodded, throwing in the spaghetti. Setting the timer, he sat down and poured us both another drink. Thirty minutes later, the buzzer went off and he got up from the table. When he reached the stove, he frowned. "Hey Mac, come over here an' see if this looks right to you." I got up and went over to look. It wasn't good. The sauce was burned and the spaghetti was mush. "Uh, no -I don't think this is right," I said. He tried to pick up a piece of pasta and it turned to liquid. "What did we do wrong?"

I picked up the spaghetti wrapper and read the directions. "It says to only cook this stuff eight to ten minutes on a medium boil." We looked at each other and sighed in unison, "Leftovers."

Noreen came in and wrinkled her nose. "What's that smell?"

"What does it smell like?" I asked.

"Smells -burned..."

"Bingo!"

Hank put his arm around her. "Never mind, honey -why don't you set th' table?"

Noreen nodded and went to get the plates and glasses. I got the turkey out of the refrigerator and when I went back for bread and mayonnaise, I found a head of lettuce and two tomatoes in the bottom that still looked edible. I got them out and then asked, "What do we have to drink?"

"There's a big bottle of coke over there in the pantry," Hank pointed. I got the coke, sliced the tomatoes and put everything along with the lettuce, on a platter.

Halfway through his second sandwich, Hank asked Noreen, "Did you find anything out on that number Ah gave you to call this afternoon?" He caught her with her mouth full, so she nodded vigorously. She swallowed and said, "Yes, but they ain't got a phone."

"Did you leave a message?"

She nodded, and I frowned. "What th' hell are you two talking about – how can you call someone who has no phone and leave them a message?"

Hank and Noreen looked at each other and smiled.

"Okay, you two -let *me* in on th' secret."

Hank sat back and let out a contented burp. "Oh, sorry," he said. "It was gonna be a secret until Ah found out more but," he sighed, "looks like we might'a hit a dead end."

"On *what*?"

Hank wiped his mouth and leaned forward with his forearms crossed on the edge of the table. "When Rose said she couldn't take th' job, Ah got a wild idea -and Ah don't know why none of us thought of it before."

"You've lost me," I said.

"Ah called Frank early this mornin'-you know, th' sheriff –an' had him see what he could find out about contacting Juan's family down in Mexico."

Suddenly a light went on and I knew where Hank was going with this. "Juan," I whispered. "Of course!"

Hank nodded. "Ah was thinking that Ah'd move his whole family up here. His mama could do th' cooking an' cleanin' -and Juan loves takin' care of Matt."

"But where would they live? They couldn't stay in here –do you know how many are in his family?"

Hank nodded. "It's not a problem," he said. "We have a four bedroom house about a mile from here, that granddad built for th' ranch hands before he built th' bunkhouse next to th' barn. We've used it for guests once in a great while, but mostly it just sits out there."

"Well, if it just "sits" out there, what kind of condition is it in?"

"Tip-top," Hank said. "Two years ago, Ah had a good year salary-wise and had to do some home improvements or pay a heavy tax. I hired a contractor Ah know, to come out. He renovated th' place, including putting on a whole new barrel tile roof, enlarging th' fireplace an' updating th' kitchen with all new appliances."

"*Damn*," I said. "Why don't I just move in there?"

"It's perfect for Juan an' his family."

"What about green cards?"

"Long as they have a place to live an' a job, there ain't a problem legally."

I fell back in my chair. "Wow, sounds like you've thought of everything...so, who did you call in Mexico?"

"Juan lives in a very small border town –about th' size of th' crossroads," he said. "Ah didn't wanna call th' local police –you know, in case it might call attention to Juan, so Ah had Frank check an' see if there might be a number for a local church. As luck would have it, th' church *did* have a phone –sort'a. Noreen called there and between his broken English, her absolutely non-existent Spanish, and a terrible connection, she was able to describe Juan and he knew who she was talking about."

My ears perked up with interest. "Yeah...?"

"Noreen had him hold on while she called me in. Ah told th' padre what Ah wanted an' he said he'd get th' message to 'em an' have them call back as soon as possible."

"Hank," I grinned. "You are *brilliant*!" I was so excited I could hardly sit still. "When did you talk to them at the church?"

"While you was out takin' in th' scenery with "Diabalo."

My grin disappeared. "Right..." I frowned. "-Diablo."

While I sat there thinking about Hank's plan to get Juan's family up here, Noreen got up and put on some coffee. It was such a great plan. I could not find one thing wrong with it –until I suddenly sat up and said, "*No*, no, no, man –**no**! It cannot be that perfect!"

"What...?" Hank frowned. "What can't be perfect?"

"This whole deal," I said. "The house just sitting out there all renovated and waitin' for someone to move in...you getting' ahold'a some padre down in Juan's fly-speck town...and bein' able to take care of their immigration problems! *Nothing* in life works that perfectly –there has to be a hitch somewhere!"

"Not if you got oil wells," Hank grinned. Then he turned serious. "Look, he said, "Ah expect to run into problems- but -Ah don't gotta be negative about it. Ah'll be th' first to admit we got a long way to go on this thing, but Ah think it's a workable plan an' can be done." "Besides," he added, " –would *you* of all people, wanna deprive Juan of this chance for a better life?"

Now I felt awful. "No," I said quietly. "No, I wouldn't."

"Ah didn't think so."

"But I *do* want to see this house you're talkin' about –it just sounds too good to be true."

Hank sat back in his chair and sighed. "Oh ye of little faith -okay, we'll ride out there tomorrow or th' next day. You can take "Diablo.""

"Ooohoho no, you don't," I warned. "I want a *real* horse –not some demon disguised as one."

Noreen served us coffee and the rest of the minced meat pie. I asked if she'd mind feeding and spending a little time rocking Matt, after we finished dessert.

"I'd like to stay by the phone in case Sam calls," I explained.

"Sure, Mac –be glad to," she said.

After we finished supper, Noreen cleared the table, stacked the dirty dishes in the dishwasher and threw out Hank's spaghetti fiasco before taking Matt his bottle. I went back to the living room and sat by the fire to wait for Sam's call. Hank put on some Christmas music and poured himself another bourbon. He brought it over to the couch, asking me if I'd like one. Shaking my head, I said, "No thanks" and looked at the ring Sam gave me for Christmas. She'd only been gone less than twelve hours, but I missed her so much. I watched the clock on the mantle. An hour passed...then another dragged by without hearing from her...and another. Around eleven, I started to worry and asked Hank, "What could be taking Sam so long to call us? It's not like her to go this long without checking in on Matt."

"She could'a been delayed on take-off, or havin' trouble getting to th' hotel from th' airport after they landed -there's a hundred reasons why you haven't heard from her." He finished off his drink and the ice cubes rattled in his glass when he set it down. "But Ah know one thing –she WILL call sometime, tonight...might be four or five in th' mornin' -but she'll call."

After he said that, I felt some better and waited up until one before finally giving up and deciding to go to bed. I crawled in and pulled the covers up over my aching body. I was so tired *and* sore after my ride on the "Horse from Hell," that I had no trouble falling asleep. Sometime later, I was deep in oblivion when Hank came in and shook me.

"Mac, get up –Sam's on th' phone."

I frowned and tried to open my eyes. "Mmmm –what time is it?" I muttered groggily.

"It's four thirty – now, c'mon, she's waitin'."

I slowly sat up and tried to find my feet, then my slippers, and finally my robe. When I got it together, I went out to the phone with Hank. The receiver was lying on top of his desk. I picked it up and said, "H-hello – Sam?"

"Sorry to call so late, sweetheart, but I just got checked into th' hotel – how's Matt?"

"He's sound asleep like he should be," I said. "Why so late getting there?"

"It took forever to get through airport security with all the luggage I have, and then we had to circle Nashville for forty minutes before we could land due to weather."

"Why –is it snowing?"

"Yeah, it is, but not bad. Th' wind picked up just as we were about to land."

"It's been nice here all day. In fact, Hank had me go for a ride on one of th' horses. I'm lucky to be alive."

"Why –which one did he have you take out?"

"Diablo."

"***Diablo**!!*" she cried.

"Yep –even let me hang onto th' saddle horn of his new saddle."

"Don't you mean, "ride" in his new saddle?"

Nope. I meant, "hang on."

"Let me talk to my brother," she said.

I smiled and handed the phone to Hank. "Says she wants to talk to you."

He sighed and took the receiver. "Yeah, sis...figured you'd wanna talk to me." I waited until Sam finished chewing him out for putting me on "Diablo," and when he handed the phone back, he said, "Ah'm goin' to bed."

I took the phone and said hello again. Sam said, "Do you know Diablo" is Hank's horse, and that NObody has *ever* ridden him?"

"Not until I got back from our little two hour jaunt," I said.

"YOU stayed on him for two hours??"

"Piece of cake," I lied.

She was speechless and sputtered; "I'm going to kill my brother when I get home."

I said, "Aaah, just let it go, Sam. I'm fine and it only killed two hours – not *me*. Besides, it wore me out to the point that I could fall asleep...well, that, along with a hot bath and four bourbons."

"Listen, what's your schedule lookin' like?"

"I haven't the faintest idea at this time. Tomorrow is dress fittings, then rehearsals and finally, a final dress rehearsal. We'll do the show live next Sunday night for New Year's Eve -no pressure *there*..."

"I'll be watching, so behave yourself."

"Yeah, right. Like I have time to do anything else."

"It's late," I said, " and as much as I hate to end this, you should try to get some sleep."

"You're right, so I guess I'll say good night. I'd give you the phone and room number of the hotel I'm staying in, but I was too tired to notice where I am."

"That's okay...you can give it to me later –get some sleep."

After we hung up, I went over and turned on the television. I sat down and flicked through the channels until I found something that interested me. It was a toss-up between "Lethal Weapon," with Mel Gibson, the Three Stooges and a John Wayne western. John won.

It was going on five in the morning, so I made myself comfortable on the couch and settled in to watch John kick some ass. I wouldn't be getting any more sleep anyway, tonight.

CHAPTER ONE HUNDRED TWELVE

We made it through the rest of the week without calling 911 from Hank's cooking -except for one night, when we rebelled and ordered pizza. (Well, it's *supposed* to be pizza -but the crap they bring you is cheap tomato sauce with melted cheese on cardboard –and makes a great frisbee.) I wanted to ride out and see the house for Juan's family, but we didn't go horseback riding again that week due to two days of it snowing heavily. Finally, Sunday rolled around and time dragged by like molasses in January. The program was scheduled to go on around midnight because of it being New Year's Eve, and I was as antsy as a cat on a hot tin roof. I paced and rearranged every magazine I could find, until Hank suggested I settle down and have a beer while he went to pick up some steaks. I seconded that motion and even offered to pay for everything -- <u>*anything*</u> to keep him from trying to fix a tuna casserole or whatever god-awful else he might find to experiment with. Besides, Hank was getting 'waaay too involved with this cooking thing and had started to think of himself as, (God help us) -a "chef."

When he came back from the grocery with three, three inch Porterhouse steaks and enough charcoal to light up Dallas, he set up the grill to start cooking on the back porch. Noreen fixed a salad in the kitchen while I sat down in one of the chase lounges to enjoy the late afternoon sun. The steaks were the best tasting meal I'd eaten in over a week, but we still had five hours to kill before show time when we finished –so we drink more beer and played, "Trivial Pursuit." (Noreen lost.) (Big time.) Around eight thirty, Hank decided to shower and shave, and I did the same in our bathroom before bathing Matt and putting on his p.j.'s. I let him nap until ten-forty then woke him and took him out with me to wait for mommy to come on television. When the hands of the clock said ten forty-five, my heart rate picked up.

Hank got up from the couch and went over to the bar. "Ah gotta have a drink –anybody else want one?" Noreen said she'd join him, but I shook my head. He came back just as the show started. "How come you aren't on this?" I asked. He leaned back with his drink and said, "Because they had the show already lined up with other entertainers."

"Then why Sam an' not you?"

"They have to have her on 'cause she has a number one song right now. Th' record company arranges these things...an' Ah'm happy as a pig in mud, Ah *ain't* on."

I said, "oh," and turned my attention back to the set. The announcer came on over the music, telling the audience who would be appearing on tonight's show. They applauded each name until he got to Sam, and then they stood up and went wild. After a "word from the sponsor," the first guest came out –then the second and so on. Since Sam was the featured guest, we had to listen to all the acts before she came on –which of course, was last. Each entertainer was great in his or her own right, but when it *finally* came time to bring her on, don't you know the bastards went to commercial! And not just one or two commercials –oh *nooooo*, they had to put on the *longest* string of commercials in the *history* of television!

After the twenty-first one, I was ready to call the F.C.C. when the show came back on and the stage lights went down. Out of the darkness, kettledrums began to beat with all the fervor of jungle drums. A primitive anticipation grew until the drums stopped suddenly and all was silent. Then the musicians played those familiar notes that I'd come to know so well, and she walked out into the spotlight. Sam was flawless in a tight fitting strapless black gown that flared out from the knees to the floor. Her long, soft, dark brown hair fell around her bare shoulders with one side pulled back over her left ear. She wore no jewelry save long diamond earrings Noreen said were called "shoulder dusters."

I sat there hypnotized –then my smile disappeared and I jumped up off the couch, yelling loudly. "Agggggggggggggggghhhhhhhh!"

"What in tarnation is the matter with you?" Hank frowned. "You almost made me spill mah drink, you crazy fool." Matt had fallen asleep and now screamed his head off.

"What th' hell has she got **ON**?" I screamed. "She looks like Rita Hayworth in "Gilda" for God's sake!"

"She looks great, you idiot," Hank said.

"She's practically *naked*!" I cried. "How can she even *breathe* in that thing –much less sing??"

"Oh, shut up an' sit down."

"What's Sid's number? "I demanded angrily. "I'm calling him tomorrow and telling him to either put some damned clothes on my wife –or *send her* home!"

Hank laughed. "You're nuts, you know that? Sid ain't got no say-so over what she wears."

"Well WHO does?"

'Th' wardrobe department...they can make her ride out on a white horse in a long curly blonde wig like Lady Godiva, if they want to. Yer married to th' public now, so sit down an' have a drink like all th' other husbands do." He handed me his and went back to get another one. Looking at the amber liquid swirling over the ice in the glass, I knew Hank was right -and it was a total bummer. I sat down again and finished the drink in two gulps. "Yeah, well, I can talk her into quitting after this song ain't number one anymore," I fumed.

"Well, you won't have to twist her arm," Hank grunted. "She's been ready to quit for over two years -that's why she showed up at your bar in th' first place. She'd had it with all this bein' on th' road an' was cracking under th' pressure..."

"No wonder," I snorted. "But I can tell you two damned things –she's gonna quit before she ever has to ride out on a white horse wearing a blonde wig -or I ever become an alcoholic."

CHAPTER ONE HUNDRED THIRTEEN

I fumed over Sam's outfit for the rest of the night. She called us around two o'clock in the morning, but I didn't mention it. I didn't want to start the year out criticizing her. However, she picked up on it in my overly phony "happy" sounding voice.

"What's wrong, Mac –is Matt all right?"

"Sure," I smiled. "He's great!"

"Okay, if it isn't Matt, then it must be you –what is it?"

"Uh, nothing, sweetheart. Just tired I guess, and I miss you like fire." There was a long silence on her end and then she said, "Ah HAH...I know what's wrong -its my dress, ISN'T it?"

She had me. I didn't say anything and she laughed. "It **is**, isn't it, Mac."

Damn women's intuition –you couldn't hide anything from them. "Yes," I sighed. "It's the dress. I'm sorry...it's just that, well...you looked so doggone sexy and –*bare*."

"Is that all?"

"No...you were absolutely gorgeous!"

"Mac –it's just a dress. It's all for show, you know that. Besides, I had on more than I would have if I wore a bikini –and it took hours longer to get into."

"Where is it, now?" I asked.

"It's back with the wardrobe mistress."

I scratched the back of my head and said, "Uh, do you think she'd loan it to you to bring home?"

Sam laughed and laughed, and it was music to my ears.

"Sam –when will you be home?" I asked, and she stopped laughing.

"I just got my schedule of one-nighters," she sighed, " –and none of 'em are in Texas, so it looks like I'm gonna be out here for at *least* the next month."

"Crap," I muttered.

"But we can still get married again in February."

"That's good," I frowned, unhappy to hear that we wouldn't be seeing each other for four more weeks.

"And since we had Matt before we had to benefit of holy matrimony, maybe I should wear that black dress for the ceremony," she teased.

"I can live with that," I smiled.

She asked how everybody was, and if Hank had found a housekeeper, yet. I told her he'd been in contact with somebody and was waiting to hear back from them. She still wanted to know who it was, and I still lied about knowing. "Just let me know as soon as you find somebody," she said.

I assured her I would and reluctantly said good-bye. I held the receiver in my hand for a minute before slowly putting it back in its cradle. A month. It might as well be a light year.

The following day was sunny and warm although there was four inches of snow on the ground. I puttered around with Matt for most of the morning and then went out to the barn. Hank was brushing "Diablo" in the corral, and the black demon snorted fire when he saw me.

"When're we gonna go out an' see that house?" I said, from *behind* the fence.

"We can go today, if ya want."

"You gonna take that crazy horse?"

"Yep."

"Great," I muttered. "Hey –here's a suggestion -why don't we just take th' truck?"

"No, Ah got *just* th' horse for you. She's old, arthritic and blind from cataracts."

"Forget it, Hank –I ain't riding no horse that's in th' same shape as my grandmother."

"Ah was just jerkin' you around," he laughed. "But Ah really do got a horse for you."

"It better not be "Buttermilk" or "Buttercup" –or whatever that horse was you gave Noreen."

"It ain't. This horse is a two-year old saddle horse that Rusty broke. She's gentle, well-trained an' Ah'd trust her with Matt on her back."

"I'm not sure what that implies," I frowned, "but –okay." Hank called Rusty out to saddle "Diablo" for him. "An' saddle up "Barbara Mandrell" for Mac," he added.

I watched Rusty's face closely for any sign of "concern" he might have about this horse, but he just smiled and nodded. "Will do, Hank."

Ten minutes later, he brought both horses out, saddled and ready to go.

"Barbara Mandrell" was a sweet, gentle mare, while "Diablo" was still the threat to all mankind. Rusty brought her over and she stood by passively, while I got in the saddle. I took the reins and was relieved to see she didn't act at all "spooky." I looked over at Hank, expecting to see him putting on the sharpest spurs imaginable to make "Diablo" submit, but the horse let Hank on, like he was just the sweetest, most lovable, little horsey in the world. I frowned and wondered if horses could be evil and eviler. If so,"Diablo" was definitely in the latter category. When we were all set to ride out, Noreen came out on the back porch and yelled for Hank.

"Telephone, Hank!" she said. "It's Mexico."

Hank reined in "Diablo" and jumped off, handling the reins to Rusty. "Ah gotta take this."

286

I handed him my reins too, and followed Hank into the house. I sat down at the table while Hank shouted, "Hello? Hello? Is this the padre?"

The connection was so poor that between it and the language barrier; the call looked like it was never going to make any headway. After twenty-five minutes, Hank hung up.

"Well, what he'd say?" I asked anxiously.

"Near as Ah could make out, he said he talked to Juan's family and they're *going to come*!!" He was so excited he grabbed Noreen and swung her around the room.

I was grinning from ear to ear. "You did it, Hank! You actually **DID** it!"

"C'mon," he said, grabbing me by my hand and pulling me out the back door. "Now we really gotta go out an' look at th' house!"

CHAPTER ONE HUNDRED FOURTEEN

We got on our horses again and lit out for the house. It was a little over a mile away just like Hank said and as we came over a hill, I saw it sitting down in a valley by a wide winding stream. The adobe house spread out beneath a red barrel tile roof with the far-off mountains pressed against the bluest sky I ever remember seeing. It was a Remington painting come to life. I reigned in my horse and whispered, "Holy cow -I can't believe this!" Hank was half a mile ahead of me. When he realized I wasn't behind him, he turned around and came back to us. "Its something, ain't it?"

"I'm speechless," I said.

The house sat in a wide empty valley at the foothills of the far-off mountains. The rolling hills were treeless and bare of vegetation. Only a few cottonwood trees grew here and there by the stream. Seeing the house from this vantage point was breathtaking and it was hard to imagine all this land belonging to one family.

"C'mon," Hank said. "Let's see what it looks like inside these days."

We ran our horses' wide open all the way. I was amazed to see that "Barbara Mandrell" held her own against "Diablo." When we tied up the horses, I leaned over and whispered, "Hah -you ain't so fast after all," ...and the black satanic spawn pawed the ground furiously giving me the Evil Eye, as he threw his head up and down. I backed away and said, "Okay, okay – you don't have to get huffy about it." Hank stood on the porch waiting to unlock the front door. "You comin'?" he frowned. "Or are you gonna stand out there an' threaten mah horse, all day?"

"I'm comin' –just hold your hor-" -I rolled my eyes and hurried up the steps. He unlocked the thick hand-carved wooden door and I followed him inside.

The interior walls were the same pale brownish/yellow stucco as outside. Mexican throw rugs were scattered here and there over terra cotta tiles. Graceful arches led from one room to the next. The living room was half the size of Hank's, but its pecan double French doors gave the room a spaciousness his didn't have. Next to them, a fireplace that qualified more as a hearth, held an array of pre-Columbian replicas on each end of its cypress mantle. Overhead, rough beams of southwestern juniper ran across the ceiling.

There were two couches and three chairs covered with sheets, but the credenzas, side tables, wrought iron lamps and chandeliers were pure Spanish. Every piece belonged –right down to the decorative pottery.

This place is amazing," I said.

"C'mon –Ah'll show ya th' bedrooms." I followed Hank down a long hall to the bedrooms. Every room was exactly the same size –even the master -and faced a courtyard with a three-tiered fountain in the center. Across from the foot of the beds, French doors opened out onto a patio. A high wall with cactus growing around its perimeter closed in the courtyard. In a far corner, a skeletal umbrella-shaped weeping willow waited for spring.

Like everything in the house, the bedrooms were furnished in true Spanish style.

"Hank," I said, "you truly underestimated this place."

"Wait'll you see th' kitchen," he said.

I followed him back down the hall into a kitchen that had every stainless steel appliance imaginable. Stainless steel gas stove and oven, double stainless sink, dishwasher, washer/dryer and refrigerator –all stainless...(except the washer/dryer.)

The kitchen was twice as big as Hank's and had a feature that his didn't –a small adobe fireplace for cooking with wood. When I saw it, I said, "I'll lay odds Juan's mama uses that little fire oven and never touches the stove."

"Yer prob'ly right," Hank smiled. "Look here..." he went over and threw open one of the cabinets. It was filled with colorful plates, glasses and bowls. The dishes were glazed Mexican pottery and the glasses were heavy hand blown bottle glass. "Those glasses remind me of the ones they serve margaritas in down in Mexico," I said.

"Ah'm glad you said that, 'cause Ah'm ready to head on back and have a drink before supper."

I sighed. "Does this mean you're going to cook?"

He nodded. "Yep. Ah got this new idea for leftover turkey, ham, and shrimp casserole."

"Well, count me out," I frowned. "It sounds awful -and I'm taking th' truck to find me a McDonald's before you kill me with ptomaine poisoning."

CHAPTER ONE HUNDRED FIFTEEN

On the ride back, I asked Hank why he named my horse, "Barbara Mandrell?"

"Simple," he shrugged. "Ah like Barbara Mandrell."

"That's the reason? No incredible backstory -like she bore your lovechild?"

"Yep," Hank said. "Ah ain't never even met th' lady."

He sat up in the saddle and with the heel of his boot, lightly kicked "Diablo" in the side. It was just what "Diablo" had been waiting for and he took off like the wind. "See ya back at th' ranch," Hank yelled–and they were *gone*. Not to be outdone, I said, "C'mon, Barbara, we'll show them you're not to be toyed with." Keeping a tight rein, I sat up and kicked her sides. She raised her head and whinnied, then took off like a bat out of hell. Leaning forward, I loosened the reins and gave her, her head. With burst of speed, she closed the distance between us quicker than I would have given her credit for. But "Diablo" _was_ the faster horse and much as I hated to admit it, his shiny black coat looked magnificent under his new silver saddle. The long fringe of Hank's black suede jacket blended in with the horse's mane and the two of them were something to see, as "Diablo" flew over the ground like he wasn't even touching it.

They reached the corral ahead of us, with "Barbara" and me only seconds behind them. Hank turned around and gave us a quick short nod. "Figured Ah wouldn't be seein' y'all 'fore midnight," he said (and I sat a little taller in the saddle when he added,) "Guess you ain't a "weenie boy" after all." Both horses were sweaty and breathing hard. Rusty came out and took the reins from us. "Looks like y'all had a good ride," he said, patting "Diablo's" frothy neck. Hank jumped down. He told Rusty to walk them a bit before he put them down for the night. Nodding, Rusty took them in the barn as we walked back to the house.

"This has been a really enjoyable day, Hank! And that house just *sitting* out there." I shook my head. "What a waste."

"That's 'cause it's so remote that whoever lived there would have to be somebody Ah knew *real well* –and trusted even *more*."

"I see your point," I nodded.

As we walked into the kitchen Noreen came running up to us. "Hank! Thank God you're back! A pipe or something busted under the sink an' there's water everywhere."

"Crap," he muttered. "Just what Ah need…"

He pulled off his gloves and followed Noreen over to the sink to show him the problem. I went along to see if there was anything I could do. There was water all over the floor. Hank opened both doors under the sink and it looked like the Flood of Noah. He checked the faucets to make sure they were off. They were, and he said, "Well, th' faucets ain't th' problem." "Did you run the dishwasher today, Noreen?"

She nodded. "I had to, I had a full load."

Hank got down on the floor. "Well," he sighed. "Wherever it's comin' from, it's stopped now."

I suggested, "Why don't I put the washer on "rinse" for you to check it out?"

"Good idea," Hank nodded, and I turned it on. Nothing happened until the dishwasher drained, then sure enough, water ran out from somewhere in back. "Okay," he said. "Shut it off again."

"Could you see where it's coming from?"

He shook his head. "No, it couldn't be *that* simple," he frowned. "Ah gotta go out to th' barn an' git mah wrench."

When he came back, he stamped his feet and said, "It's startin' to snow."

Getting down on the floor again, Hank turned over on his back and scooted under the sink. Just as he got situated, he said, "Dammit, Ah forgot mah flashlight. Hand it to me, will ya, Mac? Its over there in th' top drawer next to th'stove."

I got the flashlight and put it in his hand sticking out. He fumbled around for about twenty minutes then came out and sat up on the floor. "Ah can't see a damned thing under there," he said in exasperation. "But it's definitely comin' from th' dishwasher. Ah'll jest have'ta call a plumber Ah know tomorrow, to have him come out an' look at it." He handed me the flashlight and got up. "Don't run this 'til we get it fixed," he told Noreen, turning on the hot water to wash his hands. As he picked up the soap, the screen door opened and Jerry came in. Snowflakes fluttered around him as he took off his chauffeur cap. Hank ran his hands under the water. "Yeah, Jerry –what is it?"

"Sorry to bother you, Mr. Hank, but it's the first of the year -time to lease a new limo."

Hank rinsed the soap off and wiped his hands on a towel. "So it is," he said, rubbing his chin "Okay, take her in sometime this week –did we go over th' mileage?"

"No, we're under by twenty."

"Good - Ah hate to pay extra." Turning to leave, Hank called him back. "Lissen, Jerry, Ah want you to call over to th' airfield an' cancel th' contract on th' plane," he said. "We hardly ever use it, an' if Ah need th' Gulfstream, Ah'll just rent it back from 'em."

Jerry put his cap on again. "Will do, Mr. Hank –goodnight Mr. Mac –Miss Noreen."

Noreen stared after him. "I just *love* it when he calls me that," she said.

CHAPTER ONE HUNDRED SIXTEEN

The next day, Hank called the plumber, but he couldn't come out.

"Sorry, Hank, but it's that time of year when everybody's got busted pipes," he said. "I'm swamped right now -*and* shorthanded, so if it ain't an emergency, I won't be able to get out there much before next week."

Hank frowned. "Well, no, it ain't an emergency, Carlos, but Ah understand, so just come as soon as ya can."

"I will, Hank -an' if I get an opening quicker than expected, I'll call ya."

"No, just come on out –Ah'll be here."

"Okay, –an' how's Sam?"

"She's on th' road right now, so she ain't happy."

"That's rotten to have to go at this time'a year, but I hear her song on th' radio all th'time. It's really good."

"Yeah –that's why she's on th' road."

"Well, give her my best when you talk to her, Hank – an' I'll see you quick as I can."

"Thanks, Carlos –bye." He hung up the phone and said, "Carlos won't be able to come out here 'til next week."

I looked at Noreen and feigned pity. "Poor, baby," I said sadly. "You'll just have to wash dishes by hand –oh, boo-hoo." She didn't say a word; just came over and gave me a swift kick in the shins. "OOWWWW!" I cried, hopping around holding my knee. "Damn you, Noreen –that hurt."

She looked at me and said, "*Pooooor* baby."

"If you two are finished," Hank said, "Ah'm gonna call Rose to see if she can come out an' spruce up the house for Juan's family. Ah want her to dust an'polish all th' furniture; tidy up th' kitchen an' bathrooms, air out th' mattresses, an' put clean sheets on all th' beds..."

"That's quite a lot of heavy work," I said, "don't you think you ought'a help?"

"You mean "we" don't ya, white man?"

I sighed.

"You an' me gotta chop wood an' stack it inside next to th' fireplace."

"You're out of your mind, if you think I'm going to chop wood," I said. "I'll carry it in and stack it, but I ain't chopping it."

The phone rang. I was right next to it, so I answered and my face lit up. "Sam!"

"Hi," she said. "What's up and how is Matt?"

"Same o same o," I said. "Matt's fine, but I got some really great news for you."

"I could sure use some -what is it?" she asked.

"Hank got somebody to move here with their family to do the cooking and cleaning –*and* take fulltime care of Matt."

"WHAT?" she cried. "Who on earth –how can a whole family move into our house?"

"Hold on to your hat –are you ready for this? It's Juan and his family – and they're not moving in here; they're moving into th' little river house y'all have about a mile from here."

There was dead silence on her end and I waited for her to say something, but after a minute, I finally asked, "Sam?"

"That...is...*wonderful* news," she cried. "How on *earth* did you come up with that idea?"

I said, "I wish I could take the credit, but it was your brother who thought of it."

"So, *that's* what he had in mind when he told me not to worry about it."

She wanted to know everything. I told her about the sheriff tracking down the padre and his getting in touch with Hank.

"Are you talking about Frank –our sheriff?"

"Yes, the friend of Hank's that was out here Christmas."

She had a million more questions and I told her, "We're just waiting to hear from Juan now, so Hank can make all the arrangements to get them up here."

"And they're *all* coming?"

"Yep, his whoooooooole family."

"How many are there?"

"I can't remember, but if they double up in the bedrooms, I think they'll all fit."

"That house *has* to be better than anything they live in, now," she said.

"Seriously," I said, "they'll be over th' moon. Hell, *I* wanted to move in."

"You know, Mac –I am so homesick for you and Matt right now. I haven't taken off my cross since you put it around my neck." A pang shot through my heart and I looked down at my ring. "Same here my love, -we've had so little time together ever since we met –and most especially since we got married." She said, "You know, someday we'll be old married fogies. My teeth will start to fall out and you'll lose all your hair. You won't even remember the fun we had on our first Christmas."

I said, "You're wrong, sweetheart, I'll always remember that day -it was the day I almost got my head blown off."

"See what I mean," she huffed. "*That would* be the thing you'd remember!"

"I'm teasing you –how could I forget what a great day that was –well, the first half, anyway...the last half was just plain interesting."

"I guess you think I'm silly, Mac, but it's so important for a marriage to get off on the right footing. It's easy to be loving and not find any fault in each other right now, but as the honeymoon phase wears off and the problems of life once again seep in, men tend to forget that they once promised to love and honor the partnership –and marriage *is* a partnership. There is no "boss" –just an equal sharing of everything, whether it be fortune or trouble."

"I understand and I'll try to remember that."

"Yeah, but I want it to come natural...not 'cause you think I'll expect it," she said quietly.

"It's a bet –how much?"

"Oh...let's say, a dollar."

"Deal!"

"Mac, all I really want is you to have my back in life when things go wrong, like when so-called "friends" betray me and real friends desert me. Believe me, it happens a lot in show business; today everybody loves you and tomorrow, it's "Sam who?" It's times like that, when I'll need you to be my best friend. And silly as it sounds, I want you to love me when you *don't* understand me, because that's when I'll need you *most*."

"My precious, every moment of life is filled with betrayal and fair-weather friends," I said. "It's just worse for those in show business, because the supermarket rags know who you are and delight in making every pimple in your life public. But no one should have to take that kind of scrutiny and I'll be there for you."

"Love, honesty, loyalty and respect -that's all I ask from us," she said. "Okay, that ends the Marriage 101 speech. Look sweetheart, I have to hang up now- just know that I miss you and Matt something terrible, but feel a tremendous weight has been lifted off, knowing Juan's family is coming - and *please* let me know when they get there."

"You'll be the second to know," I said, and once again, we said goodbye.

After we hung up, I didn't know what to do next. Hank had left me alone to talk to Sam in private and the house was quiet. I went into the kitchen.

Nobody was in there either, so I walked out to the barn. I saw Rusty and asked him where Hank and Noreen were. He said they'd taken the horses out to show Noreen the house. I nodded and turned to go, when he asked if I'd like to take "Barbara Mandrell" out. "Not today," I waved, "I think I'll go in and spend some time with my son." I went in our bedroom to play with Matt, but he was sound asleep. Freeway looked at me as if to say, "Shhhhhhhhh," and I whispered, "Look, Freeway–this kid sleeps entirely too much. Are you slipping him something -like a drugged milk bone?" She cocked her head to the side and looked at me. "Not talking, eh?"

I went out on the porch. It snowed another foot during the night and everything looked clean and white. I sat down in one of the rockers and thought about what Sam said in her phone call. She was trying to tell me that for better or worse, we were a team and I should always put that ahead of any good fortune *-or* bad time. ...And she was right –we do tend to forget that over time.

I'd been sitting out there for about an hour, when I heard the phone ring again and hurried in to answer it. There was a lot of static on the line and the person on the other end sounded far, far away, but I instantly knew who it was.

"Buenos dias, Senor Mac!"

"Juan!" I cried. "Oh, I'm **so** happy to hear from you! Que pasa?"

"Nada," he laughed.

"Are you still coming up here with your family?"

"Si, si," he said. "Mi familia."

"When?"

"We are –um, how you say –readee to bee here."

"*NOW*?" I cried.

"Si," he said simply. (I wished everyone was that uncomplicated.)

"Juan," I said *sloowly*, (thinking he'd understand better -which is the same as shouting at a blind person.) "Hank-will-send-his-bus-for-you-manana, okay?"

"Como?"

Crap! This wasn't working. My Spanish had rusted since being away from him.

"Senor Hank is <u>no</u> here right now -you call back at –"

Just then I heard the kitchen door. "Just a minute, Juan –uh, un momento," I said, and yelled for Hank to come to the phone. "It's Juan calling from Mexico..."

Hank hurried in and took the receiver. He knew a bit more Spanish than I did and was able to convey his plans to have Juan and his family, picked up from my bar at the crossroads day after tomorrow. He asked if Juan thought they would have any trouble getting up there, and Juan assured him they wouldn't. Of course, he didn't tell us that they would have to *walk* the eight miles across the border carrying everything they owned...which came to three small bundles of raggedy clothes.

CHAPTER ONE HUNDRED SEVENTEEN

Hank made arrangements for Arte to leave early the next day for the crossroads. Rose came over that same morning and we took her out in the pick-up to help get the house ready. Hank spent the day chopping wood outside, while I helped Rose turn mattresses, take the sheets off the furniture and even scrubbed the toilets for her so she wouldn't have to do it. (It wasn't that she didn't want to, it's just that I didn't think she should.) Nothing was actually all that unpleasant to do –including the toilets. As far as I could see, outside of a little dust, the house was immaculate. The only thing I found objectionable was when Rose insisted all the windows needed to be washed. I took a bucket of soapy water out to do the two-hundred *thousand* windows, swearing under my breath and thinking Rose was taking advantage of me. But, while I was doing the windows, she was (-and I couldn't believe it) –busy in the kitchen washing every dish, bowl, pan and piece of silverware –by *hand*...along with scrubbing the floor on her hands and knees. I felt like a prick. But at the end of the day, the house and everything in it sparkled -and there was enough firewood inside to last until *next* winter.

On the way back to the ranch, I pleaded with Rose to *please* stay one more hour and fix us supper. "I'll eat *anything* you wanna cook," I said. "Just don't make me eat another so-called meal that "Julia Fairchild" fixes."

She looked at Hank. "*You've* been cooking?" she frowned. "Oy vey!"

"Yes, he has –and it is AWFUL!"

"Okay, so a coulpe'a things haven't come out so good," he said.

"Oh, puh-leeze," I huffed, looking out the window. "Half the time, my stomach thinks my throat is cut and the other half, it thinks I'm trying to poison it." I turned my head back to look at Hank. "Tell her about the turkey, ham, shrimp casserole!"

Rose stared at him. "You fixed such a thing?" she asked, incredulously.

Hank frowned and said, "Mmm, maybe..."

"Hank! Mixing those terrible foods together can kill you!" she scolded. "You need a Jewish cookbook."

"We need a Jewish **cook**," I muttered.

As we pulled up by the corral and got out, Rose looked at her watch and said, "It's only four, so I guess I can stay and fix you some supper." A grin spread across my face, as she looked at Hank and asked, "Do you have anything inside to fix or should I send you to the store?"

He shrugged. "What do you need? Ah got eggs, ham, pork chops, hamburger –and cheese for cheeseburgers." She rolled her eyes and opened the kitchen screen door. "I can *tell* you aren't Jewish," she said, shaking her head. Following her inside, he said, "Well, Ah didn't know we were going to have Passover."

"How much hamburger?" she asked, taking down on her apron.

"About three pounds…"

"Is it fresh –or frozen?"

"Ah took it out two days ago frozen, but it ain't been outta the fridge."

"Good, get it out, along with three onions and a two green peppers if you have them."

Luckily, Hank had what she wanted and gave her the ingredients she asked for. Tying her apron, Rose shooed us out of the kitchen and forty-five minutes later, we sat down to the most amazing skillet dinner I'd ever tasted.

What she did with three pounds of hamburger, three onions and two green peppers, was nothing short of what our Lord did with three fishes and five loaves of bread.

I said, "Rose y'all may not recognize Jesus as the Messiah, but you sure do feed th' hungry like Him." Then I turned beet red and said, "Oh, Rose, I am *so* sorry! I did not mean to offend you –I truly meant that as a compliment!" She smiled and patted me on the cheek. "I know you did, Mac. And whether Jesus is the true Messiah or just a gifted rabbi, we respect Him, so I take it as the compliment you meant." She untied her apron, saying, "Well, I must go, let me know if you need me again." Hank got up from the table as she hung her apron back on its peg by the stove.

"This is for all th' work you did today Rose," he said, handing her an envelope "-an' a little extra for a great supper…thanks."

"You don't have to pay me for any of this today," she frowned. "I'm more than happy to help you out." She tried to give it back, but he refused. "You're gonna need that one day, for when we run away together," he winked on his way to call Jerry.

While they waited for the limo, she asked, "Have you found anyone to housekeep for you, yet?" and Hank told her about Juan's family. "In fact, they should be here sometime late tomorrow night."

"Oh good, I'm so glad to hear that. They sound like the perfect answer to your needs."

"And," I smiled, "Hank is the perfect answer to theirs. They're going to live in that house out by the little river."

"OH –that's marvelous!" she grinned. "I always thought that was such a darling house -and such a waste sitting out there with no family to make it a home." Just then, headlights appeared and Jerry pulled up by the back porch. She told us goodnight and Hank walked her out to the car. He waved goodbye then came back inside. When he sat down at the table again, I said, "You know, I just had a thought!"

"*Really*?" he grinned. "You actually had a-" then he shook his head. "Naw, Ah ain't even going to take a shot," he said, reaching for another helping. "It's too easy.

"No, I'm serious! Has anybody thought to find out what *town* Juan lives in –or what his *last* name is?"

We all looked blank for a moment, then Hank scratched his head. "Might be a good idea to check on that when they get here."

CHAPTER ONE HUNDRED EIGHTEEN

Arte pulled the bus in around one thirty in the morning. We'd gone to bed a little after midnight, but Hank couldn't sleep and heard them coming up the drive. He got up, leaving Noreen asleep and greeted Juan's family in his bathrobe, but they were all so tired and happy, I don't think they even noticed.

As soon as I heard the commotion, I put on my robe and slippers and went out to the living room. "SENOR MAC!" Juan cried. He ran to me and threw his arms around my waist. Freeway heard his voice and came running too. He bent down to hug the dog and she jumped all over him as she licked his face. "Leetle Freeway!" he cried. "Oh, I have meesed you!"

His family spoke no English, outside of "yes," "no," and "okay," so, there was a lot of smiling and nodding going on. I'd forgotten how large his family was with four brothers and five sisters. All in all, counting Juan, there were ten siblings. Juan introduced everyone, but I lost count after Inez, Maria, Juanita, Teresa, Julio, Jesus, Miguel, and, oh jeese, I couldn't keep up with the others -it was one in the morning for Pete's sake.

He proudly saved introducing his parents for last.

"Theese ees mi moether y father," he enunciated carefully. His father stood humbly behind his family with his ancient torn and weather-stained hat in his hands. Juan's mother stood close beside him with her arm tightly through his. The signs of pain and hardship were etched in their faces, but their eyes sparkled with an unmistakable honesty and joy that I hadn't seen in anyone here in the States in over four decades. These people for all their poverty had something priceless that we'd given up for designer jeans and flashy cars.

Taking a step forward, Juan's father extended his hand to me. I shook it and felt the lifetime of calluses. He smiled shyly trying to hide his missing teeth –and I pretended not to see them. "Welcome, it is an honor to have you here" I said sincerely. "We're so glad you came. Mi casa, su casa."

He grinned and nodded, then looked at Juan with raised eyebrows. Juan explained what I said, and he shook his head vigorously. "Oh, *si* –gracious!" He stepped back again and put his arm behind his wife to present her. Juan translated for me and I learned her name was also Inez. I also found out their last name was Morales, and that the town they came from had no real name; it was just referred to as "Rio de la Plata" –which meant, "Silver River." (As it turns out, our underground river at the crossroads surfaced for several miles in that spot in Mexico.)

I asked Juan, "Where are your belongings -do you need to have them brought off the bus?"

"Como?" he frowned.

"Your clothes," I said, pointing to his.

"Oh, no, Senior Mac –they are here," and he pointed to three bundles on the floor.

I looked down at the three pathetic bundles, unable to believe it was everything they owned. "Okay, pick them up and I'll get you all to bed – somehow –some place...then we'll go out to your new home manana – okay?"

I showed them where the guest bathroom was in the hall. They washed up while Hank and I got out sheets and blankets to make beds on the couch and floor.

It was after four a.m. by the time the giant slumber party got situated, and I turned off the lights knowing the kids were too excited to get any sleep. I could hear them whispering and giggling all the way down the hall.

I crawled into bed again and pulled up the covers, thinking how I hadn't seen this many people under the same roof at the same time, since our last family reunion back in the early 60's.

CHAPTER ONE HUNDRED NINETEEN

I woke up the next morning to the wonderful smell of bacon and eggs - which could only mean one thing; Hank wasn't cooking. I dressed and hurried into the kitchen, taking Matt with me. Juan and his sisters were in there making breakfast and running back and forth to the dining room putting out plates and silverware. "Good morning, Senor Mac" everybody said at once. When Juan's mama, Inez saw Matt, she came running over. "OH!" she exclaimed, excitedly patting both his cheeks. She rattled off a whole string of words I couldn't understand and held out her arms. "She wants to hold thee leetle bambino," Juan laughed.

"OH!" I said, handing Matt over to her.

"Thee food, she ees readee to eet," Juan said, pointing to the dining room. "You go -we weel feed thee leetle Matt –si?"

I had just sat down when Hank came in followed by a sleepwalking Noreen. He was dressed, but she had on her robe and her hair...well. After greeting them, Juan sat down across the table from me. He had spent the night in the bar with his family waiting for Arte, so he brought me up-to-date on things -and I marveled at how well his English had gotten.

"Your English has really improved -have you been studying?" I asked.

"Si, thee padre at thee mission."

A light went on. "So *that's* how he knew you!"

"Si –I come every day to thee mission."

After the breakfast dishes were done and the kitchen gleamed, the whole family piled into the pick-up and I drove them out to see their new house. Hank followed on "Diablo" and the children thought it was great to see a real cowboy –(I guess no one taught them any Mexican history, since the first cowboys came from Mexico and were adopted by us.)

The instant the truck came over the hill and they saw the house, they got dead quiet and stared in jaw-dropping wonder. Juan's mama had both hands covering her mouth and tears running down her cheeks. Juan's papa crossed himself and mouthed a silent pray of gratitude. I pulled up in front and shut off the engine. The children were the first ones to make a sound. They jumped out of the bed of the truck and ran up to the porch, rattling off Spanish like a Gatlin gun.

Juan slowly stepped out of the truck. "Oh, Senior Mac," he whispered. "Thees...thees...ees...muy bonito!" His mother just stood there and cried in between saying a *whooole* lot in Spanish. He patted her back and looked at me. "She says she cannot live here."

"**WHAT**?" I cried. Juan shook his head. "Pay no mind, Senior Mac. She theenks eet ees –um, how you say -?" He struggled to find the right words. I stood there waiting and then he made a motion with his hand over his head. "Eet ees uh, too grande."

"It's too big?" I asked disbelievingly.

"Si –too mucho!"

I suddenly understood and rolled my eyes. "You mean, she thinks it's too *good* for her?"

Juan's face lit up and he nodded, "SI, SI."

"No, no, no, "I frowned. "The casa has been sitting out here for cinco annyos alone –uh, solo. It needs a family to make it a happy home –not stay empty." I wasn't sure Juan got all that, but he seemed to get the most important parts. He explained it to Inez and she said something back to Juan. Her face still had a look of anguish, but when Juan told me what she said, I smiled.

"You're more than welcome," I said, as she hugged me. I finally got free of her arms and walked up the steps with them. The kids hovered around the door eagerly. I unlocked it and pushed it open, then smiled as I handed the keys to Juan's father. He took them from me and I saw the humility in his eyes as he whispered, "Gracias."

I followed the family inside, and if I thought her seeing the outside was traumatic -it was nothing compared to the wailing Inez did when she saw the inside. I didn't know if I was improving their lives or destroying them. The kids scattered throughout the house, and I made an excuse to Juan, saying I had to get back to Matt. I got their things out of the truck and set them down on the tile floor, then said adios and got out of there as fast as I could!

I wanted to be as far away as possible when Inez saw the kitchen.

CHAPTER ONE HUNDRED TWENTY

It took the better part of a week for them to get settled, but Inez came to the house every morning to fix us a huge breakfast and do whatever housekeeping needed to be done and cook supper every night –thank God. Carlos (the plumber) showed up and fixed the dishwasher. He told Hank it was a worn coupling that leaked when the dishwasher drained and replaced it simple enough. So, although it only took an hour to fix the dishwasher, it was going to take much longer than that for Inez to learn how to use it. Juan took care of Matthew and spent a lot of time rocking or playing with him. Juan's father knew how to drive a stick shift and would take two of the girls in with him to do the marketing. Pretty soon, Inez had the house running smooth as silk. She learned how to use the washer and stove, but still marveled at the dishwasher. Things improved by leaps and bounds so much that I actually thought about getting away for a few days and meeting Sam somewhere on the road. I figured I'd ask her about the next time she called, so that night, I did."Do you know where you're gonna be for the next week?" I asked. "I do," she said. "I'm going from here to

Atlanta, then over to Asheville, Johnson City, Tennessee, and then let's seeee...oh, I'll be in Texas."

"*NO KIDDING –where?*"

"In Waco."

"Is that far from Dallas?"

"Not really, its kind'a in between Dallas an' Houston. Why –you thinkin' of comin' down there?"

"Just as fast as I can –even if I have to walk!"

"Get Hank to fly you down...th'plane is just sitting out there at th' airport."

"He cancelled th' contract on it last week."

"He DID –why?"

"Cause it was just sittin' out there at the airport."

"Well, you can get a flight out easy enough. Have Jerry make you a reservation and drive you to Dallas/Ft.Worth for your flight."

"Just let me know when and I'll get th' ticket," I said. Before we hung up, she asked about Matt and wondered how everything was working out with Juan's family. I told her the whole thing had been a Godsend for both parties. After that conversation, not much of interest happened between talking to Sam and Jerry driving me to the airport. When I got on the plane, I was as excited as a teenager on a date with the Honecoming Queen. I remember very little about the flight except that it was short, relaxing -and taking me to see Sam.

After we landed, I grabbed a cab straight to her hotel - took the nearest elevator up to her room and knocked on the door. When she answered, she flew into my arms and I kissed her for at least five minutes."Oh, Sam," I whispered. "It's been soooooo long." I held her in my arms and wouldn't let go. She clung just as tightly to me. "Mac, my darling Mac," she whispered in my ear. "I can't believe it. It feels like twenty years instead of two and a half weeks."

"I know, sweetheart. I know."

"I have to be at the auditorium in an hour," she said. "I can't eat before I go on –it makes it hard to sing, but you can call down to room service while I get dressed."

"I don't want a *thing* except to look at you."

"Yeah, well, I've got more in mind for you after we get back here tonight," she said with a twinkle.

"I'm putty in your hands," I smiled.

CHAPTER ONE HUNDRED TWENTY-ONE

I left an hour later with Sam for the auditorium. I'd never been to one of her concerts and it was something to see before we even got out of the limo. Fans by the hundreds where everywhere. Flashbulbs went off with blinding accuracy. Before that night, I'd never had a camera stuck in my face and I can tell you, I hope to never again. The scene at Houston city hall was enough for me; THIS was over the top and I wouldn't want to be a "star" in today's insane world for all the tea in Burbank. We made it from the limo to backstage with the help of some pretty big world-class wrestlers doubling as bodyguards. The crowds were less backstage, but it was just as insane. Longhaired musicians hurried to and fro, while half naked women *and* men shouted for wardrobe or make-up. Sam took me into her dressing room and shut the door.

"Aahhh, peace," she said, leaning against it. "Blessed peace."

I went over and sat down in the only chair outside of the one in front of the mirror. She sighed and pushing away from the door, came over and sat down in that chair. Picking up a hairbrush, she brushed her long ponytail and said, "I am so sick and tired of the road. I can't wait to finish the next eight days and come home."

When she said that, I thought it was the perfect time to talk to her about quitting.

"Sam...what would you say to quitting this whole thing?"

She stopped brushing and put down the brush. Looking in the mirror, she said, "That's exactly what I'm going to do." Then she turned to face me. "I plan on having that very talk with Sid, just as soon as this is over." I got up and went over to her. Kneeling down, I took her hand and said, "That's the best news I've heard since this whole thing started." A loud knock came on the door and a muffled voice hollered, "Five minutes, Miss Evans."

"Go get 'em, tiger," I said softly. "I'll be waiting right there in the wings."

She pinned a red rose over her left ear, threw her head to the side so her ponytail flipped behind her and gave one last quick check to her lipstick. When she was satisfied, she got up and we went out together. Sam warned me not to trip over cables and wires, and I was amazed at how quiet things had become. The musicians were sitting out on stage waiting patiently behind the curtain and as soon as they got their cue, they began to play. The curtain went up and like rolling thunder the audience started clapping non-stop for her. A white-hot spotlight pierced the darkness when Sam walked out, and the applause reached a deafening crescendo. She wore a glittering blood red dress with ruffles from the knees down trimmed in black. Her hair was pulled back into a sleek ponytail and she wore gold hoop earrings along with the big red rose over her left ear. She looked like a Barbie flamenco dancer.

Part of me was so proud that I could've burst a blood vessel, but part of me worried that all the applause signaled that her song –and popularity – might not be slowing down. But I refused to think about it and put it out of my mind for tonight. Tonight, I didn't want *anything* to spoil our time together.

The show lasted two and a half hours, but it seemed to fly by. I could've stood there in the wings and listened to her forever. She closed the show with "our song" and then embarrassed the bejeepers out of me by having me come out on stage afterwards. She introduced me to the audience and explained that the song had been written for me. They stood up and cheered and I thought I'd die before I got off. The curtain came down to cries of "More, More," and she went out for one more bow. After the show, there was another hour of signing autographs and then she was expected to show up at a late night supper in a private dining room at some country club. The governor was going to be there, along with several other dignitaries, but Sam begged off and we got out of there as soon as possible (–leaving a lot of very pissed off dignitaries.)

We got in the limo feeling like two school children that had just got away with playing hooky.

When we got back to the hotel, Sam ordered room service to bring up the biggest, thickest, rarest, steaks they had, along with a bottle of their most expensive champagne.

"Wow," I said, as she put her arms around my neck. "We're going to have a late New Year's celebration," she said provocatively. "Then I'm taking you into that bedroom –right over there –and I'm going to give you your *very own* private show tonight -the X-rated version."

"Yeah?" I said. "How about we just skip dinner?"

She laughed. "I'd say yes, but I am *starving* after a show. I burn so many calories out there on stage -plus I don't eat a thing before I go on -that I have to eat afterwards."

While we waited for room service, she went in the bedroom, got undressed and put her robe on over her nightgown. "This is the best part of the night," she said, plopping down in an overstuffed chair. "It's over and I can just relax in my jammies." But she didn't stay down long. She got up again and went over to the stereo the hotel provided. She got out a Bob Dylan album and put it on. "I love Bob Dylan," she said. "He is the most amazing artist and song writer to ever come down th' road this century. His voice, his music –the arrangements –are so plaintive yet along with his words, everything strikes something in my soul nothing else touches."

She looked at me. "Until my love for you."

The world was our oyster that night -but of course, everything has its price.

...And ours was that it all ended too soon.

CHAPTER ONE HUNDRED TWENTY-TWO

The trip back to Dallas was long and filled with both sweet memories and sad longing. Time now dragged on endlessly. I wondered if the plane would ever land and thought about asking the flight attendant if we were going back to Dallas by way of Beirut, but...didn't. Jerry asked how Miss Sam was doing as soon as I got in the limo. I told him she was homesick and although Jerry doesn't show his feelings, it wasn't difficult to see that he missed her too. When we got back to the house, it was like I'd never left. Hank and Noreen were out riding, leaving Inez and the girls to do laundry and change the beds. Juan's father was in the corral with his brothers helping Rusty fix a broken windmill pump for the horses. Juan greeted me like I'd been gone a year wanting to know in detail how Sam was. Without stopping to talk, I said she was fine. I didn't mean to be rude, but my feelings were so raw and messed up right now that I needed time to center myself.

I hurried into the bedroom and closed the door. Throwing my gym bag on the bed, I unzipped it and began to take everything out like a mad man –and I can tell you, taking it out was far less exciting than putting it in. (Perhaps that was a metaphor for this whole trip.)

I went in the bathroom putting the toothbrush and razor by the sink. I threw the underwear in the laundry basket, but instead of throwing the shirt in too, I brought it up to my face. Closing my eyes and inhaling her perfume, the vision of Sam in that red dress came flooding back.

I kept the shirt. I wouldn't put it in the laundry right now.

The rest of the day was plagued with dark, depressing-as-hell gloom. My appetite was off, my bedroom was as empty as Dracula's tomb and my heart was breaking. I sat on the edge of the bed and almost wished I hadn't gone to see her. Anything that can take you as high as I was day before yesterday, can dash you to the lowest pits of despair afterwards –and it sucked.

The day dwindled outside my window and I watched the sun go down without bothering to turn on the light. I sat in the half-darkness feeling nothing until I heard Hank and Noreen come back from their ride. When I heard their laughter and a cold rage came over me and I hated them. This kind of cruelty was what serial killers were made of -it was <u>beyond</u> the scope of humanity and I didn't want to understand anyone else's happiness when I was being denied.

I was so miserable that I lost track of time and Inez must have sensed what was wrong when I didn't come out of my room. Women are intuitive that way, but instead of trying to disturb me and improve my disposition with lame diversions, she went about her chores until suppertime –then she told Juan to call everyone into the dining room.

I was lying on the bed staring at the ceiling with my arm behind my head when he opened the door and quietly eased in the room. "Senor Mac?" he called softly. "Are you here?"

When I didn't answer, he made his way over to the bed and tried to turn on the light. I grabbed his arm and told him to go away, but he shook his head. "No, no, Senior Mac –mi madre say you *come* –<u>now</u>!" I turned my head and frowned at him. "Does that mean you're not going to go away?" He stubbornly crossed his arms over his chest and I let out a long sigh. "Crap -that's what I thought," I said, but I was too mentally beat down to fight with him. "*This* is what I get for letting you know where my bedroom is." I reluctantly got up and followed him into the dining room. Hank and Noreen were already seated at the table along with Juan's family. I was surprised to see them, but for some unknown reason I was glad they were there and sat down. The table was laid out from end-to-end with fresh baked jalapeno cornbread, gazpacho, tortillas drizzled in melted cheese and taco shells stacked next to spicy ground beef, diced fresh tomatoes, onions, lettuce and lots of grated Monterrey jack.

I wasn't the least bit interested in food, until I saw the trouble Inez had gone to. We passed around her cooking and the table became a beehive of laughter. The contagious atmosphere kept me from brooding over my misery –and thankfully, no one mentioned Sam. My appetite came back with a vengeance. I had seconds and thirds on everything, and just when I didn't think I could eat another bite, Inez (who *insisted* I call mama,) brought out her secret recipe flan covered in cinnamon caramel sauce.

The Morales had only been with us for a little over two weeks, but they fit in like they'd been with us for years. Regardless of the language barrier, I couldn't imagine life without them here and before I realized it, we were talking to each other like a real family. Juan told me that his sisters and brothers were going to enroll in school next year to learn, among other things, English. They must have understood what he was telling me, because nine little Mexican bobble heads suddenly nodded around the table. Mama got up and brought out more flan. I ate a *second* one then said, "That's **IT**! I am <u>done</u>!" I pushed away from the table and Hank looked at me, "Boy, if you weren't hungry," he said, "Ah'd sure hate ta see you when you are."

Mama shooed everybody out so she could clear the table. I was the last to leave and she pulled me aside before I went into the living room. The girls were in the kitchen rinsing and stacking dishes in the dishwasher, but Juan was there and she said something in Spanish for him to translate. When she finished talking, he nodded and then looked at me.

"Mi madre say she sabe, uh..." He made a face while he tried to think of the word in English.

I said, "Knows?" and he nodded. We stood there locked in trial and error translation, as Juan tried to relate what Inez wanted to tell me. It took some doing on both our parts, but the closest I could make out was that she understood what I was going through right now, and wanted me to remember the good time Sam and I had together –no matter how short.

I think she was trying to say, that *all time* is short when it comes to spending it with a loved one...even a lifetime. At least, I hope that's what she was saying, because it made me stop brooding and see my visit with Sam from the positive side of the coin. My face softened and I hugged her. "Gracias, mama," I nodded.

She smiled and the crinkles around her eyes lit up her face like the sun.

CHAPTER ONE HUNDRED TWENTY-THREE

I sat down in front of the fire with Hank in the living room. It was just the two of us -Noreen had gone to take a "bubble bath." He asked me if I'd like to join him in bourbon and I nodded. He poured our drinks and we sat in front of the fire, quietly watching the flames. By my second drink, I was feeling one hundred percent better. Mama came in to tell us goodnight before leaving. I got up and hugged her, thanking her for everything. She left us alone in front of the fire and after we heard the kitchen door close, Hank looked over at me and said, "So...?"

I was confused. "So -what?"

"How'd it go in Waco?"

(Great -he just *had* to ask.) I frowned and took a long draw on my bourbon. "It was heartbreakingly wonderful," I said, sarcastically. "She is the greatest entertainer, the most beautiful woman on the planet –and the best lover in the Universe -what *more* could a man ask for in a wife."

"How 'bout for her to be here?" he mused.

I looked down at my drink and sighed, "Yeah..."

"It ain't an easy life, Mac. We never get it all. There's a damn hitch or flaw in everything. Ya just gotta learn how to grab hold'a whatever ya got, while ya got it."

"Where'd you get that bit of wisdom," I frowned, "-off a greeting card?" Taking another long swallow, I added. "Did it come with any ideas on how to do that?"

"Not a one."

We dropped the subject of Sam and turned instead to the Dallas Cowboys. I didn't care a thing about football, but it was better than talking about Waco. I had one more drink with him then got up. "I'm exhausted," I said. "I'm going to bed." Hank leaned forward and set his glass on the coffee table. "Yeah," he nodded, "it *has* been a long day. Ah think Ah'll sit here 'til th' fire goes down a bit more and then hit th' hay, mahself."

We said goodnight and I left for the bedroom. I remember crawling in bed and pulling the covers up over my head, but don't remember falling to sleep. Surprisingly, I slept soundly all night and woke up the following morning feeling hungry as a bear. My starving appetite was the strongest affirmation that I'd beaten the "Blues." I dressed and went into breakfast where Mama was at the stove, humming "La Cucaracha." I kissed her and sat down at the kitchen table. She brought over ham and eggs with freshly made biscuits and red-eye gravy. She poured my coffee and said, "Bueno dias, Senor Mac." Looking up, I smiled. "*Gooood* morning, Mama."

Juan came with Matt and sat down next to me. "Hello, Senor Mac."

"Hello, Juan, hello, Matt –how're you guys this fine morning?"

"We are very well," he smiled.

"You know where Hank is?"

"Si," he nodded. "Senor Hank and Mees Noreen go for to do thee shopping." I nodded, figuring Noreen was chomping at the bit to spend some of her gift certificate. Mama poured me a second cup of coffee and I asked Juan what he was going to do today. He said he was going to give Matt a bath, take him out on the porch for some air and just spend the day with him in general.

Since everyone had something to do and somebody to do it with, I decided to go out to the barn. Rusty was in the corral with one of the horses. He had the horse's right leg bent across his knee and was working on something in his hoof. I went over to them. When he saw me, he said, "Good morning, Mac."

"Hi, Rust –what're you doing?"

"I'm trying to dig out a stone he picked up somewhere yesterday," he answered. "It's wedged in pretty tight and I'm not having much success." I watched him skillfully work his knife around the stone without hurting the horse. Ten minutes later, he got the rock out and let go of the horse's leg.

The horse whinnied and bounced up and down to show he was okay before trotting around the corral. Rusty said, "Okay, Sugarfoot, looks like you're good as new."

"Sugarfoot?"

"Uh, yeah - his name is just a coincidence." He looked at me. "You got any plans today?" he asked.

I shook my head. "Not one! I just got up and I'm bored already."

"You wanna take "Barbara Mandrell" out? She needs some exercise and you can see some of the ranch. It's a perfect day for a ride," he said, looking up, "–not a cloud in sight."

I nodded, "Okay –why not?"

I followed him into the barn and was astounded to see how clean and orderly everything was. All tack was hung up neatly on the wall and the saddles were lined up side-by-side on sawhorses. I didn't expect to see how pristine things were –for a barn, anyway. The center aisle was raked and fresh hay was spread out on the floor of all the stalls. Every stall had a window in the rear to let in plenty of fresh air and light, and roomy enough for the animal to move around in comfortably.

"Boy, you really take good care of these guys," I said.

"We try to –besides, Hank would have our hides if we didn't. We brush 'em every day and make sure they have plenty of water an' food in clean stalls."

"Do you guys do your own shoeing?"

"No," Rusty said. "We really don't have th' time, so we gotta fierier that comes out reg'lar."

"Sounds like this place keeps you busy."

He nodded. "I'll say...in fact," he added, "I could use another foreman around here. I got so much to do out there on th' range that I could use someone back here AND out there."

"Why don't you hire somebody?"

"It ain't that easy," he said, shaking his head. "Bein' th' foreman of *any* ranch isn't somethin' just anybody can do, but one this size –well, there ain't that many skilled men around that can handle it."

Harley immediately came to mind. "I know somebody who could handle any part of it," I said.

"Yeah? Well tell him to get in touch with me –th' sooner th' better."

"Wouldn't do no good," I said, "he wouldn't come."

"Why not?' Rusty asked.

"He's already th' foreman of a big spread down south of here near th' border. His name's Harley and he's been a cowboy all his life. He was born in a saddle. I'm pretty sure his mother was out ropin' somethin' when she had Harley."

"Damn," Rusty frowned. "He sounds exactly like what I want."

"Yeah," I said. "They don't come any more loyal or hard working than him."

"Look, if you talk to him, ask him if he'd be interested, will you?"

I said I would, knowing Harley would never leave where he was.

Rusty turned to go into the barn and to bring out "Barbara" when I heard the phone ringing in the kitchen. "Hold up a minute, Rusty -I hear th' phone."

"Okay, Mac –an' if that happens to be your friend, don't forget to talk to him about my offer. Hank'll pay good wages," he hollered.

"Hank knows Harley," I said, hurrying towards the house.

"Even *better*!" Rusty hollered back. I ran inside and grabbed the phone –and damned if it *wasn't* Harley. "Well," I smiled. "Speak of the devil! Man, your ears must be on fire."

"Howdy do, Mac! You talkin' 'bout me?"

"The words just came outta my mouth when I heard th' phone ring – where are you?"

"I'm at Doc's."

"What're you doing over there –not that I'm complaining."

"Had to run into Legrand's to pick up some barbed wire I ordered a week ago an' thought I'd come by here to see him -and take a chance you'd be around if I called."

"God, I'm so glad you did," I said. "It's been 'way too long since I talked to you –and I'm so sorry I didn't call on Christmas. I meant to, but we ended up having a bit of trouble here that cut into my plans."

"What happened? Doc didn't mention anything about any trouble when he said you called."

"I didn't wanna bother him about it, so I didn't say anything. Actually, it *wasn't* anything much...some crackpot phony reporters crashed th' property trying to get some photos to sell to th' supermarket rags." (I, again, left out the part about the gun.) "Hank's men were already wise to 'em, so they were down by th' road waitin' when they showed up, but the thing turned into enough of a brawl that Hank and I got into it –you know- for some exercise."

Harley laughed. "Everybody okay?"

"Yep –but you should'a been here. Hank's guys rope an' tied 'em, then marched 'em to th' house so th' sheriff could come out and throw their butts in jail."

"Shoot, wish I HAD been there, but glad to hear it all turned out okay. Now, what's this about you talkin' 'bout me?"

"Hank's foreman, Rusty, just casually mentioned that he'd like to find an experienced foreman to help out around here. I guess Doc told you how freakin' big this place is, and it's a lot for four guys to handle. Anyway, I was telling him I knew of somebody an' you probably wouldn't be interested – but, he asked me to ask you about it anyway –so, I am."

"But if Hank's man is already a foreman, what does he need another one for?"

"Rusty is young –I'd guess twenty-seven or twenty-eight -under thirty anyway. And don't get me wrong -he's very capable, but I think he'd like someone older with more experience to sort'a take over the responsibility of making the big decisions. Of course, I'm just guessing, here."

"But a foreman makes more than a reg'lar ranch hand does. You ain't tellin' me he'd take a pay cut, are you?"

"Harley, this is something we spent less than thirty seconds talking about just five minutes ago, so I have no idea what he wants to do. I DO know that you'd be a foreman and be paid a foreman's wages...otherwise, there'd be no point in you taking th' job. Why -don't tell me you're *really* considering it?"

"Naw...I was just wonderin' what he'd want a foreman for when he's already one. Hey, hold on, Doc wants to say hi." Doc got on the phone and said, "Hello, Mac –how is everything?"

"Just fine Doc - now that we don't have to eat Hank's cooking anymore."

"Pretty bad, eh?"

"It's...let's see, how can I describe it? Hank has some unique ideas about food -which is bad enough, but when he tries to cook it, *that's* where it all goes horribly wrong."

"For example?"

"You want an example? Okay, here's a couple. He mixes ham, turkey, and shrimp in a casserole for one thing, and thinks asparagus makes a good hearty soup if mixed with tomatoes and spinach. I could go on and on, but the other night he fixed a dish that's topped *anything* he's come up with yet. I call it "cheddar and porcelain.""

"What the devil -did you say Hank cooked *porcelain* for you to *eat*? REAL porcelain?"

"It was supposed to be macaroni and cheese, but it didn't come out that way. He gets out the milk, butter, and macaroni then grates a ton of cheddar cheese on top. He puts it in a casserole dish, sets the oven for 350. We wait...and wait...and wait. Finally after an hour goes by, the edges are beginning to burn, so I tell Hank to take the damned thing out before it burns any more. Hank takes it out and it doesn't look all that good, but we are *starving* and decide to eat it anyway. We sit down to eat and the very first bite we put in our mouths crunches like glass, and everybody spits it out. I look at Hank and say, "Didn't you *boil* the macaroni before you put it in the oven?" and he says, "No, are you supposed to?"

Doc laughed hysterically. "Mac, that is the funniest thing I've ever heard," he gasped, "made all the more so, because you say its true."

"Unfortunately, it is, and it was the last straw. After trying to eat that - *and* the hundred and one other fiascos he's fixed, we couldn't get Juan's family up here fast enough."

"Yes, I heard that Juan's whole family came up –how wonderful."

"It's worked out great, too - like they've been here all their lives," I said.

"What about the language barrier?"

"Oh, we have a lotta fun with that," I smiled. "People can communicate just fine an' it just shows ya how useless the U.N. is." Doc asked where they all stayed and I told him about the house down by the river at the base of the mountains. "There's a special place in God's heart for what you all have done for this family," he said, and then he asked about Sam and Matt. I told him about going to Waco, and how big Matt was getting. He asked about Freeway and I said, "She never leaves his side."

"Well, we all miss you, Mac –you think you'll get back down here?"

"I'm hoping to sometime after the first of February -Sam's only supposed to be gone a month."

"Oh, hold on, Mac...Harley wants to talk to you again."

Harley got on and asked if I was really planning on ever coming back? After telling him yes, we hung up and I felt the usual pangs of homesickness. I was a man with one foot solidly on shore here in Dallas and the other in a leaky canoe drifting further and further out to sea.

CHAPTER ONE HUNDRED TWENTY-FOUR

I didn't hear from Sam for the next two days because she was traveling. I passed the time with Juan and Matt, and riding "Barbara Mandrell." I looked forward to my rides with "Babs," seeing more and more of the ranch every time we went out. The land was even more beautiful than I imagined. However, no matter how breathtakingly beautiful something is, it isn't seen in its entirety unless shared with someone –and Sam was never out of my thoughts.

I was coming out of the kitchen with a sandwich I'd fixed when I saw a car coming up the drive. I watched it pull up to the front steps and said, "Hey, Hank- somebody just pulled up out front."

Hearing the car door slam, he got up and looked out.

"Oh jeese," he frowned hurrying to the front door. "It's my Aunt Emma."

His hand went for the doorknob but before he turned it, he said in a low voice, "Look, just act normal –no matter *what* she does."

"What th' hell does that mean?" I frowned.

"It means she's a little strange."

"In what way...?"

"She's a Jehovah's Witness," he said, peering out the window from behind the curtain. He looked at me and asked, "You know anything about the Jehovah's Witness?"

"Not a thing...wait a minute -aren't they th' ones that wear strange underwear?"

"No, dummy, that's the Mormons –now straighten up!"

He opened the door just as his aunt was about to knock. "Aunt Emma!" he grinned. "What a nice surprise –c'mon in." Aunt Emma breezed in like she owned the place and Hank was still the little boy she remembered in short pants. "Hello, Hank –where is your sister?" Easing the door closed, Hank said, "She's on th' road, Aunt Emma." She clucked her tongue disapprovingly and shook her head. "Sam should be here, not out God-knows-where with all the riff-raff." She turned and looked down her nose at me. "And just who are YOU?"

Before I could answer, Hank said, "Uh, this is Mac, Aunt Emma."

I gave her my friendliest Gomer Pyle smile and held out my hand, but she ignored it. Removing her gloves one finger at a time, she marched down the step into the living room, taking off her coat and handing everything to Hank like he was the butler. Then she went straight over to the liquor cabinet and picked up the bourbon decanter. Holding it up to scrutinize, she said, "I see you're still hitting the booze pretty hard." She set the decanter down with a loud clunk and went over to the mantle. Running her hand along the top she said, "Don't you ever clean this place?"

She did a 360 around the room, criticizing any and everything she touched. "My brother, God rest his soul, would turn over in his grave if he saw what a pig sty you've let this place become...this is *exactly* why Sam should stay at home!" My blood was beginning to boil and I looked over at Hank. He was dry washing his face like his head was in terrible pain. When Aunt Emma finished her boot camp inspection, she came over and stood in front of him with her eyebrow arched imperiously. "Hank...just *who* is this man you have here?"

I was furious and said, "Just a minute, lady...I resent your-"

Hank quickly dropped his hands and glared at me. With Aunt Emma's attention diverted, he shook his head and mouthed the words, "No, no, no!"

I shut up and she turned back to him. "Well...?"

"Mac is an old friend of mine, Aunt Emma."

"From where?"

"The road. He owns a very nice saloon a 'ways down south from here – uh, south of Houston."

She frowned at me. "Hmmm, very suspicious eyes...too close together. I don't trust him."

I could see Hank was purposefully being vague, but couldn't understand why he just didn't tell her the truth –that Sam and I were married. Since I didn't have a clue as to what was going on, I just shut up and stayed out of it...and made a mental note not to include her on my Christmas card list – ever.

"Aunt Emma, to what do we owe the pleasure of your company?" Hank smiled.

She waved him off with the back of her hand. "Oh, don't waste that flattering tone on me, Hank Fairfield. You know good and well why I'm here...somebody has to keep an eye on you, so here I am."

"Well," he said sweetly, "as you can see, Ah'm fine."

"THAT is a matter of opinion," she spat, and then she turned those cold blue eyes back to me.

Looking me up and down, she said, "Is this man running after Sam or something -is that why he's here?"

"Uh, no Aunt Emma. He ain't chasin' after Sam," and Aunt Emma sniffed, "Why - is he gay?"

That did it and I opened my mouth to tell her off, but Hank said, "**NO!** Ah mean, no, he ain't gay, Aunt Emma. He's uh, married to a very nice girl. One you'd approve of, in fact."

"I doubt it," she said. "Where is she, anyway?" Before he could come up with an answer, Mama came out of the kitchen. "Senor Hank –you come?" and she motioned towards the kitchen.

Aunt Emma's jaw dropped to her chest. "Y-You have a *Mexican* woman in this house?" she asked incredulously. "Have you completely gone to the Dark Side?"

Mama didn't understand a word Aunt Emma said, but the tone of her voice was hard to miss and her smile faded. She held the hem of her apron in both hands, looking hurt and confused.

Hank's ire was beginning to rise and he took Mama by the arm whisking her into the kitchen, leaving *me* alone with Dragon Lady. I cleared my throat and said, "I'd better come with you!"

Once we were out of her sight, Hank asked Inez what she wanted. She called Juan to come in and translate. He was in with Matt and of course, had to come through the living room –right past Aunt Emma -who let out a loud scream. When Juan came into the kitchen, he was scared to death. "W-Who ees thee crazee seniora?"

Hank shook his head and said to just ignore her. "What does your mama want?" he frowned.

Juan asked his mother what she wanted and she told him the sink must be clogged, because water kept backing up everywhere. Juan explained it to Hank and I said I'd unclog it if he'd just go back out in the living room and get rid of his aunt.

But it didn't work and Hank said, "Oooh no, you're comin' back out there with me."

I sighed and told Juan to tell Inez we'd be back to take care of the sink for her in a few minutes, then I followed Hank back out to the living room, where Aunt Emma was waiting for us with crossed arms and tapping foot.

"Sorry for the interruption, Aunt Emma," Hank said.

She glared at him, demanding to know who the hell all these Mexicans were. "Are you running a halfway house for illegals?"

By now even Hank's patience was wearing thin. "No, Aunt Emma," he said tiredly. "These folks live here and work for us. They're family and Ah don't appreciate your tone. This is mah house an' you'll treat them with respect or you won't be invited in here again, you understand? An' while we're at it, this man is Sam's husband. They were married Thanksgiving and he's family too, so you'll treat him with the same respect Ah expect you to show anybody else around here."

Hank finished what he had to say and defiantly looked at his aunt. Her face turned every angry shade of red possible –and a few I'd never seen before.

"H-How **dare** you talk to me like that!" she sputtered. "Why-why I am your father's *sister*!"

"And it's for that very reason that you'd better start acting like it. Dad would never look down on anybody, an' he'd be ashamed if he saw th' way you've behaved today."

The woman drew herself up and I was so proud of Hank, I could have kissed him. The look on her face was priceless.

Grabbing her coat off the back of the couch and opening her purse, she took out a stack of tracts. "You'd better read these and get right with God," she steamed, throwing them at him. The tracts fluttered around him, but Hank never flinched or even tried to catch them. He just let them fall to the ground, as he said, "Mah God an' me are okay...an' He ain't in *those* tracts."

Pulling on her gloves, Aunt Emma stomped up the step to the front door. Hank followed her and opening it for her, bent down to kiss her on the cheek. She pushed him away. "I'll pray for you, Hank," she said on her way out. "You do that, Aunt Emma," he said, as he closed the door. Hearing the car pull away, he nodded and muttered again, "You do that."

Coming back to the living room, Hank started to pick up all the scattered tracts. I bent down to help him. "Boy –she is somethin' else," I said.

"She ain't so bad, really. She lives all alone an' since Dad died, that church is all she's got."

"But -why'd she pick the Jehovah's Witness? Y'all are Baptist."

Hank stood up with the tracts in his hands. "Ah don't know," he shrugged. "Ah guess they fill somethin' that's missin' in her. People got a right to worship however they want to. It's just that they forget its God an' not some religion, that's to be the focus of their soul."

"Yeah but...Jehovah's Witness," I said. "Jeese, Michael Jackson was a Jehovah's Witness –and look how well that turned out."

CHAPTER ONE HUNDRED TWENTY-FIVE

That evening, Sam finally called...but it wasn't with good news. Her time on the road was coming to a close and she only had one more week -until that phone call.

"I had a meeting with the record company this afternoon," she said. "My song has finally dropped down to number six, now that another song is climbing up the charts. I don't even know who's it is, I've been isolated out here so long."

"So...that's good –right?"

"It *should* be, but since it's still in the top ten, I have to ride the wave until it goes into obscurity."

I felt my heart drop and let out a long sigh. "Just what are you trying to tell me?"

There was a long silence on her end. Finally, she said, "I have to stay on the road. They have me going to Tucson next, then Phoenix, and then Lake Tahoe. I'll get a new schedule after Lake Tahoe."

"**WHAT???**"

"There's nothing I can do about it, Mac."

"Sam –enough is enough! Can't you just tell them where to stick it?"

"I tried that already, remember? Besides, if I did that now, they would **NOT** be so forgiving and we'd be in litigation for the next twenty years. It's easier to just go on and finish my contractual obligations. They know I'm retiring, but they're gonna get every last nickel they can out of me before I walk away."

"And just how long are we talking about?"

"Three more months, Mac -just three more little ol' months."

"I'm not one bit happy about your being on the road for three more months, Sam," I frowned. "However, you're right and I guess it is better to put a period on this. But NO more after this."

"I knew you'd see it that way," she said. "Running away before was a foolish, childishly rebellious act that only prolonged the inevitable. It's time to grow up now and do it right."

There wasn't much to say after that, so I told her I loved her and would be counting the days again, until she came home. After we hung up, I sat there at Hank's desk for a long time. I hated being so damned helpless in this situation. With Sam having to fly all over the country now, I was in limbo and made the decision to go down to the crossroads. I'd open the bar and stay there until time to come back here.

At least that would take my mind off this.

CHAPTER ONE HUNDRED TWENTY-SIX

I told Hank about Sam at supper that night. He wasn't happy about it either. "Where're they sending her?" he asked.

"Further west. Arizona an' then Lake Tahoe."

He frowned. "Ah don't like it. This is th' worst part'a winter to be flyin' over them mountains."

I took a bite of meatloaf and shrugged. "We just have to get through th' next three more months and then we have the rest of our lives together. Meantime, I'm going to take this time to go down to the crossroads an' see Doc an' Harley." Reaching for another piece of cornbread, Hank said, "Good idea -how long you plannin' on stayin'?"

"I guess I'll stay 'til time for Sam to get back. I have my truck there, so all I need is a way to get down there."

"That ain't a problem –Ah'll have Jerry'll take you whenever you're ready. When do ya think ya wanna leave?"

"How 'bout tomorrow?"

"That soon, huh? Okay, but what about Matt -you gonna take him?"

"I thought it'd be best for him if I leave him here where he'll be taken good care of."

"Ah think that's a good idea."

"Okay then -guess I'll go pack after supper."

*****

The next day it was snowing and I waited with great anticipation for Jerry to pick me up on the front porch. When he pulled up, I ran down the steps with my bags. After giving him my things, I went around to get in - and there sat Hank and Noreen.

"Hey, what're you two doing in here?" I asked.

"Hurry up an' get in, its cold out there," Hank said. I climbed in and Jerry closed the door. "What made you decide to come along?"

"Me an' Noreen thought we'd ride down with ya. 'Sides, ain't you glad to have our company?"

I sat back against the seat. "Yeah," I smiled, "I guess I am at that."

I don't know what Hank and Noreen did for the rest of the trip, but somewhere around Dallas I fell asleep and slept until around midnight, when I felt the car slow down. I rubbed my eyes and sat up to look out my window. We were here. The town looked even more ghostly in the pale moonlight, as the winter wind blew a pair of tumbleweeds aimlessly down the deserted street. The saloon was closed. Dark uninviting shadows from the overhang added to its eeriness, but it was still a sight for sore eyes.

Jerry drove around back, stopping just outside my trailer. Everyone got out and stretched while I ran up the steps and unlocked the door. It was like a tomb inside –and it felt like I'd been away for twenty years. I turned on all the lights in the living room and I could almost hear the room wake up. I took off my coat and hung it up as Jerry came in with Hank and Noreen. He set our bags down on the floor while Hank took off his coat and helped Noreen with hers. He hung the coats in the closet then came out in the living room flapping his arms to get warm.

"Brrr, it's freezing in here –crank up th' heat! It ain't snowing down here, but it's still cold as mah Aunt Emma's manners."

Jerry wanted to know if there was anything else we'd like him to do.

"No, that should do it, Jer," Hank said. "Just come back tomorrow sometime between noon and three –an' have th' dust washed off th' limo if ya can find some place to do it. You need any money?"

"No Mr. Fairfield, I'm fine."

"Where are you going, if you don't mind mah asking?" Hank said.

"I stay in a nice motel I know of about thirty miles from here." Then he said good night and left us to wonder where the hell there was a "nice motel" anywhere around here.

"Okay," Hank said, rubbing his hands together, "now that we're here - where's th' bourbon?"

I pointed to the cabinet in the kitchen and he said, "Ah'm ready for a drink –anybody else ready?"

I arched my aching back and let out a long tired sigh. "Count me in –and make it a double."

Noreen said, "Me, too." While Hank got our drinks, I went back to the bedroom. I threw the quilt back, thinking, "The last time I slept in this bed –I was single."

I changed the sheets -completely forgetting I'd done that just before we left for Houston, and then went into the bathroom to put fresh towels by the sink. When I was satisfied everything was in order, I went back into the living room, where Hank handed me my drink. I took it over to a chair across form the couch. "You and Noreen take th' bedroom," I said, sitting down. "I'll sleep over there on th' sofa."

"Suites me," he said, sitting down next to Noreen.

"I guess nobody's been in here since I left," I said, running a finger across the top of the table next to my chair. "Must'a had a dust storm or two since I been gone."

I wondered if we had anything to eat and asked if anyone else was hungry? Hank looked at me and frowned. "Ah *hope* you're talkin' 'bout peanut butter an' crackers an' didn't leave nothin' in the fridge." A light went on and I made a beeline to the refrigerator. "SON-OF-A-" I cried.

One hour and two garbage bags later, I took all the rotted, liquefied, food outside to be burned the next day. I found two unopened boxes of baking soda and used one in warm water to clean the inside of the fridge – which took another forty-five minutes.

It was going on three-thirty in the morning when I finally left the kitchen. I threw a sheet, pillow, and blanket on the sofa and barely remember mumbling good night, as I turned out the light and pulled the blanket up over my head.

CHAPTER ONE HUNDRED TWENTY-SEVEN

I woke around ten thirty to the smell of coffee. It took me a moment to get my bearings and remember where I was. As I sat there scratching my head, I saw Noreen moving around in the kitchen. I threw back the blanket and headed in that direction. "Hey, Noreen," I yawned. "What's up –is that coffee ready?" She nodded, poured me a mug and handed it to me.

I said, "Thanks, an' will you put the rest of the baking soda in the refrigerator and close it up after turning it on again?"

"I already did," she said.

I looked over at the fridge. "No kiddin'? Well, thank you -how does it smell?"

"I think its gonna be okay."

"That's good, 'cause I'd hate to have to buy a new one." Hank came in the front door just as I sat down on the sofa with my coffee. "Mornin', Mac," he said cheerfully.

God, you're up early –where've you been?"

"Jest out lookin' 'round. You got th' key to th' bar? Ah'll go open it for ya."

"Over there on the table by th' front door," I said. "I'll get dressed and meet you inside."

He nodded and took the key with him as he went out. I finished my coffee and got dressed, anxious to see how things looked. With butterflies of anticipation in my stomach, I went in the back door and closing my eyes, inhaled the smell of stale beer and cigarettes.

"Won-der-ful," I smiled, taking two or three more breaths.

Hank was behind the bar. "Everything is absolutely spotless an' in apple pie order," he said. "Legrand has taken *great* care of th' place."

I pulled up a stool and sat down. "That doesn't surprise me a bit," I said.

"Ya know," Hank said, "Ah think we should go over an' see him." "Let's go," I smiled, slapping the top of the bar and sliding off the stool. We crossed the street to Legrand's store and the little bell rang over the door when we opened it and went inside. From somewhere in the back, Legrand yelled, "Be with ya in just a minute!" We waited patiently for a minute or so and he came out wiping his hands on a rag. "Sorry to take so lon-"

He stopped in mid-sentence and his jaw dropped. "MAC! HANK! Is it *really* you?"

We nodded and grinned. He hurried over to us and grabbed me by the shoulders. "W-What're you –when -?"

"Got in late last night," I laughed, shaking his hand. "Me, Hank and Noreen decided to just come on down an' see you."

"Where's Sam and Matt?"

"That's why I came down, "I said. "They got her out on th' road for three more months."

"Man, that sucks," he said and I agreed. Then he asked, "You been in th' bar, yet?"

"We just came from there –man, it looks great! You did a terrific job takin' care of it for me."

"Thanks," he said. "I actually enjoyed it."

"It does get under your skin, doesn't it?"

"Listen, not that I want you to hurry back to Dallas, but how long are you plannin' on stayin'?"

"Indefinitely, I guess. I need something to do until Sam comes back."

"So, you'll be runnin' th' saloon?"

"Yeah, I thought I'd give you a break from smoky air and dishpan hands."

"Are you kiddin'?" he said. "I'll miss them dishpan hands. Shoot, I'll have to come over an' help out just to keep 'em all pruny."

"Then let's just go ahead an' make it offical –you are now the head dishwasher of the Long Branch Saloon."

"When did you name it?" Hank asked.

"Just now..."

Legrand reached into his back pocket and took out a bankbook. "Wanna see how much you made since you been away?" I put my hand over his and said, "No, Legrand, I told you to keep whatever the bar did, so don't show me. I don't care. You earned it!"

"Okay," he sighed. "But it don't feel right. I only did what any friend would do –and friends don't get paid for their friendship."

"Yeah they do when they earn it. Fair is fair –*especially* between friends. You don't take a harvest you didn't plant." Legrand thought about that for a minute, then stuck the bankbook back in his hip pocket. "I guess that's one way of lookin' at it –if I knew what th' devil you just said."

I asked if he'd seen Doc or Harley.

"Sure, I see 'em both two or three times a week. They drop by to say hi an' have a drink. I think they miss seein' you behind th' bar, though."

"I'm gonna surprise 'em tonight –that is, if they come by."

"What's today –Wednesday? They might come in if they see th' saloon's open, but they mostly don't come by until Friday night."

"Is my band still comin' in?"

Legrand nodded. "Every weekend reg'lar as clockwork."

"Hey," Hank piped in, " it's lunchtime –how 'bout we go over to th' diner an' get somethin' to eat?"

"You buyin?" Legrand asked.

"Yep –anything your li'l ol' heart desires," he grinned.

"In that case, forget th' diner –let's go for a steak up in Houston."

CHAPTER ONE HUNDRED TWENTY-EIGHT

I opened the bar that night, but neither Harley nor Doc came by. Word hadn't spread that I was back in town yet and with me away for so long, nobody else came in either. I closed up around eight and went back to the trailer. When Jerry showed up at two-fifteen, Hank sent him to find a store and buy some groceries. There was a frozen pizza in the fridge and I asked

Hank if they wanted anything to eat while I was cooking. He said they'd both eaten something earlier, so I threw the pizza in the oven. While I ate, Hank asked me if I'd seen Doc or Harley and I told him I didn't see anybody. "Not ONE *soul* came in tonight." I finished eating and took what was left of my coke in the living room. Hank had a bourbon and asked if I wanted one. When I shook my head, he sat down on the sofa next to Noreen and turned on the television. I took the chair and wiped the dust away from the end table with my hand. Hank flipped channels until he found a good psycho-thriller. It was a real scary nail-biter and we were right in the middle of it when the phone rang, and we nearly came out of our skins. I jumped up and ran to answer it.

"Hello?" I said, and heard Sam's voice.

"Hi! You tryin' to get away from me?"

"Huh? Of course not –why?"

"I called the house an' Juan told me you'd gone down to th' crossroads. What's up?"

"Oh, that," I smiled. "No, I'm not tryin' to get away from you, it's just that when you told me you'd have to stay gone for another three months, I figured I'd come on down an' see everybody –as well as run th' bar to help keep my mind off things. It was a "spur of the moment" decision.

"I forgot to ask Juan –is Hank with you?"

"Yeah, him and Noreen."

"What about Matt?"

"No, I thought it best to leave him up there with Mama and Juan."

"Good -that was the best thing to do," she said, and then she asked how everybody was. I told her I'd only seen Legrand, but he asked about her and sent his love.

"How long are you plannin' on staying down there?"

"Right up 'til time for you to come home," I said. "But Hank and Noreen will probably go back in a day or two. Where are you calling from right now?" I asked.

"Tonight, I'm in Tucson, but I leave for Lake Tahoe tomorrow morning."

"Is it snowing in Tahoe?"

"Like a son-of-a-gun. Eight inches I think, with more expected"

"It was snowing when we left Dallas," I said. "And it's damned cold here."

"There's a Canadian front that's dumping more snow than usual all over the north and Midwest."

"Good for skiing," I said, with tears welling up in my eyes. Hearing her voice brought a pain and longing for her that nothing but holding her would heal. "I-I miss you Sam..."

"I...know," she said softly. "But when this is all over, it'll be worth the wait. Just think, other married couples would be tired of each other by now."

I whispered. "I'll never get tired of us," -and it was all I could do to say goodbye.

Hank came over to me. "You okay?"

I let go of the phone and nodded. "More or less," I sighed.

"Where is she?"

"Tucson –Lake Tahoe tomorrow."

"She say how th' weather is?"

"Yeah, It's eight inches in Tahoe with more expected."

Hank rubbed his chin and frowned. "Ah don't like it..." was all he said.

CHAPTER ONE HUNDRED TWENTY-NINE

The next night was a carbon copy of the night before. No one stopped by except Legrand –and he only had one beer before heading home. Looking around the deserted bar, he said, "Tomorrow is Friday. Your band will be here an' once they spread th' word that you're back, everybody'll be in."

"Yeah," I shrugged. "But meantime, it's just me an' th' spiders -an' it's boring as hell."

Legand picked up his beer. "Ahh, don't worry about it –things'll pick up quick." He finished his drink and waved good night. I stayed open for another hour and then called it a night.

After locking up and shutting off the lights, I went back to the trailer. Hank and Noreen were sitting in the living room with their bags packed. "What's this?" I frowned.

"We're going back tomorrow."

"WHY?"

"Ah need to git back," he said. "Ah wanna talk to Sid to find out why Sam's having to fly all over th' damned country," he frowned.

"But...I thought he didn't have anything to do with it –it was the record company."

"It is, but Sid makes all her travel arrangements an' Ah think he knows exactly what's going on - he just don't always let ya know."

I was pissed at all this deception. I went into the kitchen and grabbing the bourbon out of the cabinet, took out a glass and poured three fingers in it, tossed it down and stood there next to the counter with my eyes closed. Then I turned around to face Hank. "I feel like a man who is terminally ill and NO one is telling him the straight truth about how long he has."

I pushed away from the counter and went into the living room. "Maybe I don't understand all the "ins an' outs" of this business, but it seems to me, its got as much lying going on as a political campaign."

"It does," Hank acknowledged. "An' it's simple really –everything is about money."

"What does that mean, exactly?"

"It means there are some pretty shady underhanded deals still being made with th' devil. Ah haven't quite figured them all out yet –but this is one'a them." I closed my eyes again and rubbed my forehead. "Let me know what you find out," I sighed.

They left the following day around noon. I hated like hell to see them go -now I was really alone. The only bright spot on this bleak horizon was that it was Friday and maybe I'd see Doc and Harley. I tried to pass the rest of the day by doing a little dusting and changing the sheets, but that only managed to kill forty-five minutes. I fixed something to eat -and by three-thirty, I couldn't stand it any longer and opened the bar. I fed quarters in the jukebox, swept the dance floor, wiped off the tables and washed all the glasses. Before I knew it, it was dark outside and my band came in, happy to see me behind the bar.

"MAC, dude! When did you get back, man?" They came over and sat down. "Tell us how you been!"

"I been okay -just missed th' bar an' y'all."

"We gotta bunch'a new tunes, Mac, an' you're gonna be real surprised at how good we've got."

We talked about ten minutes before they went up on stage. I smiled and waved, as two cowboys came up and sat down at the bar. "Mac, what a nice surprise -when did you get back, buddy?"

The next two hours were spent answering that same question over and over again. They kept coming in, packing the place like old times and even though I stayed too busy to watch the time, I kept an eye out for Doc and Harley. Every time the door opened, I'd look up. When ten thirty rolled around, I was ready to ask one of the guys if they knew where they were when the door opened and they walked in.

They didn't see me right away, but when they did, they stopped and stared like they'd seen a ghost. Neither said a word, just looked at each other. Finally, they came over the bar where I was grinning like a fool. "Mac," Harley smiled. "Man –is it really you?" I nodded and Doc said, "It is so good to see you, Mac –when did you get in?"

I got them their usual drinks and brought them up to date.

Doc asked, "How long are you staying?"

"Until th' end of February or whenever Sam gets back."

"You *have* to come to dinner, Sunday," Doc said. "You and Harley. I'll fix a good New England roast with boiled potatoes and carrots."

"My mouth is watering already," I said. "Tell me what time an' I'll be there."

I refilled their glasses and we reminisced about everything from Noreen's past escapades to the times we went fishing up on Clear Mountain Lake. I was ready to pour them another drink when Doc shook his head, saying he had to get on home.

"But it's still early," I said.

He stood up. "I seem to tire more easily these days than I used to, Mac," he smiled, "but I'll see you at five on Sunday."

After he left, Harley said, "He hasn't been himself, lately."

"No? What's th' problem?"

"I don't know. He's just not as peppy as usual -an' he talks a lot about Anna."

"But Anna was the love of his life, don't you think he just misses her? Its Christmas and everyone misses their loved ones at this time."

"I don't know what it is. Anna's been gone for years an' he's never talked this much about her before -or in this way. It's like she's..." Harley shook his head. "I can't describe it."

"Well, I'm no spring chicken, but seems to me, th' older you get, th' more you don't like being alone. Life just doesn't hold much for us when we don't have our mate." Looking down at his glass, Harley slowly rotated it in his fingers. "Yeah," he said softly. "I know..."

Shit -I knew he was thinking about his wife and didn't know what to say.

Finally I said, "Hey –enough of this! How 'about another round?"

I picked up the Jack Daniels and started to pour, but Harley waved me off. "No more for me tonight," he said, picking up his old Stetson from the bar. Before I had time to recover from my surprise, he stood up and put it on. "I'll be back in tomorrow," he waved, leaving me standing there with the bottle of Jack, wondering what the hell had just happened.

Something had changed since I'd been gone. I felt it today after Hank left. I thought it was just me being antsy, but now, I wasn't sure. There was an imperceptible shift in everything.

It wasn't "just us" anymore.

Could it *be* that Sam and Matt's now being in the picture had...altered things?

I set the bottle of Jack Daniels back on the shelf and prayed this feeling of things being "out of kilter," was just a fleeting unpleasantness of my imagination. My band took a break and came over to the bar all sweaty and grinning like Cheshire cats. "How'd you like th' new songs, Mac?"

Of course I hadn't noticed, but I said, "Great, guys. You've really improved since I last heard you." I hoped that would be the end of it, but the compliment pleased them to no end and they went on with the questions. "Thanks, Mac -how'd you like th' ones by Credence an' Bob Seeger?" Before I could think of anything to say, the guitar player said, "Old Time Rock and Roll" is one'a our favorites, along with "Bad Moon Risin'" and "Fortunate Son" –but it ain't easy tryin' to get it to sound as good as John Fogerty. He's one'a th' best guitar players in rock an' roll...along with Stevie Vie."

"An' Eddie Van Halen," the bass player added.

"Hey –wait a minute!" the drummer piped in. "What about Jimi Hendrix?"

"Yeah –an' Gregg Alman?"(sp?)

Now I was really lost on top of feeling bad for lying and tried to worm myself free of this nightmare by saying, "Okay, guys, let me buy y'all a beer."

I left them to their beers and discussion on all the greats of rock an' roll, while I went down the bar to see if anyone else needed a refill. After refilling several mugs, I went back to the sink and started washing glasses. But the earlier feeling of things being out of sync just wouldn't go away. I tried to find the root of the problem, but knew there was no sense fighting what I didn't understand and gave up trying.

CHAPTER ONE HUNDRED THIRTY

Sam was standing in the wings waiting to go on stage. The bastards had once again re-routed her to some out-of-the-way town <u>not</u> on her travel schedule. She wasn't sure what town this was, but the small auditorium was packed. They weren't there solely to see her -there were other stars on the bill too. She counted six other acts on the program, but only one she knew –and he was from Stephenville, Texas. There were so many new artists coming into country that she couldn't keep up with them.

Sam patiently waited to go on and tried not to think of how much she missed Mac and home, but it was these in between times that it sneaked up on her. Absently fingering the cross Mac gave her for Christmas, she was lost in thought when someone nudged her on the shoulder. "Miss Evans...they're announcing you. You're on." Thanking the stagehand, she turned on the smile and started towards the stage. Just as she coming from behind the curtain, her shoe caught in a coiled cable she didn't see and her heel broke. She grabbed the curtain for support and swore under her breath. "Damn!" What to do now? She didn't have another pair of heels with her and there certainly was no time to find a quick fix for this pair. The emcee announced her again and looked towards the wings with a confusing frown. Seeing that there was a problem, he turned back to the spotlight and smiled broadly.

"Uh, ladies and gentlemen...Miss Evans is on her way, so just bear with me a few more seconds."

Sam heard the low rumble of whispers and groans spreading throughout the audience and knew there was only ONE thing to do. Taking off both shoes, she threw them over her shoulder and walked out on stage barefooted. Sam was a firm believer in telling the audience the truth whenever possible -and if the truth was boring then at least make it an interesting white lie.

The bright spotlight followed Sam as she walked across the stage, remembering a long ago incident where she'd been caught off guard like this down in Florida. An agent she didn't know, called one day to ask if she would take a booking in Ft. Lauderdale. It only paid scale, but it was the beginning of her career and she'd never been to Florida before -so she agreed. The agent said a ticket would be waiting at the airport and after giving her the flight number, he told her the time and address of the show. Before hanging up, he said a limo would meet her and take her to the club. Unfortunately, he failed to mention what kind of club it was or what kind of audience she'd have.

Figuring everyone knew she was a country/western singer, she threw a few things into a bag and left for the airport. Sure enough, a limo was waiting when the plane landed and when it let her off at the club that night, she changed into a new pair of jeans and a dark western shirt, opened just enough to revel a little cleavage. After one last look in the mirror she headed for the door, picking up her guitar on the way out. Making her way through the kitchen, she pushed the swinging doors open to what turned out to be a very large dining room packed with people sitting at tables. Nothing else -no stage, no curtain, no emcee - just a spotlight shining down on an open area where tables had been removed for a solitary stool in front of a microphone. But Sam had sung on the back of flatbed trucks, boxes and whatever else they had, so this didn't bother her. She confidently walked out into the spotlight and was about to sit down on the stool, when a loud gasp went through the audience. Thinking maybe she was trailing a long piece of toilet paper behind her, she quickly looked down at her shoes - then remembered she hadn't been in the restrooms. She looked out at the audience, barely making out the first row –and what she saw was enough to make her want to crawl off the "stage."

No one had bothered to clue her in to the fact that this was a very rich up-scale country club and the dress code was extremely formal. Ladies in gorgeous designer gowns, dripping in diamonds, sat next to men wearing tuxedos with black ties and three hundred dollar haircuts. Compared to them, Sam looked like she'd come in the back door and lost her way coming through the kitchen. It was **dead** quiet and Sam felt the icy cold stares. Knowing she couldn't lose control of the situation, she calmly sat down, adjusted the microphone and smiled sweetly at the audience. "Good evening, ladies and gentlemen. Well! It is an honor to be here...and I apologize for my unorthodox appearance, but when I received the call to come do this show, I was in Texas and had to catch the first flight out to get here in time."

Nothing. No one moved...(–well, one lady *did* raise a disapproving eyebrow.) Undeterred, Sam went on, "I made it here in time, but...my luggage didn't and I had to borrow something from my sibling, who lives here. Unfortunately, it's a brother." Of course it was a lie; she had no family living in Florida, but it did the job and to Sam's relief, laughter spread throughout the room. The rest of her show was a relaxed success and she finished to two encores and a standing ovation. When she took her last bow and walked off, she thought, "I'll bet this is the first time *this* place ever gave a standing ovation to Levis."

Reaching center stage, Sam stood back from the mike and lifting the hem of her gown, wiggled her toes. "Sorry to take so long, but as you can see, I had a slight problem on the way out here -a rabid fan stole my shoes." The audience burst out laughing and clapping. Without waiting for the laughter to die down, Sam signaled the band to kick off with "Rocky Top," and she didn't let them come down until she closed with the song she wrote for Mac. After the show (and a six minute standing ovation,) she took the waiting limo back to her hotel, where she rode the elevator up to her suite, unlocked the door and went inside.

The suite was silent as a tomb, but it was always like this –lonely and empty. Sam totally understood why so many entertainers drank, took drugs, and/or slept around. You had to be on such a different plane to do a show. The loving adulation of the fans took you 'waaay up here, but when you walked off that stage and out the door –boom. Coming off heroin couldn't be worse. Running a tub of hot water, Sam undressed, lit a few candles, and put on a Bob Dylan tape. She got in and sinking down in the warm water, closed her eyes and let out a long tired sigh. As she relaxed, Sam let her mind drifted back to Ft. Lauderdale and another story involving that same agent -and Florida.

She received a phone call from him at the airport, just as she was about to board a plane back to Dallas. Figuring he'd get some more mileage out of her while she was still down there, the agent wanted her to do one more booking for him at one of the hotels on Miami Beach. After the Ft. Lauderdale fiasco, she didn't want to take it, but there was more money in this one and she only had to do one thirty-minute show. Feeling like a pushover, Sam reluctantly said she'd do it and picking up her bags, got back in the limo.

Naturally the hotel was <u>not</u> one of Miami Beach's finer establishments, but at least this time the agent did provided her with a small room that had a beautiful view -of the wall of the next hotel. The central air conditioning was going full blast, but saltwater corrosion is a major problem on the beach. This air conditioner was on its last leg and Sam felt the high humidity coming in with the air. Looking around the room, she wiped the perspiration from her forehead and sighed. Along with being underpaid, this was another thing entertainers had to put up with –crummy agents and crummier rooms. She threw her bags on the bed and got in the shower. The show wasn't until eight o'clock, so she had two and a half hours to rest up before she had to get dressed.

At seven forty-five, Sam took the elevator down one floor to the lobby and got off carrying her guitar case. She asked a bellboy where the showroom was and he pointed it out to her. She started walking towards it when halfway across the lobby a short, round, balding man intercepted her. He had a cigar in his mouth and took it out. "Are you Samantha Evans?" he asked.

"Yes, I am," she said. "How do you do, I'm Grant Wilson, the agent that booked you." Switching her guitar case to her left hand, she said, "Hello, I'm glad to meet you." His handshake was limp and sweaty, but she ignored it, asking, "Do you always come out to watch the acts you've booked?" He shook his head. "No, I don't, but I got to thinking about something and thought I'd better come down to find out." He stuck the cigar back in his mouth.

"I should've asked this earlier, but you *do,* do some Jewish songs, right? Sam looked confused. "Jewish songs…?"

"Yeah –you know, popular folk songs that Jews like." He took the cigar out of his mouth again. "I ask this because this audience is made up entirely of widowed women whose husbands have passed on. Most of them live here at the hotel. They have no grandchildren or other family nearby, so they got nothing to do all day, except play Mahjong, go to the Early Bird Special, and be in bed by ten o'clock."

"B-But *I'm* not Jewish. I'm a Texan -mostly Irish/Indian –I don't know any Jewish folk songs!"

"No kiddin'?" he said. "Well, I don't usually stick around for th' show, but I think I will tonight, 'cause you're gonna bomb –BIG time." Sam tightened her grip on the guitar case, as cold panic iced her veins. This was *worse* than Ft. Lauderdale. Just as she was about to tell him to forget the whole thing, a lovely lady came up to her and introduced herself. "Hello, dear, I'm Mrs. Rubinstein," she smiled sweetly, "and if you're ready, I'll take you inside."

Mrs. Rubinstein was obviously Jewish, but she was so kind it gave Sam hope that maybe the rest of the women were too. Sam and the agent followed her into the showroom, where even in the dark Sam could see every seat was filled. The seating in this room was tiered like a coliseum and she had to walk *down* to reach the stage. Taking her guitar out of its case, Sam made her way down the wide steps dividing the audience, glancing at a few faces. The agent was right –this audience *was* all women -and they looked bored as hell. Feeling like she'd just walked "The Last Mile," she climbed on the stool with great trepidation. In the back of the room, a trail of cigar smoke marked where the agent was pacing back and forth. Knowing he was just waiting for her to fall flat on her face, she looked out at all the woman. Not one of them looked happy.

"Oh lord," she thought. "I could'a been on a nice comfortable plane back to Dallas right now, but *nooooooooo*, I had to say yes to this nightmare."

The audience was getting restless and Sam knew it was time to sing something –*anything*! Swallowing the dryness in her throat, she decided to do the best she could under the circumstances. "Good evening, ladies," she began. "It's a pleasure to be here, tonight. My name is Samantha Evans. I'm a country and western singer from Dallas, Texas and -" loud groans of disapproval went through the audience and Sam wondered where to go next with this speech. She thought about telling them she had a Jewish housekeeper back in Texas –then thought better of it. Looking down at her guitar, she nonchalantly scratched her eyebrow while waiting for the groans to stop. When things quieted again, she said, "The agent that booked me here tonight, asked me just now, if I did any Jewish songs. I told him I didn't know a one –not even Hava Nagila." (sp.) More groans -and one "oy vay." So far this was not going well, but Sam plunged ahead. "However in all fairness, I'm Irish –and I don't do "Danny Boy" either.

Nothing.

Finally Sam had had enough. Her Irish was up and she decided to hell with it, she was just going to do the songs she knew and be done with this whole thing. So sitting up straight, she wrapped her fingers around the neck of her guitar and decided to open with 'Gentle On My Mind.'-but just as she was going to announce the song, out of nowhere a thought struck her and she said, "I'd like to open with "Gentile On My Mind." She thought it was lame, but for whatever reason, that broke the ice and the audience laughed. The rest of the show was a piece of cake and when she came off, the agent came up to her and said, "If I didn't see that with my own eyes, I would have never believed it. Not *one* Jewish song and the audience loved you!"

Sam couldn't believe it either, but she just wanted to get paid and back to Dallas. The agent paid her saying he wanted to book her again, but she shook her head and said, "I don't think so -from now on, I'm staying west of the Mississippi." And she left that night on the first fight she could get back to Dallas.

Such times, Sam smiled, wondering how she ever survived them.

The water was cooling off, so she turned on the hot water again and settled back in the tub. She thought of calling Mac, but it was three in the morning and she was exhausted. She'd call him tomorrow after she found out what city and state she was in.

CHAPTER ONE HUNDRED THIRTY-ONE

Harley came by at four o'clock Sunday to pick me up to go to dinner at Doc's.

Doc greeted them with mint juleps after they sat down in the living room, explaining that dinner wasn't quite ready. We sipped the dirinks and talked. Sitting in the old flowered slip covered chair with its green piping, felt like being home again. I enjoyed the hell out of the three of us being together, but somewhere between arriving and leaving, Mac noticed everything they talked about was in the past tense. Doc would ask Harley if "he remembered the time..." and relate a story that happened in the past.

When dinner was ready, Doc got up and went in the kitchen. He brought out the roast and put it on the table, then asked them to come in and sat down. Doc had prepared a wonderful roast, with peas, carrots, and boiled potatoes. For desert, he served coffee and Boston crème pie. After they finished eating, Doc asked if anyone would like some sherry. Mac and Harley looked at each other. "Uh, none for me," Harley said, and Mac laughed. "I think Harley an' me have to draw the line on sherry."

"Of course," Doc smiled. "How about some bourbon, then?"

"Honest, Doc, I couldn't get another thing in my stomach."

"Me neither," Harley agreed. "'Sides, I gotta get up early in th' morning for a round-up, so I really should be going."

"Well," I sighed, "since I'm ridin' with Harley, I guess that means I'd better say good night, too."

"I totally understand," Doc said. "It's about my bedtime, too, so thank you for coming tonight –it was great being together again."

"Yes, it was," I said, "and thanks for one of th' best meals I've had in years."

We said goodnight and climbed in Harley's truck. On the way back, I said, "Harley, you notice anything unusual about tonight?"

"Mmmm, not really -in what way?"

"I don't know," I frowned. "But everything we talked about with Doc was stuff that has happened in the past –like there's nothin' comin' in th' future for us to look forward to."

Harley thought about it for a moment, then he said, "Doc is getting old an' with you up in Dallas now, it doesn't leave much for him to look forward to."

"But, he's got you..."

"It ain't th' same -I'm working at th' ranch an' can only spend just so much time with him. I do th' best I can, but when you were here, you filled in the other third. Now with you gone, there's a gap and two-thirds just don't fill it."

"I never looked at it that way...but I suppose you're right." "There's something else," Harley said, "I've noticed them same things you have, along with some you haven't."

"Like what?"

"Since you been gone, we sit around on Sunday an' talk about whatever comes to mind. One Sunday, he brings up a calf he had to deliver. It was a breech and he did everything humanly possible to save the calf, but both it and th' mother died. Things like that happen –it's the rule of nature, but Doc took it hard –something he never does, an' I ain't sure he's over it yet."

"What makes you say that?"

"Because," Harley said, "while he he was tellin' me about it, he got this faraway look like he was seeing something only he could see, and he said, "We think of Death as a bad thing - but lately, I've been thinking of Death as a friend...a friend that releases you from all the tiresome agony of living-" and he said it like he was thinking out loud an' didn't even remember I was there."

"Shit –what did you say?" I needed to know what he meant by that statement and asked him. He just looked at me and said, "What statement?"

They rode the rest of the way home without saying another word. When Harley pulled up to his trailer, Mac got out and said, "Thanks, Harley, see you tomorrow." Mac went up the steps, unlocked the door and pushed it open with the same feeling he'd been having all week. Tonight should have reaffirmed everything was still the same, but it had only reaffirmed that things *had* changed and he *didn't* belong here anymore.

CHAPTER ONE HUNDRED THIRTY-TWO

Mac spent the rest of the week going through the motions at the bar, but by the following Sunday he had to admit that he wanted to go back to Dallas. He had opened the bar on Monday firmly resolved to giving things time to feel like home again, but by Thursday, his resolve had dissolved into leaving as soon as possible. When Harley came in around seven on Friday night and Mac told him of his decision, Harley didn't seem surprised. "I kind'a thought you'd be goin' back soon."

"I just miss Matt and...oh hell, I don't know what's wrong with me," Mac frowned, pushing a strand of thinning hair off his forehead.

"I understand what's wrong, Mac," Harley said.

"Well, puh-leeze explain it to me!"

Harley said matter-of-factly, "You've started down a new road, Mac. It's the old "one door closes an' another one opens." Nothing stands still or stays th' same." He ran his hand through his hair. "If things stayed th' same, we'd still be listening to 50's music and tryin' to get a date with th' prom queen."

"So...you're saying I *should* go back to Dallas?"

"Yep -that's where your life is now. It's where you belong."

"*Belong.*" How odd that he should choose that exact word.

"But what about this place –an' you an' Doc?"

"We'll go on. Look, things had to change eventually, Mac. My life will always be in th' saddle on th' back of a horse, Doc's will always be takin' care'a animals, but your life is in Dallas with Sam -and you gotta follow it now -I would."

Crossing my arms, I leaned back against the cooler –and much as I hated it, the pieces were falling in place. "What you just said makes a lotta sense, Harley. I DO have a different life now, but I'm not sure I'm ready to let go of this one, yet."

"Then you're just prolonging things an' nothing can move either way."

"So what do I do, Harley? I don't want a life without you and Doc in it."

"You do what you're supposed to do, Mac –th' rest will take care of itself."

"One day at a time, eh?"

"That's all ya got to work with," he said.

CHAPTER ONE HUNDRED THIRTY-THREE

That night, I called Hank to tell him I was coming home. He asked if I needed Jerry to come get me and I said no, I'd drive my truck back -I had a lot of thinking to do. I hadn't taken Harley's advice because I *didn't* know what to do, but because I *did* know what to do! He just put it out there and the words made it real.

Hoping to get an early start in the morning, I hit the hay early, but after two hours of tossing and turning I got up, closed up the trailer and threw my bags in the truck.

It was three thirty in the morning. The town was quieter than usual with everybody home, asleep. I pulled around front and drove slowly down Main Street. I knew this would be the last time I'd see this town that had been my salvation and wanted to take my time. I also knew seeing Doc tonight, would be the last time I'd see him. This sudden awareness was painful and I was grateful no one was around to interrupt the prophecy. Three tumbleweeds rolled past me as I pulled up in front of Legrand's store. I took out a piece of paper and wrote him a note, then got out and slipped it under his door. It was a short goodbye with no explanation, because none was needed. I finally realized that I was the only one here who didn't know I belonged in Dallas -they had just been kind enough to wait until I discovered it for myself. Pulling my collar up against the wind, I got in and turning the truck around, headed towards the crossroads for the last time.

With a burning lump in my throat, I passed the saloon and turned north without looking back.

CHAPTER ONE HUNDRED THIRTY-FOUR

The drive back to Dallas gave me the time I needed to clear my head and get my priorities straight. I knew now, that I was finished at the crossroads. Harley had been right; to stay would retard any forward movement in my life, and I owed my full attention to Sam and Matt.

By the time I saw the ranch, I was my old self again. I had no doubts as to where I belonged.

This was home.

The front door opened and Hank came out with Matt. "Look, boy -it's your pa!"

I ran up the steps two at a time and he handed me my son. "Whoa!" I cried. "You've grown since I was gone!"

"C'mon," he said, "let's get inside, it's freezing out here."

We passed a warm fire in the living room on the way into the kitchen. Noreen was doing something with Juan and Mama and turned around when we came in.

"MAC!" she cried. "You're back!" and Mama said the same thing in Spanish –I think.

Noreen hugged me, as I gave Matt to Juan. "Do you want somethin' to eat?" she asked.

"No thanks -right now, I need to talk to Hank."

Hank and I went into the living room and sat down on the couch. "What's up, buddy?"

Without wasting any time, I went right into it. "I've made up my mind to sell th' saloon," I said.

"*Reeeaally*," Hank said, skeptically. "Have you thought this out?"

" I have," I nodded. "But I don't want just anybody to have it -not that they would with it being where it is, but I thought you'd be able to give me some advice."

Hank sat back and thought about it. Finally, he said, "Ah told you when Ah first met you, that if you ever wanted to sell it, Ah'd buy it – Ah wasn't foolin' an' that still goes."

"I was hopin' you'd say that."

"Just tell me how much ya want for it, an' we'll settle it here an' now."

"I'll sell it to you for exactly what I paid for it –one dollar."

"Put 'er there, ponder," he grinned, "an' put the dollar on mah account."

We shook hands and the last weight fell off my shoulders. "Now that you're the proud new owner, what do you plan to do with her?"

Hank grinned again and said, "Ah HAH! *That's* th' best part of all –Ah'm gonna do just what Ah had in mind when Ah first saw th' place –Ah'm gonna turn it into a saloon."

"B-But...it already is a saloon."

"True...but now it's gonna be **THE** saloon for entertainers. Ah'm gonna keep it jest like you had it, only Ah'm gonna book Willie, Kris, Jerry Jeff, an' a whole slew of people in there. Kind'a make it a Tex-Mex version of Nashville."

"Even Barbara Mandrell...?" I smiled.

"If she'll come," he said.

"And what about my band? I mean you can't just kick them out."

"Heck, Ah ain't gonna kick 'em out," he said. "They'll be mah house band an' open for th' entertainers. 'Course, they gotta learn a few more chords and how to play in a couple'a different keys. Not *everybody* sings in th' key of 'C'...almost...but not everybody."

"Now, I *know* I've made th' right decision -that was the last piece that needed to fall into place."

Juan came out of the kitchen just then and said, "Senior Hank –la telepohono."

"Thanks, Juan. Hang it up in there -Ah'll take it out here." Hank got up and picking up the phone on his desk, spoke briefly to whoever was on the line, then hung up and came back to me. "That was th' sheriff," he said. "Wanted to know if Ah still wanted to press charges on them pinheads that showed up here Christmas. He said all they could git 'em on is trespassing..."

"What about th' gun?" I frowned.

"Frank checked on that an' it came back clean. Only thing he could get 'em on is carryin' an unlicensed concealed weapon. So," he shrugged, "Ah told Frank Ah wasn't gonna press charges an' to jest let 'em go. Th' trespassin' charge is minor –an' th' gun charge won't stick, so-"

"But what about the attempted murder –on *me*?"

"That's a possibility. If Jerry hadn't been there, then it would just be your word against th' idiot that had th' gun, but since he *was* there, he could testify to the incident an' then we'd have to wait for a Grand Jury to say."

"Okaaaay...then why aren't we doing that?"

Hank shrugged. "We could, but it would be an endless mess if th' Grand Jury decided to indict. It'd drag on an' on -we'd be in court forever. Let somebody else go after him."

"That is just plain stupid, Hank! What if he kills somebody next time?"

Hank rubbed his chin thoughtfully. "Yer right," he said, getting up. "Ah'll call Frank back."

I grabbed his hand. "No, wait...don't do that," I frowned.

"What's wrong –you havin' second thoughts?" I rubbed my aching forehead. "Yeah –I guess I don't need to be involved in a court case for the next ten years," I sighed. "But I really *do* want to do something about this guy."

Hank sat down again. "I admire where you're comin' from, Mac, but it's a tremendous –and thankless responsibility to go after somebody, today. He may belong to a gang or he might just be your everyday psycho, but whatever he is, you gotta choose to put the rest of your life at risk or let it go. It ain't like the old west, where justice was quick."

"Yeah," I frowned, "sometimes a little *too* quick."

He looked at me. "And besides, he knows where you live."

That did it. "Shit! Shit! *Shit!*" I cried. "I can't put everybody in his crosshairs! If it was just me I'd burn the son-of-a-bitch, but you're right about justice today. This country just ain't what it used to be," I frowned.

That night, I didn't sleep a wink. My decision to let the thing drop didn't sit well and I thought about it all night. I tried to rationalize it away, but deep down I knew this guy was a menace and could possibly kill somebody one day, if he wasn't stopped. By morning, I'd made up my mind to do something. Hank had gone into Dallas on business, so after breakfast, I gave the sheriff a call and explained how I didn't feel right not pressing charges.

"I've changed my mind about it," I said.

"Okay, that's fine, but th' way I understood it from Hank, y'all had talked it over an' decided not to," he said.

"No," I said. "We didn't discuss it until after he hung up talking to you. Hank's th' one that thought it best to drop all charges."

"Mr...I'm sorry, but I didn't catch your last name."

"McIntyre," I said. "Just call me, Mac."

"Fine, let me ask you something, Mac –do you know the difference between ignorance and indifference?"

"I don't know and I don't care?"

"That's it. And that's just how most folks feel about something like this, so I'm not surprised that Hank would want to drop it -what changed your mind?"

"Well, for one thing, there's nothing quite like having a .38 or whatever it was –pressed against your head and then having the guy pull the trigger. It's only by th' grace of God that I wasn't killed. I couldn't sleep last night knowing this guy is a nut and I don't want somebody else's death on my conscious."

There was a short silence on his end and then the sheriff said, "I understand."

"What do I do now –is it too late to go ahead on this thing?"

"Well, no," he sighed, "but I had to turn them all loose after talking to Hank and they been in the wind for almost 36 hours. They could be in Canada by now, for all I know."

"Do you think you can find them...?"

"All we can do is put out an A.P.B. and see what turns up. Might take a while though..."

"Whatever it takes -just do it."

I felt a whole lot better after we hung up -and *hoped* I wouldn't regret making the decision. Maybe it was John Wayne thinking, but I could not live the rest of my life knowing I gave up and rolled over for this prick.

CHAPTER ONE HUNDRED THIRTY-FIVE

"Ah stopped in for a cuppa coffee on my way back from Dallas," Hank said, "an' *guess* who Ah ran into?"

I didn't need to guess –I knew exactly who. "The sheriff," I sighed.

"Riiiight...an' imagine mah surprise when he told me he'd just hung up from talking to -you."

"I couldn't let it go, Hank."

"So, Ah see," he smiled. He came over to me and raised his hand. Thinking he was going to deck me, I flinched, but he patted my shoulder instead. "Ah respect a man with principle, an' has th' backbone to stand up for what he believes is right."

I looked at him warily. "You –sure?"

He nodded and I frowned. "I don't believe you -you're just sayin' that."

Hank smiled and dropped his head. "No, Ah ain't." He looked up. "But, Ah gotta warn ya that this is gonna take up a lotta your time when Frank finds that fella."

"I'm not going anywhere."

"Ah jest hope it don't come back to bite you in th' ass."

"Well, if it does, it's my ass."

Sam called that evening from Provo, Utah.

"What're you doing in Utah?" I said. "I thought you were supposed to go to Tahoe."

"I was, but a storm came in from the California side. They decided at the last minute to send me here, hoping to stay ahead of it. However, soon as I stepped off the plane, it hit us too. The show is cancelled tonight, but will probably go on tomorrow night –then it's on to Salt Lake –and backtrack to Tahoe."

The more she talked, the less I liked it. "Well, just call me as soon as you know what you're doing –and by the way, you sound tired."

"I'm so tired Mac, that I'm going to come down with a case of self-inflicted laryngitis if I don't pass out on stage first."

I said, "I don't like the way they're pushin' you, Sam."

"*YOU* don't like it?? I'm going to sleep the entire first two weeks I get home, so plan on pampering me with breakfast in bed."

"I'll spoil you rotten," I smiled.

The following day, I woke up to even blacker skies. I went to the window and pulled up the blinds. Misty grey/white snow clouds practically sat on the ground as snow flurries zigzagged crazily in the bitter cold wind. I yanked on a pair of pants and pulling a sweater over my head, hurried to the kitchen without shoes. Hank was sitting at the table having his coffee and reading the morning paper. I sat down and Mama brought me over a cup. I smiled and thanked her, then said, "Hank, I'm worried about this weather." He folded the paper and laid it down. "Yeah," he frowned. "So am I."

"I talked to Sam last night and she told me they sent her to Utah."

"Utah? Why Utah?"

"This bad weather hit the west coast, so they re-routed her to Provo. She goes to Salt Lake City next, *then* Tahoe."

Hank did not look happy. "It's fucking insane to keep her out there in this!" he growled. "Tahoe is 7,000 feet, an' th' wind between Utah and there *has* to be hurricane force. They should send her home an' cancel the rest of the tour, then pick it up again when the weather clears."

I nodded in agreement. "So, why don't they?"

"'Cause her record is still in the Top Ten. If they cancel her shows now, by th' time she goes back on th' road, it'll be off th' charts."

"I don't know how much more of this I can take," I said. "I'm worried sick and just want her *home*."

Hank pushed his chair away from the table and got up. "Ah'm gonna call Sid, right now!"

He went to the phone and dialed Sid's number. When he answered, Hank said, "Sid, this is Hank –what's up with Sam? They're keeping her out there in this weather an' extending her damned tour!" Hank listened a minute and then said, "You do that, Sid, and Ah mean, NOW!"

He hung up and came back to the table. Sitting down again, he said, "Sid's been tryin' to get the record execs to bring her in, but they keep givin' him th' runaround. He said he's going to call them again an' see what he can do."

Since there wasn't much else we could do, we went in the living room and sat down in front of the fire. Lost in thought, we watched the flames leap and crackle. Finally, he flipped on the television, stopping on a sitcom and we sat there staring at the tube like zombies. Halfway through the show, a bulletin came on.

"We interrupt this program to bring you a weather advisory," the announcer said. "Blizzards have moved down from Canada, blanketing the entire western part of the country in heavy snow. Hurricane force winds have been reported as far southeast as Albuquerque, New Mexico and whiteouts have traffic at a standstill along Interstate highways 40 and 80."

"Let's go now, to our sister station in Denver, Colorado, where Peter Quinn is standing by." The camera switched from the newsroom to an outside reporter wearing a fur lined snowsuit, holding a mike in one hand and his arm wrapped around a light pole with the other. Blinding snow blew straight across in horizontal lines and the wind howled so loud, you could hardly hear him.

"As you can see, Dick, the weather here is impossible," he shouted. "Advisories are in effect warning people to stay indoors and *off* the roads, until this clears. Highway patrols in five states have called in everyone on the force and cancelled all vacation leaves." Suddenly and unexpectedly, a trashcan blew past him, just missing his mid-section by inches. Rattled by the near mishap, he took a step back, losing his grip on the light pole. Grabbing the post just in time to keep from falling, he said, "Uh, back to you, Dick or Steve-?" and they switched to a weatherman standing in front of a map holding a long pointer in his hand.

"Good evening, I'm Steve Hurrell, your weatherman..." he said, "and as you can see, all of Washington State and Oregon are in a state of emergency. Multiple blizzards have knocked out power to over half a million homes. Hospitals have switched to emergency generators, while men are out trying to restore power as quickly as possible."

"Now, down to California," he said, moving his pointer. "A record snowfall has covered the entire northern U.S., plunging temperatures into minus degrees." He moved his pointer again. "And it has now moved into northern Nevada and Utah dumping record amounts of snow, but *is* expected to lose power by the time it reaches southern New Mexico. However, another front is right behind this one and is expected to bring even more snow by the weekend. Back to you, Dick." The camera shifted again to the first announcer still sitting behind a desk, holding a few papers in his hands. He glanced down and read:

"This just in. All flights have been cancelled indefinitely for the states mentioned at the beginning of this broadcast. Meantime, keep warm as possible. 911 emergency operators are standing by for emergencies *only!* This is a serious storm and not to taken lightly –so please –stay indoors." The program came back on and I looked at Hank. "Ah don't like this," he said. "This is th' worst winter we've had in fifty years..." he didn't finish his thought, but I knew what he was thinking.

CHAPTER ONE HUNDRED THIRTY-SIX

I went to bed early, but couldn't sleep. Around midnight, the wind picked up and raged like a banshee. I got up to look out the window. The trees were bent to their breaking point.

I left the blinds open and got back in bed. Propping my arm behind my head, I watched the trees whip back and forth certain Hank wasn't getting any sleep either. This was going to be a long night for both of us. I finally drifted off sometime before morning and was awakened by a loud banging noise. An outside shutter had pulled loose in the wind and was slamming against the side of the house. Throwing the blanket back, I got dressed and went into the kitchen. Hank came in a minute later, and we sat down at the table with our coffee. He asked me if I got any sleep. "Not much," I said. "How about you?"

"Same..."

After coffee, I went along with Hank to check on things in the barn. The wind whipped around us like a demon. When we reached the barn, Hank pulled on the door to get it open, but the wind blew it shut each time he got it halfway. He finally managed to get it open far enough for us to get inside, before the wind slammed it shut again. Rusty was at the other end of the barn and met us as we walked towards him.

"I'm glad you're here, Hank," he said. "Th' horses are spooked in all this wind."

"Yeah, we all are," he said.

Just then the barn doors opened again and in walked the bow-leggedist cowboy I ever saw. He must've weighed all of 120 pounds and was singing at the top of his lungs. "Yippie ki yi yay –yippie yay –yippie yay...git along little doggie...'cause a short one won't do..."

Who is *that*?" I asked.

"Oh, that's Whitman," Rusty smiled. "He's usually out on th' range with th' cattle, but he must'a come in for some reason." He waved, "Hey, Whitman –what brings you here?"

Whitman came up to us with a big carefree smile on his face. "Hi, Rusty, Hank – long time no see." Hank grinned and stuck out his hand. "Howdy, Whit, how ya doin?"

"Oh, can't complain –'cept for this bad weather. I could take th' snow, but all this wind is a bitch." He looked at me. "An' who's this?" he grinned.

Hank said, "This is mah new brother-in-law, Mac."

"Brother-in-law -no kiddin'? So you married Sam, huh?"

I nodded and he said, "Well, put 'er there, ponder. Welcome to th' family." As we shook hands, he asked, "Where is Sam, anyway?" Hank explained where she was and he looked amazed. "Man, do NOT tell me she's *out* in all this!" Hank nodded and Whit just frowned and shook his head. "Un-freaking-believable," he muttered.

"So, what's up, Whit –what brings you in?" Hank smiled.

"This damned wind, mostly. I need to take th' cattle over to th' east side of th' mountain to get 'em outta it. It's kickin' up dust so bad out there, I can't keep an eye on th' calves. Visibility is nill an' I already been smacked in th' face once by a buzzard blown off-course."

Hank laughed. "Okay, Whit –move 'em over there to th' east side."

Whit nodded. "I just wanted y'all to know where I was in case anybody came lookin'." He waved and went out singing. Rusty watched him and said, "Man, they broke th' mold when they made him"

"You got that right," Hank grinned. "Okay, what's up with th' horses?"

"Well, I've done everything I can. I tied the windows in their stalls down tight, but this wind still howls through the barn like an old freight train. It rattles th' doors when I close 'em and kicks up a dust storm if I leave 'em open." Rusty looked apprehensive. "If this lasts much longer, we might have to call out th' vet to give 'em something to calm 'em down."

"Okay, call the vet an' see what he says…"

We went back to the house where Mama had breakfast waiting. We sat down to eat and were almost finished when Rusty came in the back door. "I called th' vet," he said. "He should be here sometime in th' next half hour." Hank wiped his mouth and throwing his napkin down next to his plate, slid his chair back and got up. "Take care of it, okay, Rust? Ah gotta wait 'round here for a phone call either from Sam, Sid, or *somebody* tellin' me where she is."

"Sure Hank, an' I hope everything is all right with Sam."

"Yeah, oh, an'Rust, tell doc to just put whatever he has to do on mah bill, okay."

Rusty put on his Stetson and headed for the door. "Don't he always?" he grinned.

Sitting down again, Hank asked Mama for some more coffee and I asked Hank where he thought Sam was right now. He said he was trying not to think about it, but he'd call Sid if he didn't hear back from him first. I tried to find some comfort in that, but whatever I found wasn't much -and short lived. The thought of them sending Sam *anywhere* in this weather, was too much for me to wrap my head around.

By nightfall, the weather turned as bad at the ranch as everywhere else. Murphy's Law went into overtime. Phones were out, power was out – nothing got through. Some places were worse off than others, but the entire western half of the country was locked in some state of emergency. The worst part was not hearing from Sam. Wherever she was, the phones were out. By some miracle, our phone and electric were still on, but who knew for how long with the wind never letting up for a second. After two days of it hammering the house, I became nervous as a cat left alone with a roomful of pit bulls.

By day three, I was about to go out of my mind and asked Hank to call Sid and see if he'd heard anything. "Ah'll call him, but Ah'm sure Ah won't get through." He picked up the receiver, and dialed, and to his surprise, the phone rang -but went to his answering machine. Hank left a message to call back a.s.a.p. Another day went by with no word from either Sam-*or* Sid.

Hank was annoyed that he hadn't heard anything out of him and *I* was ready to get in my truck and drive up to Utah. "Where do you think Sid is in this weather?" I asked.

"That's just it –he wouldn't be out in it," Hank said. "If Sid had to be snowed in, he'd do it sitting behind his desk."

That night, I went to bed dreading another sleepless night. I tossed and turned until I finally gave up and turning over on my back, put my arm behind my head and stared at the ceiling. I was listening to the wind howl outside, when something I'd said to Hank today came back. It was said out of frustration, but now going to Utah seemed like a damned good idea...and the longer I lay there, the better it sounded. I looked over at the clock. It was five-thirty. I threw back the blankets and got up. Getting dressed, I pulled on my boots and grabbed my coat.

With the exception of Hank's snoring, the rest of the house was quiet. I tiptoed over to his desk and wrote a short note explaining where I'd gone, leaving it on the kitchen table where he'd be sure to find it. Then putting on my coat and gloves, I headed for the front door. Quietly closing it behind me, I got out my keys and hurried down the steps.

The sky hardly showed any signs of daylight due to the weather, but that wasn't going to stop me. This was the first time since the wind started up that I had something positive to do with all this energy. I got in my truck and pulling away from the house, headed out to find my wife.

CHAPTER ONE HUNDRED THIRTY-SEVEN

Twenty miles out, it was coming down so hard I had to pull over. I wasn't familiar with this part of the country and got out the map. I wanted to find the fastest way to Utah, knowing a lot of the smaller two-lane roads would probably be closed or impassable –but it was a chance I was willing to take. I mapped out my route and was about to pull back on to the road, when a sheriff's deputy pulled in behind me. Wondering what the hell he wanted, I shut off the engine and took out my wallet. He turned off the siren before getting out of his car and coming up to my window.

"Good morning, sir," he said, touching the brim of his hat. "May I see your license and registration, please?" I held up my wallet to show him my license. "Would you take it out of your wallet for me?"

I was pissed, but did as he asked and handing him my license, I said, "My registration is in the glove box –okay if I get it out?" His arm casually went to his side and he rested his hand on the butt of his gun. "Do you have any weapons in there?" he asked politely.

"No, of course not," I huffed, reaching over and getting out the registration. He scrutinized both the license and my registration very carefully then he looked at me. "Is your name Matthew Sean McIntyre?"

"My mother calls me that," I frowned. "Everybody else calls me "Mac."

"That's all I needed to know," he said, opening my door and taking a step away from the truck.

"Step out of the vehicle, Mr. McIntyre."

Now I was *really* pissed!

"WHAT –*WHY*?" I yelled. "What th' devil is this all about -what are you stopping me for, anyway?"

"I've been instructed to take you back to Mr. Fairfield, so please step out of your vehicle."

I closed my eyes. Hank. I was livid and would kill him when I got back. Angrily unbuckling my seat belt, I got out and demanded hotly, "What're we going to do with my truck –I don't want to just leave it out here!"

"Lock it. Mr. Fairfield will send someone to drive it back to the ranch."

"Great!" I mumbled. "Just *&%$# great!"

He escorted me back to his patrol car, where I got in the front seat.

"Please fasten your seat belt," he said, closing the door. I buckled it and he got in on the driver's side. He turned the car around and we headed back to the ranch. Halfway there, I folded my arms definitely across my chest and said, "You still haven't told me what this is all about –and just why th' hell, couldn't I drive my own truck back?"

"Sorry, but I wasn't advised why," he said, keeping his eyes glued on the road. "My instructions were just to find you, bring you back in the patrol car and leave your vehicle for someone to drive back, but...if you don't mind my saying so, this is no weather to be going *anywhere* in."

"I can manage it," I grumbled.

"Maybe," he said, "but visibility is only about eight feet or less."

"So?"

"Eight feet isn't much distance if you have to stop quickly."

"Big deal –I've got good reflexes."

"Did you know a large tree blew over last night taking out the bridge you were headed for less than two miles away?"

I didn't know -and didn't say anything.

"I've been working this part of th' state going on sixteen years, and I've seen some pretty bad things happen to overconfident folks in *regular* weather. But I've never seen weather like this -and I can tell you, Mac, you never would have seen the bridge was out. However, if by some miracle you *were* able to handle the bad visibility, the sudden hit on your brakes on this icy road would've been enough to send you skidding right over into the river."

There was no sense fighting it. "I guess you're right" I mumbled. "Thanks for...you know."

Twenty minutes later, we pulled up in front of the house. As I got out of the car, Hank came out on the porch –and he didn't look happy (-which made *two* of us.). Slamming the door, I shot him a look that could kill. "What on earth are you doing, Hank?" I said.

"Ah could ask *you* th' same question," he said coldly. The deputy got out and followed me up the steps. "Here he is Mr. Fairfield. You'll need to send someone back for his truck. It's sitting on the side of the road about twenty miles out."

"Okay, Jim, Ah'll get Rusty to bring it back, if you don't mind givin' him a ride out there."

"Yes sir, no problem." Hank went to the end of the porch and yelled for Rusty. He came around to the front and said, "Yeah, Hank?" Hank explained what he wanted and asked me for my keys. I threw them to Rusty. He caught them and got in the car with the deputy. After they left, Hank suggested we sit down on the porch until they got back. I was still so mad I sat down without saying a word to Hank.

Three minutes of frost biting silence went by before Hank broke the ice by saying, "Ah don't know if you realize there's a mandatory alert in effect right now an' no one is to go out in this storm. Th' deputy could'a arrested your ass for pullin' this stunt. What th' hell were you *thinking* going off half-cocked in this bloody mess?"

I glared at him. "WHAT was *I* thinking?? Maybe YOU'RE content to just sit around here and wait, but I can't take it **one** day longer! *ENOUGH is ENOUGH!*" The emotional dam broke and I unleashed all my fury. "*I* want Sam home *NOW* -and if that means I have to go get her, I *will*!"

I was gripping the arms of the rocking chair so hard my hands hurt. Sitting back, I closed my eyes, took a deep breath and relaxed my death grip. Hank settled back too. "Look," he said softly, "Ah know how ya feel – an' this weather ain't helpin' any, but if you were to take off, you'd just be makin' things worse, Mac." I opened my eyes and saw Rusty coming up the drive in my truck with the deputy right behind him. Hank saw them too and got up. Rusty stopped up in front of the steps and got out. He threw the keys to me and asked Hank if he needed him for anything else. Hank shook his head and Rusty went back to work. "And if there's nothing else, Mr. Fairfield, I'll be going too," the deputy said, coming up on the porch. "Thanks, Jim an' tell Frank Ah really appreciate it." He shook his hand and the deputy left.

When we were alone again, Hank turned to me. "Ah need to talk to you, Mac. Let's go inside." I didn't want to talk and sat there with my arms crossed. Hank went to the front door and turning around, he said, "*Now*, Mac! Trust me, it's important –*more* important than your li'l ol' pouty hurt feelings." I reluctantly got up and followed him inside. Sitting down on the couch, I waited to see what Hank had on his mind. Unless he'd heard from Sam, I had no interest in hearing anything he had to say.

There was no fire going and it was a bit chilly sitting there in front of the fireplace. From time to time a strong gust of wind blew down the chiminy, stirring the ashes. I was still waiting for Hank to sit down, but he went over to the bar instead and got out the bourbon. Taking out two glasses, he filled them halfway, then came back and held one out to me.

"Its only eight-thirty in the morning, Hank," I frowned. "Ain't it a bit early to be hittin' th' sauce?"

"Take it," he ordered. "You don't gotta drink it, but just humor me an' take it."

I took the damned drink from him and set it down on the coffee table. Crossing my arms again, I sat back against the couch and waited to hear what this was all about. I expected a lecture and was all set to launch into a strong defensive rant, when I noticed a strange tired look on his face. Sitting down on the couch, he opened his mouth to say something but the words caught in his throat and he emptied his glass instead. After draining every last drop, he got up and went back to the bar. He refilled his glass and I watched in amazement as he downed it one swallow. Filling it again, he brought the drink back to the couch and sat down.

"What th' hell...?" I said, expecting a shit-eating grin from all the booze, but he was sober as a judge. "What's *with* you, this morning?" I frowned.

After a long pause, he finally said, "Judgin' from the time on your note this mornin' Sid called not long after you left." Hank had my full attention now, and I waited for him to go on. "He ain't been in th' office 'cause he's been up in Utah...with a search party."

Search party? That didn't sound good and my eyes popped wide open. My mind raced in a thousand different directions, but none of them once considered anything worse than thinking Sid's being in a search party was because he'd lost his wallet...or...something...like...that.

Funny how the mind can come up with the most absurd things to avoid reality...

"Why would Sid be in a search party in Utah -he lose his wallet or something?"

I knew my words didn't make sense, but at that moment I felt giddy thinking of Sid out looking for his wallet with a seach party. Riduclous.

Looking at me with the deepest concern, Hank said, "Mac...Ah...Ah...listen, why don't you take a long swallow of your drink?"

"Because I don't want a drink," I smiled, wondering why my head felt so light and funny. Reaching over and picking up my glass, Hank held it out to me. "Here, just drink this –please?"

I still didn't want it but was tired of fighting him and took the glass, downing the entire thing. As the bourbon sent a warm glow through my bones, I shook my head and said, "Wow-okay, are you happy now?" I sat back grinning, noticing that same tired look I'd seen earlier –but now his eyes were red and brimming with tears. "No," he said. "Happy is not th' word that best describes how Ah...feel," -and it still wasn't getting through my thick skull that something was seriously wrong. He got up, went over to the bar and came back with a fresh unopened bottle. Opening it, he refilled both our glasses –to the brim. He handed me mine and without waiting, drank his down to the last drop. I did the same although not exactly sure why. When our glasses were empty, I said, "What's up, Hank – why are we drinking like condemned men?"

Letting out a long tired sigh, he said, "Try to follow me here, Mac. Sid's call wasn't good news." Before I had time absorb that and say anything, Hank continued. "Another cold front blew in behind this one out west, and for a few brief hours, it was clear blue skies and warm sunshine."

I listened, feeling wonderfully mellow and nodded. "Great...so -Sam is on her way back, right?"

Unable to go on, Hank stood up rubbing his legs nervously and said softly, "Oh, God..."

He paced anxiously to the end of the couch and back again before he sat down.

"No, Mac, she isn't. For whatever reason," he began," the record execs – in all their incredible wisdom, decided to take advantage of the clear weather and..." he stopped and rubbed his chin so hard, I thought he'd rub all the skin off.

"And they're flying her home?" I finished for him.

"No...they flew her to Tahoe. Right into it."

Whatever Hank was trying to tell me was NOT getting through, and I sat there grinning like the slightly drunken idiot I was. "Now -why on earth would they do that?" I giggled. "That's just plain stupid! Fly *into* a storm?? Oh puh-leeze...why, the very thought of Sam flying in a little plane straight into a bliz-" my face went ashen and I sat straight up. Turning to Hank, I grabbed him by his collar and said, "What are you trying to say, Hank?" I couldn't finish and he gently removed my hand. "Everybody warned th' pilot not to fly, but throw enough money at some fool with more greed than character and they'll do anything."

The words still weren't real to me and I heard myself ask, "What happened –an'-where?"

"Somewhere over th Sierra's –in th' most lonely, desolate part of the state." Hank stopped and took another long swallow. "When th' plane went missing," he sighed, "Sid was called instead of us, because they hoped to find out that th' pilot set down somewhere safe." His voice was barely a whisper as he struggled to finish. "Sid's been in a heicopter for the last three days, searching for her plane."

I was too stunned to move.

"The pilot couldn't control th' plane in eighty mile an hour winds and got disorientated in th' blinding snow. They f-flew into the side of a mountain and were killed instantly. The search party found 'em when th' weather broke on th' third day."

Suddenly all the air went out of the room. "YOU'RE *LYING*!!!" I screamed. "WHY are you DOING THIS –what kind of **MONSTER** ARE *YOU*??" I threw my glass against the mantle, shattering the glass and sending bourbon everywhere. I paced, pulled my hair and ranted like a madman. "I WANT SAM BACK RIGHT **NOW**! OH, God –**PLEASE**!" I went on and on and on. Hank didn't try to stop me -he just let me go until I finally fell to my knees. Noreen came out and joined Hank. They later told me they tried to talk to me, but I didn't say another word –for five days.

CHAPTER ONE HUNDRED THIRTY-EIGHT

I didn't know how long I was in a catatonic state before I finally opened my eyes to find an elderly man standing over me holding my eyelid open, shining a pin light in.

"W-where am I?" I asked weakly, trying to throw off the blanket and get up. "Say, just why am I in bed, anyway?" I couldn't see Hank, but I heard him ask, "Is he comin 'round, doc?"

"Is that you, Hank?" I asked. "What's going on?" I tried to get up again, but the man gently pushed me back down. "Take it easy," he said. "You've had quite a bad shock."

I looked at Hank and frowned. "What's he talking about?"

The man called doc, took out a syringe and filled it with a clear liquid. Taking my arm, he bent down and carefully forced the needle into my vein. When he finished, he stood up and smiled. "There -that should keep you calm for a while," he said.

"Mac, this is our family doctor, Doctor Reese," Hank said, "Doc was kind enough to come out here to take care of you after –"

"After? After –what?"

Hank pulled a chair up next to the bed. "Do you remember anything that's happened in the past five days?" I thought back –then shook my head. Looking exhausted, Hank sighed and rubbed his forehead. "Mac," he said, beginning to tell me all over again -and when he got to the part about the plane crash, it all came rushing back. I couldn't stay still and threw back the blanket, this time determined to get out of bed. I swung my legs over the side and stood up. They immediately gave out and I fell straight to the floor. Hank helped me back into bed just as my mind went fuzzy and the rest of my muscles went rubbery. I fell back on the pillow and remember very little else, except for a vivid Technicolor dream of Sam smiling at me, totally unaware of the bright red blood that slowly dripped down her face onto her white wedding gown. The mind is a mystery to me and I don't know how it works, but after a while some kind of coping mechanism began to take over. Doc Reese quit giving me those shots and I was able to sit up in bed and eat a small bit of solid food.

During my more lucid moments, I could hear the news of Sam's death playing non-stop in other parts of the house, and the phone rang every time it was hung up. There was no escaping it –it was big news and the world reveled in hearing it, but she was more than a news story to us. Sam was my wife and the mother of my son and a sister to Hank. I tried to block out the circus as much as I could, but it was pretty much impossible. One afternoon, Hank came in to talk to me. Pulling up a chair, he said, "Mac, it's been over a week now since the accident." He paused for a moment and then went on. "Sam is over at the morgue waiting to be put to rest. We need...to do that."

I had resisted thinking about this and when I said nothing, he sighed and started to get up. I waited until he reached the door and then said, "I want to see her." He came back and sat down again. Clearing his throat, he said, "No...you...don't, Mac."

But I was insanely insistent. "Yes –I DO!" I shouted.

Looking horrified, Hank said, "Mac -she hit th' side of a *mountain*! There ain't much left of-" his voice cracked. When he could speak again, he said, "You need to remember her the way she was –not -like this. If you see her now, you'll never be able to get th' image outta your head for th' rest of your life. Let it be, Mac -for her sake. She would *never* want you to see her now."

I lay there staring at the ceiling trying to connect the dots of what he was saying, but Hank's words were all jumbled up. It didn't make sense for me not to see her -after all it would be my last time. Suddenly, I was *very* angry and cried, "**NO**! How *dare* you –or <u>anyone</u> to try and keep me from seeing her." I must have looked as crazy as I'm sure I was, because Hank said, "Okay, Mac...we'll go see her." I settled down again and nodded. "All right, then..."

I was so lost in my own grief that it never occurred to me how horrible his must've been. If I'd bothered to look at him, I'd seen the tears streaming down his face, but I saw nothing and felt nothing.

CHAPTER ONE HUNDRED THIRTY-NINE

Hank, of course, never took me to see Sam's remains and it was some months before I realized how grateful I was that he didn't. Old friends like Rose, came as soon as they heard about Sam. They closed ranks around us, giving us time to do what had to be done. Rose was a special Godsend helping Mama prepare vast amounts of food for the endless friends that came by to pay their respects. Hank and Noreen handled the funeral arrangements, while I, of course, was as useless as tits on a wart hog. I wanted to help out, but between my physical weakness and the tranquilizers, I was a bag of wet sand.

Doc called as soon as he heard the news. Hank brought me a cordless phone from his bedroom so I could talk to him. Harley and Legrand were there too, and they all felt so bad that I ended up undoing any progress I'd made in my own depression. I couldn't really talk about losing Sam and thankfully, they understood. Before we hung up, Harley asked if there was anything they could do...which naturally, there wasn't.

The day came for Sam's funeral and I finally had to face that it was time to say goodbye to her.

I got up that morning, moving in a trance. I managed to take a shower by myself, but Hank had to shave and help me into my one and only suit – the same one I wore at our wedding, which still had what was left of the boutonniere on the lapel. Rose came in and tied my necktie and combed my hair, reminding me of my own mother helping me as a thirteen-year-old going on my first date. She was coming to the funeral with us and as soon as I passed inspection, we went out to join the others in the living room. Juan, along with the rest of his family, asked if they could stay home with Matt, explaining that they felt it was important for us to be with Sam. Hank told them it was perfectly all right and we went out on the porch to wait for Jerry to drive us to the church.

The ride wasn't long, but it gave me time to collect my thoughts. It was like I was stuck in some kind of limbo-I hadn't cried since Sam's death and couldn't help thinking this was what it must feel like to be a zombie...not really dead and not really alive. The limo stopped in front of three wide steps leading up to an enormous gothic church. I got out of the car, awed by the seventeenth century English architecture. Its high bell tower, flying buttresses and twelve stained glass windows, made the church an intimidating fortress against evil. "You ready to go inside?" Hank asked. I nodded and starting up the steps, noticed hundreds of cars parked everywhere. When we reached the arched entrance of the church, I saw an enormous crowd waiting to get in and panicked. "W-who are all these people -and why are they here?"

"They're just some of Sam's fans," Hank said.

"B-But I don't want them here," I cried, pulling away as Hank grabbed my arm. "Mac! You have to get hold of yourself! This isn't about you –it's about Sam! C'mon, you can *do* this."

Shaking my head wildly, I said, "no, no, no..." over and over and tried to go back to the car. Rose came up then and took my hand. "Sam is inside waiting for us, Mac," she said softly. "Make her proud." She smiled at me and I felt a calmness come over me. I nodded and holding my hand tightly in hers, Rose led me inside, where the foyer was packed. The crowd immediately closed in on us and my panic was back. People rudely pushed and shoved themselves against us so hard I thought we'd be crushed. My eyes darted from one face to another, hearing them whisper, "Look, there's Hank Fairfield -and *who's* that with him?" Someone else said, "The woman is his wife I think, but I don't know who the man is..."

Then a woman screamed, "HANK! HANK!" setting off every other woman. "*WHERE'S* HANK?" one yelled, as another cried, "OVER THERE...C'MON!" and just as the crowd got out of control, four bodyguards came out of nowhere and escorted us through the madness.

Taking us down to the front pew, we sat down -and *there* it was! -Sam's casket, just six feet away. The natural cherry's highly polished wood gleamed beneath a blanket of white baby's breath -and it did not escape me that this was the closest I'd been to Sam since Waco.

I wanted to cry –thought I *should* cry, but I was so overcome by the flood of people, the insanity of the crowd, the magnificence of the church -and the way a single shaft of sunlight fell on her casket, that I could hardly breathe. I stared at the halo around her casket, fighting every urge to run up and take her in my arms once again. It killed me that I couldn't see her...touch her...feel her.

The funeral home had given her ring to Hank and he gave it to me. I slipped my hand inside my coat pocket and wrapping my fingers around it tightly, felt some small comfort knowing it had been on her hand. I remembered how her face looked when I'd put it on her finger. What a day that had been. If I forgot everything else that ever happened in this life, I would *never* forget when I saw her waiting for me in that white dress, how I knew heaven was missing an angel -and it was little wonder that they wanted her back.

People were still crowding into the sanctuary and it was surreal to watch them push each other out of the way, so they could have the seat. I sighed. What were we coming to? I needed something to take my mind off this ugly display of humanity and noticed a simple wooden cross hanging suspended over the choir loft. In my wandering state of mind, I wondered why the cross was bare and asked Hank."Why is that cross bare?" I mused. "Isn't there supposed to be a figure of Christ hanging from it?"

"No, that's th' Catholic church" he whispered. "We're Presbyterian. Christ no longer is on the cross. He's risen and is in heaven and we don't put Him back on it."

"Oh, I thought this *WAS* a Catholic church –it looks like one."

Hank shook his head. "No, it ain't, but it *was* modeled after th' old churches in England...and Ah guess they were Catholic. Th' man who donated th' money to have this one built was from a small English shire outside of London. He might'a been Catholic an' left th' Catholic church for whatever reason – Ah don't know, it was before mah time, but he asked that this church be built exactly like th' one he grew up in over there. Money was no object, so he had th' original plans sent over here for th' artectect..." and raising a suspicious eyebrow, Hank asked, "Say...are you all right?"

"Yeah, why?"

"You're jest talkin' about some really odd stuff."

"Really –am I? I was just wondering...that's all."

"It's okay," he smiled. "Ah jest wanted to make sure you're doin' okay..."

Unknown to me at the time, Hank was very aware of the strained condition I was in and was watching me closely. He knew I hadn't really let go and realized I'd talk about things that either made no sense or were completely unrelated to the circumstances -and he was right. My muddled mind went in and out of reality. I would focus on her casket one minute and then anything that caught my attention the next. Except for movies, I'd never seen a church like this and was somewhat taken by its opulence. The inside was as extravagant as the outside. The vaulted ceiling had to be at least three stories high. Six large wrought iron round chandeliers –twelve in all –hung on long chains suspended from wooden beams spanning the open space over the congregation. I really couldn't fathom the cost –or the fact that one man had paid for it.

The sanctuary was the size of a football field with row after row of long highly polished wooden pews. It was everything a church should be- awe inspiring, holy, and quietly intimidating.

Suddenly, I realized where I was and all the air went out of the room. My jaw dropped and I couldn't breathe. Grabbing my tie, I yanked it loose from my neck. Noreen gasped, "Mac –what's wrong?" I stood up but Hank grabbed me, pulling me back down in my seat. "What's wrong with you?" he growled. "This church," I whispered, having a hard time catching my breath. "What about it?" he frowned. "Its *your* chuch, isn't it –the one you and Sam grew up in!" A light went on in Hank's head and he knew where I was going with this. "Yes," he said matter-of-factly, "it is."

"Oh-my-God," I whispered. "What complete irony."

CHAPTER ONE HUNDRED FORTY

Before I had time to processs everything going through my mind at the speed of light, a hush fell over the crowd. A middle-aged woman crossed the stage and I watched mindlessly, as she sat down behind an immense organ. Placing her feet on the bass pedals and her hands over two of the three keyboards, her fingers touched the keys and the church resonated with the timeless music of Mozart. I vaguely remember thinking how the mammoth organ dwarfed the woman and yet, she had complete control over it.

As I listened to the music, my eyes drifted over the stage, whose size would rival anything in Carnegie Hall. Dark burgundy drapes hung on either side of the stage, and three high back chairs sat behind an antique mahogany podium in the center. The organist stopped playing and an old black man I hadn't noticed before, got up from one of the chairs behind the podium. As he shuffled to the stage, another black man holding an old beat-up F-hole guitar came out and pulling up a wooden chair, sat down behind him. A trio of black women followed him, taking their places in front of the choir loft.

All eyes were rivited on this man now standing in front of the podium. Wearing an old wrinkled suit, a badly knotted black tie and shirt with frayed cuffs, his tired yellowed eyes spoke of days gone by...of picking cotton and living with all the segregated misery of shantytowns. A hard life –harder than anyone should ever have had to live through. The man behind him hunched over his guitar and his gnarled rheumatoid fingers began to strum the strings –and I never dreamed anyone could ever get such music out of a guitar –*any* guitar.

But NO one could have guessed the voice that would come out of the man standing before us. It was a deep rich baritone –not quite a bass, but when he began to sing, a shiver ran through me like all the angels of heaven had just touched me. The song was called, "The End of the Rainbow," and I heard the words as clearly as if I'd written them myself.

"I went runnin' to the end of a rainbow...
Lookin' for a treasure they said I would find...
I found nothing but heartaches and trouble...
An' now I'm about to lose my mind.

On the way, the load got heavy...and the burdens got hard to bear...
None'a my friends was there to help me...an' they left me standing in th' middle of nowhere.

With a heart full of pain, I was lost...So blind I couldn't see a thing...
So far down in misery, I couldn't even remember my own name.
But it soon became loud'n clear...Every word my ears could hear.
My heart was so heavy, I couldn't move...so I just stood there like a silly fool.

I believe I'll go on home...
An' start all over again...
I left my rainbow behind me...
Right where I began...
Goin' goin' goin' home...
I'm goin' home...
To the end of the rainbow..."

He sang with weariness that reached the deepest part of the heart –the part where few things in life ever touch. His raspy voice told of an intimate closness with pain –pain that lay just beyond what we THINK is pain. The lump in my throat swelled until it choked off my air. Suddenly a broken sob burst from my lips and unable to stop myself, the tears came. The song - and his voice -had done what nothing else had been able to do; they split me through and through, setting my grief free. If ever I thought I'd suffered before now, believe me, it was nothing compared to this. When he finished, several people were crying –otherwise, you could've heard a pin drop. No one said anything for a long time. Minutes went by before anyone could even breathe again.

The minister got up but by the time he spoke, I was no longer there. I was back at the crossroads and Sam was running in the back door with Freeway. They'd been out in the desert and her cheeks were on fire from the cold fresh air. Her smile was like that of a child's, as she sat at the bar and told me all about their climbing rocks, finding lizards and seeing an eagle overhead.

There would never be another day like that -or another like her.

...And I wanted to remember her just the way she was that day.

CHAPTER ONE HUNDRED FORTY-ONE

After the service was over, the funeral director came up to us and asked if we were ready to go to the gravesite. I didn't feel up to battling the crowd waiting for us outside and said I would drive over in the limo with Jerry. Understanding what the problem was, he asked if we would follow him. I was too drained to argue, so I nodded and got up with the rest of the family. To my eternal relief, we avoided the insane crowd by leaving through a private exit on the side where the funeral home had a long white limousine waiting. We got in behind the darkened windows and the driver by-passed the crowd –which had tripled in size now and grown into a mob.

As we drove away from *the* church Sam-and-I-were-to-have-been-married-in-next-month (–but were holding her funeral in instead,) I asked Hank which cemetery we were going to. He said we were going back to the ranch. He wanted to bury Sam on a small hill underneath a big oak tree overlooking the river. "That was her favorite place when we were growing up as kids," he said.

I liked that idea, plus I could ride out often and visit with her. When we reached the gravesite, I saw the grave had already been dug. The hearse was in front of us and stopped next to the site. Three muscular men got out and went around to open up the rear doors. Two of them removed Sam's casket while the third stood by to help. The wind whipped the hem of my coat as I followed them. They gently laid her down by the open grave and went back to the hearse. I stared at the coffin. The stark contrast of the baby's breath next to the to the dry soil of the earth was some kind of oxymoron.

I took a step back and looked up at the clear blue sky. It was late afternoon and the sun was low on the horizon. A spring wind was sweeping winter away and tiny leaves were budding out in all the trees. I stood there wondering why it couldn't have been a day like this when they decided to send Sam to Tahoe.

I knelt down and ran my hand lovingly over the smooth cherry. Tears found their way down my cheeks again, but this time, the pain was not as fierce. I touched the baby's breath lightly and whispered, "This isn't goodbye, my love...it's just an adios until we meet again."

I stayed by her for some time, unaware of the two men with shovels standing some yards behind me. When I stood up again, I turned around and saw the tears streaming down Hank's face. In that instant, I saw his heartbreak and wanted to take it away for him so badly. Instead, I moved away to let Hank, Noreen and Rose have their time with her. I walked several yards away to watch the river's blue water roll by. It was peaceful here -and the perfect place for Sam to find her long overdue well-deserved rest. "You're finally home now, Sam. No one will ever take you away from me again," I whispered.

The sun went down and brilliant pinkish/gold twilight backlit the mountains. Turning around, I saw that Hank and the rest were still by Sam's grave, so I didn't interrupt them. The wind brought the perfume of flowers from somewhere. I walked down the hill to a small stand of trees by the river's edge. I was almost there when I thought I saw the dark silhoutte of someone leaning his shoulder against a tree and his arms crossed over his chest. Thinking it must be a trick of the shadows I ignored it, but as I got closer, the dark figure dropped his arms and moved. It was definitely a man wearing boots and a Stetson. He reached up and took it off. Frowning, I went over to challenge him.

"Who's there?" I said. "How'd you get on this land –are you one of those crazy fans from back at th' church?"

The man said, "Yeah, you could say I'm a big fan of Sam's...an' it wasn't hard to get on this ranch -*if* ya know th' right folks."

"*HARLEY!*" I cried, hurrying over to him. "You ol' son-of-a-gun," I laughed, grabbing him in a bear hug. "H-How...when...I-I..."

He laughed and put on his Stetson again. "Got in early this afternoon, but too late for th' funeral. I met Rusty, told him who I was and he told me y'all would be comin' out here afterwards."

"He let me park my truck an' horse trailer next to th' barn. Even took my horse out an' fed him. That Rusty's a right nice fella," he smiled. "You didn't tell me that."

"I'm...speechless," I said and taking a deep breath, let it out in a whoosh. "Where's Doc –why isn't he with you -an' how long can you stay?" Harley's smile disappeared and he looked down at his boots. He kicked at some dirt then looked back up. "Doc...died two days after we talked to you. Had a massive heart attack...was gone before he hit th' floor."

I felt like I'd just had all the wind knocked out of me. My knees buckled, and I grabbed the tree for support. Tears welled up in my eyes and I opened my mouth to say something, but looked like a guppy when nothing came out. Finally, I just let go and slid down the trunk into the tall grass. Harley sat down beside me. We neither one said anything for a long time, then he said gently, "I didn't want to tell you over th' phone with all you had right now with Sam...so, I drove down here to tell you in person." Leaning my head back, I closed my eyes and tried to absorb this new punch to the gut. "I'-I'm glad you did, Harley."

It was dark now. Crickets chirped around us and lightning bugs flickered in and out of the grass. I heard Hank calling me. "I guess they're ready to go back now," I said and yelled, "I'm down here by the river, Hank. Y'all go on back without me...I'm gonna stay a while longer."

He heard me and yelled back, "Okay, but Ah'm gonna send Jerry back in half an hour."

"Fine -I'll be ready." I heard the car leave and looked at Harley. "You want to go up an' say goodbye to Sam?" He nodded and we got up. As we walked back up the hill, I looked up at the night sky. A kjillion stars were out and the wind carried the sweet smell of Nature. We stopped by Sam's grave, now covered in a warm blanket of soft earth. Harley removed his Stetson and bowing his head reverently, stood there for a long time. Finally, he put his Stetson back on and said quietly, "She was quite a lady...there won't be another like her."

"Amen," I nodded.

We walked away and went over to sit down on a log and wait for Jerry. While we waited, I asked, "So, how long you gonna be able to stay, Harley?" Harley brought his leg up and resting his arm on his knee, he squinted out at the countryside. "Oh...I ain't in no big hurry," he said. "Don't seem like there's much to go back to."

I was confused. "Okaaaay, what does that mean?"

Harley leaned back on his elbows and stretched out his long legs. "It means, I left my job and was wonderin' if that foreman offer up here, is still open?"

I grinned from ear to ear. "Welllll, let's just go talk to Rusty tomorrow an' find out."

THE END

Author's note

Since beginning this book, I have lost two very dear and special friends. Most notably, is Marty Caidin and most recently, is Scott Crossfield.

These two men are without peer and how I came to be so blessed to have them in my life is beyond my understanding, but I will be eternally grateful that we became lifelong friends of over 40 years.

The merits of these men are much too long for me to go into, but I would suggest anyone interested in rocket flight (especially the X-15) check the Internet on Scott Crossfield.

Martin Caidin is one of the foremost writers of science fiction of the 20th Century. Among his over 300 books, are "Cyborg" –later turned into the television show called, "The Six Million Dollar Man" starring Lee Majors.

This is my tribute to them –and thanks for their friendship and the friendship of others through knowing them. And last but certainly not least, for Scotty's nickname for me, "Destiny's Tot." Which sez it all.

www.ingramcontent.com/pod-product-compliance
Lightning Source LLC
LaVergne TN
LVHW091213080426
835509LV00009B/971